EMERGING PERSPECTIVES ON

MARYSE CONDÉ

EMERGING PERSPECTIVES

ON

MARYSE CONDÉ

A Writer of Her Own

Edited by

Sarah Barbour and Gerise Herndon

Africa World Press, Inc.

P.O. Box 1892  P.O. Box 48
Trenton, NJ 08607 Asmara, ERITREA

Africa World Press, Inc.

P.O. Box 1892
Trenton, NJ 08607

P.O. Box 48
Asmara, ERITREA

Book design: Saverance Publishing Services
Cover design: Roger Dormann
Cover Photo: Courtesy of Jacques Sassier/Mercure de France

Library of Congress Cataloging-in-Publication Data

Emerging perspectives on Maryse Condé : a writer of her own/ edited by Sarah Barbour and Gerise Herndon.
  p. cm.
 Includes bibliographical references.
 ISBN 1-59221-222-0 (cloth) -- ISBN 1-59221-223-9 (pbk.)
 1. Condé, Maryse--Criticism and interpretation. I. Barbour, Sarah. II. Herndon, Gerise.
 PQ3949.2.C65Z63 2005
 843'.914--dc22
                                    2005030952

dedicated to

Lucrecia Becerra Freebairn
1940–2003

TABLE OF CONTENTS

INTRODUCTION

1. Maryse Condé: A Writer of Her Own   3
Sarah Barbour and Gerise Herndon

TRANSLATING CULTURE AND CROSS-TALK OF NARRATIVES: FROM TRANSLATION TO DIALOGUE

2. Translating Maryse Condé: A Personal Itinerary   33
Richard Philcox

3. Crossing the Bridge of Beyond: Translating the Mangroves of French Caribbean Identities   39
Pascale De Souza

4. On the Untranslatability of Tituba Indian, An Intercultural Subject   63
Kathleen Gyssels (Trans. by Victoria Bridges Moussaron with additions by the editors)

5. Talking the Cross-Talk of Histories in Maryse Condé's *I Tituba, Black Witch of Salem*   87
Jennifer R. Thomas

GENEALOGIES AND GENDER: HISTORY'S ROUTES, IDENTITY'S RHIZOMES

6. Not Enough Shade under the "Royal Kaïlcédrat": Maryse Condé's *Hérémakhonon* or the Difficult Search for Ancestors   107
Serigne Ndiaye

7. "I'm No Mayotte Capécia": Engaging with Fanon in
Hérémakhonon   127
Jennifer Sparrow

8. In the Face of the Daughter: Feminist Perspectives on
Métissage and Gender   143
Gloria Nne Onyeoziri

9. (Up)rooting the Family Tree: Genealogy and Space in
Maryse Condé's Fiction   159
Johanna X. K. Garvey

TRANSGRESSING BOUNDARIES, CHALLENGING
CATEGORIES

10. Maryse Condé: Historian of the Black Diaspora   181
Laurence M. Porter

11. Monstrous Readings: Transgression and the Fantastic
in *Célanire cou-coupé*   201
Dawn Fulton

12. Oedipus and Oedipa according to Condé   217
Christiane Makward (with Anne Oszwald)

PROBLEMATIZING POSTCOLONIAL HISTORIES

13. History's Theft and Memory's Return in Maryse Condé   241
Katherine Elkins

14. Maryse Condé Creolizes the Canon with *La migration
des cœurs*   253
Maria Cristina Fumagalli

15. Rewriting the Postcolonial in Maryse Condé's *La
migration des cœurs*   275
Carine Mardorossian

Bibliography   291
Notes on contributors   311
Index   315

ACKNOWLEDGEMENTS

We thank the editors of the journal *SITES: The Journal of Contemporary French Studies* for permission to reprint Richard Philcox's essay, which first appeared in Volume 5, no. 2 of *SITES*, fall 2001. Kathleen Gyssels' essay was originally published in French as "L'intraduisibilité de Tituba Indien, sujet interculturel" in the on-line journal *Mots Pluriels* (23 March 2003), and translation of that article is presented here with the kind permission of the editors.

As is always the case, the time and support of many people allowed us to complete this volume. Valerie Loichot helped us clarify some questions about Créole, as did instruction in "le français aux antilles" with Muriel Gabourg at CIRECCA in Martinique. In addition to her translation of the Gyssels essay, we appreciate the helpful, thoughtful editing Victoria Bridges Moussaron provided throughout. We also thank Natalie, Roger, Pango, and Marfa for hosting us for a week of marathon editing in Ithaca, New York. Friends at Wake Forest and in Winston-Salem offered guidance, editing advice, and inspiration—among them, Debra Boyd, Jill Carraway, Mary DeShazer, Julie Edelson, Gillian Overing, Elizabeth Phillips, and Eva Rodtwitt. A Wake Forest University research leave of absence, as well as the Nebraska Wesleyan University Faculty Development Committee scholarship releases and funding allowed for completion of this project in a timely fashion. Thanks to Larry McClain for demonstrating that *Tituba* can be studied as early American literature, and to Hal Wylie for introducing many University of Texas students to Afro-Caribbean literature. Mike Rambo helped us not to take ourselves too seriously, and his observations enriched the seriousness of our work.

INTRODUCTION

MARYSE CONDÉ: A WRITER OF HER OWN

Sarah E. Barbour and Gerise Herndon

"VIE PLURIELLE/A PLURAL LIFE"[1]

We borrow the title for this section from Françoise Pfaff's *Entretiens avec Maryse Condé* [*Conversations with Maryse Condé*], first as a gesture of gratitude to Pfaff for providing this rich resource to Condé's readers, and second, as a way of inscribing dialogue in this volume, much as the author herself has done in her numerous interviews. Over the course of her writing life, interviewers and critics have ascribed a public identity to Maryse Condé through various epithets describing her role in West Indian and global literature: from simply "a Guadeloupean writer" (Fratta) to "Grand Dame of Caribbean Literature" (Nunez), to more polemical titles like "Une nomade inconvenante" [A Nonconformist Nomad] (Cottenet-Hage and Moudileno) and "Une écrivaine politiquement incorrecte" [A Politically Incorrect (Female) Writer] (Araujo). In spite of the fact that she has repeatedly stated she simply wants "la liberté d'être moi-même" [the freedom to be myself] (Moudileno 126),[2] we admit that the richness and complexity of her literary and critical writings inspire such projections. The author who emerges from the essays in this volume could therefore be called "a witness to her time," to borrow from Pfaff again (1996, xvi), and to borrow from one of the volume's contributors, "La Grande Marronne du Tout-Monde"[3] (Makward 2002).

Standard biographical summaries place the beginning of her *marronnage* just after she had completed her *bacculauréat* in Guadeloupe, when her parents sent her to study at the Lycée Fénélon in Paris in 1953. She may not have known at the age of sixteen that this first step outside the confining upper middle class milieu of colonial Guadeloupe would initiate her nomadic life—for as she describes in an autobiographical essay, she felt she had simply traded one prison for another.[4] Interviews indicate, however, some incipient awareness of her desire to wander. In a society divided strictly along race lines, she recalls how her parents did not allow the Boucoulon children to "speak to other Negroes on the street" in Pointe-à-Pitre, nor to "socialize with mulattoes because they were illegitimate children of Whites," or "to mingle with Whites" because "they were the enemy." "We lived in isolation . . . totally bored, because being by ourselves all the time was not very enriching" (Pfaff 2; 10-11). Born in 1937, Maryse Boucoulon thus passed the early years of her adolescence bored in Pointe-à-Pitre and the later ones in Paris, first at the Lycée Fénélon and then at the Sorbonne (Clark interview 97). With her circle of West Indian friends outside the classroom, she was soon sharing her writing, short stories and cultural articles, already describing and engaging the world around her in critical and creative ways.[5]

By the late fifties, Condé's life in Paris had brought her into contact with the African community there. At a rehearsal of Jean Genet's *Les Nègres/The Blacks* she met Mamadou Condé, a Guinean actor whom she married in 1959. Her world now included Africa in a personal way at a moment in history when many nations, like Condé herself, were on the threshold of independence. She went first as a teacher to the Ivory Coast, then to join her husband in Guinea, which had become independent two years earlier and where she discovered the culture and civilization of the ancient Mali Empire. She describes her introduction to political theory, specifically Marxism, through acquaintances and the reading she did in Guinea as an evolution "from political daydreaming to a true political consciousness" and "a kind of euphoria" (Pfaff, 9-10; 21). As Sékou Touré's regime imprisoned acquaintances and colleagues who dared to question its repressive policies, however, she soon began to understand what she would later call "the real face of African Socialism" (Clark interview 103). In spite of the three daughters they had together, differences in expectations at home and in the world wore down her marriage to Mamadou Condé (Pfaff 11-13; 23-26). It was over by 1964. She accepted a teaching job in Ghana for personal reasons—she "could not see why [she] was staying" in Guinea—but Maryse Condé's personal journey would always intersect with political realities (11; 23). Ghanaians were also experimenting with socialism, though differently than in Guinea. At Kwame Nkrumah's Institute for Ideological Training, she worked with other teachers to write "textbooks adapted to Ghana that did not bear the imprint of colonial ideology" (14; 27). Although she would stay only two years, it was in Ghana that she recalls beginning to "reflect more deeply on Africa, its reality and myths, the future and problems of socialism. . . [,] to grasp the interplay of power and conflicts in a newly independent country" (14; 27). When Nkrumah's power ended in 1966, her involvement in the Institute and her Guinean passport made her suspect to the new government, and she and her children were deported to London. She returned briefly to Ghana in 1968, but too much had changed in the interim, personally and politically, so she and the children moved on to Senegal. It was there that she met Richard Philcox, the British teacher who would become her second husband.

In 1970, feeling that she was "stagnating in mediocre teaching jobs," Condé decided to leave Africa and to resume her studies in Paris (18; 32). Like Veronica, the protagonist of her first novel *Hérémakhon*, Condé may not have known what she was looking for when she first went to Africa in 1960. When she left, however, her ten years of living and working in the Ivory Coast, Guinea, Ghana, and Senegal during this vibrant and sometimes violent time had divested Maryse Condé of any myths she might have had about this overdetermined region of the world. Her extended stay on the continent had also developed in her an unflinchingly critical eye for political agendas that promise liberation and deliver oppression. All of this would be expressed through her writing. Most immediately, her experiences in Africa constituted the ground from which she began her doctoral research on "the definition of the Negro in the Negritude movement" ("Autobiographical Essay") and her first novel. In 1976, she defended her dissertation with honors and published *Hérémakhonon*.

During her stay in Paris, her contact with Africa continued and was enriched through her work as editor at Présence Africaine and as organizer of conferences for the Société Africaine de Culture. When she later took a position as lecturer at the Université-Paris VII and then Nanterre, she also developed literary programs for Radio France International and interviewed contemporary writers from Africa who were themselves reflecting on cultural production in the dynamic period of post-independence. Her research included West Indian literature as well. After defending her dissertation, she published two anthologies in 1977 (*La poésie antillaise* and *Le roman antillais*), two book-length essays in 1978 (*La civilisation du Bossale: Réflexions sur la littérature orale de la Guadeloupe et de la Martinique* and *Cahier d'un retour au pays natal: Césaire*), and a third in 1979 (*La parole des femmes: Essai sur des romancières des Antilles de langue française*).

Condé's first novel received such negative reviews that she recalls swearing that she "would never write again" ("Autobiographical Essay"). Her work had attracted the attention of French departments in the U.S., however. Throughout the late seventies and early eighties she was invited to lecture and teach about literature from *la francophonie*.[6] In the meantime, she was writing. In 1981 she published *Une saison à Rhiata*, and after two extensive trips to Niger and Mali, the *Ségou* volumes in 1984/85. Proceeds from *Ségou* allowed Condé and Philcox, now married, to buy a house at Montebello, Petit-Bourg in 1984. An award as Fulbright scholar at Occidental College delayed their return to Guadeloupe, however. It was during her year in Los Angeles (1985/86) that she began writing *Moi, Tituba*. The novel is inflected with both her homesickness for the Caribbean, as Richard Philcox mentions in his essay in this volume, and her frustration with the intolerance and racism she was seeing in the U.S. ("Autobiographical Essay"). When they moved to Montebello in 1986, as she tells Vèvè Clark, it "was a long-standing dream finally realized" (105).

Montebello still held the beauty of her childhood, but it was impossible to recognize anything else. "Hills had been cut through to build roads or low-cost housing projects," she writes. "The mangrove swamp had been filled in to build a garbage incinerator. Gosier and Ste. Anne, once peaceful fishing villages, had become tourist paradises, bristling with four-star hotels, golf courses and marinas" ("Autobiographical Essay"). The land of her birth would not escape the critical eye she had turned on the emerging nations in Africa; she began writing *Traversée de la Mangrove* "in a frenzy" to describe the changes she saw in Guadeloupe ("Autobiographical Essay"). The novel came out in 1989, the same year Jean Bernabé, Patrick Chamoiseau, and Raphaël Confiant published *Éloge de la créolité*, a call both for a revisioning of the concept of "Caribbeanness" as a source of solidarity among peoples of the Caribbean and for an "authentic" language in which to express that vision.[7] For some, an urgent question of debate was whether to write in French or Creole, and as Condé recalls, *Traversée de la Mangrove* "put me right at the center of the controversy" ("Autobiographical Essay").

In an essay that appeared the same year, "Habiter ce pays, la Guadeloupe," Condé reflects on how her return to Guadeloupe had led to her rethink her relationship to this land and to her writing: "To live in this land is to learn to write all over again. To change almost entirely one's way of writing. To live in this land is also to learn a certain social fabric all over again. To live in this land is to solve an enigma, the enigma of the cultural particularisms which persist. . . . To live in this land is to speak of it in the present. It is to write of it in the present. . ." (qtd. and trans. by Lionnet, *Postcolonial Representations* 72). *Traversée de la Mangrove* not only portrays the complexities of reality in present-day Guadeloupe that Condé witnesses on her return. From her position as outside-insider (or as inside-outsider), Condé creates in the novel what Françoise Lionnet calls "a space in which new configurations [of identity] can begin to be glimpsed" (80); in which, for example, "the longstanding cultural pluralism of the postcolonial world" becomes a "positive point of departure" (73). In this sense, *Traversée* represents Condé's own expression of *créolité*, that is, her own "relationship with oral materials and the oral tradition" of the West Indies (Pfaff 114; 165).

After three years in Guadeloupe, Condé left again: she accepted an invitation to teach in the land she had sworn she would never return to, the U.S. She describes being happy enough to leave the "quagmire" of the *créolité* debates, but she went to her teaching position at Berkeley "reluctantly, expecting the worst." She fell in love with the Bay area, however, perhaps, as she reflects, "quite simply, I had been bored to death in Montebello!" ("Autobiographical Essay"). She also lectured around the country during this time; English translations of her novels began to appear and her name was becoming known. She left Berkeley in 1992 to live in the Washington D.C. area, teaching at the University of Maryland and the University of Virginia, before going to New York City in 1995 to teach at Columbia University. She retired from her position as Chair of the Center for French and Francophone Studies in 2002. As she reflects in her autobiographical essay, a realization was taking place as she lived between Guadeloupe and the U.S., she had a developed a "certain taste for the nomadic life": "I realized that being rooted in one spot is a form of death. One has to carry one's roots from place to place and, without knowing it, I had adopted Édouard Glissant's theory of the rhizome identity."

Continuing to explore the depths of this identity, Condé also perhaps carries two lessons from childhood that Kate Elkins observes in her discussion in this volume of a scene from *Le cœur à rire et à pleurer*. During one of their vacation visits to Paris as children, young Maryse and her brother are interrupted in their play by the voice of their mother calling them home. When her brother tells her not to go, calling their parents "une paire d'aliénés" (14) [a pair of alienated individuals (6)], she ponders both the possibility of not going home and the meaning of this term. Once she decided what it was, she swore "un serment confus de ne jamais devenir une alienée. [C'est-à-dire] . . . une personne qui cherche à être ce qu'elle ne peut pas être parce qu'elle n'aime pas être ce qu'elle est . . ." (16-17) [in a confused sort of way never to become an alienated person . . . (that is,) someone who is trying to be what he can't be because he does not like what he is (7)]. Thus Condé reiterates in numerous conversations that travel, the nomadic life allows one to spread out, like a rhizome, to be open to others and to continue to feed the creative imagination. Her "nomadism" is in part literary. Writing for herself, she doesn't cling to roots in her native country of Guadeloupe or even to her experiences as a black woman. Her writing reflects this determination never to go "home" if home means an obligation to be what one's family, social circle, peers, or contemporaries expect one to be.

THE EXAMINED LIFE AND THE PLEASURE OF DISPLEASING

> *Writing to me is not about audience exactly. It's about living.*
> *It's about expanding myself as much as I can and seeing myself*
> *in as many roles and situations as possible.*

–Alice Walker (in Tate, *Black Women Writers at Work*, 185)

In frequent interviews and numerous articles and essays, Maryse Condé states clearly that she does not write to please any audience; she writes for herself (Pfaff 30; 49). In "The Role of the Writer" (1993), she recalls one of her first memories of writing and the response it provoked. After reading the one-act play she had written "illustrating the many facets of [her mother's] character," her mother was upset not to recognize herself. "She nearly cried," Condé writes, which led the writer to discover "at a very young age . . . that writing is a very perilous exercise" (697). Something similar happens at school, as seen in one of the stories she tells in *Le cœur à rire et à pleurer* of her teacher's response to one of her homework assignments. Asked to "Describe Your Best Friend," she does: "Yvelise n'est pas jolie. Elle n'est pas non plus intelligente"

(41) [Yvelise is not pretty. She's not intelligent either" (32)]. "Avec la même maladresse, je m'efforçais ensuite d'expliquer le mystère de l'amitié entre la cancre et la surdouée" (41) [With the same clumsiness, my essay tried to explain the mysterious friendship between a dunce and an exceptionally gifted pupil (32)]. Needless to say, Yvelise was "blessée par cette franchise brutale" (41) [hurt by this blunt candidness (32)], and the teacher punished young Maryse with eight hours of detention for writing these "méchancetés" (41) [nasty things (32). "Méchancetés?" the narrator asks. Yvelise's mother continually told her how plain she was, and everyone at school knew she was no star. "Qu'est-ce on me reprochait? D'avoir dit la vérité?" (41-42) [What was I being blamed for? For having told the truth? (33)]. Such moments from Condé's childhood offer a glimpse at the role writing would play in her life and the way she approaches it: writing is first of all an honest response to what she sees around her in the world, and it is secondly an effort "to explain, to elucidate, to journey through that 'I'" (Pfaff 74; 109).

Writing includes something else, however. "If you write what you believe to be true, you displease," she says in regard to her mother's response to the play. "You are in danger of being beaten or jailed or even killed. At the same time, by making my mother cry, I felt a very intoxicating kind of power. I decided to renew the experience. Writing is largely enjoying the pleasure of displeasing" ("Role" 697). She writes for herself and also "to provoke people, to force them to accept things they don't want to accept and to see things they don't want to see. . . . Critics miss the essential point if they don't see this" (Pfaff 30; 49). The "pleasure of displeasing" is not a gratuitous gesture, not even simply a means to a predetermined end, that is, a "message" or lesson Condé seeks to impose on her readers.[8] Some readers may respond as her mother and the teacher did; they are made uncomfortable by her frank and unsentimental treatment of the subjects that interest her. The subjects Condé engages in her novels range from personal stories of male and female characters seeking to establish a cultural identity while living between cultures in the African Diaspora to narratives that recast historic periods, events, and Western canonical works from an African-Caribbean perspective. Within these contexts, she often invokes an ironic style that challenges formulaic thinking, be it the Marxism of newly independent African nations in the 1960s or the Black Pride movement in the U.S., while creating (often simultaneously) compassion for and confusion about characters who struggle to know themselves in the midst of political and historical realities.

Making visible the africanist presence (many critics note resonances with Toni Morrison's *Playing in the Dark*), Condé sometimes restores the voice of the other through irony or parody, or she rewrites historical narratives and canonical literature in sometimes shocking ways. Condé has the so-called witch Tituba meet Hawthorne's Hester Prynne in prison and discuss feminism; *Wuthering Heights* is retold in *Windward Heights* as a story of the fear of racial pollution and the dissatisfaction with heroes who advocate race pride; and as Dawn Fulton argues in this volume, *Célanire cou-coupé* reworks Mary Shelley's *Frankenstein* to create a story that "expose[s] the fundamental anxiety of race as a fear of the unknown" and challenges her readers to consider hybridity as "a monstrous simultaneity of unknown worlds." While giving voice to marginal figures who never had the chance to tell their stories (which is partly the case with Tituba), Condé also complicates that voice by refusing to conform to the formula of the courageous victim who overcomes all obstacles. She critiques everyone and everything, even the marginalized other who has suffered racism, sexism, imperial domination, colonial education, and slavery. The search for a lost identity is usually frustrated, incomplete, leaving the reader with the same sense of dissatisfaction that the characters feel. Unsentimental yet sometimes gentle, her novels mirror the frustrating, disappointing and irritating experiences we've lived.

Her characters may not be likeable; but Condé likes them because they are genuine human beings, flawed people not unlike the individuals or states of mind she has known.[9] Readers of her works will not find satisfying role models or easily accessible formulas for her characters. Quite the opposite: they annoy, they surprise. They do not represent tradition, indigeneity, or cultural pride; they are in between fixed, static positions where others would prefer to place them. They may fancy themselves revolutionaries and turn out to be racists. They may see themselves as intellectuals and turn out to be tourists. They may resist discrimination while participating in their own oppression. They may strive for importance as writers, artists, thinkers, or politicians and end up bogged down in sordid scandals or affairs. They desire love and find abuse, manipulation and neuroses.

Not only do the characters frustrate readers' expectations, but the narrative surprises, too. Condé's narratives tend to ignore the comfortable, linear, unitary route, wrapped up tightly with obvious closure. Hers is the crooked and spiraling path of irony, satire, parody, risk, defiance, and iconoclasm. Not conforming to any aesthetic expectations, she does not attempt to write canonical or "universal" works. While her writing may seem pessimistic, it is often comical. With an innovative use of multiple narrative voices in a single text, free indirect discourse, and elements of the epic, mock epic, and fictive autobiography, her works open up critical spaces for imagining identity and narrative as dynamic and evolving cultural experiences. Although Condé's novels have elicited much scholarship about her female characters, she also writes easily from a variety of perspectives, male and female, old and young, and she does each believably. As the characters in her novels question the basis for their cultural identity, often as it relates to gender identity, Condé's readers acquire a new understanding of the relationship between official and oral history and discover the complexity of realities both familiar and unfamiliar.

PAROLES DES FEMMES/WOMEN'S VOICES

Published in 1979, *Parole des femmes: essai sur des romancières des Antilles de langue française* can be seen as a continuation of the research Condé did for the dissertation on stereotypes of Blacks in West Indian literature that she had defended three years earlier.[10] As Marie-Denise Shelton observes so eloquently, the title *Parole des femmes* is "evocative" of the intention of this project (719). In the introduction, Condé frames the discussion as a dialogue, prefiguring the intimate conversations she would claim with Tituba ten years later: "Nous avons pensé qu'il serait intéressant d'interroger quelques écrivains femmes des Caraïbes francophone pour cerner l'image qu'elles ont d'elles-mêmes et appréhender les problèmes dont elles souffrent. . . . (5) [We thought it would be interesting to question some women writers from the francophone Caribbean about the image they have of themselves and about the problems in their lives. . .]. The image that emerges from this study does not correspond to the ways in which other (West Indian and African male) writers and (American feminist) critics had portrayed the West Indian woman: she is neither victim nor idol (Hewitt, *Tightropes* 170). These women's discourse is "full of anguish, frustration, and revolt," it is "neither optimistic nor victorious" (Shelton 720).

Condé notes that West Indian women share with women world-wide exploitation from and dependency on men, but that this condition has its own particular expression in a Caribbean reality (*Paroles*, 113). She concludes that "c'est cette différence qu'il impor-tait d'appréhender" (113) [It is precisely this difference that it was crucial to understand].

Condé's study also revealed to her that in addition to discussing the "often negative and always ambiguous image that people have of them," West Indian francophone women writers explore subjects in their works that are dear to them, that is, the difficulties they face in their own lives and the complexities of their relationships with men (Pfaff 37; 60). Unlike male writers, they don't address "political demands or political consciousness that leads to struggle" or "such large issues as racism, exploitation, or ideology," and they do not "talk about feminism as defined in the West" (37; 60). Often con-fronting "color issues and relationships with men and children," the writers in *Parole des femmes* "seem interested in matters com-monly defined as intimist but that are, in fact, societal problems (37-38; 60). In sum, "their writings imply that before thinking of a political revolution, West Indian society needs a psychological one" ("Order" 131). Condé's project in *Parole des femmes* furthers what Leah Hewitt calls "the American feminist project of creating and reforming literary canons . . . [by enlarging] the audience for women writers" (*Tightropes* 170); at the same time, it represents "an affirmation of the Caribbean existence and the recognition of the specificity of women's voices" in that existence (Shelton 719).[11]

Condé's deep commitment to critiquing the socioeconomic and sociocultural conditions that restrict women's lives and limit their possibilities in the world, combined with her creation of female characters whose stories and travails raise questions about the rela-tionship of gender to identity and to power, have led many inter-viewers to ask if she is a feminist. Her answer (often exasperated and frustrated) is almost always a resounding "No!" She admits being drawn to Alice Walker's concept of "womanism": "C'est-à-dire," as she explains to Monique Blérald-Ndagano, "une manière pour la femme de ne renoncer à aucun aspect de ce qui peut faire sa personnalité et de renoncer non plus à ce qui fait son épanouis-sement dans la société à laquelle elle appartient" (385) [in other words, a way for a woman not to have to give up any aspect of her personality or to renounce anything that will allow her to develop fully in the society in which she lives]. Indeed, Condé's female characters, never unproblematic or simplistic, often express themselves through an unabashed and unashamed sexuality, heterosexual and bisexual. Condé's nonjudgmental representation of black women enjoying their bodies and their pleasure represents an affirmation of women's bodies and of women as sexual agents, even in the face of rape. With Morrison's *Sula* or Jeannette Winterson's *Written on the Body*, Condé's novels offer complex literary examples for discussion and scholarship about gender and sexuality.

Like the women writers she discusses in *Parole des femmes*, Condé too is drawn to "matters commonly defined as intimist," which lead some critics to observe, as Michèle Praeger does, that "la position 'intimiste' de Maryse Condé . . . paraît plus proche de celle de la 'womanist' que de celle de la féministe (blanche, cela va sans dire) . . . " (210-11) [Condé's "intimist" position . . . seems more "womanist" than feminist (which, it goes without saying, is white)]. As Jennifer Thomas contends in this volume, Condé challenges what the term "Western feminism" has come to represent for many global feminists: a perspective exclusively white, middle-class, Amer-Anglo-Eurocentric that advocates equality at the expense of difference.[12] Instead of claiming affinity with any school of thought, Condé creates narratives that present "the woman of color as being intersectionally positioned between competing discourses of identity and difference" (Manzor-Coats 744). Writing for herself about what she sees, Condé challenges her readers to engage with the world the way she does, with skepticism, suspicion, and rigorous thinking. If that displeases, her readers must ask themselves why.

"A BORDER IS A VEIL NOT MANY CAN WEAR" (EDWIDGE DANTICAT, *THE FARMING OF BONES*)

For some readers displeasure may stem from Condé's refusal of the feminist label, for others it is her refusal to engage in identity politics. Her characters have no fixed identity based on race or gender, even though they may make that the object of their quest. Their identity remains fluid, dynamic, and unstable because what interests Condé are "cultural encounters and the conflicts and change that come with them" (Pfaff 29; 47). Just as Condé complicates any essentializing gesture based on gender and race, she also argues against the "essentialism of language," that is the "opposition between 'colonial language' and 'mother tongue'" ("O Brave New World," 5). Frequently asked about her relationship to the French and Creole languages, she describes writing in "ma propre version du français qui n'est pas la langue qu'on entend en France." "C'est un mélange entre la langue d'une personne née en Guadeloupe," she continues, "à l'écoute des nombreuses sonorités différentes du langage, et mon langage personnel" (Nunez 2) [my own version of French, which is not the language you would hear in France. . . . It's a mix of the language of a person born in Guadeloupe with an ear for the various different sounds of the language, and my personal language]. Condé's idiolect, her writing, indeed her very self-definition are above all faithful to the flux she perceives in the world around her and the realities within her self, beyond binary categories imposed by the very syntax of the questions, feminist or womanist, French or Creole.

In her essay "O Brave New World," she asks her readers to imagine a world in which "the notions of race, nationality, and language, which for so long have divided us, are reexamined and find new expressions; where the notions of hybridity, metissage, multiculturalism are fully redefined." Acknowledging her borrowing from Shakespeare's Miranda in *The Tempest*, she envisions "the mapping of a new world, a brave new world," and predicts that "with the help of the creators, writers, musicians, and dancers, backed by a new generations of politicians, it will be possible to overcome the challenge of the future" (6-7).[13] Condé's novels already envision this "brave new world." Since 1986, she has spent half her time in the U.S. though her relationship with it is ambivalent. She has also lived and visited various parts of Europe and Africa, and her own nationality is complicated by the DOM Caribbean's relationship with France and Africa, experiences that inform her novels and enrich her characters.[14] All her narrators have some African ancestry, though no character would necessarily agree with another on what that means; and just as her fiction moves with stylistic ease between genders, ethnic groups, cultural communities, and political positions, her characters frequently crisscross national boundaries. They journey from Guadeloupe, Martinique, Barbados, Panama, Peru to California, South Carolina, Paris, London, Senegal, Guinea, South Africa—all corners of the African diaspora. As Johanna Garvey proposes in this volume, the black Atlantic, the ocean, may be the only home common to them. Christiane Makward (with Anne Oszwald) also proposes fluidity as a metaphor for home—la mer [the sea] and la mère [the mother] are homonyms in French—and the warm liquid of the womb is the home many of Condé's characters seek.

Maryse Condé: A Writer of Her Own

Set in France, the Caribbean, in parts of West Africa and Southern Africa, North America, Central America, and South America, Condé's is truly a literature of the African diaspora and the globe, one of the many reasons she deserves greater renown among readers of literature in English. Her work illustrates a new global literature demonstrating the fluid nature of current identities, resulting not only from colonialism and slavery, but as Pascale De Souza observes in her essay in this volume, from various patterns of migration and movement that are part of postmodern life. Nationality is no longer clear; home is not stable. Indeed, as Gloria Oneyoziri argues, ethnicity is not even static as characters discover the African ancestry within themselves, or accept the European branches of their family trees. Condé's characters are mobile, geographical nomads, expatriot wanderers, symbolically in exile, or immigrants who later attempt to return "home." They help make up the new communities and ethnoscapes that challenge both our conventional perceptions of nations and borders and our comprehension of cultural references.

On one level, the various references, metaphors and allusions in her novels testify to the "concern" Condé says she shares with Vèvè Clark "for 'diaspora literacy'" (Pfaff 98; 144). Condé weaves into her narratives the names of historical and cultural figures whom she feels "that we, the people of the Black Diaspora, should know and recognize . . ." (98-99; 144); and which, by extension, all readers need to understand to fully comprehend the text. At the same time, Condé's references go beyond simply cataloging figures from the Black Diaspora and invite her readers into what Clark would call "a sphere of cultural difference" that "demands a knowledge of historical, social, cultural, and political development generated by lived and textual experience" ("Developing Diaspora Literacy and *Maroon* Consciousness" 41-42). Beyond E.D. Hirsch's limited notion of "cultural literacy" and Condé's own interpretation of Clark's "diaspora literacy," her novels perform truly multicultural, global literacy. They implicitly call on readers to look beyond the reference on the page: not simply to go look it up (checking the Atlas for the exact location of N'Dossou when reading *Histoire de la femme cannibale*, for example), but to experience what is *dessous* ("behind" it, in the sense that Bernabé et al. use this word in *Éloge de la créolité* when they write "*nous sommes Paroles sous l'écriture* [*we are the Words behind writing*], 38) and to glimpse and ponder the lived experience behind the reference on the page. Her references ask us to reconsider, as Kathleen Gyssels does in this volume, what we think "hoodoo" means and what we learned in school about the Salem witch trials; they make us rethink with Jennifer Sparrow any unconditional admiration for Fanon. Condé goads us to reread *Wuthering Heights*; she inspires us to question received accounts of what started the Spanish American War as Maria Cristina Fumagalli does in her essay. Reading Condé is an education in ever-changing transhistorical and global social formations.

QUILTED NARRATIVES, CROSS-TALK OF THEORIES

Carole Boyce Davies and Elaine Savory Fido describe the term "quilted narrative" in their introduction to *Out of the Kumbla* as "braided or woven," a narrative that "alters the language and mode of fictional . . . discourse" (6). Quilting suggests resourcefulness, making beauty and warmth out of what others have discarded, and in some respects, Condé's global perspective evolves from and "quilts" intellectual developments that began during the decade she was born in Guadeloupe. What develops in her work can also be called, borrowing a term Jennifer Thomas uses in this volume, "a cross-talk" of theories.

Unlike Maryse Boucolon, bored in Pointe-à-Pitre without contacts to the larger world, the generation of young West Indian students in Paris in the thirties were awakened to the richness of a part of the world they had barely heard of in the French schools where they learned history beginning with "our ancestors the Gauls." Through the acquaintances they were making with other students from around the French colonial empire, and from the works of the Harlem Renaissance poets and the academic studies of Maurice Delafosse and Leo Frobenius, they encountered the continent of Africa as they never had before.[15] The result was *Négritude*, initially a cultural movement calling for and expressing racial pride and solidarity among Blacks worldwide as children of Africa.[16]

In the introduction to *Poésie antillaise* (1977), Condé outlines the major moments of this movement. The journal *Revue du monde noir*, founded in 1931 by Paulette Nardal (Martinique) and Léo Sajou (Haïti) as an outlet for literary, artistic, and scientific writing by black intellectuals and "amis des Noirs" [friends of Blacks], "présentait l'Afrique comme une sorte de Terre Sainte" [presented Africa as a kind of Holy Land]. Publishing articles commemorating the suffering Blacks shared, editors invited readers to "se connaître et à s'aimer" (7) [know and love themselves]. The following year,

1932, a group of young West Indian students produced *Légitime défense,* a manifesto denouncing Western capitalism and its cultural hegemony and calling for new inspiration derived from Marx, Freud, and surrealism and for a rehabilitation of the cultural value of non-Western civilizations.

The final stop on the road to *négritude* was the literary review *L'Étudiant noir.* Aimé Césaire (Martinique), Léon Gontran-Damas (French Guiana), and Léopold Sédar Senghor (Senegal) were among the editors who proclaimed in the first issue in 1934: "On cessait d'être un étudiant essentiellement martiniquais, guadeloupéen, guyanais, africain, malgache pour n'être plus qu'un seul et même étudiant noir. Terminée la vie en vase clos" (qtd. in Condé, "Introduction" 9) [We've stopped being Martinican, Guadeloupean, Guyanan, African or Madagascan so that from now on we can be one and the same black student. Life lived in a vacuum is over]. Refusing European aesthetic models and liberating themselves from the confines of assimilation (grounding ideology of French colonialism), the co-founders of *négritude* embrace Africa and beckon fellow writers and artists to return "aux sources" [to (African) sources] for artistic and cultural inspiration. In 1939, Césaire would publish *Cahier d'un retour au pays natal* in a little known journal *Volontés,* and his neologism *négritude* was inscribed forever in the history of West Indian and world literature.

As revitalizing as it was for its founders and many of its proponents, however, *négritude* would not remain long without facing serious debate. Maryse Boucolon arrives in Paris in 1953 (a year after Frantz Fanon's critique of *négritude* appeared in *Peau noire, masques blancs*), perhaps unaware of the particulars of the debate surrounding this movement; but she is certainly heir to the questioning it provoked. As she explains in the 1977 introduction, constituting an identity based solely on ethnic heritage struck many as essentialism; and the mythic return to the African "homeland" ignored (naïvely and dangerously) past and present realities in African nations that dispel any notion of "black unity." Three years before publishing *Poésie antillaise,* Condé had already reflected in print about these notions. Calling *négritude* "a sentimental and empty trap" that starts "from an illusory 'racial' community founded upon a heritage of suffering" and "obliterates the true problems that have always been of a political, social, and economic nature," she writes that "the Black ('Nègre') does not exist. . . . Our liberation will come through the knowledge that there will never be any Blacks ('Nègres'). There has only ever been human exploitation" ("Négritude césairienne, Négritude senghorienne," qtd. by Nesbitt, "Negritude").[17] Condé has since spoken pointedly about the great "disillusionment" most of her generation felt by *négritude*'s promise that Africa would be "a home," and she questions the "likeness" that this consciousness imposed on so many different black realities (Clark interview 117). Her first novel *Hérémakhonon*, as Serigne Ndiaye discusses in this volume, presents an ironic critique of these aspects of *négritude*, especially the belief that returning to Africa can be a means for a West Indian to establish ethnic identity. For many West Indians, the African essentialism apparently inherent to *négritude* denied the Caribbean difference that should itself be valorized through a recognition of the uniqueness of *créole*, an evocative manifestation of the specificity and plurality of the region. Other heirs to *négritude* in the Caribbean have had their own dialogue with the "Founding Ancestor," most importantly, in the movements of *antillanité* and *créolité*, which Laurence Porter describes in his essay in this volume.[18]

Articulate and stalwart in her critique of certain aspects of *négritude*, Condé nevertheless recognizes the historical importance of the movement and continues to remind us that "you have to consider [Césaire] within the context of his era. Without Césaire we might not be what we are." "I think we are all Césaire's children," she says to Pfaff, he is the "Founding Ancestor" in that "he was the first to give [West Indians] racial pride, racial consciousness, and the awareness that the West Indies are not insignificant dots, 'specks of dust,' in the Caribbean Sea"; and he gave to Blacks worldwide consciousness of: "their connection to a continent like Africa" (38; 61). Like her nonlinear narrative, Condé's analysis of literary theories refuses to adhere to an easily traceable path. While affirming the fundamental importance of Césaire, her fiction still questions *négritude* as a clear affirmation of blackness as a race or Africa as a source of identity; in this sense her novels can be said to illustrate principles of *métissage* and creolization, the cultural quilting, braiding, blending, and building of various cultural elements.

For Gloria Onyeoziri in this volume, *métissage* has the added sophistication of recognizing gender as an element just as important as race, ethnicity and culture, and she sees the *métissage* performed in Condé's texts as a feminine response to *créolité*. While the concept of creolization is inclusive—creation of a new culture drawn from African, Asian, Indian and other cultures in the Caribbean, even incorporating European colonial elements—it tends to neglect the persistent social reality of racial difference that results in everyday experiences of racism. Use of the concept *métissage*, on the other hand, recognizes that the braiding of cultural forms is not without suffering. English speaking readers may be more familiar with Homi Bhabha's notions of hybridity, as Laurence Porter uses it here. Bhabha prefers this botanical metaphor rather than *métissage* because of the latter's more charged etymology denoting race-mixing. Bhabha also contributes the notion of the third space which breaks down binaries between black and white, African and European, etc., and as Porter argues, it is from that third space that many of Condé's narrators seem to speak.

The border crossings found in Condé's works touch on all domains—cultural, literary, linguistic, political, social, and critical; and Carine Mardorossian's discussion of *La migration des cœurs* in this volume demonstrates how this novel can be read as "a rewriting of the assumptions and tropes that motivate analyses of postcolonial rewritings." Inhabiting while questioning concepts of *négritude, antillanité, métissage, créolité,* African diaspora consciousness, and postcolonialism, Maryse Condé has, as Monique Blérald-Ndagano observes, "su rechercher et trouver sa voie (voix) propre qui fait d'ailleurs d'elle l'une des écrivains antillais les plus lus et les plus traduits... (7) [learned how to seek out and find her own way (voice), which is what makes her one of the most read and translated West Indian writers]. In a transformative echo of the statement made by the editors in *Étudiant noir* (1934), Blérard-Ndagano concludes that what distinguishes Maryse Condé from her contemporaries in the Caribbean is that her work "ne sera ni africain, ni guadeloupéenne, ni américaine, ni française. Elle sera tout cela à la fois" (10-11) [will be neither African, nor Guadeloupean, nor American, nor French. It will be all of these at once]. Condé's novels invite her readers to entertain a variety of possibilities, privileging only the questioning that is at the heart of her identity as woman, as writer, and as global nomad from the Caribbean.

TRANSLATION: CANNIBALISM, DISJUNCTIONS, REVELATION, DIALOGUE

The opening group of essays address the complexities of translation, and in a sense the entire collection was conceived as an attempt at translation. As Maryse Condé's work as writer, scholar and teacher has gained in stature for readers and scholars over the last thirty years, her novels have been translated into English almost as quickly as they appear in French. Access to her novels in English has led to them being studied in a variety of fields at all levels of the university curriculum as faculty in a variety of disciplines seek to design courses that are both more interdisciplinary and more culturally diverse. Her works enrich discussions of narrative practices and themes in world literature, at the same time that they offer literary examples outside of the field of literature (the relationship between Official History and personal history, cultural identity in postcolonial realities, the writer *engagé*, to name a few).

We who have read Condé in both French and English, have heard her speak and studied her in various venues, we wish to translate Condé for the teacher or scholar who may not be familiar with the many contexts from which her writing springs. In this attempt, we are aware that every act of translation is an interpretation fraught with possibilities and perils, for as Richard Philcox has said elsewhere, a novel by Condé is "déjà la traduction en français, une langue européenne, d'une culture non européenne. Le livre en anglais est donc la traduction d'une traduction . . . " (in Araujo 230) [already a translation, in French, a European language, of a non-European culture; so the English version is a translation of a translation]. And Condé's words to Emily Apter about any translation of her novels ring in our ears: "For me, it is another work, perhaps an interesting one, but very distant from the original" ("Crossover Texts/Creole Tongues"). Condé the person might not recognize herself in some of these attempts to elucidate her work. We believe, however, that through these essays the reader "should be able to hear Maryse Condé and understand her character and her culture are fundamentally different," as Richard Philcox writes of the preface to his translation of *The Last of the African Kings* [org. *Les derniers rois mages*] (vii). We have selected essays that introduce Condé to an English speaking readership (Laurence Porter provides an excellent overview of the literary/historical background), as well as ones that provide new perspectives on her work. Some are contradictory, some complementary, but they are nonetheless enlightening when read alongside one another because each brings a slightly different critical perspective to reading this writer and appreciating what makes her different.

The essays on translation, particularly, bring to light the nuances, obstacles, and complications of crossing the various cultural, literary, and historical contexts that nourish Condé's writing as we seek to reach English-language readers in academic circles. Richard Philcox describes translation as "a form of cannibalism" in the preface to *The Last of the African Kings* (iv). In his essay reprinted in this volume he takes the metaphor further and reflects on how he himself is cannibalized, transformed, and reborn as the Other through translation. In order to translate he must become not only Maryse Condé, but Maryse Condé's characters, black, African, Caribbean, female, or whomever she writes. We hope readers of this collection and of Condé will keep Philcox's analogy in the back of their mind as we have while preparing the volume.

The essay reprinted here is one of many instances when Richard Philcox, Condé's husband and most consistently her translator, has reflected publicly about what is at stake when translating a text from the Caribbean. He observes in the preface mentioned above that "to translate the Caribbean text is doubly cannibalistic since the Caribbean work of fiction is, according to Césaire, Glissant, Depestre, already a cannibalization of the Western canon" (iv). To elaborate on the "palimpsests of Caribbean discourse" that he finds in Condé's novel, he cites Antonio Benitez Rojo's words from *The Repeating Island* : "[The Caribbean novel] is a double performance, a representation containing another representation. The first, or rather the most visible, is directed toward seducing the Western reader; the second is a monologue that returns towards the I, toward the Caribbean self, intending to mythify and at the same time transcend symbolically its unnatural-natural genesis, that is to assume its own marginality vis-a-vis the West and to speak of its Calibanesque Otherness, an Otherness deriving from the violence of conquest, colonization, slavery, piracy, war, plunder, occupation, dependence, misery, prostitution, and even tourism" (vi-vii). Drawing on three novels from the Caribbean in her essay "Crossing the Bridge of Beyond: Translating the Mangroves of French Caribbean Identities," Pascale De Souza fleshes out the multiple complexities, issues, and problems inherent in any attempt to translate the diversity of Caribbean culture and Creolized French into English. Some of her examples bring to light instances when the absence of a cultural equivalent in the target language results in a loss of meaning. More importantly for a discussion about translation, however, other examples alert her readers to the danger of oversimplifying the opacity of the Caribbean subject's "Calibanesque Otherness." As De Souza aptly concludes, one must experience some challenge in reading Condé or one is not reading Condé.[19]

Kathleen Gyssels's essay "On the Untranslatability of Tituba Indian: An Intercultural Subject," as the title suggests, takes the discussion of translation to another discursive space. Gyssels's close reading of different paratextual elements reveals the struggle of the narrative voice to establish out of an echoless history an "affirmative subjectivity" for a historical figure about whom a lot will no doubt remain untranslatable. Gyssels's depiction of Tituba Indian, *sorcière noire de Salem*, as an individual (mis)translated from one culture to another (in this case, from the Caribbean to Puritan New England) could apply to many of Condé's characters. And as Gyssels argues in regard to Tituba, by writing them into being, Condé gives them the opportunity to speak for themselves or for others whose voices history has stifled, but also perhaps for the author who through her subtle intervention raises questions about sexuality, racism, notions of cultural superiority, and possibilities for hybridity.

Broadening Gyssels's discussion of the subject in/and History as seen through the novel *Moi, Tituba*, Jennifer Thomas's essay "Talking the Cross-Talk of Histories" departs from the linguistic focus. Her essay extends the concept of translation beyond the metaphors of cannibalism and a (potentially flawed) bridge between cultures and shows how Condé creates a literary space in this novel in which different histories talk to, rather than at, one another, and where silenced voices may be heard. As Thomas demonstrates, Condé's validation of Tituba's experience does not mean that she seeks to write a final and definitive translation of this figure's life: it emerges instead as an ongoing song that challenges dominant historical narratives and denounces the myth of Caribbean alterity.

Philcox's metaphor of translation as cannibalism has special resonances for the Caribbean writer, for as Peter Hulme explains, the word "Canibales" was a form of "Carib" (365). With the essays in this section, we begin to see the relationship between Carib/Cannibal and Caliban, who learned English so that he might curse. Condé goes beyond quoting the canon or cursing the colonizer; to read Condé is to deepen the complexity of one's understanding of the multiplicities of Caribbean and African diaspora identity, and of history itself.

The next essays, grouped under the heading "Genealogies and Gender, History's Routes, Identity's Rhizomes," address issues raised by the Black diaspora subject's search for origins and identity, especially as it is complicated by gender. The metaphor of finding one's roots, according to Condé, is not without pitfalls, and a precolonial past cannot be romanticized. As Serigne Ndiaye announces in the title of his essay "Not enough shade under the 'Royal Kaïlcédrat': Maryse Condé's *Hérémakhonon* or the difficult search for ancestors," he examines how Condé's first novel challenges both the "royalness" and the "rootedness" of the legendary African tree that Aimé Césaire uses as a metaphor for a dignified racial identity rooted in Africa. Ndiaye's close reading of *Hérémakhonon* highlights Condé's implicit critique of *négritude* by revealing the novel's creation of a dense canvas of challenges that make the construction of a unitary black world fragile and problematic.

Whereas Ndiaye focuses on Condé's critique of *négritude* in *Hérémakhonon* in terms of the inadequacy of the Founding Ancestor Césaire's metaphor, Jennifer Sparrow addresses a theoretical founding father, Frantz Fanon, as indicated in her title, "'I'm no Mayotte Capécia': Engaging with Fanon in *Hérémakhonon*." Drawing on Condé's inscription in her first novel of the heroine of the Martinican novel *Je suis martiniquaise*, Sparrow challenges Fanon's critique of Mayotte by examining what Condé's novel tells us about "gender formation in relation to the construction of race for the Caribbean woman." Gloria Nne Onyeoziri's essay also engages with Fanon's critique of Capécia's heroine. As Onyeoziri's title suggests, however, her essay "In the Face of the Daughter: Feminist Perspectives on *Métissage* and Gender" examines the relationship between gender and the theoretical concept of *métissage*. Onyeoziri's close reading of *La vie scélérate* [*Tree of Life*] demonstrates that *métissage* can be "a useful term of analysis of certain forms of racial and sexual oppression and their continuing influence" rather than a "temptation of lactification for black women" as Fanon describes it. Onyeoziri proposes that Condé's multiracial character Claude offers a new metaphor for the incorporation of the complexities inherent in constituting a cultural identity.

Finishing out this section, Johanna Garvey's essay, "(Up)rooting the Family Tree: Genealogy and Space in Maryse Condé's Fiction," returns us to an examination of the (masculinist) imagery associated with the search for roots that Ndiaye addresses in the opening essay; at the same time that it continues the discussions by Sparrow and Onyeoziri about what an analysis of gender brings to identity construction. Garvey's reading of *La vie scélérate* in conjunction with two later novels, *Les derniers rois mages* [*The Last of the African Kings*] and *Desirada*, reveals both a persistent concern for patrilineage on the part of Condé's characters and more and more concerted attempts on the part of the author to relinquish patrilinear models for the "family tree." Garvey's analysis of Condé's female characters proposes that "contemporary daughters can begin to trace a path that is not genealogical, as they turn to writing-as-becoming and claim new spaces in which to shape a new identity." In the end, Garvey offers the possibility of the ocean that surrounds the Caribbean islands as a new metaphor for identity origin. Questioning founding ancestors, established theories and myths of origin becomes a kind of literary/critical transgression in these essays, and other metaphors emerge—rhizome, ocean, womb—though none is posited as a clear alternative.

The section "Transgressing Boundaries, Challenging Categories" opens with Laurence Porter's essay "Maryse Condé: Historian of the Black Diaspora," which in its systematic and comprehensive review of Condé's work as it has been read in the context of Caribbean philosophy and literature provides a *bilan* for the analyses presented thus far. Porter's analysis of *Desirada* unravels the assumption that Guadeloupean women write fiction and Martinican men write theory by showing that whereas the male authors' inspiration diminishes when they try to ground themselves in one place alone, "Condé's synthetic vision achieves an overarching, open-ended diasporic consciousness that imposes no conditions for membership, and that perpetually renews itself through its steady expansion."

One element of this expansion can be seen in "Monstrous Readings: Transgression and the Fantastic in *Célanire cou-coupé*" [*Who Slashed Celanire's Throat?*], an essay in which Dawn Fulton discusses how Condé takes the concept of a "monstrous" identity elaborated in her previous novel *Desirada* one step further by incorporating it into the genre of the fantastic. Drawing on Mary Shelley's *Frankenstein* and theories of the fantastic and of cultural hybridity and *métissage*, Fulton proposes that through the monstrous and ultimately unknowable figure at the heart of her narrative, Condé insists on contradiction as a creative process, a quality as essential to contemporary understandings of cultural identity as it is to the fantastic narrative. "Oedipus and Oedipa according to Condé" by Christiane Makward (with Anne Oszwald) also revisions canonical border crossings. The nuanced analysis in this essay of several "excessive" Oedipal ties in mother-child dyads in two recent Condé novels, *La Belle créole* and *Histoire de la femme cannibale* ferrets out possible answers to the question, "Caribbean Oedipus, Black Oedipa, do they exist, like Black Orpheus and Black Venus?" The essay's interrogation of the role of the mother in identity construction, on several levels—as function, introjection, and metaphor—reveals that a "Black Oedipa" does indeed exist, and that she has no need to "destroy herself nor tear out her eyes to see the internal light."

The analyses in the essays of the final section, "Problematizing Postcolonial Histories," talk back, in a sense, to history, personal and collective, and to theory by revealing the ways in which historiographies are stolen or appropriated and by contesting the foundations of postcolonial critiques. Kathleen Elkins begins her essay, "History's Theft and Memory's Return in Maryse Condé," with a discussion of the ways in which Condé's work engages in a dialogue with other Caribbean Francophone writers, especially Glissant and Bernabé, to explore the relationship between memory and history. Elkins's close reading of Condé's novella *Nanny-ya* in conjunction with her own history as told in *Le cœur à rire et à pleurer* [*Tales From the Heart*] reveals that for Condé, literature is always the theft of another's History, both to relieve the other's burden and to return it remembered as a personal tale of Memory.

In her analysis of *La migration des cœurs* [*Windward Heights*], Maria Cristina Fumagalli shows how Condé rewrites Bronte's canonical novel by setting it in the Caribbean and highlighting the racial dimensions involved in forbidden romance. Taking into consideration the historical, political, social and economic contexts of Condé's novel, Fumagalli's essay, "Maryse Condé Creolizes the Canon in *La migration des cœurs*," demonstrates how this novel helps move Caribbean writing from narratives of existential fragmentation to ones that admit the possibility of new multifaceted and ultimately liberated Creole identities.

Carine Mardorossian's "Rewriting the Postcolonial" provides an apt conclusion to our attempt to translate Condé to Anglophone readers as it examines this author's re-vision of Emily Brontë's *Wuthering Heights* in relation to the larger context of postcolonial revisionism. Mardorossian's article reaches beyond a textual analysis of *La Migration des cœurs* as a rewriting its colonial source-text; she shows how Condé's refusal to provide the reader easy opportunities for admiration and identification or to provide satisfying narrative conclusions forces us to question many premises on which postcolonial literary analyses have been based.

While the contributors to this collection may use different approaches or methodologies, they represent the broad spectrum of scholarship Condé's work elicits. Her *œuvre* has increasingly become the subject of scholarly articles and book chapters in the U.S. and abroad. Four volumes dedicated to her works have appeared in French since 1995: *L'Œuvre de Maryse Condé* (Lydie Moudileno) and *L'Œuvre romanesque de Maryse Condé : féminisme, quête de l'ailleurs, quête de l'autre* (Monique Blérald-Ndagano) are book-length studies; *L'Œuvre de Maryse Condé: A propos d'une écrivaine politiquement incorrecte* (Nara Araujo, ed.) is a collection of presentations made at the international conference "l'Autre Regard" en hommage à Maryse Condé (Pointe-à-Pitre, 1995); and *Maryse Condé: Une nomade inconvenante: Mélanges offerts à Maryse Condé* (Madeleine Cottenet-Hage and Lydie Moudileno, eds.) brings together personal and scholarly essays on Condé's life and her work. A special issue of *Callaloo* (summer 1995) edited by Delphine Perret and Marie-Denise Shelton offers a selection of articles in both French and English, as does the issue of *World Literature Today* (Focus on Maryse Condé) two years earlier (autumn 1993). *Emerging Perspectives on Maryse Condé: A Writer of Her Own* brings together for the first time a collection of essays in English. We have limited the focus to Condé's novels for the sake of unity, and we were not able to include discussion of all her novels. Condé's other prose fiction, drama, and nonfiction, as well as her autobiographical *Le Cœur à Rire et à Pleurer* [*Tales From the Heart*] deserve further study.

Given the growing interest of students, teachers and scholars in Condé's work, *Emerging Perspectives on Maryse Condé: A Writer of Her Own* represents an effort to share the delights and complexities of her novels with a broader readership, and we hope that the critical introduction situates Condé's novels within larger political and theoretical discussions about her contribution to women's writing, to writing from the African diaspora, and to world literature. The bibliography of criticism on Condé's writing complements the "selective bibliography" found in Françoise Pfaff's *Entretiens avec Maryse Condé* and updated in the English version, *Conversations with Maryse Condé*. For a more complete list of works about Condé in French and English from France, the U.S. and the francophone world from 1971-95, we refer readers to Pfaff's text. *Emerging Perspectives on Maryse Condé: A Writer of Her Own* celebrates an exciting, prolific, disconcerting, and yes, appealing writer who has influenced our own work and our ways of reading. Engaged and engaging in literary criticism and the diffusion of world literatures, Maryse Condé has come to represent for us an urgent voice in debates on culture, writing, and identity, within and outside the academy, both in the U.S. and abroad. Her works explore old questions and open up new spaces of inquiry; and as the essays in this collection suggest, they envision a myriad of answers.

Notes

1.   Françoise Pfaff entitles the first section of her published conversations with Maryse Condé "Vie Plurielle" [A Plural Life]. In 1996, Pfaff made these conversations (1982-92) available to an English audience, augmented by an additional interview from 1994. In this introduction and throughout the volume, citations from these conversations are from *Conversations with Maryse Condé*, followed by a semicolon and the corresponding page number from the French edition.

2.   This and other translations from French to English are our own, unless a standard translation is indicated.

3.   "Maroon Nanny for All Worlds" or "Maroon Nanny for the Global Age" or "Maroon Maryse" [trans. Christiane Makward, referring to Édouard Glissant's concept of "Tout-Monde"].

4.   This essay appears as part of the "Contemporary Authors" series available on the Gale database (see bibliography). Further reference to this essay will be indicated in parentheses as "Autobiographical Essay."

5.   Condé has spoken about her life in numerous interviews (see Bibliography), but much of this information is culled from Pfaff's conversations, as well as from the comprehensive interviews with Vèvè Clark and from Condé's autobiographical essay (*Contemporary Authors Online*).

6.   The term was first coined in 1880 by French writer Onésime Reclus as a way of referring to the community of people worldwide who spoke French. In 1960, Léopold Sédar Senghor reappropriated the term for his own use, to invoke solidarity among the French-speaking African nations after independence and to invite them to assume their place in the larger domain of influence still held by France. (The preceding description has been culled from the definition for *francophonie* from the database Hachette's *Dictionnaire Universel Francophone*.) For some, Senghor's use of the term never adequately reappropriated it from its political reference to French imperialism. Not only does it "impose the domination of the French language," as Condé explains to Pfaff, but it also keeps former French colonies "culturally dependent, always awaiting France's opinion of their literary and artistic production" (22; 37-38). Jeannie Suk's observations should also be consid-

ered: "The term 'francophone,' widely used in the context of literary groupings, is a remnant of the now unfashionable *francophonie*, . . . [but] 'francophone' is the only French analogue that has developed in parallel function to 'postcolonial' in the Anglo-American world" (18).

7.   Briefly, *créolité* can be described as an acceptance of all parts of the Caribbean cultures including African, European, Asian, indigenous, etc. It thus enacts a mixing of the languages, races, religions, and customs of uprooted, transplanted peoples who nonetheless form a totality and have created a new culture. Characterized by cultural adaptation and confrontation between people in the same space and by a rootedness in orality, *créolité* comes to represent a syncretic, complex, diverse whole with a geopolitical, anthropological solidarity. In *Éloge de la creolité/In Praise of Creoleness*, the authors define *créolité* as: "the interactional or transactional aggregate of Caribbean, European, African, Asian and Levantine cultural elements united on the same soil by the yoke of history" (87).

8.   See Mekkawai: "Asked about the meaning (valeur et signification) she consciously or unconsciously intends to produce through writing and public speaking, Condé says: 'Je ne suis pas un "écrivain à message." J'écris d'abord pour moi, pour m'aider à comprendre et supporter la vie. En racontant des histoires que j'espère signifiantes, je souhaite aussi aider les autres, ceux de mon peuple en particulier, à comprendre et à la supporter à leur tour'" [I am not a writer with a message. I write first of all for myself, to help me understand and live my life. I write stories that I hope are meaningful to people, especially my own people, in an effort to help them understand and live their own lives].

9.   See, among other references, Pfaff 105; 153.

10. See Mekkawi.

11. Shelton goes on to write: "With regard to the gender question, the novelist shares the ideals of emancipation and freedom expounded by feminists. However, afraid to be boxed in, she has exhibited a certain mistrust toward *feminism* as a call to action or as a catchall word which in the end eludes the specificity of the Caribbean woman's situation" (721-22).

12. See among others, *Out of the Kumbla: Caribbean Women and Literature*, eds. Carole Boyce Davies and Elaine Savory Fido (esp. notes to the Introduction); Françoise Lionnet, both *Autobiographical Voices. Race, Gender, Self-Portraiture* and *Postcolonial Representations: Women, Literature, Identity; Playing in the Dark: Whiteness and the Literary Imagination*, Toni Morrison; *Third World Women and the Politics of Feminism*, edited by Chandra Talpade Mohanty, Ann Russo, and Lourdes Torres.

13. In reference to this "brave new world," Condé also cites Stuart Hall's description of diaspora in *Culture, Globalization and the World System*: "Diaspora does not refer to those scattered tribes whose identity can only be secured in relation to some sacred homeland to which they must return at all costs. Diaspora identities are those which are constantly producing and reproducing themselves anew through transformation and differences" (4).

14. With Martinique, French Guyana, and Réunion, Guadeloupe became a French *Département d'outre mer* (DOM) shortly after World War II, in 1946. In principle, the DOM were "to have the same laws and rights applied to their peoples as to all other French citizens. In practice, the majority of laws and benefits were not extended to the Antilles until well into the 1950s and 1960s, with many not being extended until the 1970s and 1980s" (Haigh 5).

15. For an excellent overview of this period, especially for use in the classroom, see Euhzan Palcy's documentary, *Aimé Césaire: une voix pour l'histoire/Aimé Césaire: A Voice for History*, in three parts, 150 minutes, 1994. Available from California Newsreel.

16. For the standard history of the *négritude* movement, readers have the rich resource of Lilyan Kesteloot's *Écrivains noirs de langue française: Naissance d'une littérarature* that came out in Bruxelles in 1961. This study has since been translated by Ellen Conroy Kennedy as *Black Writers in French: A Literary History of Negritude*. First published in 1974, by Temple University Press, Kennedy's translation was reprinted in 1991 by Howard University Press; this revised edition includes a new preface by the author and supplementary bibliography.

17. Nesbitt remarks in relation to this quote: "Condé's critique implies that Césaire's Négritude cannot remain a mere invocation to black identity politics; instead, the shock of its alienating gesture must serve to illuminate the very constructedness of 'blackness' itself" ("Négritude").

18. See Glissant's *Discours antillais* (and Michael Dash's translation of selected essays by Glissant, *Caribbean Discourse*), and the bilingual edition of Bernabé et al., *Éloge de la créolité*.

19. For more discussion about translating Condé's novels, see two essays in *L'Œuvre de Maryse Condé*, edited by Araujo: Doris Kadish's "*Tituba* et sa traduction"; and "La question de la traduction plurielle ou les traducteurs de Maryse Condé," by Françoise Massardier-Kenney. For a discussion about Philcox's relationship to the author and to publishers, see his interview with Doris Kadish in *The French Review*, "Traduire Maryse Condé: entretien avec Richard Philcox."

TRANSLATING CULTURE AND CROSS-TALK OF NARRATIVES: FROM TRANSLATION TO DIALOGUE

TRANSLATING MARYSE CONDÉ: A PERSONAL ITINERARY[1]

Richard Philcox

Quince: Bless thee, Bottom! Bless thee! Thou art translated!

Exit

Bottom: I see their knavery. This is to make an ass of me. To fright me if they could. But I will not stir from this place, do what they can. . . . I will walk up and down here, and will sing, that they shall hear I am not afraid.

–*A Midsummer Night's Dream*

The above quotation from Shakespeare caught my eye because of the use of the word "translated" in regard to the actual person. Bottom has become someone or rather something else. Translation implies a change, a transformation, but of what and of whom? Not only does the text, the very subject of the translation, undergo a major upheaval, but the translator in person is transformed in the process. Does the translator take charge and manipulate the text or does the author of the text play a dominant role and have the last word?

Nothing gives me more pleasure than to read my translations in front of an audience and become the actor I always wanted to be. I then become the author and my translation becomes the text. I thus become Maryse Condé—"Maryse Condé, c'est moi"—and perform the greatest ventriloquist's act there is, taking over from the author and playing to the gallery. There she sits on the stage beside me, silent and composed, while I can reach an English-speaking audience with a translation she does not recognize of a text she once wrote in another language. And yet she should know what it's like, taking an author and adapting her to one's own voice. After all, she did it to Emily Brontë and *Wuthering Heights*, and I did it to Maryse Condé and *Windward Heights*. Nowhere do I feel this more than when I read my translation of Cathy's wake: "While I was on earth, I had the feeling you were inside me, always there, in my head, in my heart and in my body. I even got the impression I was you." In this particular book, not only am I rereading one of my own literary canons, but rewriting it through a Caribbean filter.

I can remember taking Maryse to a particular spot on Grande Terre in Guadeloupe that for me corresponded exactly to the setting of *Windward Heights*. It was an old sugar mill, set amidst a great expanse of cane fields, and it would be difficult to find a more desolate spot. The actual house had long fallen into ruin and all that remained were a few stone walls and the tower of the windmill that ground the sugar cane. Throughout the translation process my mind would concentrate on that spot and it was as if the island itself was helping me find a voice. The same can be said for the translation of *Crossing the Mangrove*. Although, as I said in the introduction to the translation, Virginia Woolf's *To the Lighthouse* gave me the music to the monologues, it was the village of Montebello, where we live, alias Rivière-au-Sel, that was speaking to me. I only had to sit in front of my computer and transport myself back to Montebello, our neighbors, the trees, and the forest, to see exactly what I was translating. I wonder if Moise, our postman, or the rum guzzlers at Chez Christian, the local rum shop, ever realized they were being immortalized in print. You can't translate unless you understand it, was the motto I went by when I worked as a technical translator in Paris. I had to visit the factories, study the machines, understand how they worked before even daring to translate a manual or a technical description. Literary translation for me is somewhat similar. I have to hear, smell, touch, and see, and in this respect I am privileged since there are not many places in Condé's novels where I have not been by her side: San Francisco, Charleston, Dominica, Marie-Galante, Guadeloupe, La Désirade, France, West Africa, New York, Barbados, Salem, Boston, Martinique. My one regret is that I never got a chance to translate *Segu*, another region of the world we traveled together from Segu to Mopti to Timbuktu to Gao, twice, by boat and by land. I do feel I would have made the translation more three-dimensional than it actually is, and instilled in it a sense of time and place.

And this is where the author/translator experience becomes interesting. Although Maryse loses interest once her texts are translated, the actual genesis of the novel is a shared experience. I am there when the first flash of inspiration comes. No need to be a postcolonial scholar, no need for applied translation theories, the intimate exchange between author and translator occurs during the very moment of creation and this for me is essential.

I can remember living in Los Angeles with Maryse and watching her pine like Tituba for her lost island while she endured her "long solitude in the deserts of America." In *I Tituba, Black Witch of Salem*, Tituba fills a bowl of water in which she imagines the landscape of her island: "The bowl of water managed to encompass the entire island, with the swell of the sea merging into the waves of the sugarcane fields, the leaning coconut palms on the seashore and the almond trees loaded with red and dark green fruit." And however much Maryse says *Tituba* should be read with tongue in cheek, there is a profound melancholy that infuses the entire book, a shadow at the back of her eyes.

I can remember driving into Charleston, South Carolina, one rainy December evening in 1989 and, like her, being surprised at all the blue tarpaulins covering the roofs. Hurricane Hugo, which had flattened Guadeloupe a few months earlier, had taken its toll on Charleston, and this became the inspiration for her novel *The Last of the African Kings*, where the Caribbean meets America, not only historically, but geographically.

While translating *Desirada* I can remember taking the boat from Saint-François to cross over to the island of La Désirade and climbing up "the mountain" with Maryse to the spot where Nina, the grandmother, might have lived. There on a flat ledge that looked as if it had been balanced above the ocean stood a cabin, blackened and shapeless, capped by a patched roof that sat somewhat askew under a gray mapoo tree. You could hear the commotion of the waves buffeting below, mingled with the roar of the wind and the cries of the seagulls.

The temptation to adapt and challenge the original text is great. I am a great admirer of Tony Harrison's 1979 adaptation of *Phèdre* by Racine, where he sets the play in British India and Phèdre has become the Memsahib, the governor's wife and Hippolyte, Thomas Theophilus. The Greek pantheon has been transformed into the gods of Indian mythology. How tempting it is for the translator to rewrite and cannibalize and become an author in his own right. How I would like to reshuffle chapters and do some serious editing to the text, but there we would contest the whole question of the moral duty of the translator to the contemporary reader and as Susan Bassnett-McGuire states in *Translation Studies*: "The cannibalistic notion of translation involves a changed idea of the value of the original text in relation to its reception in the target culture." To take liberties is a dangerous thing. And yet I feel so attuned to Maryse's way of thinking and seeing the world, that I do take liberties and refuse to become a slave to the text. Given Maryse's attitude to the translated text, I feel free to cannibalize it. Once her text is translated, for her it is empowered with another music, another language that she no longer recognizes.

Walter Benjamin wrote in *The Task of the Translator*: "The task of the translator consists in finding the intended effect upon the language into which he is translating which produces in it the echo of the original." Nowhere did I find this more challenging than in *Windward Heights*. The original French title is *La migration des cœurs* (literally, "migration of the hearts") but something had to speak to the English-speaking reader of that other text, *Wuthering Heights*, which echoes throughout the book. Hence my use of the term "windward," as in the Windward and Leeward islands of the Caribbean, which felt so right. One of the chapters in the book is called "Belle île en mer," referring to the island of Marie–Galante, taken from the French song by Laurent Voulzy. For my translation, I needed another song referring to another island, and I chose "O Island in the Sun" by Harry Belafonte. These, I think, are good examples of Benjamin's Intention, producing the echo of the original.

To go back to the second question in the opening commentary, am I not the one in the end who has been translated? As a white, English-speaking male, brought up in the narrow confines of a parochial English family, belonging to a culture used to dominating the world and, at the time, grappling with a fading sense of superiority, I have had to undergo serious translation to confront the worlds of a black, female writer from the French-speaking Caribbean. As a member of a dominant culture my first transformation was to see the world through the eyes of a dominated culture. I have learned the virtues of empathy and placed myself in the minds and souls of an entire set of characters that until now have never been allowed to express themselves. My favorite author to translate has allowed me to walk through Africa, the Caribbean, Europe and the United

States, singing my language and giving voice to a self that needed expression. I have been translated into many things: a woman, a Caribbean, an African, an African-American, I have changed colors and sex, I have crossed borders and cultures. As Madhi says in *Windward Heights*:

> I know I've lived ten lives, I've lived a hundred lives before I came to live this one. I have been a toad in the mud, a slug on the rotten wood of the trees, I have been wild pine growing in the armpit of the candle-wood tree and quetzal bird feeding off fruit redder than my crest. I have been a dairy cow, I have been a goat, I have even been a woman and had two children.

> . . . I have lived in many countries. In China. In Japan. In Belarus. Sometimes I remember all these lives, the loves and misfortunes, and there is a great commotion in my head and I have to stand still, without breathing a word, until it's over.

I have had to tackle four cultures—British, American, French, and Creole—all of which are present in the novels of Maryse Condé, from the Brontës to Boston via Paris and Point-à-Pitre, and although there is no commotion in my head, I have had to deal with an intertextuality that has often influenced the translation process. Not only the intertextuality of the author, but also mine, not only that of an author well versed in the Bible, raised with a Catholic French schooling, fond of cinematographic references and possessing the unbridled imagination of the novelist, but also that of a translator steeped in French and British classics, raised on Anglo-American culture, fond of wordplay and possessing an unbridled taste for travel. Such a world of intertextuality can but have sweeping consequences for the translator's decisions, and despite the feeling of freedom to cannibalize and manipulate, in the end I am the one who is cannibalized, I am the one being forced into a world that is not my own. When I was growing up, I never thought I would be translated into a black witch from Barbados living at the time of the Salem witch trials; I never dreamed I would become a single mother from La Désirade or the descendant of an African king from Dahomey living in Charleston. In the end the author has the last say and I have become the real dummy. And I am wiser, more understanding, and more tolerant from the experience. Loving the English language as I do, I have learned to place it at the service of another culture and force it from its dominant position into a labor of love. My one last wish is that, when hearing my translations, Maryse Condé will think of Titania in *A Midsummer Night's Dream* and declare: "I pray thee, gentle mortal, sing again:/mine ear is much enamored of thy note."

Note

1.   This essay first appeared in English in *SITES: The Journal of Contemporary French Studies*, 5, no. 2 (fall 2001)(http://www.tandf.co.uk). Translated by Lydie Moudeleno as "Traduire Maryse Condé: Un itinéraire personnel," the essay was also part of the collection *Maryse Condé. Une nomade inconvenante*, edited by Cottenet-Hage and Moudileno.

CROSSING THE BRIDGE OF BEYOND: TRANSLATING THE MANGROVES OF FRENCH CARIBBEAN IDENTITIES

Pascale De Souza

I then become the author and my translation becomes the text.

The author has the last say and I have become the dummy.

–Richard Philcox

Francophone Studies enjoy increasing popularity on campuses throughout North America, as evidenced both by the number of positions offered in the field and the number of texts used in courses taught in French, as well as in introductory, cross-listed or post-graduate courses taught in English. This popularity, fueled by accessible and affordable English versions of French texts, undoubtedly increases readership and scholarship in Francophone Studies. As a critical analysis of paratextual and linguistic elements in three French Caribbean novels will show, however, the rifts and disjunctions that inevitably occur in the translation process (be it from life to art or from language to language) raise issues regarding the 'authenticity' of the texts being studied.[1]

What are some of the issues raised for Francophone Studies by the availability of texts in translation? First of all, under the influence of recent migration trends and globalizing effects, assigning literary authors a nationality becomes an increasingly difficult endeavor, as seen by the emergence of hyphenated identities such as Haitian-American, Moroccan-Belgian, Sri-Lankan-Canadian or Turko-German, to name but a few. Edwige Danticat, born and raised in Haiti until age 12 but now residing in New-York and writing in English, is a case in point. The hegemony of English has probably contributed to offering Danticat a wider audience than if she had written in Creole or French. Given, to quote a Haitian colleague, that she writes in "Haitian images," should she however be included in a course on Haitian literature taught in French, or should her work be limited to an American literature course taught in English? This particular example points to the increasing complexity of a field where both the 'nationality' of the text is often challenged and the language in which the text was originally written is no longer a defining label.

It seems that translating Danticat's texts into French would solve the dilemma of their inclusion into literary courses; the original could feature in a course open to English speakers while its translation could be studied in a course offered to French speakers. The solution yet soon appears eminently controversial as several aspects of the translation process call into question the accessibility and reliability of translated versions.

Second, financial concerns skew the issue. Depending on the return on investment publishers may expect from a translated text, some texts are more likely to be translated than others and some target languages more likely to be selected. A renowned writer writing on a topic deemed likely to attract an audience beyond speakers of the language used in the original version will thus be more readily translated and published in a foreign language. Likewise, the higher number of potential readers in English, French, or Spanish will mean that a text written in Dutch is more likely to be translated into such 'world' languages than an English text into Dutch. Given these parameters, critics of Caribbean literature who wish to explore Caribbean texts within a regional context are faced with a particularly complex situation. While Dutch-speaking critics interested in a regional approach need to read another language, given the limited number of translated texts available in Dutch, English-speaking critics can more easily have access to English translations.[2]

The issue of critical publication further complexifies the debate. Critics who submit essays written in English not only widen their opportunities for publication but also increase the readership and scholarship for the text they are studying. Editors rather than critics, however, dictate whether quotes in critical essays should be taken from the original text, from a translated version, or from both, and whether a personal translation is acceptable. The decision to work on a translated version affects critical conclusions because, as Philcox notes, translation slippages create, in effect, a new text rather than a translated clone of the original. Two series of articles entitled "The Caribbean that isn't" and "The Caribbean that is" and recently published in *The Journal of Caribbean Literatures* illustrate the challenges of dealing with a multi-lingual region. All the essays are written in English, and English translations of quotes from Haitian Creole, Spanish, Dutch, or French reveal some rifts in the translation process that problematize the analysis of linguistic forms and narrative tactics, as well as their impact on the construction of discursive identity. Editors are often at a loss to deal with such slippages if they are not fully cognizant of one of the languages used; and even if they are aware of the slippages, recommendations for rectifying them are limited by differences inherent in the languages.

An essay I published in *MaComère,* the yearly journal of the Association of Caribbean Women Writers and Scholars, entitled "When Anancy meets the Desaragnes: an arachnean reading of *The Bridge of Beyond,*" further underlines the dangers inherent in this cultural dialogue. The critical analysis of animal imagery and creolisms in *Pluie et vent sur Télumée-Miracle* by Simone Schwarz-Bart based on quotes from the original text becomes much weakened, or even irrelevant, when quotes from the English version of the novel, *The Bridge of Beyond,* are used. A character defined in French as a "un cheval de diable" (26) [literally, a devilish horse] is described in the English as "pig-headed" (19), which changes the cultural references: the horse being associated with malevolent forces in the novel while the pig is an animal traditionally butchered for Christmas.[3] Key passages likewise lose their Creole identity in the English edition (see below). Despite these slippages, journal editors required that only English quotes from standard translations be used. The slippages were such that footnotes had to be added to the published essay to indicate that the French version differed and that the claims made were better substantiated by the quotes in French.

The selection of a translator is another salient issue. A sound experience of the languages used in the original and the translated versions is not the sole requisite for an effective translation. An experience of and sensitivity to both of the cultures represented are also needed. As Richard Philcox, Maryse Condé's British husband and translator points out in this volume, "I have to hear, feel, touch, and see." Accurate translations of 'local' terms for architecture, cooking, fauna and flora are not incidental, for they feed into the imagery of the novel and contribute to an intricate web anchored upon local traditions. Within the Caribbean context, a solution could be to select one person from the region either to help in the translating process or to assume full responsibility for it. While such an approach would indeed allow for increased sensitivity to regional issues, it would raise other concerns. First, the Caribbean pool of bilingual candidates trained in translation is more limited than the American or English pools. Secondly, a Caribbean author would bring to the debate his/her own island's expertise. Which word is one to select when, depending upon the Caribbean island selected as a point of reference, a single fruit can be called guinep, chenette, akee, canep, chenep, kenip, mapo, skinip, Spanish lime or tjennét? Thirdly, such an approach may lead one to dismiss a potential translator who, though not native to the Caribbean Basin, may be intimately acquainted with its culture.

Creolisms pose another kind of challenge to translators. Authors will often select to creolize the language imposed by the (former) colonial powers, not only to add 'local flavor' but to differentiate between levels of acculturation among characters and offer an ongoing commentary on identity issues in the Caribbean. Translating creolisms into a standardized form of English then leads to a misrepresentation of the author's intent. Indeed, during various readings of 'his' work, rather than 'her' work, Philcox underlines the challenges he faced in selecting the appropriate vocabulary and creolized expressions when translating Condé's novels. Access to the author can contribute to avoiding major pitfalls and mistranslating key ideas. Even in such cases as Condé's novels, however, the author may be at a loss to help due to a lack of reference in the target language. A Caribbean person fluent in the Creole based on the target language would then need to provide valuable insights. Island specificity is always a concern, as in the case with terms referring to flora or fauna; but in the case of the translation of a French, Dutch, or Spanish Caribbean novel into English, an English Caribbean Creole term would be a more culturally appropriate match than the African-American terms sometimes found, that is, as Philcox would say, a better "echo of the original."

Finally, the publication of (translated) texts can also contribute to the distortion of the original message through the selection of different paratextual elements, such as jackets, illustrations for the front cover, quotes for the back cover, forewords, introductions, appendices, or afterwords.

The discussion that follows illustrates the challenges faced by translators more specifically within the Caribbean context. These challenges are elucidated by focusing on the selection of paratextual elements and the translation of Creole expressions or creolisms in three Guadeloupean novels, *Moi, Tituba sorcière…Noire de Salem* and *Traversée de la Mangrove* by Maryse Condé and *Pluie et vent sur Télumée-Miracle* by Simone Schwarz-Bart and their respective English editions *I, Tituba, Black Witch of Salem, Crossing the Mangrove* and *The Bridge of Beyond*. While the challenges posed by using creolisms in French and translating them into English are clearly illustrated in all three novels, the selective impact of paratextual elements is particularly salient in Condé's novels, and the translation of dialogues hinging upon Creole and French as indicators of power play between characters is more conducive to (mis)readings in Schwarz-Bart's work. Four levels of translation are put into play in this discussion: French publishers/editors translating authors' text/intention with covers that will sell books; English publishers/editors doing essentially the same thing but aiming for a different audience; Condé and Schwarz-Bart translating Caribbean identity/culture; their English/American translators providing a further translation of the authors' Caribbeaness. An analysis of the rifts and disjunctions inherent in the publication and translation of these texts illustrates how translation may indeed be naught but the failed crossing of a mangrove to an elusive beyond.

The two French editions of *Moi, Tituba sorcière…Noire de Salem* were published by Mercure de France in 1986 and Folio in 1990, and the two English versions were produced by University Press of Virginia in 1992 and 1994. In her readings of the first three editions, Lillian Manzor-Coats points out what she describes as the "untranslatability" (737) of the language used in the original version, supporting her view with a detailed analysis of the French and English titles selected. Manzor-Oates argues that this linguistic 'untranslatability'—as well as paratextual elements such as an introduction, prologue and appendix and the selection of various illustrations for the front covers—all point to a marketing strategy targeted to a specific (here gendered) audience. Editors may choose to keep the paratextual elements of the original version, translating any prologue or appendix and keeping the same cover. However, they often choose, as they did with *I, Tituba, Black Witch of Salem*, to add an Introduction, to 'invite' a different critic to contribute a Prologue and/or Afterword, and to modify the front cover with a different illustration and a different lay-out for the author's name, the translated title, and any other information they deem pertinent.

Expanding on Manzor-Oates' argument, one could argue that the "untranslatibility" represented by these changes does not so much derive from an unmet linguistic challenge as from a purposeful decision to 'adapt' the text to an anticipated audience. Manzor-Oates discusses how paratextual elements are selected with a view to attracting a gendered audience. But an editor's selection of paratextual elements can also serve a more complex purpose; as seen, for example, when editors include an introduction or afterword by a critic who is well-known to readers of the translated version, and/ or if they choose an illustration for the front cover that plays into readers' expectations of a Caribbean novel. As will be seen in the case of the English versions of *Moi, Tituba sorcière...Noire de Salem* and *Traversée de la Mangrove*, paratextual elements are not so much untranslatable, as they are translated to convey a different meaning from the original elements selected in the French version. In the case of *Moi, Tituba sorcière...Noire de Salem*, editors highlight connection to the African-American experience and female rebellion; while in *Traversée de la Mangrove*, they offer a front cover aimed at both eliciting interest in a mystery novel and reinforcing stereotypical images of Caribbean islands.

An analysis of the front covers of the two French editions of *Moi, Tituba sorcière...Noire de Salem* illustrates how publishers of the first edition 'translated' Condé's text in such a way as to sell the novel as a "Histoire romanesque," and how publishers of the second edition shift focus from the historical period of the Salem trials to female witchcraft. Mercure de France opted to feature on the front cover of the first edition a rural scene with dark forests in the foreground, a village in a clearing and a fire raging just beyond the first row of houses. Clouds of billowing smoke fill up half the page, which creates an oppressive, ominous landscape. Though Condé originally wanted to call her novel *Moi, Tituba* and rejected the label "Histoire Romanesque," "the publishers [who] said that it was a bit laconic as a title" (Scarboro 1992, 205) prevailed. The 'new' title *Moi, Tituba sorcière...Noire de Salem* appears in white and red letters within the clouds on the front cover, and "Histoire Romanesque" is printed in smaller letters against the backdrop of the forest at the bottom. The rather odd presentation of the title (see below on the left-hand side) focuses the reader's attention on Tituba's 'status' as a witch, perhaps targeting interest in such a sulfurous topic, and creates a link between the author's name and "Noire de Salem." This link is mirrored but also challenged by the first epigraph, in which Condé states that "Tituba et moi, avons vécu en étroite intimité pendant un an. C'est au cours de nos interminables conversations qu'elle m'a dit ce qu'elle n'avait confié à personne" (7)[4] [Tituba and I have lived in close proximity for a year. During our endless conversations, she shared with me what she had never divulged to anyone]. On the one hand, the epigraph "destabilizes Condé's own authorial position" (Manzor-Coats 737) in relation to Tituba, as author and character seem to merge and Condé becomes the 'Noire de Salem.' On the other hand, Condé asserts her mastery of subversion in relation to her publishers by establishing an impossible link between Tituba, who lived during the Salem trials, and herself, a 20th-century Guadeloupean writer, and thus destabilizing the meaning of the title and label they imposed on her novel. *Moi, Tituba sorcière...Noire de Salem* can neither be a historical novel—Condé points out in a historical note at the end of the novel that hardly anything tangible is known of the 'real' Tituba—nor a testimonio, because Tituba died long before Condé was born.

The next few pages further complexify the potential reading of the novel. Readers are reminded on page 3 that the work figures in the collection "Histoire Romanesque," on page 5 that they are about to read a novel called "Moi, Tituba, sorcière...," and finally on page 7 they are given the information as provided below on the right-hand side.

Title on the front cover of the Mercure de France edition	Title on page 7 of the Mercure de France edition.
Maryse Condé	Maryse Condé
Moi,Tituba **Sorcière**	Moi, Tituba, sorcière... *Noire de Salem*
Noire de Salem	

At this point, the ambiguous genre, topic, and status of the novel have been "clearly" established. It is a historical novel that apparently takes place in New England during the Salem trials, it is not a historical novel because the author denies the label with her historical note; it is a testimonio according to the first epigraph, but it cannot be a testimonio because Tituba and Condé are not contemporaries. As it is announced on the first page, the novel is clearly focused on "Moi, Tituba," who is a "sorcière," but Condé may also be a "sorcière" if we 'misread' the term "moi" here. The novel may deal with color issues, and yet it may not: on page 5 the title simply states "Moi, Tituba, Sorcière…," while on page 7 "Noire de Salem" is printed in italics and relegated to the second line. This complex presentation of the novel—which, as we shall discuss, illustrates the tensions between author, editor and publisher—has but one objective: to sell more books. The cover features a bonfire, and billowing smoke is sending an ominous message; witchcraft is being practiced but no image of the witch is offered, though we suppose she may be black. This romanticized view of a historical period would appeal both to history buffs and to readers of mystery novels, and all of this is offered by an author who might be black and from Salem. Who could resist such a tantalizing presentation?

The front cover of the second edition published by Folio downplays the location of the Salem trials and emphasizes the prominent role of witchcraft as a sales pitch. The qualifier "Noire de Salem" has disappeared, and the title appears as *Moi, Tituba Sorcière*…(see below). The elimination of the comma between *Tituba* and *sorcière* confirms that Tituba is indeed a witch; while *Moi* is now isolated on one line and followed by a comma, which emphasizes that the novel is indeed a first-person narrative.

Maryse Condé
Moi,
Tituba sorcière….

The title itself is printed on a clear sky above an ominous landscape featuring a few dark branches on the left and a pine forest on the right. Contrary to the first edition, the witch is now pictured, a black woman dressed in black, her hair in an Afro, her intense glowing eyes looking straight at the reader. She is holding a walking stick, or is it a broom?

The Folio edition gives scant reference to Salem (a pine forest?), focusing instead on sorcery as a way to increase readership. The fact that the novel deals with a black woman is no longer indicated by a reference in the title but illustrated by the image of a defiant figure challenging the reader to open the book. This front cover veers even further from Condé's intentions for the novel than the first one. Both within the novel itself and in the afterword to the English edition, Condé emphasizes that *sorcière* is a problematic word, and that Tituba is most definitely not a *sorcière* if readers attribute a malevolent meaning to the word. Yet, the first English edition continues in this vein, its front cover featuring elements from the French editions that present Tituba as a black malevolent witch.

On the front cover of the first edition of *I, Tituba, Black Witch of Salem*, readers find simply the face of a black woman "whose outline is achieved through variations of the colors red and orange out of what appears to be a wire fence" (Manzor-Coats 738). Salem has now vanished. There only remains an even more ominous figure than on the Folio edition. If the Folio figure could be read as a guide looking for a path and leading the reader with her walking stick, this face belongs to a witch ready to set the world ablaze. Who is this witch, may we now ask?

Some likely answers appear to be offered by the title, and translation of the title into English apparently offers little opportunity for any slippage. *Moi, Tituba sorcière…Noire de Salem* becomes *I, Tituba, Black Witch of Salem*. Three changes, however, are noteworthy. First, a pronominal shift occurs as the disjunctive pronoun *Moi* becomes the subject pronoun *I*, thereby emphasizing the work as a first-person narrative. Secondly, the adjective *Black* now comes before the noun *Witch*, which gives the color issue much more emphasis than was the case in the two French editions. Thirdly, due to grammar rules in English regarding the placement of adjectives, *Black* and *Witch* can no longer be separated as *Sorcière* and *Noire* are in the French title. If indeed as Manzor-Coats argues, "linguistic constraints point to the untranslatability of the French title" (737), they also contribute to appealing to a new readership. This publication is no longer an "histoire romanesque" about a (black) witch tried at Salem but a novel about a black woman practicing witchcraft to rebel against an oppressive world and set it ablaze. Such a novel published in the United States would likely attract the attention of scholars and students interested in the African-American history of resistance. The front and back covers further point in this direction. The former mentions a "Foreword by Angela Y. Davis" while the latter features remarks by Charles Johnson and Henry Louis Gates, but neither gives any information about the critical afterword by Ann Scarboro.

Pascale De Souza

Scarboro's afterword provides fascinating insights into the novel because it also includes an interview with Condé. Indeed, this afterword offers an example of a paratextual element that enhances the reader's appreciation for the complexities inherent in translation, at all levels. In the interview, Condé emphasizes that her novel is neither to be read as a story of resistance through witchcraft nor to be taken at face value; she describes it instead as a parody aimed at deconstructing social expectations regarding historical novels and the practice of witchcraft. Condé also explains to Scarboro her use of the term *sorcière*: "Tituba was doing only good to her community. Could she be called a witch? I don't think so, and the book is there to prove it" (Scarboro 206). If indeed the book is there to prove it, the front covers, especially the one for the English edition, contradict the author's agenda and set up false expectations among readers. This may in turn lead to misguided readings that take the novel at face value, or rather at front cover value, and fail to take into account the parodic dimension intended by the author.

Interestingly enough, the second English edition of the novel brings this analysis of paratextual and linguistic markers to a close in some respects. Contrary to the other three editions, the focus is no longer on the fiery art of witchcraft. The new edition is rather subdued with a pale yellow and red cover featuring the full title in green and a picture of a woman being tried during the 17th/18th century. A female figure in the foreground points an accusing finger at the woman on trial, while men dressed in black sit in the background listening intently to 'testimonies.' A quote from the *New York Times Book Review* is presented below the title; and the name of the author, of the translator, and the reference to the foreword by Angela Y. Davies are printed below the picture. The focus has indeed been changed: the 'black' identity of the heroine has less prominence and the novel's 'universal' appeal is promoted with words from a *New York Times* critic who praises it as an "exhilarating understanding of the human heart" (front cover, Condé 1994). Other elements suggest that *I, Tituba, Black witch of Salem* is a noteworthy historical novel focusing on the trial of a woman for witchcraft, and readers are brought back full circle to the Mercure de France's "Histoire Romanesque."

Despite the 'clues' offered on the covers of two editions, *Moi, Tituba…Sorcière…Noire de Salem* hardly focuses on the Salem trials per se. Instead, the novel traces the migration of Tituba, a Bajan slave of Ashanti parentage, from her native Barbados to Puritan

48

New England and back. Though the novel is written in French, some characters are described as speaking Ashanti, Bajan Creole, Bajan English or American English, and none of them speaks French. This may explain why the translation of creolisms in this novel does not provide as many avenues for fruitful exploration of Caribbean culture and identity as other novels featuring only Caribbean characters. The few examples of French Creole do, however, provide opportunities to explore Condé's interest in maintaining a certain level of opacity within her work. Condé pursues a dual objective here, to echo the opacity of Caribbean history (especially of the slaves' experience, given the lack of records) and to illustrate its 'untranslatability' into French.[5]

Condé's approach ranges from underlying the 'otherness' of Creole by setting words and expressions within quotation marks and providing a clarification to incorporating Creole expressions with no further clarification. Expressions such as "«mal sortie»"[6](19) or "«grangeks»" (224) thus appear within quotation marks and are respectively explained within the text and in a footnote, while "un pantalon konoko" (37) and un "canari" (38) are used without any quotation marks but explained in footnotes. Finally, several expressions are inserted in the text with neither quotation marks nor clarification. The context may sometimes help a French reader grasp the meaning of the words, when for example, Abena digs up "des trous d'ignames dans un carreau de terre" (20); but several expressions remain opaque to readers not familiar with the Caribbean context or with Creole. Tituba meets "une haute chabine en madras calendé" (34) and "deux bossales" (248); she sees Yao as a "Mapou aux pieds larges et puissants" (219); maroons ring "l'abeng" (251). The lack of clarification that disorients readers is Condé's own 'abeng,' a call for rebellion against the silence of the past and the hegemony of the French language.

Despite the limited use of Creole in *Moi, Tituba sorcière... Noire de Salem*, the English translation provides interesting insight into the rifts and disjunctions inherent in the translation process. Making the novel more accessible to non-Caribbean readers can ultimately deny Condé's call for rebellion and her right to opacity. The translator adopts two approaches to deal with creolisms in the novel:

– Creole words and expressions are left in French Creole but italicized and explained in a glossary such as *acomas* (157), *grangeks* (144), *konoko* (19) or *bossales* (161). The clarification provided in the glossary may include the origin of the French word and an English equivalent; *acoma* is thus "commonly known in the Anglophone West Indies as mastic bully" (185).

- Creole expressions are sometimes eliminated altogether: the Creole term "«mal sortie»" (19) is thus rendered simply as "the color of my skin was far from being light and my hair was crinkly all over" (6); "ma canari" (38) as "my earthenware pot" (19); and the "haute chabine en madras calendé" (34) becomes "a tall yellow girl with a pleated madras head tie" (16). At other times, a standard English term is used as an equivalent: as with "un carreau de terre" (20) or "a plot of ground" (7), the "mornes" (20) or "hills" (7), the "abeng" (251) or "a conch" (163), the "mapou" (219) or "a silk-cotton tree" (141).[7]

Although *Moi, Tituba, Sorcière…Noire de Salem* provides fewer examples of creolization than *Traversée de la Mangrove*, it still presents challenges to the translator who wishes to respect the author's intent in selecting Creole expressions and in providing, or failing to provide, clarification. The absence of any English Creole, and the glossary and the translation/explanation of several terms into (British) English make the English version much more readily accessible to a non-Caribbean English-speaking reader than the French text is to a non-Caribbean French-speaking one. Does this not in some sense diminish Condé's intention to represent the specificities of Caribbean identity through an opaque or referential text? The reader familiar with Caribbean history will not miss the choice of "mornes" (272) as a last word in the novel, a reference to the times of marooning and a claim to victory for Tituba. The English equivalent "hills" (179) carries a far less potent message.

A brief study of *Traversée de la Mangrove*, a later novel by Maryse Condé, further underlines the slippages that occur, not only through the selection of paratextual and linguistic elements but also within the novel itself, as the focus on the accurate translation of 'local' terms for flora masks more complex shifts of meaning from creolized French to English. The novel was published both by Folio and Mercure de France in 1989.[8] The cover of the Mercure de France edition features a pale blue background and bears the name of the author at the top in black, the title of the novel in a bigger red font in the middle, and the logo and name of the editor at the bottom. The absence of images neutralizes any attempt to ascribe a particular interpretation of the content of the novel prior to reading it.

The cover of the Folio edition, on the other hand, serves to give the potential buyer some inkling of the themes explored in the novel. The cover features an impressionist illustration depicting a woman sitting in an anchored boat on an apparently stagnant or slow-moving river with heavy foliage on both banks. Both the name of the author and the title appear above the illustration against a white background. At first sight, the scene is rather innocuous and might be set in a temperate country. Yet, the boat is anchored and the woman is hence going nowhere, a subtle reflection of the impossible 'Traversée de la mangrove' presented in the novel.

Several interesting slippages occur with the cover of the English edition published in 1995 by Doubleday. First, the scene on the front cover is now clearly set in an 'exotic' country identified by such 'clear' markers as exuberant strange vegetation, multicolored flowers, colorful houses lost amidst a sea of green on hillsides, a shimmering blue sea, and a straw-hat similar to the ones used in Guadeloupe by cane cutters. The hat floating on the calm sea under a shining full moon and sending ripples through the water could recall the effect of Sancher's arrival in Rivière-au-Sel in the novel. Yet, the village of Rivière-au-Sel is not built along the shore, Sancher does not drown but dies in the forest, and a mangrove is not a wide-open bay of clear blue sea. What purpose would an illustration so at odds with major features in the novel then serve?

The objective recalls the case of *Moi, Tituba sorcière...Noire de Salem*, insofar as in both cases the front cover stands at odds with the focus of the novel. While the foreboding scene in the first English edition of *I, Tituba, Black Witch of Salem* is aimed at attracting readers to a novel featuring sorcery, the 'exotic' landscape and the abandoned straw hat that illustrate *Crossing the Mangrove* lead readers to expect a mystery novel set in the tropics. No interpretation could be further from Condé's representation of Rivière-au-Sel. As a character states in the novel, Guadeloupe is no longer such an 'exotic' country; it has become instead a microcosm of global trends, "ce pays-là est à l'encan. Il appartient à tout le monde à présent" (139) [this country is a lost cause. It belongs to everybody now]. As for this being a mystery novel, Condé adopts this apparent format better to subvert it. The novel indeed begins with the suspicious death of a stranger called Sancher; but the death is never solved, and the focus soon shifts from tracking a murderer to exploring the life, hopes, and dreams of each villager attending Sancher's wake. The first question in the novel is *not* "Qui l'a tué?" [Who killed

51

him?], but "Y a quelqu'un?" (15) [Anybody here?], pointing to the search for solidarity that will structure the novel as a whole.

The presentation of the title and the author's name on the cover of the English edition also points to a shift in emphasis when compared to the French edition. In the Folio edition, the author's name in a slightly smaller font is printed with the title in black at the top of the novel's cover. In the English edition, the author's name is given much greater emphasis at the expense of the title. "Maryse Condé" appears in large letters on a golden background at the top, whereas *Crossing the mangrove* is written in smaller letters against a background of foliage at the bottom. The publisher seems to be first and foremost selling "Maryse Condé, author of *Segu*," as stated on the cover.

The translation of the title from *Traversée de la Mangrove* to *Crossing the Mangrove* raises more serious issues in regard to form, content, and context. First, in a surprising play with grammar, Condé chose not to use an article with the noun "traversée." Uneasy with the absence of this article, many scholars make the mistake of referring to the novel's title as "*La" Traversée de la Mangrove*. Her choice strongly suggests that she omits the article to recall another French Caribbean 'detective' novel, *Solibo Magnifique* by Patrick Chamoiseau, which also fails to shed light on a suspicious death and uses a criminal investigation as a means to explore issues of Caribbean identity, and also omits an article. Chamoiseau did not entitle his novel *Solibo "le" Magnifique* as one might expect, but *Solibo Magnifique*. This linkage is completely eclipsed by the English translation of Condé's title as *Crossing the Mangrove*, for her noun "traversée" is now replaced by a verb "crossing." In addition, Condé's choice of the noun "traversée" in the original focuses attention on the *resulting state of things* rather than on a *process*, as implied by the verb. As one character explains, it is impossible to complete a 'crossing' of the mangrove, "On s'empale sur les racines des palétuviers. On s'enterre et on étouffe dans la boue saumâtre" (192) [You get impaled on the roots of the mangrove trees, you sink and choke in the brackish mud]. The irony of the title in French is lost in the English title: "crossing the mangrove" suggests that the novel is about the process of crossing, the endeavor itself rather than its doomed result.

Issues raised by the translation of the narrative itself echo those discussed above with *Moi, Tituba sorcière…Noire de Salem*, insofar as in both cases the opacity of Condé's text is partly lost through the translation of creolized French into standard English. The following extract and its translation offer one of the most salient examples of such a shift in meaning from French to English. It is the beginning of the chapter focusing on Xantippe, a 'man spirit,' dweller of the forest, harbinger of Creole traditions, preserver of the Creole language.

> J'ai nommé tous les arbres de ce pays. Je suis monté à la tête du morne, j'ai crié leur nom et ils ont répondu à mon appel.
>
> Gommier blanc. Acomat-boucan. Bois pilori. Bois rada. Bois trompette. Bois guépois. Bois d'encens. Bois pin. Bois la soie. Bois bandé. Résolu. Kaïmitier. Mahot cochon. Prune café. Mapou lélé. Arbre à lait. Malimbé.
>
> Les arbres sont nos seuls amis. Depuis l'Afrique, ils soignent nos corps et nos âmes. Leur odeur est magie, vertu du grand temps reconquis. Quand j'étais petit, ma maman me couchait sous l'ombrage de leurs feuilles et le soleil jouait à cache-cache au-dessus de ma figure. Quand je suis devenu nèg mawon, leurs troncs me barraient.
>
> C'est moi aussi qui ai nommé les lianes. Siguine rouge. Siguine grand bois. Jasmin bois. Liane à chique. Liane à barrique. Liane blanche des hauts. Les lianes aussi sont des amies depuis le temps longtemps. Elles amarrent corps à corps. Igname à igname. (241)

> [I named all the trees of this island.
>
> I climbed to the top of the hill and cried their name, and they answered my call.
>
> Candlewood. Mastwood. Bladderwood. Golden spoon. Trumpet wood. Myrtle. Incense tree. Magnolia. Cigarox cedar. Crabwood. Resolu. Star apple. Saltfish wood. Sweet plum. Manjack. Marmalade tree. Mapou.
>
> The trees are our only friends. They have taken care of our bodies and souls since we lived in Africa. Their fragrance is magic, a power recaptured from times long gone by. When I was little, Maman used to set me down under the shade of their leaves, and the sun would play hide-and-seek above my face. When I became a Maroon, their trunks barricaded me in.

I too named the vines. Bird's nest anthurium. Oilcloth flower. Little star jasmine. Goosefoot. Morning glory. Firecracker. The vines too are our friends from long, long ago. They tie body to soul. They lock creeper to creeper. (201-2)]

The long list of trees and vines is one element that contributes to Condé's construction of an opaque discourse in this extract, and the main challenge for the English translator apparently lies in finding the appropriate terms for this wide array of vegetation. What's more, the reference to the highly emblematic 'igname' [yam] plays a major part in setting Xantippe apart from the other characters in the novel and linking him to a Caribbean heritage. The difficulty for the translator lies not so much in finding the appropriate word for "gommier blanc," a French word at any rate, but in identifying the instances of creolization which should *not* be translated into (British or American) English and the images which should *not* be tampered with. In effect, the real challenge here is to understand and translate Condé's construction of Xantippe's Caribbean identity.

Four expressions suggest creolizing processes at play in French. "Crié" is a creole word used to designate "speaking." The phrase "j'ai crié leur nom" hence means that Xantippe "cried" their names, as the English translation reads. But more importantly, in a creole context, the phrase means that he *gave* them an identity by *speaking* their name. His use of the word "crié," which is lost in the English, denotes both his rootedness in Creole traditions and language and Condé's attention to creolization processes. Likewise, the spelling of "nég mawon" originated during a time when slaves escaped plantations to assert their right to an identity fully theirs through the rejection of the master's trope. The calibanizing process at play here is completely lost when "nèg mawon" is translated into the English term "a Maroon," meaning simply "a fugitive slave," which ignores the linguistic import and history of Creole. "Le temps longtemps" is not an expression used in metropolitan French, whereas 'from long, long ago' is common in English. Finally, the structure that concludes the second paragraph, "leurs troncs me barraient," is unusual in metropolitan French. The expression is normally followed with a direct complement such as 'la route', 'le passage' [the road, the way], 'me' being then used as an indirect pronoun. Here, Xantippe is the direct object pronoun. He is indeed a prisoner as the English clearly states, but he is also a free wanderer protected from slave hunters by "un barrage d'arbres."

A reference to an emblematic Caribbean element is also missing in the English text. The "igname" [yam] is both a staple of the Caribbean diet and a rhyzomatic plant used by Édouard Glissant to characterize the Caribbean archipelago, each island being linked to the others through an array of underground vines like yams via their root systems. The word "creeper" not only misses the point entirely but suggests a different image. Rather than being part of a strong rhyzomatic Caribbean network, Xantippe is seen here as a "creeper" lying low when confronted with (post)colonial threats to his identity. The slippage from the "igname" to the "creeper" leads to totally divergent images of the character, which in turn affects the critical reading of Condé's approach to issues of Caribbean identity.

Similar slippages occur in *The Bridge of Beyond*, the English version of *Pluie et vent sur Télumée Miracle* by Simone Schwarz-Bart. A discussion of two elements analyzed above in regard to Condé's novels—the front covers and the creolizing of French structures— reveal how the selection of a front cover can minimize opportunities to misread the novel; while a standardization of creolized French into English contributes not only to a misinterpretation of characterization but to a complete reversal in the power play between two female characters. The illustrations on the front covers of both editions of *Pluie et vent sur Télumée Miracle* and of the English version *The Bridge of Beyond* reflect a different focus from Condé's novels. Whereas Condé's publishers emphasized the historical setting of *Moi, Tituba sorcière…Noire de Salem*, and/or its focus on a witch as a potential figure of rebellion, Schwarz-Bart's publishers adopt a more subdued approach, one ultimately more respectful to the Caribbean setting of the novel. The first French edition, published by Seuil in 1972, features on the cover the photo of a young black washerwoman and a bareback boy sitting on a rock in the middle of a river. Though the picture was provided by an international photo agency, it does reflect Télumée's life and a particular passage in the novel where she sings to preserve her identity while washing clothes. The second French edition, published by Points in 1995, features a drawing of a black woman wearing a yellow dress and a necklace, similar to clothing and jewelry that may be found in the Caribbean. The English version, published by Victor Gollancz in 1975, features a light-skinned mulatto woman sitting along the water's edge against a backdrop of sea and bluish coastal hills. Though it does not peddle the novel to a specific audience as was the case with *Moi, Tituba sor-*

cière…Noire de Salem or *Traversée de la Mangrove*, this illustration is less true to the novel than the ones selected for the French editions on several accounts. Télumée was, according to Schwarz-Bart, so dark-skinned as to be almost blue. She came from a rural village not built along the sea; and her daily toll is completely contrary to the idle pose and impeccably clean white shirt of the woman on the front cover. This visual 'slippage' betrays Télumée's identity as the proud descendant of slaves who successfully asserts her identity despite poverty and personal hardships.

Two conversations between Télumée and Mme Desaragne, the mistress of the plantation where she seeks employment, offer the most salient illustrations of what is at stake in the translation of creolization processes, as seen in the above discussion of Xantippe's speech in *Traversée de la Mangrove*. The conversations are particularly striking in the French version because Télumée asserts her identity by becoming a Caliban: she shows her mistress-to-be how adept she is at mastering her language and experience before forcing her back into her Creole world.[9] Here is part of the first conversation, in the original, between Télumée (T) and Mme Desaragne (MD):

> MD- C'est une place que vous cherchez?
>
> T- Je cherche à me louer.
>
> MD- Qu'est-ce que vous savez faire, par exemple?
>
> T- Je sais tout faire.
>
> MD- Vous connaissez cuisiner?
>
> T- Oui.
>
> MD- Je veux dire cuisiner, pas lâcher un morceau de fruit à pain dans une chaudière d'eau salée.
>
> T- Oui, je sais.
>
> MD- Bon, c'est bien, mais qui vous a appris?
>
> T- La mère de ma grand-mère s'était louée, dans le temps, chez les Labardine.
>
> MD- C'est bien, savez-vous repasser?
>
> T- Oui.
>
> MD- Je veux dire repasser, c'est pas bourrer de coups de carreaux des drill sans couleur.

> T- Je sais, c'est glacer des chemises en popeline avec des cols cassés. (90)

Télumée's laconic answers—which Bernabé characterizes as her "dignity" (123)—force Mme Desaragne to reveal her own familiarity with Creole traditions, syntax, and lexical terms. She refers to the preparation of local fruit, "lâcher un fruit à pain dans une chaudière"; the style of local clothing, "des drill"; and she uses local terms such as "carreaux." Her syntax reveals the influence of Creole, "c'est pas bourrer" (direct translation from the Creole *sé pa* + verb). Aware of Télumée's familiarity with both languages, Mme Desaragne is reluctant to let Creole take over. After stating "vous connaissez cuisiner," a direct translation from Creole, she tries to 'over-correct' herself by reverting back to a 'proper' French verb meaning to know how to do something (*savoir* as opposed to *connaître*) and by asking the question with subject-verb inversion: "savez-vous repasser?" As the whole passage reveals, however, she fails to keep Creole at bay.

Conversely, Télumée is the one explaining to Mme Desaragne what French cooking and ironing entail in 'proper' French. The process at play here is similar to the one outlined by Philcox when he argues that "despite the feeling of freedom to cannibalize and manipulate, in the end I am the one who is cannibalized." Télumée's refusal to communicate in French, despite her ability to do so, forces Mrs. Desaragne to revert to Creole. Likewise, the opacity of the text to be translated forces the British translator to abandon his position of privilege, to adopt a Creole identity. If Philcox was often cannibalized, thereby providing an echo of Condé's text, Schwarz-Bart's translator does not let herself become a Caribbean 'dummy,' does not let Caliban win. Indeed, the 'calibanesque' reversal of power is lost in the English version:

> MD- You're looking for a situation?
>
> T- I want to hire myself out.
>
> MD- What can you do?
>
> T- Anything.
>
> MD- Can you cook?
>
> T- Yes.
>
> MD- I mean cook, not just drop a bit of breadfruit into a pan of hot water.

T- Yes, I know.

MD- Good, but who taught you?

T- My grandmother's mother once worked for the Lab-
ardines.

MD- Good, Can you iron?

T- Yes.

MD- I mean iron, not just thump old rags into shape.

T- I know. Putting a gloss on poplin shirts with wing
collars. (84)

The reference to Creole cooking remains in the English version, but
Mme Desaragne's grasp of local syntax and lexicon are lost. "Can
you cook?" bears no Creole influence, contrary to "Connaissez-
vous cuisiner?"; while local terms such as 'chaudière' or 'carreaux'
have either been translated into English or eliminated.

The second conversation between the two women hardly quali-
fies as one. It is more of a ranting monologue by Mme Desaragne
who eventually concludes: "Regardez vous-même, comme vous
êtes, je vous parle et vous ne répondez pas…. Que faire, Seigneur,
que faire avec des gens pareils, que vous leur parliez et c'est
comme si vous leur chantiez!" (94). Several terms here call for a
pertinent translation: the use of the polite form 'vous,' which points
to the distance Télumée has been able to maintain between Mme
Desaragne and herself; the comment "des gens pareils" used to
debase people of African ancestry; and the reference to the verb
chanter [to sing], as singing was one of the weapons Toussine taught
Télumée to use when feeling threatened. None of this information
carries into English: "Look at yourself – I talk to you and you don't
even answer, you haven't got anything to say for yourself…Good
Lord, what's one to do with such people- might as well talk to a
brick wall" (88). The distance created by the 'vous' has vanished,
and the derisive connotation of the expression "des gens pareils"
is more subdued in the phrase "such people." Mme Desaragne's
phrase, "c'est comme si vous leur chantiez"—literally, 'it's as it you
were singing to them'—is translated with a ready-made phrase in
English that may convey the woman's exasperation, but loses the
significant thematic reference mentioned above, namely that for
Toussine and Télumée singing is a fundamental means of expressing and preserving their identity.

Tejaswini Niranjana argues that translation can be seen as "the noble task of bridging the gap between peoples" (Niranjana 47) by providing increased exposure to authors writing in different languages and from different cultural perspectives.[10] In this essay, I have not explored the gap with a view to narrowing it but rather probed some reasons for its existence and exposed the dangers inherent in any attempt to bridge it. Bridging the gap includes several strategies, such as the iconographic translation of the novel into an illustration on the front cover, the presentation of a title, and the inclusion of an introduction, a glossary, footnotes, and/or an appendix all aimed at 'clarifying' the author's intent and the 'meaning' of the novel. One would hope that bridging the gap between Creole and French cultures will inspire Condé and Schwarz-Bart to continue to write opaque texts and thus provide translators the opportunity to offer English speakers some access to processes of creolization. Readers of the English versions would then view these texts not as equivalents of the original, but as one translation of the diversity of the Caribbean.

Given the commitment made by some authors to write opaque texts in order to reflect on the gaps in Caribbean history and on the untranslatability of the Creole experience into French, however, how can such 'clarifying' endeavors not be betrayals, that is, not another way to translate the authors' text into a (post)-colonialized product. In this sense, the process of transforming the original text by translating it into another language is no crossing of the mangrove to an elusive beyond but an opportunity to contain such calibanizing endeavors. French Caribbean authors who follow Caliban's lead and mis/use the French language to better curse its hegemony may be partly denied their right to differ in translation. As the Caribbean archipelago moves towards increased political and economic linkages, readers, translators, and critics need to be aware that while literature in translation may on the one hand enable dialogues, translated texts also have the potential to alter, or indeed subvert the message, leading to increased rifts rather than fruitful exchange, making the mangrove even more impossible to cross and the beyond more elusive.

Notes

1. The audience who attended the panel at the African Literature Association (Richmond, April 2001) where a version of this essay was presented as a paper raised several issues that greatly contributed to this essay in its published form.

2. In some seminal cases, such as the *Cahier d'un retour au pays natal* by Aimé Césaire, several English versions are available.

3. It must be noted, however, that spider imagery was translated faithfully into English. This animal imagery is all the more important as Anancy stories came from Western Africa and can be found today not only throughout the Caribbean, irrespective of the language spoken, but also in the United Sates, Canada, and several South American countries.

4. I originally wished to provide no translation of the French quotes unless the translations themselves taken from the English editions were the focus of the analysis. Editors pointed out that some English readers might be at a loss to follow the argument, which illustrates the difficulties inherent in critical writing. To limit some pitfalls, and open others, my own translations are provided when the study of translated passages is not the focus of the analysis.

5. Condé's decision to use mostly French terms for local flora apparently contradicts her stand on French as an inadequate means to convey a Caribbean experience. A comparison with a later novel, however, provides some clarification. Contrary to Xantippe who, in *Traversée de la Mangrove,* lists the local names of trees and vines to underline his own rootedness in Guadeloupe, Tituba never uses local terms, preferring instead "le papayer, l'oranger, le grenadier" (222) [paw-paw, orange and pomegranate trees (143)] and "un fouillis de goyaviers, fougères, de frangipaniers et d'acomats" (241) [a tangle of guava trees, ferns, frangipani and acoma trees (157)]. Condé's use of French terms points to Tituba's own alienation from Barbados, as she first opts for an isolated life in the hills, then leaves to follow John Indien overseas, and returns only to die. Her own death will open up an ultimate passage to Barbados as she inspires future rebellions.

6. English translations of Creole expressions taken from the 1992 English version of the novel are provided further on.

7. The glossary also includes "literary inventions by the author" (185) such as *"Populara Indica," "passiflorinde," "persulfureuse," "prune taureau."*

8. All quotes are taken from the Mercure de France edition.

9. My purpose here is not to offer an extensive analysis of creolisation processes in the novel but to focus on translation issues. Such an analysis can be found in Jean Bernabé's essay "Contribution à l'étude de la diglossie littéraire: le cas de *Pluie et vent sur Télumée Miracle"*

(1979). In his essay, Bernabé researches the strategies set in place by Schwarz-Bart to resist the hegemony of French. His analysis of several passages proves conclusively that although "the socio-linguistic norm of the dominant language is not easily contaminated by the intrusions of the dominated language" (104), Schwarz-Bart successfully weaves Creole into French to assert the strength of her character as a "Guadeloupean woman who has faced many hardships but never lost her dignity" (118).

10. In *Siting Translation*, Niranjama's own analysis inadvertently illustrates why translation provides at best a rickety bridge. In order to explain the problems raised by three translations of a South Indian text, she needs to provide five pages of explanations regarding context, content, and author, thereby pointing to the untranslatability of the original text.

ON THE UNTRANSLATABILITY OF TITUBA INDIAN[1]: AN INTERCULTURAL SUBJECT

Kathleen Gyssels

My race began as the sea began,

With no nouns, and with no horizon,

With pebbles under my tongue,

With a different fix on the stars. . . .

and my race began like the osprey

with that cry,

that terrible vowel, that I!

–Derek Walcott, "Names" in *Sea Grapes* (1976)

In "Names," dedicated to the Bajan poet Kamau Brathwaite, Derek Walcott retraces the origin of the Caribbean "race."[2] It began, he writes, without nouns, with pebbles under his tongue, with the cry of "I." The allusion to a cry and the struggle to enunciate foreshadow the verses of Martinique's Édouard Glissant in *Le Discours antillais*, where he calls for transforming the soundless countryside into an affirmative subjectivity:

> Vois ton pays. Entends les pays, derrière l'îlet. Du point fixe d'ici, trame cette géographie.
>
> Du cri fixe d'ici, déroule une parole aride, difficile. Accorde ta voix à la durée du monde. Sors de la peau de ton cri. Entre en peau du monde par tes pores. Soleil à vif. Nous entassons des salines où tant de mots miroitent. (1997, 27)

[Look at your country. Hear the countries, behind the tiny isle. From *this* point, interweave the geography.

From *this* scream, comes an arid, difficult speech. Tune your voice to the world's enduring. Come forth from the skin of your scream. Enter the world's skin through your pores. Sun, burning. We pile up saltworks where so many words shimmer.]

Along with Édouard Glissant, Derek Walcott of St. Lucia and Martinique's Aimé Césaire[3] have also wrestled with the meaning and creation of a specifically Caribbean language and literature as distinct from and in relation to the that of the colonizers. These and many other Caribbean authors continually remind us of the struggle for the genesis of the creative word [4] in the Caribbean context, coming as it does out of the chaos of slavery, colonization, and the world of the plantation. This same struggle manifests itself in the opening words of the autobiographical fiction *Moi, Tituba sorcière...Noire de Salem* (1986), by Maryse Condé. [5] Although the first-person narrative does not purport to be spoken by the author, *Tituba* is nevertheless based on an historical personage. This fictional narration by an historical character records the difficulty of communicating the life of Tituba Indian.

RIGHTING AMERICAN HISTORY

Tituba's life cannot be translated: the actual black woman Tituba had no opportunity to record her own story—its only recognized, factual record is to be found in the Essex County Archives in Salem, Massachusetts, where documents from the witch trials are preserved. History's Tituba remains unreachable by writer and reader: differences not only of language, but of culture, history, and power prevent readers from knowing her life story. Though Tituba is untranslatable, Condé has boldly written her autobiography (not unlike Dominica's Jean Rhys writing the life of *Jane Eyre*'s Bertha in *Wide Sargasso Sea*), and by doing so she places herself for the first time in a tradition of black female autobiographies. At the same time, an analysis of different paratextual and textual elements of Condé's novel reveals how it represents a possible variation on autobiographies written by Caribbean women, for this autobiography oscillates between an author's minimal intervention (seen in the title, *Moi, Tituba*) and her maximal intervention (seen in the epigraph, "Tituba et moi"), and it takes into account the history of older generations (by beginning with "Abena, ma mère, un marin anglais la viola").[6] Thus Condé composes a necessarily mixed form, a hybrid autobiography in which the author is inscribed, invested as it were, in the fictional autobiography even as she unmasks herself as its creator.

Although the genre of autobiographical writing has been abundantly studied in Caribbean and African-American literature,[7] the ex-slave autobiography in Condé's writing does the unexpected in that it undermines (Puritan) power by reversing the role of Knowledge: Tituba-as-autobiographer successfully argues her case by directing the narration from her own point of view, thereby obliging us to listen to her sometimes stumbling, stuttering language. As Homi Bhabha's theorizing of hybridity reminds us, Foucault's concept of power relations can equally well be reversed, suddenly inverting the colonizer's dominant position: "Power/Knowledge places subjects in a relation of power and recognition that is not part of a symmetrical or dialectical relation—self/other, master/slave—which can be subverted by being inverted....[It] is difficult to conceive of the process of subjectification as a placing within Orientalist or colonialist discourse for the dominated subject without being strategically placed within it too" (72). Condé's Tituba is placed in the role of slave and other, yet Condé rewrites her voice to enable her to claim power and become master of her own narrative. Tituba, accused, misnamed and distorted by history, has overturned the Puritans' power and knowledge by speaking for herself.

The novel can be read in light of the author's reasons for writing or the author's suggestions for determining meaning, but perhaps the author's conscious intention is not the last word on interpretation. In an interview with Françoise Pfaff, Condé speaks of how fast she wrote this novel on "intolerance and racism" and how much she wanted to "get rid of [her] frustrations" with "Los Angeles, this huge tentacular city" (23; 39). In the same series of interviews, as well as in the interview with Ann Scarboro, Condé confesses that one (that she) always writes the same novel, that Tituba should not be taken too seriously, and that the novel is fully intended as a "mock epic" ("Afterward" 216). Based on these paradoxical, if not contradictory assertions, let us consider the following question: given that her first American[8] novel takes up the questions and problems that she addresses in prior novels—"encounters between cultures and civilizations," to paraphrase Michel Leiris, colonization and the struggle for independence, racism and the condition of women, Blacks' search for identity in the African diaspora,[9] etc.—and in light of her own assertions that *Moi, Tituba sorcière... Noire de Salem* should not be measured against truth nor considered a "serious" novel, then to what extent does the autograph character, she who is supposedly telling her own life story, translate, not her life, but some of Maryse Condé's deeper convictions?

To say "to get rid of her frustrations" is to express the desire to give free rein to her frustrations with her adoptive country, America, to set straight a few misunderstandings concerning certain movements and myths (about the West Indies in particular), and to rebuff a certain American mentality (Scarboro, 203). What if Condé simply wanted to explore the question: "By what right does the author think he or she can/must translate the life of an Other?" Conscious of her authorial position, Condé manipulates "le mensonge romanesque" [the novel's illusion], to the point of giving a lie to what's left of the "historical" in the novel.[10] In so doing, Condé raises questions about the author's own power and knowledge when faced with the lacunae in her protagonist's history. On three occasions that will be analyzed here, the protagonist with this stumbling, titillating name—Titibe/Titiba/Tittapa and Tattuba—explodes the syntax.[11] Autobiographical subject with an indefinite name, Tituba stuttering and titillating nearly topples the language. In this way she inscribes the near impossibility of translating her life, her journey.

After the title's *"Moi, Tituba,"* which signals the paradigm of a *testimonio,*[12] Condé confronts us with a chiasmus in the novel's first epigraph, "Tituba et moi, . . ." [Tituba and I, . . .], followed by its ungrammatical comma.[13] Reading the first page, the reader is faced with the incipit, yet a third instance where the punctuation, even if not ungrammatical, again invites reflection. The first comma in *Moi, Tituba* can be read as indicating a minimal distance between the narrator-character (Tituba) and the author; whereas the conjunction in the exergue "Tituba et moi" of the epigraph is its opposite, reversing the certitude of that identity. The incipit, or opening words, suggests yet a third variation, relegating the narrative "I" to the background and emphasizing a biographical project.

Although she found in Tituba Indian a superb subject for a fictional autobiography, Condé is far from the first to take an interest in the Salem trials, held between March 1691 and 1692.[14] She is interested in them because they point to encounters between cultures and to the difficulties such encounters engender: from the very founding of the New World, conflicts arose between the colonizers and the colonized, and between the new inhabitants of America and their rivals, that is, the "savages" (Indians as well as slaves brought across the Atlantic). In order to give full measure to cultural differences, to make tangible the dialogue of the deaf, or rather the absence of a translator between the Puritans (who have the power) and the non-Puritans (the so-called voodooists), between Whites and people of color, between men and women, Condé shapes her work within the generic limits of fictional autobiography. As her own interpreter, Tituba traces a life full of surprising events, intentionally beginning with the history of her mother, an Ashanti deported to the New World. Raped on board a slave ship, Man Abena never recognized the bastard fruit of her womb. Young Tituba is brought up by Yao, her adoptive father, and later by Man Yaya, a "healer," which makes her a witch in the eyes of the Whites. After her mother's hanging, Tituba becomes without complaint the property of Susanna Endicott and then of the Puritan Samuel Parris, all out of love for John Indian. It is in Parris' house in Salem that the heinous accusations of witchcraft begin: as the governess of the minister's daughters, Tituba told them terrifying stories about people in league with the devil; she gave them ritual herbal baths (102) made from magical powders and potions. Accused of witchcraft, along with Sarah Good, Sarah Osborne, Anne Putnam, Mary Walcott, Elizabeth Hubbard, Susanna Sheldon, Sarah Churchill (125), Tituba is first thrown in prison and later pardoned and released by Governor Phips. This (chapter II, 7) is as far as the authentic summary of her life goes.

Thereafter, Condé invents a second life for her character, the life of a freed slave, a desired woman, the nominally happy companion (if only briefly) of an Ashkenazi Jew, Benjamin Cohen d'Azevedo. Attacked and ruined by anti-Semites, Benjamin agrees to let Tituba return to Barbados. There she lives among the Maroons, whom she eventually leaves. She then falls in love with young Iphigene, who is soon sacrificed on the altar of yet another aborted Maroon insurrection. Tituba's fate is equally sinister: she is hanged with the other rebels. There follows a posthumous note wherein Tituba (267-73) claims to have survived in the songs and legends of her island, exactly like the eponymous heroine, *The Mulâtresse Solitude* of André Schwarz-Bart (1972).[15]

Clearly, this eventful life becomes entirely unbelievable when Tituba meets Hester Prynne, the protagonist of *The Scarlet Letter* (Nathaniel Hawthorne, 1853)[16] in a prison cell! Like other postcolonial authors (Toni Morrison in *Beloved* and Bharati Mukherjee in *The Holder of the World*), Condé deliberately transgresses the rules of verisimilitude, disregarding both authenticity and historicity. It remains nevertheless the case, despite the author's words of caution, that many readers continue to consider Tituba as historical fiction.[17]

But the appeal of the novel is to be found elsewhere. It questions the possibility of translating a life that is not the author's, of putting into the author's own mouth the words of a different woman. A discussion of the three levels of meaning offered by the following phrases will help clarify what is at stake here: the title: *"Moi, Tituba sorcière...Noire de Salem"* (Tituba as she is translated by/into the early North American culture of the Puritan era); the opening words of the author's first epigraph: "Tituba et moi, avons vécu en étroite intimité pendant un an [Tituba and I lived for a year on the closest of terms] (the historical record as it is translated by/into Condé's writing); and the first words of Tituba's narrative: "Abena, ma mère, un marin anglais la viola" [literally, Abena, my mother, an English sailor raped her] (Tituba translating the history of her mother's rape). The significance of these phrases can be analyzed in relation to their (un)grammaticality and thus enrich our understanding of the relationship between historiography and imaginative literature.

THE TITLE : *MOI, TITUBA SORCIÈRE...NOIRE DE SALEM*

The autobiography of the black witch of Salem "perverts" (in the etymological sense of derailing or distracting from its end), if it does not subvert, the genre of autobiography. That Condé hands us an un-conventional autobiography is already clear from the title and subtitle of the novel, paratextual levels that become problematic for several reasons.[18] First of all, the title, as it appears on the cover of the 1986 French Folio edition (n° 1929), is *"Moi, Tituba sorcière...."* This title appears again on the title page with, below in italics, what appears to be a subtitle, *"Noire de Salem,"* creating a caesura (represented by an ellipsis) between the substantive *"sorcière"* and *"Noire,"* an ungrammatical break if *"Noire"* functions as an adjective. To be grammatically correct in French, the title should read *"Moi, Tituba, ... sorcière noire de Salem."* On the other hand, reading *"Noire"* in the subtitle as a substantive (translated into English as "a Black Woman") inscribes Tituba within a racial category, added at the editors' request to exploit the curiosity French readers might have about race in North America.

This ethnic indication, *sorcière noire*, is moreover inexact: not for the reason that Condé probably was not aware of at the time of composing the novel—namely that Tituba Indian is believed by some have been Amer-Indian (Breslav 1996)—but because different terms are used to refer to a witch in the Caribbean, depending on the locale: in the French West Indies, the term would be "quimboiseuse" or "séancière"; in Jamaica, "obeah-woman"; and in Surinam, "winti"; etc. Coming from Barbados, Tituba Indian was not at all a "voodoo" or "hoodoo" priestess. Rituals of African origin were practiced there, and are called today "obeah," but the word "hoodoo" is inappropriate in Barbados. To this should be added that Tituba herself seems to recognize that the term in the Puritan lexicon used to describe her—"witch," in the past, present, and future—was, is, and would be a mistranslation of her life and her art: "Il me semblait que je disparaissais complètement. Je sentais que dans ce procès des Sorcières de Salem qui feraient couler tant d'encre, qui exciteraient la curiosité et la pitié des générations futures et apparaîtraient à tous comme le témoignage le plus authentique d'une époque crédule et barbare, mon nom ne figurerait que comme celui d'une comparse sans intérêt. On mentionnerait çà et là «une esclave originaire des Antilles et pratiquant vraisemblablement le 'hodoo'» [sic]....On m'ignorerait" (173) [It seemed that I was gradually being forgotten. I felt that I would only be mentioned in passing in these Salem witchcraft trials about which so much would be written later, trials that would arouse the curiosity and pity of generations to come as the greatest testimony of a superstitious and barbaric age. There would be mention here and there of "a slave originating from the West Indies and probably practicing 'hoodoo'".... I would be ignored (110)]. With the use of the term "hoodoo" and Tituba's reflection, did Condé want to suggest that the colonizer was alternately indifferent or careless when it came to knowing the different religions, beliefs, or mentalities of dominated cultures?[19] The magic-religious amalgam continues today in the U.S.: all that resembles "witchcraft," however vaguely, when it comes from the Caribbean is labeled as "hoodoo"; and as Hollywood films such as Val Lewton's *I Walked with a Zombie* (1943) attest, the stereotype of the Black from the islands portrays him as a dangerous intruder, a wild and bewitching element.[20] When the Other is named or depicted, that is, "translated," as practicing religiously tinted magic, the colonizer neglected to listen or to take careful notes. Tituba/Condé's use of the expression "çà et là" [here and there] indicates the lack of care or rigor that she imagines the judges took in submitting their reports about this *sorcière noire*.

Questions about the referential nature of language or the power of the narrator of history become implicitly unanswerable in the memoirs of slaves from Barbados exiled in the New World. And consequently, the question of how to translate an unrecorded life of bygone times becomes crucial for postcolonial authors. As Alice Brittan has noted in her analysis of *Remembering Babylon* (David Malouf, 1993), the same semantic volatility affected the Aborigines' lexicon, which Brittan describes as "the problem of naming oneself and speaking referentially about the world of imported objects in a national context of acute and sustained material anxiety" (1159). In the context of slavery in the Americas, a word such as "hoodoo" becomes the "marker" of colonizers and chroniclers used to justify their claims to superiority by debasing the Other in his/her linguistic and cultural otherness. Condé's use of the term "hoodoo" in this novel reminds her readers just to what extent Africans or those of African descent transported onto the American continent were stigmatized as cannibalistic by an atrophied discourse. It is as if the oppressed had to be quelled even at a linguistic level, not allowed to exist in the language of the oppressor as anything more than a "cultural menace."[21] If historians have been negligent as to the accuracy of the term "hoodoo," essential to the Puritans' accusation that Tituba Indian was practicing witchcraft, how can the modern day author hope to render justice by correcting it? We know from interviews with the author that she initially presented her editors with the title *Moi, Tituba*, but that they asked her to lengthen it.[22] Is the strange ungrammaticality of the break between "*sorcière*" and "*Noire*" in the title evidence of this same inattention on someone's part?

Condé's preferred title, *Moi, Tituba*, allows her novel to echo a genre that is absent in Caribbean literature, that is, "the slave narrative." Marie Guillemin Benoist's very beautiful, noble, melancholy *Portrait de négresse* [*Portrait of a Negress*], though it bears no relation to the contents of Condé's novel, appears on the cover of the Folio re-edition, and serves to further such an association. Portraits and/ or medallions on book covers are typical of the genre of ex-slave autobiographies in abolitionist America.[23] All narrative traditions, and "History" is one of them, recall or translate the past through a variety of means. What would be the significance, then, in the cultural memory of a people, if the memory of enslavement was or was not told as a slave narrative?

There are virtually no autobiographies of African slaves: either because they were forced to live in inhumane conditions, or because captives did not have access to the master's language, or because they had to trick him into teaching them to read and write. Teaching slaves reading was, in particular times and places, forbidden by law, so the "colored" subject wrote with the "master's" permission, which modified an already self-censored work. Most slave narratives have come to light through the combined efforts of white abolitionists, Protestants and Quakers (Helen Thomas 7). The foundation of a very rich African-American literature in the United States, the slave narrative is, however, traditionally studied as a male genre, with as its prototype the famous *Narrative of the Life of Frederick Douglass, an American Slave, Written by Himself* (1845). There are a few feminine exceptions[24]; and in the West Indies the genre is necessarily an avatar, intended for slightly different purposes.[25] As the inscription of the "death of the author" (see Mudimbé-Boyi), the utterance "*Moi, Tituba*" also implies a self-generating discourse, without any mediation other than Tituba's gestures, her stuttering, her "nonstandard" speech. Indeed, the odd comma between the pronoun "*Moi*" and the proper noun is readable as the trace of the subject's determination, now that she has the right to speak, to translate exactly what she has undergone and how she has faced multiple humiliations and accusations.

In Condé's writing, the autobiography of the ex-slave acquires a new intention: it becomes the appeal of a defendant on trial and thus illustrates the fundamental "problem" of intercultural communication. Tituba, in defending herself against the accusation of witchcraft, tells the story of her culture and identity, necessarily unfamiliar to the contemporary reader. Her plea of innocence recalls the words of the African-American, W.E.B. Du Bois, according to whom, "the emancipated slave, [is] barred from court" (1935: 721, qtd. in Hesse 152). As an act of "rememorization," in the sense Toni Morrison intended "rememory" ("Memory..." 385),[26] that is, a conscious effort to re-imagine the life of a slave in Barbados and Salem in the seventeenth century, "autobiography, as testimony, a plea, justification and requisition, belongs to the legal domain, from which it takes its *mise en scène*, roles, and enunciation. The judicial and the theatrical are inextricably linked here, theatre being the privileged locus of a trial, as in a Greek tragedy, and a courtroom being analogous to theatre" (Mathieu-Castellani 21).[27] Through the intervention of fiction, Tituba's trial is dismissed, and the *non locus* replaced by another locus of speech. The different stages are traced, from the discovery of the Other to the discrimination against and accusation of the Other with emphasis placed on the arbitrary meaning of words—in Tituba's trial, "*sorcellerie*" [witchcraft], "*magique*" [magic], "*art*" [art], "*prière*" [prayer], "*servir*" [serve], "*blesser*" [hurt], and "*Satan*" [the devil].

With the title "*Moi, Tituba...*" a reversal occurs: it is for the defendant, whose voice is so rarely heard in a court of law, to fully recount her version of the facts. Even though the Puritans focus on the trials as part of a struggle against Satan, Tituba, the defendant without weapons, with no "freedom of speech" other than that of enunciating the lies her torturers have dictated, will nevertheless reiterate her question, "Où était Satan? Ne se cachait-il pas dans les plis des manteaux des juges? Ne parlait-il pas la voix des juristes et des hommes d'Eglise?" (182) [Where was Satan? Wasn't he hiding in the folds of the judges' coats? Wasn't he speaking in the voices of these magistrates and these men of religion? (116)]. And what if the Puritans were witches? That is doubtless the real question, which would explain the title's three suspension points after "*sorcière*." Condé shows that the Puritans are guilty of exactly the same crimes as those they have accused the "*sorcière noire*" of committing. Tituba's testimony makes use of an arsenal of clichés, systematically replacing the Whites' accusing words with their Black equivalents: when the Puritans cry "*sorcellerie*," Tituba speaks of her "*art*," when the former speaks of "*des formules magiques*" [magic formulas] and "*incantation sorcières*" [witches' incantations], Tituba speaks of "*prières*" [prayers].

Most significantly and on several occasions, she redefines the word "*sorcière*," thereby putting language into question as the tool to which ordering the world of God's creation, the universe, is entrusted. John Indian calls her a "*sorcière*" during one of their first conversations and she reflects on the term: "Je m'apercevais que dans sa bouche, le mot était entaché d'opprobre. Comment cela? Comment? La faculté de communiquer avec les invisibles, de garder un lien constant avec les disparus, de soigner, de guérir n'est-elle pas une grâce supérieure de nature à inspirer respect, admiration et gratitude?" (33-34) [I noticed that when he said the word, it was marked with disapproval. Why should that be? Why? Isn't the ability to communicate with the invisible world, to keep constant links with the dead, to care for others and heal, a superior gift of nature that inspires respect, admiration, and gratitude? (17)]. Given Tituba's interpretation of "*sorcière*," it should be a term of honor rather than disdain. "En conséquence," she decides, "la sorcière, si on veut nommer ainsi celle qui possède cette grâce, ne devrait-elle pas être choyée et révérée au lieu d'être crainte?" (34) [Consequently, shouldn't the witch (if that's what the person who has this gift is to be called) be cherished and revered rather than feared? (17)].

Tituba's initial encounter with the Puritans evinces their definition of difference as evil: hardly propitious for intercultural exchanges. As soon as she arrives in Salem, Tituba, one of the rare black slaves, realizes that the rural community is steeped in superstitions and unable to think of the unknown other than as dangerous. Their inclination to believe in irrational, magical forces, the very inclination for which they reproach the colonized Other, makes them blind, frightens them, and thus unleashes such violence and terror that they maximize the distance between themselves (the "Founding Fathers") and all others (Africans, Indians and Jews). As Morrison demonstrates in *Playing in the Dark. Whiteness and the Literary Imagination* (30), the settlers combated their own fears by stigmatizing Blacks. "Africanism" (see Manzor-Coats, Dukats) was invented to assuage the conscience of colonizers looking for a scapegoat. Uncertainty—about the forces that controlled their fate, from inclement weather to their relationships with Native Americans (see Hawthorne's *The Scarlet Letter*)—combined with ignorance to create the community's distrust of Blacks. Threatened by the presence of people they themselves had brought to the new world (and Blacks would outnumber Whites a century and a half later), the Bay Colony warded off "Evil" with propitiatory rituals and gestures. When Tituba arrives in Salem, a town of around two thousand, she is surprised to see the cows crossing the street and notices "des bouts de chiffon rouge…fixés à leurs cornes" (91) [pieces of red cloth attached to their horns (56)]. As she discovers the Puritans' superstitions, Tituba attends numerous ceremonies analogous to exorcisms, weddings among them.

The leaders of the community persist in desperate efforts to control difference and sexuality. Samuel Parris, convinced that the color of her skin indicates that she is the Anti-Christ of Salem, futilely attempts to tame and punish Tituba and John after finding them kissing on the bridge of the boat. He tries to exorcize his own

73

fear of the Other by invoking the Bible and imposing marriage and prayers, telling them that ". . . tant que vous serez sous mon toit, vous vous comporterez en chrétiens! Venez faire les prières! (68) [as long as you are under my roof, you will behave as Christians! Come and say your prayers!" (41)]. The mouth that utters the word — be it "*sorcière*" or "*prière*" — determines its meaning.

Tituba clearly descends from African healers with her "gentle medicine" and prestidigitation, but the white witch Judith White initiated her as well. The burgeoning "new world" soon shows itself in the novel to be an intercultural zone in spite of the sectarian doctrine of the Founding Fathers. And in spite of the so-called religious (and racist) segregation of the Puritans from the Other, exchanges do take place. Blending the occult techniques learned from the Whites with those of Man Yaya, and aided by Man Yaya and Man Abena, her *marassa* mentors who appear to her from the spirit world as birds (Kasongo 1994), Tituba creates a laboratory of creolization in the Puritan colony. When she learns that two women have lost their lives in the upstairs bed, she hurries to exorcise the double death with a purification ceremony (T. 94); and like Télumée, in Schwarz-Bart's novel *Pluie et vent sur Télumée miracle* (1972),[28] Tituba casts out the troubles and afflictions rampant in the small congregation. From gazing into a bowl of water to revive a Barbados for the moment lost to her, she will go so far as to concoct a "witch's cake" out of several drops of the invalid's urine. Here Tituba attempts to integrate Africanist knowledge into a healing ritual for European Puritan culture, though the attempt is unsuccessful.

At times when she compares these two "visions of the world," Tituba concludes in favor of her own ethno-cultural origins. For example, cats are not foreboding, but rather a blessing for her: "Ils miaulaient, se couchaient sur le dos, élevant leurs pattes nerveuses, terminées par des griffes acérées. Quelques semaines auparavant, je n'aurais rien trouvé de surnaturel à ce spectacle. A présent, instruite par la bonne Judah White, je compris que les esprits de l'endroit me saluaient. Qu'ils sont enfantins les hommes à peau blanche pour choisir de manifester leurs pouvoirs au travers d'animaux comme le chat! Nous autres, nous préférons des animaux d'une autre envergure: le serpent, par exemple, reptile superbe aux sombres anneaux! (94) [Hordes of cats were chasing each other in the grass, meowing and lying on their backs, nervously raising their paws that ended in sharp claws. A few weeks earlier, I would have found nothing supernatural in such a sight. Now, instructed by Goodwife Judah White, I realized that the spirits of the place were greeting me. How childish white folks are to choose the cat as a manifestation of their powers! We others, we prefer animals of a nobler breed: the snake, for example, a magnificent reptile with dark rings (58)]. Even though both these interpretations of the world may be considered equally naïve and superstitious by some of Condé's readers, the gap between them and the incompatibility of Euro-American and Africanist explanations for their troubles will only grow.

Tolerated because of her difference at the beginning of her stay in Salem, Tituba eventually attracts a collective hate when she comes to care for Parris' wife and two daughters as a *da* ("governess," "nanny" or "nursemaid" in West Indian Creole). In taking on their medicinal and spiritual care, she excites much gossip and loose talk, and before she knows it, she acquires the reputation of a witch who knows all and sees all (99). Her maternal ministrations introduced something hybrid into a culture that claimed to be homogenous, opened up as it were a "third space" where cultural identity could be renegotiated (Bhabha 38). Wild contrary values were infiltrating the Puritan household and Tituba, preferring hybridity to assimilation, suffers from the Puritans' efforts to maintain sameness. As Condé's "*sorcière noire*" unfolds the tale of her life, Tituba's rhetorical questions often challenge her readers to join her in this third space challenging preconceived ideas: "Quel était ce monde qui avait fait de moi une esclave, une orpheline, une paria? Quel était ce monde qui me séparait des miens?"(81) [What kind of world was this that had turned me into a slave, an orphan, and an outcast? What kind of a world that had taken me away from my own people? (49)].

Once readers have reflected along with Tituba in this third space, we then wonder about the failure of one individual to create a hybrid culture in this place and time. Tituba cares for the Parris' child Betsey, who becomes a substitute for her aborted child, but this affection is betrayed. She uses a confessional tone to proclaim her faith in the interracial friendship that fooled her: "Je confesse que je suis naïve. J'en étais convaincue, même une race scélérate et criminelle peut produire des individus sensibles et bons, tout comme un arbre rabougri peut porter des fruits généreux. Je croyais à l'affection de Betsey, passagèrement égarée par je ne savais qui, mais que je ne désespérais pas de reconquérir(121-22) [I confess that I am naïve. I was convinced that even a race of villains and criminals could produce some good, well-meaning individuals, just as a stunted tree can bear some healthy fruit. I believed in the affection of Betsey, led astray by some unknown force, but I was sure of winning her back (76)]. When her experiment with creolization (as interracial friendship and mothering beyond racial lines) has failed, Tituba notes, ". . . je ne pourrai jamais décrire l'impression que je ressentis. Rage. Désir de tuer. Douleur, douleur surtout" (142-433) [. . .the impression I had was indescribable. There was rage. There was a desire to kill. There was pain, especially pain (90)].

THE EPIGRAPH : "TITUBA ET MOI, . . ."

The narrative of the novel is an act of recollection, and Condé replaces the traditional topos of a lost manuscript with the following epigraph:

> Tituba et moi, avons vécu en étroite intimité pendant un an. C'est au cours de nos interminables conversations qu'elle m'a dit ces choses qu'élle n'avait confiées à personne.
>
> Maryse Condé
>
> [Tituba and I lived for a year on the closest of terms. During our endless conversations she told me things she had confided to nobody else.][29]

The comma after "Tituba et moi," separating as it does the plural subject from the verb, is an awkward construction that serves to mirror the splitting already suggested by the chiasmus in the title, *Moi, Tituba sorcière…Noire de Salem*. Claiming to have had several conversations with the (defunct) eye-witness of the "Peculiar Institution," Condé proclaims the fake and fictional nature of the autobiography by insisting on intimacy as the grounding of their exchange.

Can Tituba then be read as the translator of Condé's (conscious or unconscious) convictions? If so, the narrative's presentation of Tituba's sexuality illustrates Condé's attempt to raise questions about representations of black women's sexuality, as she has done since her first novel *Hérémakhonon*. In the imagination of Whites, black sexuality has been seen as an exotic, forbidden taboo, and thus desirable.[30] White men's stereotypes, especially in Puritan New England, of black women combined the "dark continent" of Africa with the "dark continent" of women's bodies into a seemingly infinite mystery, usually associated with Evil. A Caribbean woman writer can not translate the sexuality of black women for a European and North American audience already steeped in these stereotypes. Historically, issues of sexuality were muted in slave narratives written in the nineteenth century. Freed and literate slaves told of the atrocities and humiliations, but shame prevented them from revealing more intimate 'disasters' of 'breaking-and-enterings.' Consequently, their writings were interwoven with shadows and the unspoken. Consider Harriet Jacobs' shame, reluctance and indirection when recounting her choice to have sex with a white man other than her master in order to escape being raped by him.

Tituba, in complete contrast to this tradition, not only describes the act of rape in minute detail, she also becomes a slave who ardently desires men. But her libertine attitude opens the way for her being stigmatized, reduced to filling the role of scapegoat in a culture where the bodily and the sexual are marked with the letter "A" for adultery. In prison Tituba meets perhaps the most famously stigmatized character in American fiction, Hester Prynne, punished for having passionately loved a man of her own choice. The two women talk at length together about their sexual needs, and after Hester's death, she comes from the spirit world to lie down with Tituba and bring her a sexual pleasure that surprises her: "Peut-on éprouver du plaisir à se serrer contre un corps semblable au sien?" (190) [Can you feel pleasure from hugging a body similar to your own? (122)]. Admitting her great sexual appetite, Tituba is frequently criticized by the spirits of both Man Yaya and Man Abena for being too dependent on men. "Pourquoi les femmes ne peuvent-elles se passer des hommes? (31) [Why can't women do without men? (15)], Man Abena continually asks her; and Tituba reflects candidly on the question herself: "Qu'avait-il donc, John Indien, pour que je sois malade de lui?...Je savais bien où résidait son principal avantage et je n'osais regarder, en deçà de la cordelette de jute qui retenait son pantalon konoko de toile blanche, la butte monumentale de son sexe" (36) [What was there about John Indian to make me sick with love for him?...I knew all too well where his main asset lay and I dared not look below the jute cord that held up his short tight-fitting *konoko* trousers to the huge bump of his penis (19)]. Excluded from Puritan society, labeled as a "creature of the Anti-Christ" because Black and a woman, Tituba is above all condemned for the pleasure she takes in her body. When masturbating, Tituba runs her hand over "les renflements et les courbes" [curves and protuberances (15)] of her body, imagining that it is not her hand but the hand of John Indian caressing her to orgasm: "Jaillie des profondeurs de mon corps, une marée odorante inonda mes cuisses. Je m'entendis râler dans la nuit" (30) [Out of the depths of my body gushed a pungent tidal wave that flooded my thighs. I could hear myself moan in the night (15)].

In this post-colonial revision of the *sorcière*, "commerce with the Devil" is nothing other than absolute sexual freedom. This is a freedom the author has defended with equal conviction in subsequent novels (*Desirada, Colonie du nouveau monde*, and *Célanire cou-coupé*) in which certain passages seem to confirm Condé's "diabolical intentions"[31]; that is, they are seen as shocking (for some) and "politically incorrect" (for others). With Tituba, Condé has invented a heroine who breaks down all the social barriers that this (American) society, from its Puritan beginnings, smugly thought it had established: language, religion, race, and even sex. Tituba is less a "hoodoo" priestess than a free woman living out a "*géolibertinage*" (as practiced by René Depestre, Raphaël Confiant, and Dany Laferrière). Unbridled sexuality, pleasure as an anti-depressant during the reign of the institution of slavery, becomes another fundamental component of this *mock* epic. Condé tries the patience of any reader who comes looking for a novel with a semblance of truth, for something fantastic, or for magical realism.[32] She strikes out as well at those who would condemn gay culture, homosexuality or bi-sexuality. In her own way, Condé declares war on WASP America, still puritanical, bigoted and hypocritical. Full of postmodern irony, Tituba's masturbation scene recalls the love, anger, and madness portrayed in a similar scene in *Amour, colère, et folie* (1968) by Haitian Marie Chauvet.

Seemingly incongruous is the reflection that follows this ecstasy: Tituba wonders whether Abena, her mother, had also moaned in spite of herself during the rape. Taking full advantage of her liberty as an author, Condé shows Tituba experiencing sexual pleasure and then contemplating rape. The author thus shows, first of all, the depth of the violation that rape represents, in that this unwanted sexual act takes one's own pleasure out of one's control. Second, by juxtaposing the rape of Tituba's mother and Tituba's own masturbation, Condé takes her readers into a forbidden territory where rape victims may indeed experience sexual pleasure during rape and then feel shame for that pleasure. Conflating rape and pleasure, while seemingly problematic, is just one more boundary that Condé insists on crossing. Rather than calling for compassion and pity,

Maryse Condé shocks and irritates, dispensing with the mournful, martyr's tone sometimes heard in African diaspora literature.

THE INCIPIT: "ABENA, MA MÈRE, UN MARIN ANGLAIS LA VIOLA" [ABENA, MY MOTHER, WAS RAPED BY AN ENGLISH SAILOR][33]

The opening words of the novel, the incipit, immediately confront the reader with Abena's rape aboard the slave ship named "Christ the King,"[34] all of which presents a third element in Condé's syntax: the fictional origin of this autobiography and the flagrant crime of rape committed against thousands of black women in the colonies. The supposed autobiography deals with experiences that Tituba only infers and could not herself have witnessed. She gives voice to Abena, and by extension to all the slave women whose rapes were never reported, to their silenced voices, to their symbolically amputated tongues. This sentence, represents a third syncope[35] in Condé's syntax: by introducing a sequence of commas, it displaces the autobiographical narrating subject and accentuates the first term of the phrase (the direct object of the verb), "Abena," the victim of the opprobrium, the mute mother.

The rape that opens the narrative functions as a synecdoche for the lacunae in black feminine autobiography, for the untranslatability of the feminine experience under slavery: "Abena, ma mère, un marin anglais la viola sur le pont du *Christ the King*, un jour de 16** alors que le navire faisait voile vers la Barbade" (13) [Abena, my mother, was raped by an English sailor on the deck of *Christ the King* one day in 16** while the ship was sailing for Barbados (3)]. Whether readers want to or not, they follow this *pariade*,[36] their gaze riveted on the victim of the rape, on the lowly, voiceless subject, *Abena*. Only the possessive adjective "ma" [my] communicates to us that Tituba is speaking of herself, or rather, that she is speaking for her mother. As autobiographical subject, Tituba begins the story of her life not with her own birth, but with the sexual "death" of her mother, Abena the African.

But if we consider this incipit in relation to the title, something else is happening here, more easily appreciated when the first words of each are written as Walcott might, as a verse of poetry:

Abena, ma mère, . . .

Moi, Tituba sorcière...

Read this way, the structure of the incipit evokes the title by creating a chiasmus (once again) that links "Moi" and "ma mère" (the equivalence between the self and the mother belonging to the self) and the two proper names Tituba and Abena. The structure of the phrasing shows the connection between the self and the mother—the speaker and she whose tongue was figuratively cut. Tituba is Abena; "ma mère" is "moi." In this phrasing—"Abena, ma mère"—we see three performative acts: *ma* refers us back to the title of the novel (with its echo *Moi*); the mother is foregrounded (her name opens the narrative); thus the narrator, the daughter, speaks for her mother who cannot speak. Interestingly, Abena's name also begins with the (scarlet) letter "A" reminiscent of the one Hester Prynne was forced to don to announce her sin of adultery. Abena's sex was not consensual, however, and her crime goes unmarked by history. As her character Tituba announces her own birth as the product of this violating and violent act, the author creates an echo of Walcott's cry: for her (and her mother), violence is the alpha and omega of the feminine condition. And historically, as we know, too many black women's cries have been silenced, smothered, or choked back in an untranslatable moan.

If Maryse Condé opts for a fictive autobiography (where the character who says "I" is not she), is it not perhaps out of a desire to create a broken speech, a syncopated syntax in an eminently intimate, feminine story where the mother's voice is absent, her speech having been mutilated or amputated. Abena is finally hanged for attacking her master as he attempts to rape her. "On pendit ma mère…On pendit ma mère…On pendit ma mère…" [They hung my mother], Tituba makes the words a litany in her narrative. "Je vis son corps tournoyer aux branches basses d'un fromager…la nuque brisée" (20) [I watched her body swing from the lower branches of a silk cotton tree…her neck…broken (8)]. Later, as she turns over in her mind the question about whether or not to return to the world of "le Blanc" to be with John Indian, Tituba remembers the lynching, and with it recalls the English sailor's rape of her mother and Abena's master anticipating the pleasure of the rape he had in mind: "Ma mère avait été violée par un Blanc. Elle avait été pendue à cause d'un Blanc. J'avais vu sa langue pointer hors de sa bouche, pénis turgescent et violacé" (37) [My mother had been raped by a white man. She had been hanged because of a white man. I had seen his tongue quiver out of his mouth, his penis turgid and violet (19)]. His pleasure denied and his power threatened, he hangs Abena. The white man's sex becomes the weapon that breaks her mother's neck, amputates black women's speech: muted, or in any case diminished, by the physical and psychological violence of such atrocities, the survivor turns inward in total silence.[37]

CONCLUSION: "I IS A LONG MEMORIED WOMAN"[38]

Although Condé has written of her first eighteen years in *Le cœur à rire et à pleurer* [*Tales from the Heart*], readers will find her opinions, however shocking or politically incorrect they may be, throughout her novels. Re-writing from a post-colonial and autobiographical perspective the first trial in early U.S. history to inspire so much fiction, Condé chooses to modify the historical character, making of her a resolutely emancipated woman of color. As a prisoner trapped in multiple conflicting relations (between religions, "races," sexes and generations), the "sorcière de Salem" settles several accounts with America. If the title *"Moi, Tituba"* underlines the need for a Caribbean feminine autobiography, freed of all constraints, "Tituba et moi" recalls the author's translation and refers to a dialogisme, "gendered as feminine because Condé's female characters main-tain dialogic relationships with their socio-historical context and are at the same time independent thinkers, speakers, actors who desire, love or hate" (Malena, "Le Dialogisme" 249). As an author and theoretician at the crossroads of several languages and cul-tures—along with other major voices, such as those of Assia Djebar and Régine Robin—Condé uses fiction to articulate her own fric-tions with her adopted society (Hewitt 1998). Haunted by what History has "forgotten" and by the roots of racism, Condé stands in a polemical place: "Nomade inconvenante" [Inconvenient Nomad], as the title of a recent collection of essays describes her (Cottenet-Hage and Moudileno), she maintains that one must be "errante, multiple, au-delà et au-dedans" (Pfaff 46) [errant and multifaceted, inside and out, nomadic (28)]. Condé decries the evils of our sup-posedly modern societies and civilizations. Perhaps Jeannie Suk sums it up most succinctly: this author remains "a particular breed of writer that one could call postcolonial. Her position of ironic distance from the West Indies, her active role in American academic criticism of Caribbean literature, her fluency with the theoretical stakes of contemporary literary criticism, and her extreme self-consciousness and self-distancing might bother those who hold a romantic view of the creative artist" (21). Disobliging and disobe-dient, Condé has played with Tituba, bewitching her readers with penetrating criticism of ancient and modern intolerance, of ethnic and religious sectarianism, and of a certain literature that prides itself on being politically correct.

Translated by Victoria Bridges Moussaron,
with additions made by the Editors

Notes

1. This article first appeared in French in the online journal *Mots Pluriels* (23 March 2003) (http://www.arts.uwa.edu.au/MotsPluriels/MP2303kg.html). [The word *Indien* is an example of this untranslatability: as Tituba's married name, a proper name, it should not be translated; however, it also means "Indian" (or "Amer-Indian") as Richard Philcox translates it. Condé would seem to leave it in between a proper name and an ethnic origin: Tituba's husband, "John Indian," is indeed half Indian. It is, however, only his first name "John" that functions as an English proper name; his family name, very probably originally "*the* Indian," remains in between a name and an epithet, which Condé therefore translates as "Indien." But what to do with Tituba, who is not Indian? In her case, his race has become her married name. (Trans.)]

2. This stanza elicited the following commentary from Homi Bhabha, "Walcott's purpose is not to oppose the pedagogy of the imperialist noun to the inflectional appropriation of the native voice. He proposes to go beyond such binaries of power in order to reorganize our sense of the process of identification in the negotiations of cultural politics....Against the possessive, coercive 'right' of the Western noun, Walcott places a different mode of postcolonial speech; a historical time envisaged in the discourse of the enslaved or the indentured" (233).

3. See Daniel Delas, "Aimé Césaire ou « le verbe parturiant »."

4. [From the *Book of Genesis*, "In the beginning was the Word..."; "Au commencement était le Verbe...." (Trans.)]

5. All citations are taken from the first edition, Mercure de France (Coll. Folio), n° 1929, which is identical to the second edition, except for the latter's cover illustration, a detail taken from the famous "Portrait of a Negress" by M.B. Guillemin (*cf. infra*). All English translations of citations from the novel are from the standard Philcox edition (Ballantine Books, 1992).

6. [The English translation is not given here because it will be discussed later in the essay. (Eds.)]

7. For the former, see Lionnet, *Autobiographical Voices*, and Hewitt, *Autobiographical Tightropes*; for the latter, see Braxton, *Black Women Writing*

Autobiography, and Brodzki and Schenk, eds., *Life/Lines*, as well as articles in numerous journals such as *Studies in Autobiography*.

8. [That is, the first novel primarily concerned with rewriting and critiquing U.S. history and cultural development. Eds.]

9. Condé imagines a scenario that clearly resembles African-American Toni Morrison's project in her fifth novel, *Beloved* (see Peterson; Gyssels). Although *Beloved* (1987) is based on the actual historical person, Margaret Garner, *Moi, Tituba…* profoundly reworks the genre of Black autobiography.

10. See Kadish, *Slavery in the Caribbean Francophone World*, and Manzor-Coats, "Of Witches and Other things: Maryse Condé's Challenges to Feminist Discourse."

11. See Jane Moss's article, "Postmodernizing the Salem Witchcraze: Maryse Condé's *I, Tituba, Black Witch of Salem*" (10).

12. The testimonial *Me Llamo Rigoberta Menchú Y Asi Me Nacio La Conciencia* was translated as *I, Rigoberta Menchu An Indian Woman In Guatemala* and offers an example.

13. [A chiasmus is a grammatical figure by which the order of words in one of two parallel clauses is inverted in the other, for example, "never let a fool kiss you or a kiss fool you" (OED). (Eds.]

14. See Wilson J. Moses, "Sex, Salem, and Slave Trials: Ritual Drama and Ceremony of Innocence." While Arthur Miller was inspired by the trials to denounce the McCarthyism of the Cold War ("the hunt for Communists" in *The Crucible*, 1958), Condé re-imagines Tituba as an innocent woman who, in the Puritan colony, has no choice other than to defend herself, "beak and claws," against their racist, sexist and religious attacks. If the Afro-American Ann Petry, a militant for Black Civil Rights, reveals the sad condition of Black women in the economic superpower's society, Condé shows how she who is accused of witchcraft resembles the Founding Fathers, who, in their own way, venerated God fanatically and intolerably as they practiced certain superstitious customs. [For French readers, the author cites the following edition: *Les Sorcières de Salem*. Trans. Marcel Aymé. Paris: Grasset, 1959. (Eds.)]

15. For more on this subject, see my study *Filles de Solitude. Essai sur l'identité antillaise dans les [auto]biographies fictives de Simone et André Schwarz-Bart*.

16. [For French readers of Hawthorne, the author cites the following edition: *The Scarlet Letter. La Lettre écarlate*. Trans. Lucienne Molitor. Paris: Coll. Marabout Bibliothèque, 1975. (Eds.)]

17. See for example, Moss (16).

18. [It is difficult to render the next point in English: in French, adjectives, for the most part, come after the noun they modify – "sorcière *noire*"– whereas in English, adjectives come before the noun they

modify – "*black* witch"– and the issue becomes even more complicated when one remembers that "Black" is also a noun, a synonym for "African American." (Trans.)]

19. It is true that the written form of *vaudou* in French remains uncertain even today. *Vodun* is etymologically from Dahomey (Benin), it can also be written as *vaudou, vaudoo, vodou* or in English, *voodoo*, sometimes plural and sometimes not.

20. Set in the 17th century, Condé's novel foreshadows the hysteria of exactly a century later (1791) with the slaves revolt in France's richest colony, Haiti. The massive exodus of the plantation owners to the American colonies (Louisiana, especially New Orleans), resulted in a generally denigrating stereotype of Haitians.

21. As Steiner writes: "[T]he frequency and sclerotic force of clichés, of unexamined similes, of worn tropes…[imprisoned] their users in an atrophied speech" (qtd. in Brittan 1167).

22. The subtitle *Noire de Salem*, was added by Condé at the editor's request, Mercure de France (Scarboro, "Afterward" 205). A similar paratextual amendment can be found in the latest publication of Edwidge Danticat, in a new Crown Books collection of travel writing, *After the Dance, a Walk through Jacmel, Haiti* (2002), where "Haiti" has been added to make clear to the reader that this book deals with carnival in a Caribbean island, thus creating particular expectations and in doing so attract more readers.

23. For the anthology *Extravagant Strangers. A Literature of Belonging*, the editor and author Caryl Phillips intentionally chose the portrait of Olaudah Equiano (1789) and extracts from famous slave narratives (Gronniosaw, 1770; Ignatius Sancho, 1776). This image has also been used on the cover of several re-editions of works from the West Indies (e.g. *Le Voyage aux isles. Chronique aventureuse des Caraïbes* 1693-1705 du Père Labat).

24. The two known examples in America are Harriet Jacobs, *Incidents in the Life of a Slave Girl, Mrs. Harriet Brent Jacobs. Written by Herself* (1861); and Mary Prince: an abolitionist African-American, she traveled in Jamaica in 1840 and married a Russian Jew, who in turn founded the first Black Masonic lodge in Boston, see *A Black Woman's Odyssey through Russia and Jamaica. The Narrative of Mary Prince* (1850). There is also one Caribbean exception: the work of Mary Seacole, a Scottish-Jamaican mulatto who as a doctor traveled to Panama, where she fought cholera, and later to London (1854), where she sought acceptance as a nurse in order to alleviate the suffering of British and French soldiers in the war against the Russian Tsar. See *The Wonderful Adventures of Mrs. Seacole in Many Lands* (1857).

25. Several Caribbean testimonial works exist: the ethnologist and sociologist Dany Bébel-Gisler has given us *Léonore, l'histoire enfouie de la*

Guadeloupe (1985), an autobiography of an ex-slave, but this work is rarely read as a "'novel." In the same anthropo-cultural domain, it is worth mentioning the beautiful book, halfway between journalism (interviews) and anthology, by Gisèle Pineau (text) and Marie Abraham (photos): *Femmes des Antilles, Traces et voix* (1996) published for the 150th anniversary of the abolition of slavery in the West Indies (1848-1998). As part of "reparations" literature (Amnesty International, Droits de L'Homme,…), the Nobel Prize for Peace, on the 5th centenary of the discovery of America, was awarded to the Caribbean Rigoberta Menchú.

26. [For French readers, the author cites the French translation of Morrison's novel by Pierre Alien (Paris: C. Bourgeois, 1993). (Eds.)]

27. The French text reads: ". . . l'autobiographie, qui est à la fois témoignage, plaidoyer, justification, et réquisition, s'inscrit par là dans le judiciaire, auquel elle emprunte sa mise en scène, ses rôles, et les modalités de son énonciation. Le judiciaire et le théâtral ont partie liée ici, tant le théâtre est le lieu privilégié du procès, comme dans la tragédie grecque, tant le tribunal ressemble à un théâtre."

28. See Gyssels, *Filles de Solitude* Chapter III. 5.

29. [Richard Philcox's translation here "corrects" the grammatical awkwardness of the French which would be rendered in English: "Tituba and I, lived for a year…." (Eds.)]

30. To name a few literary works that address this question, see Condé's *La Belle Créole*, as well as Jean Toomer's *Cane*, James Alan McPherson's "Elbow Room," Ferdinand Oyono's *Une vie de Boy*, and Carl Van Vechten's *Nigger Heaven*. Films include: *Imitation of Life, Blonde Venus*.

31. See Condé's recent interview with Lydie Moudileno (*Women in French Studies*, 2002) for the author's response to this association (126).

32. See for example, Onyeoziri's article, "L'Ironie et le fantastique dans *Traversée de la mangrove* de Maryse Condé" (405).

33. [For the discussion that follows, a literal translation: "Abena, my mother, an English sailor raped her." (Trans.)]

34. « Christ the King » appears in English in the original text.

35. [In grammar, an elision of one or more letters or sounds from the middle of a word, as in *Wooster* for *Worcester*, is the second definition of "syncope" (*Webster's New Twentieth Century Dictionary*). The first syncope is the ellipsis in the title "*Moi, Tituba sorcière…Noire de Salem*." The second is the missing *nous* from "Tituba et moi, [nous] avons vécu en étroite intimité." (Eds.)]

36. For readers familiar with *La Mulâtresse Solitude* by André Schwarz-Bart, this scene echoes "l'étrange coutume de la Pariade" that opens the novel.

37. [After much discussion, the editors decided to use Philcox's version of this passage, in which he translates (emphasis added) "Ma mère avait été violée par un Blanc. Elle avait été pendue à cause d'un Blanc. J'avais vu *sa* langue pointer hors de *sa* bouche, pénis turgescent et violacé" as "My mother had been raped by a white man. She had been hung because of a white man. I had seen *his* tongue quiver out of *his* mouth, *his* penis turgid and violet." For the record, however, and in keeping with Gyssels's original text, another translation is offered here, with the addition of the sentence that follows in the text, "Mon père adoptif s'était suicidé à cause d'un Blanc": "My mother had been raped by a White. She had been hung because of a White. I had seen *her* tongue sticking out of *her* mouth, a violet and turgid penis. My adoptive father had killed himself because of a White." The vision rendered in the second translation reflects the trauma for the child of the initial rape, of Abena's hanging, and of Yao's suicide, and is much more powerful psychologically if she sees her mother's tongue as the symbol of the penis that killed her (and Yao). This translation of the possessive pronouns turns one particular man's tongue/penis into a metonymy which functions on an unconscious and therefore universal level, more in keeping with Condé's intentionally violent style in the scene; and the translation of "le Blanc" as "a White" is more crude and violent, it carries more anger. Although the Philcox translation can still be used to support Gyssels's imagery here, to read the pronoun as *his* penis is to weaken the scope of the scene. In addition, the sentence that follows in the text, referring to Yao's suicide "because of a White," adds to the anger of Tituba's vision/memory and expands her mother's hanging to a larger racist act. The repetition of "because of a White" makes a litany in this scene as well, echoing "on a pendu ma mère" seen earlier (Trans.)]

38. [The title of a collection of poetry by Guyanese poet Grace Nichols (1983). (Eds.)]

TALKING THE CROSS-TALK OF HISTORIES IN MARYSE CONDÉ'S I, TITUBA, BLACK WITCH OF SALEM

Jennifer R. Thomas

The Caribbean writer's engagement with history is frequently a complex process of challenging dominant historical narratives and denouncing the myth of Caribbean alterity. Maryse Condé enacts this process in her novel *I, Tituba Black Witch of Salem* as she interrogates the memory of colonial history through her affirmation of the subjective presence of forgotten selves like her protagonist Tituba. Her validation of Tituba's experience, however, does not mean that the text seeks to declare fiction historical fact. Condé's work is more concerned with chronicling her commitment to expanding historical consciousness through a dialogue that engages the (not always clear) convergences and divergences of various histories.

Edouard Glissant's notion of "nonhistory" in *Caribbean Discourse* helps to elucidate Condé's engagement with histories in her novel. Nonhistory for Glissant represents the Caribbean experience of "brutal dislocation," "shock," and "painful negation" which prevents the "collective consciousness" of the colonized from absorbing the totality of this tortuous genealogy (61-62). Understanding Caribbean identity, however, requires accessing these violent and disjointed beginnings. Furthermore, Glissant explains that nonhistory exists outside of "History," or European meta-historical discourse, in that it problematizes dominant historical models through its presence and affirms value in articulating the effaced experiences and complex origins of Caribbean peoples.

The duty of the Caribbean writer according to Glissant is to reveal and explore nonhistory, which he also recognizes as "obsessively present" in dominant historical discourse (63-64). Nonhistory can emerge as history for peoples of the Caribbean with the help of the writer who cultivates a historical consciousness unlimited by the traditional chronological and hierarchical understandings of experience.[2] By representing nonhistory, literature functions as a medium through which the writer attempts to fulfill the passionate *"longing for the ideal of history"* [his emphasis] by representing nonhistory (79). In this sense, writing nonhistory is a struggle to reorient the evolution of meta-history through the recovery of a *"primordial source"* [his emphasis] and is a process of revelation which has the "peculiarity (like myth in the past) of obscuring as well as disclosing" (79). The mythical nature of the writing process reflects both its ability to "open up the full range of the unknown" and its limits, since clarification emerges through a recognition of and interaction with constantly shifting ambiguities (69-84). Nonetheless, for Glissant this dilemma enables Caribbean writers to prepare a way for denied and broken histories as their texts display the "repertoire of responses" to the colonial encounter (70).

Condé's text *I, Tituba, Black Witch of Salem* challenges and affirms Glissant's notion of the writer and nonhistory. Drawing on the legacy of African slavery in the diaspora, on Caribbean history, Puritan history and the Salem Witch Trials, on Jewish persecution, and on American fictional literary history, Condé affirms the presence of Caribbean nonhistory while demonstrating that there is no "ideal history." In this sense, her understanding of historical consciousness reveals the "unknown" as described by Glissant, but she does so through a representation of these histories as linked within a web of experience. Such an approach supports a textual exploration of nonhistory by engaging Glissant's acknowledgement of "concealed parallel histories" (63). Condé's narrative spotlights these historical relationships as the starting point for cultivating an alternative understanding of history. While this novel does exhibit the struggle implicit in any process of rethinking historical consciousness, it does not suggest that Condé's links represent Glissant's "full range" of the unknown. The "full range" for Condé can only be attained when histories enter into the dialogue she represents in her text. These linked histories are her "primordial *sources*" [my emphasis] that allow her to enact an imaginative exploration of the forgotten histories, or nonhistory of black people (Scarboro 1992, 201). Searching for "self," "identity," and "origin" through the first-person voice of Tituba allows the author to affirm the significance of articulating nonhistory while also placing this experience in specific relation to other histories (203-04).

In this sense, Condé invokes imagination for the purpose of what Toni Morrison refers to as *"becoming"* [her emphasis] (4). Condé's writing of Tituba is Condé's recognition of the frequently omitted "Africanist presence" integral to her envisioned extension of history and literature into what Morrison calls a "wider landscape" (3-5). The collective narration by author and character presents an Africanist presence capable of establishing coherence as it releases forgotten experience from the "margins of the literary [and historical] imagination" (5-6). This literary strategy, however, has also been criticized for disrupting the "reader's sense of the truthfulness of [Tituba's] testimony" (Bernstein 2). Such a disruption is actually a discomfort readers may experience when asked to accept fictional history. However, this criticism is misplaced because the alleged rupture is not caused by textual weakness; it results from the reader's uneasiness with being complicit in Condé's fictional history. The collective narration, like the text's epigraph, highlights the fictitious nature of the narrative, while ironically also operating to make the reader believe this created history. The alleged propensity for Tituba's voice to "slip...into a false authenticity" (2) does not represent Condé's interrogation of her literary project per se; it denotes instead a struggle between the reader's possible flirtation with suspending belief while attempting to sustain a clear awareness of the absolute division between history and fiction.

Condé recognizes that her writing is also a "very perilous exercise" which will inevitably "displease" or "disturb," as seen with the aforementioned criticism regarding the text's first person narrative structure ("Role" 697; "Order" 161). Though disturbing, this disorder is part of a valuable creative process that helps her cultivate an increased historical awareness ("Order" 160-62). Engaging a dialogue with multinational narratives of history, Condé links Tituba's story to global histories in an effort to help develop a more comprehensive historical consciousness. In this sense, she enacts Glissant's "exploded [literary] discourse" (*Caribbean Discourse*, 159). Condé gives Tituba's effaced subjectivity a reality, albeit a fictional one. Her text is not a sterile "nostalgic lament" (64); it is an intimate dialogue with the historical moments her narrative traverses. This process, however, is not neat, consistent, or always accurate; it is wrought with tension, ambivalence, and paradox. For Condé, these are problems associated with recovering forgotten selves, in both actual history and in the realm of fiction. Her acknowledgment of these issues is not a "question[ing] [of] her own literary project" (Bernstein 3); rather it is an acknowledgment of the inherently ruptured nature of the emergent historical consciousness to which she attempts to give expression (Glissant, *CD* 64-65). Engaging in this type of historical dialogue, whether as a traditional historian or a fictional writer, lends itself to creating narratives that are neither seamless nor straightforward. An attempt to recover and articulate violent ruptures and effaced experiences cannot create a linear conclusive narrative. The dialogue between histories will contain gaps and questions as we continue to grapple with the problems of meta-history.

One way Condé illustrates the problems associated with creating a narrative of historical dialogue is by linking Tituba's history with the experiences of the Jews as well as with maroon resistance in Barbados. The relationship between Tituba and her Jewish master Benjamin Cohen d'Azevedo highlights their shared experience of oppression. Tituba ponders their situations when she considers his contemplation of her horrific experience in the Salem Witch Trials as a similar "basic cruelty that seemed to characterize those he called Gentiles" (123). Nevertheless, Benjamin's attempt to create a competition for the more oppressive history supercedes Tituba's desire for understanding. While Benjamin interrogates her to see if she knows how many Jews died during the Inquisition, he also ignores her question about whether he knows "how many [Africans] bled from the coast of Africa" (127). Some may view this dialogue as a mutually beneficial conversation about their respective peoples (Bernstein 6), but it is not. Benjamin disregards Tituba's attempt to demonstrate that the African diaspora deserves equal consideration with the Jewish diaspora.

This unequal exchange marks the encounter between Benjamin and Tituba as one about Afro-Caribbean history versus Jewish history. The characters' verbal battle depicts the tensions frequently implicit in the attempt to rank oppressions. Through Benjamin's and Tituba's interaction Condé exposes the tensions inherent in an attempt to launch a "cross fertilization of histories." She reconceptualizes Afro-Caribbean and Jewish experiences to enact an "unprecedented" revaluation of power that affirms each one's "time and identity" non-hierarchically (Glissant, *CD*, 93). However, Condé demonstrates her simultaneous ambivalence about this reconfiguration of power through her depiction of the maroons in Barbados.

Although heralded as a manifestation of the slave's "commitment to [all] 'things African'" (Gikandi 20) through what Glissant refers to as a "cultural" and "systematic opposition" to colonial order (1981, 612), *marronnage*, as depicted by Condé, emerges as a co-opted strategy divested of its power to engage in effective resistance.

Maroon society in Barbados at the end of the novel functions primarily as an appendage of colonialism. Contrary to their original revolutionary impetus, the maroons only enjoy a "precarious freedom" as long as they denounce any attempts at revolt (Condé, 163). Condé struggles with this paradox, questioning the maroon's ability to claim autonomy. She cannot reconcile the intent of *marronnage* with stifled consciousness and the replication of colonial domination by the cigar-smoking maroon leader Christopher. His power, gained through complicity in the colonial project, however, does not render Condé hopeless. She juxtaposes him with the young revolutionary maroon Iphigene whose commitment to freedom from colonial oppression keeps him from accepting the "fatalism of misfortune" dictated by the changed face of slave resistance (169).

Juxtaposing maroon and Jewish history not only creates tension and ambivalence; it also depicts the complicated, frequently irreconcilable sexual politics "intertwined with the wider politics of history" (Wilson-Tagoe 251). Tituba's intimate involvement with Benjamin, which she admits places her in an odd role as both mistress and servant, reflects Condé's awareness of numerous complexities at work as she celebrates Tituba's sexual agency within the context of slavery. Condé does not divest Tituba of the sexual enjoyment she experiences as she "pitched and heaved...on the sea of delight" with her Jewish master, nor does it place a value judgment on women's sexual pleasure (127). Not only does Condé's text vehemently support "a woman's right to enjoy sex and to say it," but her creation of so sexually empowered a character marks Condé as a liberated (Caribbean) writer committed to exploring what she recognizes as "taboo[s]" in West Indian literature ("Order" 163). Moreover, engaging these taboos infuses the text with a power to deploy a complex notion of history, one conceptualized as a "conscious intertwining of [various] aspects of [individual] existence" (Wilson-Tagoe 233).

Tituba's sexual encounter with Iphigene reveals Condé's elaboration on the relationship between sexual history and other histories. This encounter also marks Condé's further exploration of what some may consider a sexual taboo since Tituba views Iphigene like a son. The character's feelings of shame and intrigue portray Glissant's "obscuring" and "disclosing" of realities as the political and historical come to bear on the personal. In other words, this sexual encounter reveals the underlying fear, need for reassurance, and passionate "desire to taste pleasure" also implicit in their struggle against colonial oppression (169). However, this union of the personal, political, and historical also resists being named as Tituba struggles to reconcile the sexual act as oblivious "love" which "rolls back the torment and fear" of slavery, or as a sign of her sexual frivolity (169-70). Admittedly, some may view this act as incestuous, but the text remains purposely ambiguous as it places the reader at a complex intersection of Condé's dialogue of histories.

Incorporating a Foucauldian analysis of Tituba's sexual history, Michelle Smith explains that the character's contemplations about her sexual nature are a type of "talking sex" that situates "sex as history,…signification [,] and discourse" (604). Smith's analysis of sex as a body of experience engaged in and reacting to other realities is consistent with Condé's concept of sexual history as part and emblematic of larger historical and political discourse. Condé thus inscribes Tituba's sexual history within a larger Caribbean discourse; sexual violence signifies the exploitation suffered by the islands of the Caribbean at the hand of the English, French, Spanish, and Dutch (604). Her body becomes the landscape of West Indian history that can now express a self-conscious identity inextricable from the inherent violence, contradictions, and ambiguities of Caribbean reality.

Smith's discussion of Tituba's sexual identity illustrates these contradictions. She asserts that Tituba's musings about how men like Benjamin can "instill…the desire to be a (sexual) slave" (Condé 140) demonstrates the character's concealing of "the meaning of her sexual being(-ness)" (604). This concealing, therefore, is a response to Tituba's discomfort with her sexuality, and it also marks her search for a sexual identity different from and better than the sexuality she possesses (604). Smith's argument about concealment helps explain Tituba's inability to reconcile her roles of mother and lover with Iphigene. This analysis, however, also reflects the problems of an unnamable Caribbean sexual identity within nonhistory and meta-history. Rather than hiding sexuality, Condé's representation of black female sexuality within the colonial context is necessarily ambiguous; she challenges readers to grapple with understanding how sexuality can operate within the complexities of race, gender, history, and politics.

Tituba personifies the complex links between sexual violence, history and politics. Her "moan[s]" during an autoerotic experience cause Tituba to wonder if her mother Abena "moaned in spite of herself"when she was raped by the English sailor (15). Condé's mixing of sexual pleasure and violence within the colonial moment complicates the attempt to reconcile the two. Tituba's conflation of these experiences is consistent with Smith's Foucauldian reading of Tituba, as sexuality comes to signify complex meanings. Smith confirms that this commingling of violence and pleasure denotes a departure from the "clear roles of shattered victim and all-powerful perpetrator," thereby making it "exceedingly difficult" to "read the limits of choice, will, and desire" because the concepts become "too convoluted" (606). However, one solution may be to dialogue with histories, as Condé does throughout the text, reading sexual violence, history, and politics together.

A provocative starting point for this analysis is Tituba's dream toward the end of the novel when she envisions Samuel Parris, John Indian, and Christopher wearing black hoods and raping her with "a thick, sharpened stick" (164). The scene links all of these male characters to the Ku Klux Klan, while also blurring the lines of patriarchy. This linkage is an effective technique because the dream contains an allusion to the Klan, namely the hood and all the horror historically associated with it, but it eviscerates the binary racial (il)logic implicit in Klan ideology by implicating John Indian and Christopher in the violence. However, gender binaries empower Condé's new black and white "klan" to wield a joint violence on the black woman, displaying the author's abhorrence for all forms of patriarchy. Tituba's contemplations in the dream about having previously endured this ordeal reflect the piercing resonance in her psyche of prior experiences of actual sexual violence.

Earlier in the text, the Puritan minister Samuel Parris and three of his followers, all dressed in black hoods, rape Tituba. As in her dream, they thrust a sharpened stick into her body in an attempt to elicit a confession of witchcraft from her for the upcoming witch trials. They inflict sexual violence not only to affirm Puritanism's vehement condemnation of her spiritual practice, but also to dictate her submission to the legal system. In addition, these experiences link Tituba to her moment of conception when her mother Abena was raped on the ship *Christ the King* (3). Religion in both of these scenes figures prominently as it condones sexual violence in the name of religious intolerance, in the scene with Samuel Parris, and in the name of colonialism in the scene with Abena. Condé also suggests that sexual violence assumes new forms under colonialism when she conflates Puritanism and *marronnage* through the detestable Christopher who "take[s] [Tituba] without removing his clothes" (154). As he does so, Tituba recalls "Elizabeth Parris's complaint: "'My poor Tituba, (my husband) takes me without either removing his clothes or looking at me'" (154). As in the earlier examples of sexual violence, Condé asserts a color-blind notion of patriarchy which inflicts sexual domination.

Condé's weaving of sexual history within the narrative personalizes traditional history by challenging the reader to consider Tituba's historical absence, and fictional presence, as real and specific. As mentioned above, Tituba was born as a result of Abena's rape which takes place on the slave ship *Christ the King* "one day in the year of 16**" (3). Unlike many victims of the slave trade, Tituba knows her mother's name and is even able to locate her place in the Middle Passage, the ship on which Tituba herself was conceived. She also shares the experience of sexual violence with her mother: both women were raped. This sharing of sexual violence reaffirms the paradoxical nature of Condé's dialogues. Tituba's claim to identity through her maternal blood line requires a painful embrace of the violence implicit in that familial legacy. Such a claim represents a way to access the experience of nonhistory Glissant explains as initially inaccessible to consciousness (*CD* 61-62). Condé's depiction of Tituba's accessing and embracing of nonhistory emphasizes the finite known and infinite unknown horrors of the Middle Passage. The slipperiness of nonhistory is a crucial part of what Condé uses to preserve the history and identity of Tituba and Abena.

Placing Tituba's beginnings sometime during the seventeenth century marks the absence of specific historical data. More importantly, however, Condé's deliberate inclusion of the two asterisks reaffirms the importance and necessity of establishing a place in time for the unknown. Two asterisks also appear at the end of the novel when she refers to the time of "the unsuccessful rebellion of 17**" (175). Like Tituba's birth date, the revolutionary movement marking her death is an equally important moment. Condé's asterisks function like place holders in math. When doing multiplication, the placement of zeros in certain positions helps maintain an order while working to find the answer. Her asterisks are by no means zeros in the sense of total absence; they represent instead the range of temporal possibility, ninety-nine years, more or less, which must be accounted for to gain a more comprehensive understanding of the colonial encounter. These asterisks metaphorically represent Condé's entire work, and her fictional account emerges as a place holder in history for unacknowledged selves.

Within this indeterminate place in time, Condé further explores how identity ensnared within the cross-talk of histories can be grossly misunderstood and violently denigrated for not fitting into the dominant order. Tituba's experience of sexual violence is one manifestation of dehumanization and subjugation. Puritan society's naming Tituba a witch is another. This act erroneously projects an identity contrary to her consciousness of herself as one who wants to heal, not frighten. To survive, she has to perform this identity during her deposition at the witch trials. In this sense, when the deposition becomes a pre-scripted dialogue affirming the supremacy of Puritan religion, it stifles Condé's working for a mutual understanding of experience. Tituba must ventriloquize the lie her narrative counters, namely Caribbean alterity.

Tituba's survival within the entanglement of the cross-talk of Puritanism and African religion reflects Condé's subversion of the lie. The protagonist's performance of the Puritan concept of *witch* renders the concept itself a fiction that thrives only because of a neurotic belief in that fiction. In "Demythifying the Witch's Identity as Social Critique in Maryse Condé's *I, Tituba Black Witch of Salem*," Lisa Bernstein confirms this cultural creation of the witch. Tituba's ability to heal Elizabeth and Betsy Parris using the practices of an African based spirituality challenges the traditional concept of "witch" and transforms it into a sterile "social construct created to disparage and contain powers of healing [and] communicating with the unseen world" (Bernstein 13). According to Bernstein, the deconstruction of the term witch in the novel "humanises [sic] [Tituba] as it exposes the ways in which dominant discourses construct and manipulate the epithet of 'witch' to dominate and contain individuals who are different" (4-5). The need to define and control identity also represents a fear of difference. The Puritan fear of Tituba's spirituality is entangled with a simultaneous attraction to her powers. Ironically, this attraction reflects a desire to engage a dialogue with the same history that Puritanism painstakingly attempts to silence.

Presuming Tituba's access to a knowledge she does not have, Goodwife Rebecca Nurse connivingly smiles with Tituba as she petitions for her help to punish neighbors whose hogs ruined her vegetable garden (69). Tituba's alleged evil becomes good when it can be used for the Puritan benefit. The embrace of Tituba's witch status is all the more complicated by her Jewish master's acceptance of her spirituality. For Bernstein, this acceptance occurs in light of Benjamin's and Tituba's shared oppression (6). To some extent Bernstein's analysis is well-founded; but Benjamin's acceptance may also be influenced by Tituba's use of her powers to help him communicate with his dead wife Abigail. Tituba's witch status, like her slave status, serves a particular purpose for her master. Proclaimed his "beloved witch," Tituba is still Benjamin's property (131). Condé's placing of these belief systems in dialogue underscores her critique of dominant white Christian dogma as claimed by Bernstein (6). In a broader sense, however, with this juxtaposition Condé challenges the superficial embrace of a belief system different from one's own primarily for the benefit it can confer, rather than for a true appreciation of an alternative spiritual expression.

While Benjamin suggests an appreciation for Tituba by claiming that the Jewish God does not privilege a particular race, he nonetheless suggests that she should convert to Judaism so that she can pray with him and his family (131). Temporary acceptance of Tituba's spiritual identity gradually diminishes, revealing the underlying compulsion to reject difference and privilege traditional religious expression. His creation of a religious competition resembles the historical competition that emerges during Benjamin's and Tituba's discussion about their respective oppressions. The dialogue breaks down as one religion or history talks past the other, ultimately wanting to recreate or erase the unacknowledged one in the interest of the more dominant. Tituba's experiences with both Goodwife Rebecca Nurse and Benjamin reveal that they use her as a malleable body of knowledge capable of being molded for purposes of satisfying their narcissistic "ambitions, dreams, and desires" (146).

Condé also 'speaks' through Tituba. She consciously creates the character to allow the voice of a forgotten subject to speak on behalf of herself. This speaking releases Tituba from the realm of unnamed historical object, as she proclaims herself to be a person whose reason for existence far exceeds the purposes established by Goodwife Rebecca Nurse and Benjamin. Condé's re-creation of Tituba in this manner not only emphasizes the effacement that has occurred within the cross-talk of histories; it also demonstrates the author's complicity in manipulating knowledge and shaping experience in order to foster a dialogue that addresses this erasure. Modifying existing historical narratives enacts the shift needed to account for omitted realities. Condé's development of a more comprehensive story through her creation of Tituba is different from Benjamin's and Goodwife Rebecca Nurse's engagement with the character, for the author acknowledges an affinity with the histories Tituba's story traverses. Echoing Glissant's notion of "cross-fertilization" (CD 93), Condé's text cultivates a symbiotic notion of histories, shaping dialogue to affirm the value of the diversity of human experience.

Mara L. Dukats confirms the text's power to shape experience. She asserts that Tituba's narrative gives the character an opportunity to expose the falseness of the identity imposed on her by her oppressors; more importantly, however, she notes that Tituba's control of the narration reveals that she has also shaped her oppressors and their view of themselves (5). Dukats' provocative analysis illuminates the reconfiguration of roles that takes place when Tituba becomes the subject acting upon the oppressor. While there is no textual support for claiming Tituba's awareness of her influencing her oppressors, Condé manipulates the character in a way that cumulatively causes Tituba to have this impact. Tituba's dealings with Benjamin and the Puritans demonstrate her ability to shape her oppressors. These individuals covet Tituba's alleged demonic powers because of her ability to bestow benefits they cannot attain. In this sense, Condé inverts colonial ideology as the white master becomes subservient to the black slave. Dukats' methodology effectively displaces normative constructions of histories and complicates notions of subjectivity. Her analysis highlights Condé's desire to develop a superior historical consciousness in her reader. Tituba's history, like any other, should not be privileged; instead, it should be contextualized within a complex web of historical intersections, ultimately fostering an understanding of experience which enriches all parties participating in the dialogue.

The relationship between Tituba and Hester Prynne from Nathaniel Hawthorne's canonical text *The Scarlet Letter* depicts such a moment of sharing in the historical web. Hester befriends Tituba in prison, and consistent with her canonical good nature, she cares for Tituba by washing the welts on her face (95). Condé's recreation of Hawthorne's Hester as a feisty feminist, however, is a savvy subversion of the classical text. This reconfiguration of Hester interrogates a literary history with which Condé is clearly allied, while simultaneously sensitizing her reader to the parallel histories of two ostracized literary characters. Here, Condé follows what Glissant refers to as the "latent signs" of literary history as she enters the memory of the American literary canon to engage a dialogue (*CD* 64). While some may argue that Condé's Hester represents a capricious manipulation of Hawthorne's character, the manner in which Condé recreates Hester reflects a fine attunement to the latent signs Hawthorne places within his text.

Although Condé's pregnant Hester commits suicide in prison, unlike the Hester of *The Scarlet Letter*, Hawthorne acknowledges Hester's propensity to "perpetuate violence on herself or do some half-frenzied mischief" to her child while in prison (178). In the classical text Hester leaves prison with her child to live her own life, but with her departure Hawthorne contemplates whether her wild nature might have led her to assimilate with people "whose customs and life were alien from the law that had condemned her" (186). Condé's linking of these two literary characters in prison brings Hawthorne's speculation 'to life.' Her reading of his literary signs and subsequent creation of a Hester who adopts a path her original creator contemplated demonstrate a sensitivity to the subtext of other histories, as well as an awareness of how readings of that subtext can innovatively link experience. Creating a Hester with a total disregard for what Hawthorne said about her would erase the character, ultimately reenacting the omission of experience Condé works so hard to reverse in her work. Comprehending the breadth of experience is precisely what she wants to convey to her reader through the creation of Tituba and her interaction with Hester. Condé is not trying to replace Hawthorne's original creation; instead, by introducing Hester the author can engage a dialogue with the American literary canon of fiction.

Condé's provocative recreation of Hester also illuminates the absence of Tituba in history and literature. Hester's character in Condé's novel is a representation of what lurks in Hawthorne's mind, as well as a manifestation of Morrison's "dark, abiding, signing Africanist presence" that hovers in *The Scarlet Letter* and much of American literature (5-6). Conceptualizing Hester as an Africanist presence should not be understood literally as an attempt to transform her into an African-American character, or to trivialize the history of the African diaspora Condé painstakingly works to validate. Hester functions more like a dual link, or what Morrison terms as a "mediating force" between the reader and the forgotten Other (46). First, she is a Hester whom most readers would not envision because her identity and subjectivity in Condé's text lie dormant in the recesses of Hawthorne's work. In this sense she is a Hester who emerges out of canonical silence. Second, the presence of Condé's Hester is directly linked to the presence in Hawthorne's text of different cultures she could potentially join upon her release from prison. Such a culture is acknowledged in Hawthorne's text through the "Indian" man Hester sees standing on the outskirts of the crowd at her public display on the scaffold (169). It is through Hester's uncanny emergence in Condé's novel that the reader becomes acquainted with the peripheral Africanist presence of Hawthorne's text. With Hester, Condé effectively 'imports' both the Native American man and the alien cultures at the margins of Puritan society in Hawthorne's work and places them with Tituba at the center of the novel.[3]

By bringing these characters in from the margins, Condé subtly calls for an articulation of whiteness as a racial category. Unearthing Hester's submerged identity from Hawthorne's text exposes a deviant whiteness in Puritan society, or in the Puritan lexicon, something akin to 'blackness.' The shared experience of domination conflates racial categories traditionally viewed as opposites. Even Hester's dark physical features, her black hair and eyes, as well as her appreciation for the "magnificent" color of Tituba's skin, links her to blackness (Snitgen 71). This mutation of whiteness contradicts traditional meanings of race through the emergence of white as something almost totally counter to the essence of its non-Other core to which Morrison refers. Being white in Condé's text is an identity far more tainted than in Hawthorne's classic. It can be doubly deviant, embodied in Hester as a potentially black adulteress. While the novel's focus on slavery underscores the centrality of considering class status in the analysis of Tituba's and Hester's identities, as well as their relationships to patriarchy, gender, too, plays a pivotal role. The negation of whiteness as portrayed through Hester links her to stereotypes of black female sexuality.[4] Condé's skillful disruption of fixed racial identities through this character enacts a much-needed analysis of whiteness as a category.

Condé's use of Hester works because the reader's familiarity with the character helps the author demonstrate how unfamiliar he or she may be with Hester's identity in the subtext of Hawthorne's work. If one were to read her Other presence in the canonical text, an undeniable dialogue with parallel histories emerges. Once Condé successfully convinces her reader to suspend belief momentarily in the canonical Hester and to consider the existence of a different Hester, one which Hawthorne did contemplate to some extent, it becomes easier to believe in the existence of Tituba. Historical consciousness expands, as previously erased (or yet to be considered) histories are brought into focus. Moreover, Condé's reading of the canon serves not only to expose the range of possible histories; it also emphasizes the importance of reading those narratives in a way that successfully charts the relationships between histories on the map of human experience. Such an approach, as Condé's representation of Tituba's sexuality also illustrates, will give rise to a sometimes partially incomprehensible but nonetheless useful and expanding notion of human identity and history. In this sense, the map of human experience does not limit history to a particular temporal space. The map chronicles the ongoing development of a historical consciousness that traverses time to reveal the intersections of experience that meta-history often effaces.

Condé's dialogue with Hawthorne also depicts a similar writing experience for both authors. Her claim in the epigraph explaining the close relationship she had with Tituba that inspired the text seems to echo Hawthorne's experience. Although Hester's spirit does not communicate with him, Hawthorne nonetheless claims to have been charged by the ghost of Mr. Surveyor Pue to publicize "his mouldy and motheaten lucubrations" about the treatment of Hester in order to give her memory due credit (147). Both authors possess an ancestral type of muse figure who wants them to tell a story as an act of redemption. Like Condé, Hawthorne also invokes imagination when he describes becoming the "citizen of somewhere else," as "the haze of memory" causes his "old native town [to] loom upon him" (157). In this sense, Hawthorne also experiences Morrison's process of *"becoming"* (1992, 4). Through his writing of Hester he enters the past to return a dignity to her that he could only bestow by telling a story history never told. As the representative for his Puritan ancestors, Hawthorne accepts their shame and prays that they are forgiven and released of any curses incurred as a result of their mistreatment of Hester (127). His writing enacts a quasi-cleansing process not only for their actions, but also of the decaying remains of Hester's story in Mr. Pue's "lucubrations." Condé does not respond to Hawthorne's request with a blanket pardon; she offers instead a petition for a dialogue acknowledging the multiple atrocities of the period as depicted through their treatment of Tituba. Understanding and accepting these realities cannot change what happened, but it can foster an appreciation for the intersections of these histories.

Condé's fictional discourse with Hawthorne extends beyond the confines of the Afro-Caribbean colonial moment and the Salem Witch Trials to initiate a conversation with the radical strand of Western second-wave feminism. Hester's radical feminist perspective, reflected in her desire for a total separation from men, is alien to Tituba because of the different spaces they occupy within the web of patriarchy and colonialism. Tituba's participation in revolution toward the end of the novel marks her as one who envisions liberation primarily in terms of a release, for both men and women, from the grip of colonialism. Jeanne Snitgen interprets this action as a reflection of Tituba's commitment to Alice Walker's notion of womanism (69). However, citing an excerpt from Condé's text *La Parole des femmes*, Snitgen asserts that Condé's portrayal of Hester reflects a reductive view of Western feminism as primarily separatist (68). She further claims that Tituba does not become a feminist, despite the feminist discourse criticizing patriarchal power incorporated within the text (67).

Snitgen cites Tituba's "unfortunate relationships with men" in an admittedly colonial context as one explanation why the character cannot achieve feminist status (67). Although she acknowledges the historical context, Snitgen still severs that context from the personal, and this separation limits her definition of feminism. Snitgen's echo of Hester's claim that Tituba is not a feminist is precisely the concern expressed by Condé and by global feminists. While many debate the efficacy of even using the term "feminist," Condé wants to release it from the limits Snitgen and Hester articulate. Liberating the term "feminist" would infuse it with a more comprehensive meaning capable of characterizing a myriad of experiences. Condé's critique of Hester does not support the argument that she views all of Western feminism as merely separatist. She does view a branch of it as such, and critiques that manifestation of feminism. More importantly, however, Condé's questioning of the term "feminist" parallels her deconstruction of the term "witch."

She challenges their meanings to engage her reader in a dialogue to liberate historical and feminist consciousness. Feminists and witches do not have to submit to the stereotypes portrayed in the text, which means that these identities can assume new meaning in light of historical and political realities.

Once again, as in Condé's exploration of the complexities of Tituba's sexual history, the author's examination of feminisms in this novel reflects how entangled the personal is with the historical and political. Cultural constructions of gender cultivate diverse forms of feminisms, each of which becomes an external manifestation of an internal process negotiating the personal, political, and historical. For Hester this process unleashes her desire for an all-female society. Although Tituba admits that she does not know what a feminist is and certainly does not want to disassociate herself from men, she is acutely aware of what it means to be a black female slave in colonial America.

Tituba's consciousness, whether one calls it feminist or not, informs her vision of self as an agent of revolutionary liberation. The text cannot disengage Tituba's gender from her race or her activism within the colonial context. Analyzing Tituba in this manner supports a fluid reading of feminist consciousness, one accounting for perspectives which are always filtered through historically specific racialized and gendered identities. Snitgen is clearly aware of the diversity of feminist consciousness when she reasons that Hester's rejection of the patronymic concept and Tituba's embrace of her patronymic name are cultural expressions of divergent understandings of the characters' relationships to power and the masculine gender (72). Consequently, Snitgen asserts that a comparison of their opposing perspectives cannot occur because of the totally different contexts informing these perspectives (72). Unfortunately, and perhaps unknowingly, Snitgen does just that when she says Tituba is not a feminist. The critic seems to be trapped in a quandary polarized by opposing notions of feminist consciousness that she struggles to reconcile through an exclusive alliance with one.

Condé's text disrupts this compulsion to situate consciousness within binary constructions of identity. She creates a space in Tituba's narrative for two perspectives to exist simultaneously: Hester's Western feminist abhorrence for a patronym and Tituba's embrace of her name bestowed by Yao in an attempt to symbolically memorialize and empower the disenfranchised of the African diaspora (5).

Such a juxtaposition allows the reader to examine each perspective on its own terms, rather than to try to make these experiences fit into sterile categories within some predetermined hierarchy. Condé wants to expose how unproductive this hierarchy is through an encounter between Hester and Tituba that allows for debates about feminisms to be acknowledged as a component of larger dialogues of histories.

Condé ends the narrative of Tituba's earthly life at the threshold of the destiny met by numerous African-Americans, the lynching gallows. Echoing Billie Holiday's blues song "Strange Fruit," which analogizes the lynched bodies of African-Americans to fruit on trees, Condé sensitizes Tituba to her surroundings as she approaches her final moment: "All around me strange trees were bristling with strange fruit" (172). The author's use of this reference from the song also marks an interesting twist of Holiday's "strange fruit" theme. Throughout the text, Tituba is an empowered 'strange fruit' who claims the subjectivity she lacks in the history reflected in Holiday's song. Tituba emerges on the stage of the novel as a different lady; one who sings the blues of silenced historical dialogues. Tituba's blues become discordant in the moments before her hanging. Resonating in the background music of this lynching is Christopher, the maroon leader who informed the white planters of the revolt Tituba and Iphigene are organizing. Christopher's tolling of the death knell for Tituba disrupts her revolutionary crescendo *in medias res*, also reiterating Condé's ambivalence about the role of *marronnage* in the movement for liberation. This complication of essentialist constructions of Caribbean history and identity through *marronnage* supports an understanding of Tituba's blues as more than a rewriting of what Glissant terms as "History," or the West's "highly functional fantasy" (*CD* 64). Moreover, with its complex web of frequently irreconcilable Caribbean realities, Tituba's blues are given perpetual life in the epilogue, as her memory and spirit resonate in the consciousness of those who know the story.

The reader's conversation with Tituba in the novel bestows a knowledge of how to sing histories' blues. While sadness permeates the experiences retold in the dialogues of Condé's text, the blues the author sings are not self-defeating. They continually refresh consciousness with expanded dialogues and new tellings of histories. Navigating the narratives of colonialism and slavery in the Afro-Caribbean diaspora, of religious persecution, feminism, and the canon of American fiction, Condé penetrates the realm of the forgotten Other to claim this space as a part of the historical continuum. That her story is "merely" fiction fades into the background of her song as she returns the notion of personhood to the erased subjects whom Tituba represents. It is not as important to believe her story as it is to acknowledge the presence of such figures in history. Condé's goal in creating this dialogue is to open up a space for comprehending the experiences that lie within the complex interstices of history. Adjusting consciousness in this manner quiets the crosstalk, enabling one to hear the other songs yet to be sung by the voices preserved within Condé's two asterisks.

Notes

1. The English edition of Condé's novel is the source for this essay. The parenthetical page references refer to the Ballantine Books edition (1994).

2. Glissant does not suggest that the writer is the only person who can cultivate such a consciousness or deny that there are other ways of achieving such an awareness. His emphasis on the Caribbean fictional writer and literary imagination spotlights the important role of literature in the re-creation of Caribbean history and identity.

3. Incorporating Morrison's idea about the "imaginative encounter" in literature between the white writer and the "Africanist presence," Dukats suggests a provocative paradigm for analyzing the relationship between Condé, Tituba, Hawthorne and Hester (5-6). I do not agree with her analogy, however, because the analysis diverts from the premise of Morrison's argument which emphasizes how the encounter between the white writer and Africanism reaffirms the writer's essentialist self-conception as superior.

4. See Patricia Hill Collins' discussion of the stereotype of the alleged hypersexual nature of black women and other stereotypes in "Mammies, Matriarchs, and Other Controlling Images" and "The Sexual Politics of Black Womanhood" in *Black Feminist Thought*.

GENEALOGIES AND GENDER: HISTORY'S ROUTES, IDENTITY'S RHIZOMES

NOT ENOUGH SHADE UNDER THE "ROYAL KAÏLCÉDRAT": MARYSE CONDÉ'S *HÉRÉMAKHONON* OR THE DIFFICULT SEARCH FOR ANCESTORS

Serigne Ndiaye

In Aimé Césaire's *Cahier d'un retour au pays natal*, the poet-narrator's imaginary quest for a genealogical connection with the "Motherland" (Africa) prefigures the trope of "rootedness." Césaire's return to roots also implies the metaphor of the enormous tree, the "*royal Kaïlcédrat*," that represents a dignified racial identity.[1] For Césaire's narrator, identification with and "rootedness" in his claimed African origins suggest the symbolic creation of a genuine sense of self. In her first novel, *Hérémakhonon*, Maryse Condé critically echoes Césaire's trope by telling the tale of a return *manqué* to the "Motherland" that serves to question any hasty cloaking of continental Africans and their diaspora relatives under the indiscriminate mantle of a congruous Black World.

In literary discourse and in *Négritude* in particular, emphasizing this filial connection between Africa and the Caribbean has come to resemble a rite of passage seemingly inescapable for many Blacks seeking to re-member their fragmented racial identity. As Condé reiterates in an interview with Françoise Pfaff, at its inception the notion of *Négritude* operated as an important vehicle for racial consciousness and pride by establishing a strong sense of connection with Africa: "Without Césaire we might not be what we are. He was the first to give us racial pride, racial consciousness.…[and] connection to a continent like Africa, where history is so rich and diverse. I think we are all Césaire's children. I consider him to be the Founding Ancestor" (38; 61). Despite the "Founding Ancestor's" transmission of racial pride and consciousness to his "children," his message of diasporic identification with Africa, along with its affective correlates of "likeness" and "similarity," has largely turned out to be an inveigling fixation that Condé also acknowledges: "We were led to believe that Africa was an ideal home. When we discovered it was not, we suffered. Without *Négritude*, we would not have experienced the degree of disillusionment that we did. The issue of 'likeness' or 'similarity' is erroneous even in the Antilles" ("Pan-Africanism" 60). Coming a generation after Césaire, Condé's writing counters this disillusionment by challenging uncritical notions of identity founded on the notion of a homogeneous Black world.

In her essay "Mediations of Identity through the Atlantic Triangle: Maryse Condé's *Hérémakhonon*," Leah Hewitt explains Condé's impassiveness toward such representations as a refusal to give in to the luring appeal of the sirens of racial self-congratulation. Yet such an attitude, Hewitt suggests, does not automatically induce capitulation into racial self-loathing. It operates instead as a critical mechanism attempting to find its way between the extreme articulations of stereotypes and clichés. As Hewitt argues: "Condé sees in *Négritude's* affirmation of racial pride and a black cultural aesthetic the danger of complacency, of glossing over, for example, the aspects of black history that do not support a positive image…And she reacts vehemently against any essentialist position that recognizes the 'Negro' ('nègre') as a real category rather than a false mythology invented by the Europeans" (*Tightropes* 168-9). In *Hérémakhonon*, the protagonist's reluctance to embrace one-dimensional values may be read as a refusal of any overly sweeping images of identity, images often articulated by proponents of *Négritude* as well as by its detractors. The novel thus articulates a critical and ironic outlook on racial identity, which, to use Hewitt's words, "erodes [the] noxious potential" of stereotypes and clichés (179).

Produced in part to explore the ineffective efforts of its protagonist Veronica Mercier to achieve self-realization through identification with Africa, *Hérémakhonon* recounts the story of this Guadeloupean woman who leaves her home in France to go to an unnamed African country and embark on what Condé calls her "initiatory self-quest" (Pfaff 39; 63). Once in Africa, Veronica finds herself in the midst of a conflict opposing on the one hand the oppressive ruling elite spearheaded by her lover Ibrahima Sory, Minister of Interior, and on the other the oppressed masses, represented by both Saliou, a progressive high school principal, and Birame III, a student activist. When Birame III mysteriously disappears in the end, all indices point to the government as having orchestrated his murder; the same with the death of Veronica's friend, Saliou, who has reportedly committed suicide in his cell after several days of detention and torture inflicted by the government. Disenchanted by the horror of her experiences in Africa, Veronica puts an end to her quest and returns to France. As the novel draws to an end, she is convinced that her search for ancestors has proven unproductive. Instead, she has found "assassins" who have foiled her dream of getting in touch with what she imagines as her lost identity.

Inscribing her identity quest in a sequence of ironic twists, the narrator seeks from the outset to convince the reader that if she must be perceived as a tourist, then she is a unique kind of tourist: "Touriste peut-être. Mais d'une espèce particulière à la découverte de soi-même. Les paysages, on s'en fout" (20) [I'm…perhaps a tourist, but one of a new breed, searching out herself, not land-scapes" (3)]. At the beginning of her journey, Veronica describes her trip to Africa as totally detached from the fashionable desire to discover the exotic: "Franchement on pourrait croire que j'obéis à la mode. L'Afrique se fait beaucoup en ce moment. On écrit des masses à son sujet, des Européens et d'autres. On voit s'ouvrir des centres d'Artisanat Rive Gauche. Des blondes se teignent les lèvres au henné et on achète des piments et des okras rue Mouffetard. Or c'est faux. Je n'obéis pas à la mode" (19) [Honestly, you'd think I'm going because it is the thing to do. Africa is very much the thing to do lately. Europeans and a good many others are writing volumes on the subject. Arts and crafts centers are opening all over the Left Bank. Blondes are dying their lips with henna and running to the open market on the rue Mouffetard for their peppers and okra. Well, I'm not! (3)]. Veronica's defensiveness in regard to her trip betrays her painful efforts to convince herself that her journey has meaning, at the same time that she recognizes the ambiguity of her project. "Mais enfin, pourquoi?" (19) [Why am I doing this?], she asks herself as she arrives. "À présent tout se brouille et l'entreprise paraît absurde" [At the moment, everything is a mess, and this whole idea seems absurd (3)]. By questioning the integrity of her quest, yet embarking on it, Veronica displays a layer of ambivalent feelings that confirm what Hewitt calls this protagonist's "long[ing] for a secure sense of self" (167). Veronica's ambivalence also por-trays identity as a complex assemblage of questions rather than an array of ready-made answers.

Veronica's inability to communicate successfully the object of her quest—to others whenever she is engaged in dialogue, or to herself in recurrent monologues—demonstrates her inability to discover the meaning of her search and foreshadows the disenchantment awaiting her. As Hewitt argues, in *Hérémakhonon* Condé stages a communication breakdown between Veronica and her surroundings in order to highlight the abrasive confrontation between the exigencies of collective theories and her claim to personal affirmation. Veronica's attempt to reconcile the apparently contradictory poles of the communal and the personal illustrates her determination to probe what Hewitt calls "the possibility of a self rooted in a cultural heritage, but still free to move in societies without being labeled or stereotyped" (171). By inscribing her quest in the interstices of the communal and the personal, Condé places Veronica on a slippery ground where any word she utters or any action she takes leaves little room for interpretation outside the performance of her politics of race or gender. Consequently, nothing about this performance lends itself to a static perception of the self. On the contrary, it opens onto a field of ambivalence where Veronica becomes an unreliable character.

As part of her identity quest, Condé's protagonist sets out in search of an Africa that differs from the image usually presented through the deforming prism of clichés and stereotypes; but the first observations she makes about the place assumed to be symbolic of the Motherland echo the so-called "true Africa" seen in tourist brochures: "je remarque des femmes qui font la queue à la fontaine, bébé au dos. Des hommes qui dorment sur des pliants devant leurs cases en banco, mal assises sous leurs toits de paille. Images déjà aperçues dans les catalogues offrant à des gogos la découverte de la 'vraie Afrique' . . ." (20) [I noticed women lining up at the fountain with babies on their back. There were also men sleeping on folding stools in front of their unsteady grass huts. These are images I have already seen in catalogues offering fools the discovery of the "true Africa".... (my translation)]. This passage, which does not appear in the English translation, relates to something more than a simple description of the landscape that unfolds in front of Veronica. Without giving herself time to understand what she has just encountered, Veronica's gaze zooms in on the decayed road, transportation, and housing conditions in Africa, as well as on the inactivity of men contrasted with the industriousness of women. But Veronica is an unreliable narrator. Does Veronica buy into the stereotypical images of the "true Africa" she evokes? Does she allude to the gender division of labor out of spite or out of genuine concern for African women? One answer is certain: even though Veronica is candid about her observations, her comments reflect the position of a stranger and confirm her as an exotic tourist despite her refusal of this label.

Such an incongruity in both Veronica's feelings and choices underscores the nature of her character as a repository of contradictions. The text illustrates both this discrepancy and Veronica's psychological instability by presenting her experiences in a chaotically dizzying pattern. In an almost cinematic fashion, the narrative randomly zooms in and out from Veronica's childhood memories to her present condition, and from one geographical location to another. As Hewitt points out, Veronica's confusion reflects her situation, as she "becomes a filter or mediator of the multiple, often contradictory, discourses that traverse her existence" (174). The dense clutter of images not only mirrors Veronica's confusion, it also reveals her inability to put enough order into her thoughts to construct a coherent sense of self as a haven of inner peace.

One of the threads of discourse that Condé emphasizes is that Veronica's African journey will help her retrieve the part of her self untainted by slavery and by various resulting psychological complexes. Hence her curiosity to find out which narrative of her "ancestors" she can pick up and adjust to her own condition: " – Nous étions en Afrique. / Je sais. Alors qu'est-ce que nous y faisions? Nous devions bien y vivre de quelque façon? Manger, dormir, élever nos enfants?…Faisions-nous tous cela si sauvagement, si laidement qu'il vaut mieux que nous en ayons perdu le souvenir?…Qui me renseignera? Personne…. C'est d'abord pour cela que je suis ici…Pour essayer de voir ce qu'il y avait avant" (31) ["We were in Africa." I know, I know. What were we doing there? We must have lived, *somehow*. Eaten, slept, raised children? Was it so savage and horrible that it is better forgotten? Who can tell me? No one… that's mainly why I'm here. To try and find out what was before (11)]. As Veronica seeks to locate what "was before" ["ce qu'il y avait avant"], she inevitably engages in an endeavor that is bound to fail. Her persistent questions as to who will inform her about her "ancestors" are followed by a surprising "no one," which questions the conclusiveness of any narrative of origins attempting to stitch together the fragments of a history that has already taken its toll on identity construction in the Caribbean.

Part of the reason for Veronica's resolve to "re-connect" with Africa may be traced to her ardent desire to settle a score with the insolent configuration of the racial power structure that invaded her childhood memories and branded her as an outcast. "Et pourquoi?" she asks in one of her many reflections, "Parce que le sang noir, chez eux tellement dilué et dont on pouvait nier la présence, gonflait mes veines" (184). And her own criteria for beauty was thus shaped: "Et toutes les femmes me paraissaient plus belles que ma mère qui pourtant était aussi bien vêtue.... Elles me paraissaient plus belles avec leur peau à peine cuivrées, à peine bronzée, leurs cheveux souples et ondulés que ne martyrisait pas le peigne à décrêper chauffé sur la braise et trempé—pschtt—dans la *petroleum jelly*. Elles me paraissaient plus belles parce qu'elles étaient claires" (184) [Why? Because their black blood was so diluted, even nonexistent, whereas mine swelled in my veins... All the women seemed more beautiful than my mother, who was just as well dressed... They appeared lovelier because of their slightly coppery, slightly tanned skin, their soft wavy hair spared by the straightener, heated over coals and dipped—ssh!—in petroleum jelly. They seemed more attractive because they were light-skinned. (123)].[2] The body imagery Veronica invokes here reverberates with parallels to the places that stereotypes of Africa and Europe occupy respectively on the aesthetic spectrum. Her mother (Mother Africa) *seems* to be less beautiful than the "others" (Europe, in particular) simply because of her darker complexion. Racist notions of beauty complicate Veronica's identity quest. The frustration engendered by the disparagement of her racial identity as a child serves as a catalyst for her efforts to know herself by trying to find a more acceptable meaning of her blackness.

By asserting her connection with a racial community, Veronica performs a double-edged task of identification that aims both to obliterate certain memories and to avoid the obliteration of others. This duality engages on the one hand Veronica's desire for undoing her personal history as a descendant of enslaved Africans, as she wishes she could "exchange childhoods" with Sory. On the other hand, she knows that coming to terms with herself requires her return to her "island specks"—where slavery forced her ancestors to land. Ironically, as suggested by her constant wondering about what meaning to attribute to the past and what rationale to attach to her project, Veronica *at times* does not realize that the symbolic memories she wants to retrieve are illusory and that her desire to attach a contemporary face to the indeterminate character of what "was before" in the person of Ibrahima Sory is hopelessly flawed.

Condé's metaphors present Veronica's existential void as a series of ailments for which she *must* find a therapy. As Veronica discloses the panoply of ailments affecting her, she *literally* defines herself as a patient, "une malade… à la recherche d'une thérapie" (53) [an invalid… seeking therapy" (26)]. Her infirmity is mainly psycho-affective, since she suffers from both a "chagrin d'amour" (49) [a broken heart (24)] and a mental imbalance: "Il faut que les rabs quittent mon esprit et retournent à la pointe Sangomar. Pour moi quel *ndöp*?" (55) [I must rid myself of these *rab* and send them back to Sangomar. Which is my *ndöp*?" (28)[3] Veronica seems to need both a cardiologist for broken hearts and a therapist for psychic troubles to restore her mental balance. She also needs a *"marabout"* —a person endowed with a psychic power—because Western medicine has apparently proven incapable of curing her. Of all people, Ibrahima Sory is the "doctor" she identifies to administer her curative therapy. Convinced in advance she has found the antidote, Veronica proclaims: "Je suis venue pour me guérir d'un mal: Ibrahima Sory sera, je le sais, le gri-gri du marabout. Nous échangerons nos enfances et nos passés. Par lui, j'accéderai enfin à la fierté d'être moi-même. Il n'a pas été étampé" (71) [I came to find a cure. Ibrahima Sory, I know, will be the marabout's *gree-gree*. We'll exchange our childhoods and our past. Through him I shall at last be proud to be what I am. He wasn't branded (39)]. Veronica's efforts to find a past untainted by slavery resemble *Négritude*'s invitation for Blacks to revisit their racial past. Condé, aware of the challenges embedded in such a project, creates Sory as a problematic and paradoxical character.

Ibrahima Sory, as Veronica comes to picture him, is the embodiment of the connective thread that must reconcile her with the lost part of herself. She discovers, however, that the story of his aristocratic family is problematic. "Que leur histoire est compliquée!… l'agent le plus zélé des colonisateurs…. Collecte d'impôts, travaux forcés de construction de routes, ou de cultures industrielles arbitraires, rien n'y manque. Fouet en main, ils pressuraient les masses pour le profit des Blancs. Et aussi pour le leur" (46) [Their history is so complicated…the staunchest ally of the colonial powers…. Taxes, forced labor for building roads or cash crops, nothing is missing from the picture. Whip in hand, they forced the laboring masses to work for the profit of the whites. And theirs too (22)]. In addition to having such a ruthless family background, Ibrahima

Sory is the Minister of Interior in a government masterminded by himself and infamous for knowing no other means of interacting with its citizens than by torture and repression. Thus, Veronica's friend Birame III calls Sory "un assassin" [an assassin] who has "les mains rouges du sang du peuple!" (47) [hands...dripping with the blood of the people (22)]. In spite of Sory's history, Veronica sticks to her choice as if to mock any uncritical connection between Africa and its Diaspora.

Veronica's problematic choice of ancestors is reflected in the staccato style and dubiousness that (de)regulate her discourse whenever she tries to clarify the purpose of her journey, as is the case in the first instance when she identifies Ibrahima Sory as "ce nègre [qui] a des aïeux" (47) or her "nigger [who] has ancestors" (22): "Est-ce que vous ne savez pas que c'est pour vous que j'ai traversé les mers? Rien que pour vous.... Est-ce que vous pouvez comprendre? Et d'abord est-ce que je sais expliquer? Reprenons" (63) [I crossed the seas for you, you know. Just for you.... Do you understand? But am I making myself clear? Let's start again (33)]. Veronica is confused and unable to put together a coherent narrative that elucidates her choice of ancestors, precisely because she cannot clearly conceptualize the goal of her quest. The questions and contradictions that shape her speech can be described as Hewitt does in terms of "a language of negativity within the subject [which speaks to] the doubled subject's ongoing battle with herself as well as others" (186-7).[4] Veronica thus seems to be destined to spin around in circles instead of moving on towards her stated goal of finding her ancestors.

Several instances in the novel emphasize this vagueness by associating the presence of Ibrahima Sory with a ghostly image lurking in the penumbra. At one point in the text, for example, Veronica recalls how she used to be frightened by playful plots of ghostly apparitions contrived by her family maid Mabo Julie, and then she suddenly describes hearing "un pas derrière moi. Je sursaute": "Je vous ai fait peur?" Ibrahima Sory asks (63) [footsteps behind me. I jumped. Did I frighten you? (33)][5] The ghostly analogy raised by Sory's "apparitions" into Veronica's life suggests her involvement with an insubstantial image produced by her own imagination. Her initiatory quest has no solid foundation and is therefore bound to fail.

Even though Sory has not been branded with slave marks, he has been branded by his people as an "assassin" responsible for the devastation to which Veronica has opted to remain blind (47). Just as the hands of Ibrahima Sory's father and grandfather were sullied, his own hands are dripping with the blood of the oppressed masses. Yet all Veronica cares about is the comfort of self-reconciliation that Ibrahima Sory *seemingly* offers. For the reader, her desire to plunge into "la nuit utérine" [the womb] of her existence, to be born again "sans honte, ni mépris secret" (103) [free of shame and hidden contempt (62)] through Sory is highly compromised by his ruthless behavior. Veronica tries to acquire a noble birthright so that she can put it on display and exclaim that her ancestors were not savages as she was told they were; they were real aristocrats. What does it matter the number of their crimes: "Mais avouons franchement que des crimes passés et présents de cette aristocratique famille, je n'ai cure! Parce qu'en fait, c'est cela que je suis venue voir. D'authentiques aristocrates. Pas des singes. » (47) [Quite frankly, I don't care a damn for the past and present crimes of this aristocratic family. They are the ones I came to see. Genuine aristocrats. Not monkeys. (22)]. By focusing her attention on Ibrahima Sory as a repository of African aristocracy, Veronica enacts a search for a homeland that is marked by her indifference to and disassociation from the political realities taking place in the immediate world around her. As Simone Alexander rightly argues, this isolation precipitates Veronica's disillusion: "Divorcing her personal problems from the real political problems of the African people constitutes Veronica's crucial mistake and eventual downfall. Frozen in the past, she rejects the present" (110). Veronica's contradictions are all the more exacerbated as she deliberately keeps her distance from the people among whom she explores the meaning and origins of her identity.

As she disassociates herself from the people, our narrator ends up spending much of her time with Ibrahima Sory at "Heremakhonon," the name ironically given to his residential island mansion.[6] At Heremakhonon the mere comfort of a sofa transports Veronica into a sort of sensational sedation: "Brusquement comme je m'assieds, quelque chose cède en moi.… Peut-être l'extrême fraîcheur de la pièce ou son silence?… Heremakhonon est une île.… Dans ce fauteuil je sombre dans un extraordinaire bien-être. Le temps s'arrête. Le temps recule en arrière. J'ai cinq ans" (52, 61) [Suddenly, as I sit down, something gives inside me.… Perhaps it is the utter coolness of this room or its silence?… . Heremakhonon is an island.… This armchair gives me an extraordinary feeling of

well-being. Time stands still. The clock is going back. I'm five…
(25, 32)]. The feeling of calm and well-being, and perhaps childhood innocence that Veronica enjoys at Heremakhonon cannot be
permanent, and the transience of the soothing sensation that Sory's
mansion provides testifies to the impossibility of blocking the clock,
going back, and retrieving such innocence. No matter how idyllic
"Heremakhonon" seems to be, it is most certainly not a sanctu-
ary of spiritual rebirth. The picture of human life that unfolds at
Heremakhonon serves as a counterpoint to the spirit of the dignified and noble ancestry she hopes to recover in Africa. For the
reader, Sory's ruthlessness does not conjugate well with nobility. If
Veronica has come to Africa to seek happiness and inner peace, at
Heremakhonon she will have to wait forever in order to experience
that happiness. At Heremakhonon Veronica can easily dampen her
mind with whiskey, forget about the problems of the people, jump
into Ibrahima Sory's bed and prepare to be "possessed," as she calls
her sexual affair with him.

Veronica admits that she feels "une secrète et malsaine volupté
à être traitée en objet"(131) [a secret unhealthy voluptuousness in
being treated like an object (85)] and persists in her belief that sex
with Sory will help maintain her psychological equilibrium amid
the chaos of the situation; or, as she puts it: "En somme ce qu'il me
faut pour voir la vie presque en rose, c'est *a good fuck* (177) [What
I need to see life through rose-colored glasses is a *good fuck* (119)].
Indeed, that seems to be all Sory needs from her. He clearly has no
interest in knowing anything about her, even after they begin sleeping together. Unlike a traditional psychiatrist, Ibrahima Sory is not
interested in knowing what brought his "client" to his couch, or his
bed, to be precise; while she notes with pleasure that she is in his
eyes "un arum dans un vase; je dis arum. Car la plante, comme moi,
est exotique. Elle ne pousse pas sous ces cieux" (151) [I'm an arum
in a vase. I say arum because the plant is exotic like me. It doesn't
grow here (99)]. Sory does not really *see* Veronica, even after grati-
fying himself sexually, but Veronica is so alienated from herself and
her environment that she does not see Sory either. Beyond the pleasure principle guiding Veronica's delight in her status as an object,
Sory's refusal to recognize her complicates her quest. Not only does
his refusal mock her quest for psychic unity, it also disembodies her
and casts her into the objectification of a being devoid of spiritual
and self-consciousness. The abortive search Veronica is determined
to enact will continue to be fraught with such tensions, especially

when Sory draws a parallel between Veronica and Shirley, whom he calls "une jeune Noire américaine, qui avait… des problèmes du même genre" (86) [a young black American girl…who had the same sort of problem (49)]. Refusing to admit in Veronica any notion of personal identity, he sloppily lumps together all Blacks from the diaspora in the same mold.

While recognizing that she belongs to the so-called community of neurotics from the diaspora, Veronica adamantly refuses to succumb to a facile identification with the image and does not want to be identified by those around her as "une cinglée de plus" [just another idiot]. "Car ce pays regorge de cinglés," she explains, "je veux dire de cinglés étrangers. L'espèce la plus courante, celle qui… [considère] l'Afrique comme le bain de jouvence de leur âme-d'Occidental-épuisée-desséchée-par-la-civilisation-technique" (150-51) [This country's overflowing with idiots, I mean foreign idiots. The most common species is the one that… considers Africa the rejuvenation of his (sic) Western soul, exhausted and dried up by the technological age (98)]. She wants to convince herself that her dreams are more profound and spiritual than those of the many other "névrosés de la diaspora" [diasporic neurotics] who rush to the "Motherland" to reconnect with their "ancestors" (86; 52). In her mind, she is driven neither by a desire to flee from mechanistic Western civilization nor by a longing for exotic places and realities, as she assumes is the case with many of the other "neurotics." Veronica believes that she and her "nigger with ancestors" can "exchange childhoods," that she can reinvent herself and throw off her defiled past to acquire a historical virginity.

By choosing Sory as her "ancestor," Veronica identifies Africa with a virile sex symbol, which opens the way for the author to question the racial and Pan-African bonds that underlie the principles of *Négritude* and its call for a mythic return to the African Motherland. Simone Alexander supports this view when she argues that in *Hérémakhonon* Africa functions as both "a mythic home space" and is "equated with a phallus": "For [Veronica] Africa is a phallocentric world where the phallus is the law of the land. She fools herself into believing that the love of and for a man can sustain her love of and for the mother('s)land" (103). The incommensurability between Veronica's "love of and for a man" and that "of and for the mother('s)land" falls in direct line with Condé's response to the *Négritude* discourse that refers to Africa in gendered terms. Condé problematizes *Négritude*'s image of the black woman as analogue of the African continent by having Veronica associate the continent with a male figure, and a corrupt one at that, and herself (Veronica) with this masculine and patriarchal version of Africa.

Alexander astutely points out that the masculine bent perceptible in Veronica's search is a testimony of a lack of and desire for a "Father." "Equating Mother Africa with the phallus," Alexander argues, "is Veronica's need for a Father('s)land rather than a mother's land" (107). As Susan Z. Andrade observes, in male writers' depiction of Africa "the land itself, whether it be so-called 'mother' Africa or a newly refigured Caribbean island, is fundamentally gendered, both feminized and (hetero)sexualized. Often the relationship between female characters and the land or nation appears unmediated, the latter standing for the former, rendered as either maternal and inviting or virginal and rape" (214). Veronica's case enacts Condé's reversal of the pervasive paradigm that Andrade has signaled in male writings.

Veronica's Africa is indeed gendered, but in a masculine rather than a feminine form. Andrade further stresses her point by arguing that even though "*Hérémakhonon's* metonymic displacement is not stubbornly single but instead is comprised of constantly shifting signifiers," Ibrahima Sory "represents a metonymic substitution for the entire continent... his phallus filling in for the epistemic void, or the whole that is Caribbean history" (217). Veronica's need for a "Father('s)land" underlies her sexual obsession with Ibrahima Sory because Africa is single-handedly embodied by her African lover. He thus functions as what Andrade calls "a metonymic displacement" for the continent (216). This displacement operates on two levels. It not only suggests the virile connection that Veronica wants to establish with Africa (as opposed to the traditional maternal one), but it also alludes to the love that she would like to have received from her own father. Speaking about her relationship with her father, whom she calls the Mandingo Marabout, Veronica recognizes the role he plays in her identity quest: "En vérité, si le marabout mandingue m'avait fait sauter plus souvent sur son genou en m'appelant ma petite perle,... je n'en serais peut-être pas là où j'en suis. Car c'est avec lui, et lui surtout, que j'ai un compte à régler. Ma mère ne m'a jamais beaucoup impressionnée. Elle n'était rien que reflet de l'astre paternel" (48) [Had the Mandingo marabout bounced me more often on his knee and called *me* his little pearl... I would most likely not be here today. He is the one with whom I have an account to settle. My mother never impressed me very much. She was just a moon round the paternal planet (23)]. Condé here plays with the Electra complex. Between Veronica and her father there is clearly a void that she wants to fill and Ibrahima Sory serves as a substitute for the father she never had. By the same token, she refuses to identify with her mother just as she fails to identify with the women she encounters in Africa. Ironically, searching for her identity through a masculine image of Africa propels Veronica into the same shadowy zone on Ibrahima Sory's "planet" that her mother occupies in her father's world.

In this respect, many of our unreliable narrator's decisions indicate her lack of feminist consciousness, which, according to Alexander, shows both a deprivation of agency to women in the novel and a strengthening of men's power. "Not actively participating or taking control of the narrative discourse," Alexander writes, "Veronica condemns and sentences herself to a symbolic death, voicelessness… [Her] identifying with the phallocentric society gives the patriarchy, appropriately represented by the men, agency and voices, while it further stifles the already silenced females in the novel" (107, 111-112). For Alexander, Veronica's voicelessness is thus a result of her own doing, and "the shackles which bind her exist within herself" (114).[7] Alexander's point about Veronica's lack of feminist consciousness is quite valid, although one also needs to realize that Condé's portrayal of Veronica as apparently naïve and self-destructive is replete with irony. Condé's characters rarely model ideal behavior. Critics should refrain from a rather facile attribution of ideological tags to creative authors. However, one could argue that Alexander's assessment is also relevant, in that it shows the potential for any search for roots to take part in the "conspiracy of silence" ("Pan-Africanism," 57).[8] If Condé's protagonist is indeed voiceless, then her own complicity is largely accountable for this voicelessnes which results more from confusion than from a deliberate choice, for as Condé explains in an interview, Veronica "is so confused about her life, she never speaks…. You have to guess exactly what she thinks, what she feels" (Taleb-Khyar 361). Veronica remains in a situation of confusion dictated by the complexity of her identity crisis, and the reader can discern the paradox of her simultaneous search for identity and lack of voice.

When Veronica first embarked on her voyage of self-discovery, she was willing to pay whatever price it took to get a "cure" for her "ailment" and regain her inner peace. She ultimately finds out that she has chosen the wrong therapy; she realizes her entire project has been an enormous sham: "Me voilà ramené à Ibrahima Sory qui en vérité est au centre de tout. Au centre de quoi? Il y a belle lurette que j'ai abandonné ma quête. Au fait qu'est-ce que je quêtais? Alors, au centre de quoi?" (187) [This brings me back to Ibrahima Sory who in fact is at the center of everything. In the center of what? I've given up looking a long time ago. What was I looking for in fact? In the center of what? (125)]. What she finds is the impossibility of answers, certainties, or attainment of goals. Her failure to answer questions raised by her existential void on one hand, and by her relationship with her "nigger with ancestors" on the other, also signifies the distance separating Africa from its so-called diaspora.

Maryse Condé corroborates this argument in her preface to the second edition of *Hérémakhonon,* where she addresses the gap between Africa and its diaspora as an aberration that consists in subscribing to the notion of a comprehensive black world today. In other words, the author of *Hérémakhonon* calls for a critical reevaluation of the vertical relationship suggested by the *"royal Kaïlcédrat"* trope, while constructing the character of Veronica in a way that pits her against her African "ancestor" and negates the possibility of communication between them,. Condé contends in her preface to the French edition: "Ses démêlés sentimentaux avec son 'Nègre avec aïeux,' son incapacité à communiquer avec lui, à être à ses yeux à peine plus qu'un objet divertissant, un peu pathétique et ridicule, matérialisent la distance aujourd'hui connue entre l'Afrique et ce qu'il est convenu d'appeler ses diasporas, et éclairent l'absurdité qu'il y a à parler en plein XXe siècle de 'monde noir'" (13) [The romantic problems she faces with her "Nigger with ancestors" and her inability to communicate with him or be hardly anything other than a rather pathetic and ridiculous plaything mark the gap, now unquestionable, between Africa and what is conventionally called its diasporas. All this illustrates the absurdity that consists in speaking about a "black world" in the middle of the 20th century (my translation)]. *Hérémakhonon* thus offers a counter-reading of *Négritude's* reduction of blackness to a concept suggesting uncomplicated unity among those identified as "black." It is, in Condé's words, a response to "the idea perpetuated by *Négritude* that all Blacks are the same" ("Pan-Africanism" 60). In sum, Condé's dispelling of the Pan-Africanist ideology that lumps all black people into the same mold serves as a way for her to expose—through what Wa Nyatetu-Waigwa calls a "subversive, fictional quest" (554)—the romantic notion of the existence of a unified black world, the so-called "lie" propagated by *Négritude*.

By exposing this "lie," the novel also refutes the perception that Africa is automatically an ideal home for Blacks everywhere. In Maryse Condé's account, such a perception is as close to fiction as one can get. This is why in both her life and her work Condé has vigorously tried to affirm the erroneousness of the fiction that posits Africa as a natural home for all Blacks, regardless of their cultural and historical experiences. As she argues, "[C]ulture, unlike Césaire's definition… is something that you live and not a phenomenon you simply discuss in detail" ("Pan-Africanism" 62). Having experienced the differences between Africa and its diaspora by personally enduring what she calls the "sort of cultural terrorism" (Pfaff 12; 24) that she suffered in Guinea, Condé is in an appropriate position to address these differences in a fictional form. *Hérémakhonon* may, therefore, be read as more than mere fiction with no bearing on social issues (assuming such a category of fiction exists).

Moreover, what does it really mean for Veronica to claim an African identity? What Africa would she identify with? What pieces in the multifaceted jigsaw puzzle constituted by the notion of Africa are there to be put together? In a word, what is Africa? It would take us far beyond the scope of this essay to speculate on these questions. Given the gigantic, ambiguous and complex elements that form the so heavily charged notion of Africa, any will to retrieve the essence of what this notion stands for can only confront the ineluctable vagueness and incompleteness of what is invoked. As much as one would like to identify with a homogeneous idea of Africa, one can always and only identify with bits and pieces, which is far from providing a full picture. In *Hérémakhonon* the best assemblage of fragments that such a picture could offer remains the emotional charge embedded in the rehabilitative desire carried by the protagonist's imaginary affirmation of her ties with Africa. Yet such an assemblage is hardly more than a tableau of fog.

As part of the vagueness of her quest, Veronica is engaged in an existential search that completely brackets off the present in favor of a nebulous image of the past. Her project constitutes an impossible attempt to undo history: a process that implies, as Jonathan Ngaté has argued, a reversal of the Middle Passage.[9] Condé's protagonist meditates on the fruitlessness of her search: "Mon entreprise est-elle absurde? Comme celle d'un homme qui, traversant le Sahara, essaierait de s'imaginer ce qu'il était avant sa désertification" (89) [An absurd undertaking? No worse than a man crossing the Sahara who can't help imagining what it was like before its desertification (51)]. The image of a traveler crossing the Sahara desert and imagining what it used to be like *before* compellingly describes Veronica's predicament, for it would be a platitude to observe that the mere act of treading the dry sandy fields of the Sahara is not enough for them to regain their fertility. As Frantz Fanon warned in a passage to which Maryse Condé is fond of referring, and one which she probably had in mind while contriving the circumstances of Veronica's disenchantment in and with Africa, "[T]here can be no two cultures which are completely identical. To believe that it is possible to create a black culture is to forget that niggers [sic] are disappearing" (*The Wretched of the Earth* 234). Near the end of the novel, Veronica realizes that too many centuries separate her from her ancestors and she will not find them, nor will they find her (193; 136). Veronica also realizes that the fracture between Africa and its diaspora is too wide for her to even attempt to mend, for in the process she recognizes the irreversible dissimilarity generated by this fracture.

As the novel draws to a close, Veronica is predictably ready to *flee* from Africa, the place where time, characterized as having "ce train de roi fainéant" (242) [this sluggish pace] (165), has "s'est totalement arrêté" [has totally stopped (131)]. What Georges Ngal calls the "eschatological time of the ancestors" (207) is no longer relevant for Veronica, and Africa no longer represents her spiritual inspiration: "Je me suis trompée, trompée d'aïeux, voilà tout. J'ai cherché mon salut là où il ne le fallait pas. Parmi les assassins" (244) [My ancestors led me on. What more can I say? I looked for myself in the wrong place. In the arms of an assassin (167)]. Her avowal clearly marks the turning point of what Simone Alexander has dubbed "the impracticality of this call to a return home," which forces Veronica to "take flight into dreams and illusions" (97, 102).

In coming to grips with the stark truth about her experience, namely that her journey was propelled by fantasies and dreams, Veronica articulates her need to reorient her focus to her "speck of islands" rather than to a Mother Africa whose connection with her tends to recede with time: "Si je voulais faire la paix avec moi-même, c'est-à-dire avec eux, c'est-à-dire avec nous, c'est chez moi que je devrais retourner. Dans ma poussière d'îles (*dixit* le général)" (110) [If I want to come to terms with myself—i.e., with them, i.e., with us—I ought to return home. To my island specks (dixit the general) (67)]. Maryse Condé seems to concur with her heroine in the sudden spark of insight that it is from their "speck of island" that they should try to find the rebirth they have been seeking throughout the continents. As Condé asserts, "after thirty years of living in Europe, Africa and the United States… I had to be born again" ("Pan-Africanism" 61). Condé's "revival" coincides with recognizing the need to seek her roots within her Caribbean experience. Illustrating her skepticism vis-à-vis a broadly panoptic African sodality with a West Indian proverb, Condé argues that "[i]t is only when you have swept your house that you can go out." She goes on to add: "I believe we are in the process of sweeping our houses, achieving our independence. Only after that can we begin to think about something more ambitious" ("Pan-Africanism" 64). In Condé's mind, this more ambitious "something" cannot be achieved through an emphasis on a logic of sameness that overlooks dissimilarities. Instead, it is possible only through the recognition of diversity because the need for unity in Pan-Africanism cannot be materialized "[i]f we are not allowed to be diverse and different." Thus, "[d]iversity within unity is," for her, "the definition of our shared objectives… " ("Pan-Africanism" 65).

Veronica finally becomes aware that she is a stranger in Africa, and cannot find her true self there. At the same time, she discovers that this challenge is a measure of her fragmented historical experience, meaningful *only* when it takes account of *all* the fragments that compose it, including the Caribbean. Anything short of recognizing the multi-dimensionality of this experience would be self-denial: "Je suis un animal ambigu mi-poisson, mi-oiseau, une chauve-souris nouveau modèle" (193-94) [I'm an ambiguous animal, half fish, half bird, a new style of bat. (130-1)]. Veronica's trip to Africa may seem to be a total waste, but it is not. At least she has come to realize that Africa alone cannot provide all the answers to her self-exploration. The trip has given her the tools to reorient her existential search and take into consideration the need to include Europe and her Caribbean homeland in the broad and complex picture of her identity. Before heading to the Caribbean, Veronica makes a "stopover" in Paris, where it is spring time. Europe seems to be, at least temporarily, the place that could offer her the rejuvenating force she failed to obtain in Africa. Yet, if Veronica pursues her quest for inner peace, spiritual strength and self-reconciliation in her Caribbean island, one may wonder why she prefers to take a detour through Europe.

Pondering this apparent diversion, Wa Nyatetu-Waigwa writes: "One could argue… that since the connection between Africa and the Caribbean has from its very beginnings existed through Europe, Veronica's going back to Paris is a logical and necessary step in her implied return to Guadeloupe. Her return to Paris would then highlight the lack of a direct connection between Africa and the Caribbean and point up the role of Africa as a 'detour,' as Édouard Glissant would say, in the Caribbean person's quest for an identity" (556-57). This double detour through Africa and Europe thus suggests, as Elizabeth Wilson has argued, a Caribbean reclamation of "three *potential* 'homelands'": Africa, Europe, and the Caribbean (48; emphasis added). However, for Veronica it is clear that Africa can only be a *potential* homeland *in* which she feels exiled just as she, as an Afro-Caribbean person, felt exiled *from* it by the historical experience of slavery.

Like her fictional mother and many other Afro-Caribbean subjects—real and fictional—Veronica is not alone in taking this "African" detour. The idea is commendable; however, in many instances, the outcome has been the same: disenchantment. For beyond the affective desire to trace one's Caribbean identity to Africa, the gap is still wide enough that any diasporic connection with the "Motherland" cannot be bridged without acknowledging that, in addition to their respective *internal* differences, Africa and the Caribbean form distinct and complex clusters of cultural zones. Therefore, the desire for connection can hardly make up for the historical, cultural and geographical differences. Yet, the chimes of the "journey home to Africa" are sometimes so appealing that the partisans of such a journey may remain deaf to the obviously jarring notes also contained in the score. Perhaps, *Hérémakhonon* is, after all, a call for a different orchestral score.

Notes

1. The Kaïlcedrat, or Cailcedrat, may grow as high as 25 meters tall. The tree loses few of its leaves during the dry season but it does not always provide a substantial shade. It also serves many purposes: the trunk is used as furniture or in construction work, and the bark is said to have numerous curative functions, as it is used to heal small-pox, diarrhea, headaches, rheumatism, and so on.

2. One could infer from this passage that the psychological roots of Veronica's desire to discover Africa go back to her childhood memories. The way she thinks about skin color and racial phenotypes as the main criteria for beauty in this passage is reminiscent of the type of self-loathing displayed by Pecola, Toni Morrison's child protagonist in *The Bluest Eye*. Without forcing the intertextual relationship between this passage and the motif of Pecola's racial self-loathing, it is noteworthy Condé's stated preference for Morrison's early works, namely *The Bluest Eye* and *Sula*, over the more recent ones, which she finds "somewhat hermetic" (Pfaff, 115-16; 167).

3. Here Maryse Condé is making a direct reference to the therapeutic rite customary among the *Lébou* of Senegal. *Ndöp* is a traditional healing practice used by the *Lébou* to treat people with psychological disturbances caused by spirit (*rab*) possession. It is a complex therapeutic process, which culminates in the patient's articulating the name and favorite songs of the *rab* that possesses him or her. When the patient is cured, the *rab* is said to have left for *Sangomar*, a bay located off the *Petite Côte*, a few kilometers south of Dakar, and which, according to the legend, is the favorite abode of the *rabs*.

4. I would like to thank Sally Barbour for drawing my attention to the constant need to look at Veronica as a "doubled subject." Her insightful comments and suggestions have been very helpful in my thinking.

5. See also, among others, the scene on page 82 [47].

6. Reflecting on the nuances embedded in the title of the novel, Vèvè A. Clark reports: "[according to a Malinké native speaker], Heremakhonon indicates that one has overcome hardships and moved on toward happiness. That Ibrahima Sory so names his villa suggests that after the Revolution in his country, a new era of peace and friendship will prevail" (1990, 318, note 9). Ironically, nothing in Ibrahima Sory's methods suggests his devotion to either peace or friendship. The effect of this misnomer is to highlight the hiatus between what it *ideally* stands for and what it *actually* represents. For more details about the meaning of the word "Heremakhonon," see Condé's preface to the 1988 second edition of the novel.

7. Alexander is using a phrase from Joycelynn Loncke's, "The Image of the Woman in Caribbean Literature with Special Response to *Pan Beat* and *Hérémakhonon*."

8. To put this statement in context, it is necessary to note that Condé does not use it in reference to Veronica specifically but to the public's indifference to things Caribbean, in general.

9. His very useful article, "Maryse Condé and Africa: The Making of a Recalcitrant Daughter" is cited by Wa Nyatetu-Waigwa (554).

"I'M NO MAYOTTE CAPÉCIA": ENGAGING WITH FANON IN HÉRÉMAKHONON

Jennifer R. Sparrow

"It is useless to invent a myth of origin for the Antilles when one knows that in 1492 Christopher Columbus arrives in Guadeloupe, and that a few years later a slave ship unloads hundreds of Africans," Maryse Condé asserts, given that the Antilles lack the "serious or sacred" oral literature that is the foundation of a creation myth (qtd. in Hewitt 1990, 182). She adds that because both vegetation and people in the Antilles have been "imported," "the Antilles are totally creations of the capitalist system."[1] Separated from Africa and a lost past by the Middle Passage, estranged from Europe by the fear that assimilation would entail joining the ranks of the "mimic men," cut off from a virtually extinct indigenous culture, intermingled with laborers from Asia, Antilleans inhabit a socio-cultural no-man's land neither wholly African nor wholly European. As such, quests for personal and collective identity, rather than being considered outmoded and "essentialist," are crucial political projects for writers throughout the Caribbean. In particular, Condé's protagonists, often created with the intent to displease, can be read as antagonists; but that doesn't warrant their dismissal on the grounds of their unattractive (and often unappealing) identity quests, particularly when we consider gender formation in relation to the construction of race for the Caribbean woman.

Francophone Caribbean women's writing shares this preoccupation with the identity crises pervasive in West Indian writing. However, as Elizabeth Wilson notes, when the quester is female, the journey tends to end in withdrawal and isolation or flight and evasion rather than in confrontation (45). In her discussion of the journey as an archetypal symbol, Wilson argues that rather than being a journey-of-initiation (to self-knowledge and/or integration into a community), "[i]n Francophone female Caribbean writing, the journey, except in rare instances…takes the form of journey-as-alienation"(45). Indeed, in a study of the works of the first-generation of female Antillean writers [Mayotte Capécia (Martinique, 1928-1953), Michele Lacrosil (Guadeloupe, 1915-), and Jacqueline Manicom (Guadeloupe, 1938-1976)], Lizabeth Paravisini-Gebert notes that out of the seven novels published among them, only one protagonist has not committed suicide or left her island by the novel's conclusion. The other six (mostly light-skinned and middle-class) protagonists, denied acceptance in the *béké* (white colonial) world because of racial prejudice and reviled by the island's black population as *"assimileés"*[2] turn to Europe to escape the sense of alienation and placelessness experienced at home (74).

The alienated "tragic mulatta" heroine appears as a recurring theme in the Francophone literary tradition (Mordecai and Wilson). The phenomenon of Francophone alienation has its roots in the French colonial policy of assimilation, which sought not just political and economic control over its territories, but cultural hegemony as well.[3] In contrast to colonial subjects in France's South Asian and African possessions, this assimilationist policy promised Antillean colonial subjects that education could overcome any cultural difference between the Antillean Frenchman and the Frenchman from the *métropole*. The French policy of assimilation worked all too well, and the result of this "unreflected imposition of culture," as the Martinican theorist Frantz Fanon argues, is that the "Antillean partakes of the same [anti-Negro] collective unconscious as the European" (*Black Skin,* 191). Indeed, in Martinique and Guadeloupe, the word "African" or "black" was usually meant as an insult (Glissant, 16). When Condé discusses her own childhood in Guadeloupe, she describes being raised in an insular, well-to-do community of Blacks who were "racists in their own way," as they remained aloof from less-affluent Blacks while believing that "mulattoes were bastards and Whites, the enemy" (Pfaff 5; 14). Her first novel, *Hérémakhonon,* provides some reflections on this childhood experience. Although the novel is not strictly autobiographical, Condé admits that the protagonist's account of her West Indian childhood and family milieu are drawn from life. Of the black bourgeoisie Condé says, "they are proud to be Black, but they don't even know what it is. In the final analysis, to be black, for them, is to act like a white person, to become 'whitened.'"(40; 63).

As Condé writes in "Order, Disorder, Freedom, and the West Indian Writer"; female writers from the West Indies have been neglected and misunderstood because their work treats the theme of Francophone alienation with candor: "There is nothing West Indian society hates more than facing the reality of color prejudice, which reminds it of the days of slavery, of the times when to be black was a curse and to possess fair skin was regarded as a blessing" (131-32). Because their texts addressed taboo issues like color prejudice, mental illness, female sexuality, and gender oppression (rather than approved topics like colonial oppression, celebration of the masses, messianic male heroes and their brave hardworking women), these early women writers have been unfairly blamed for the problem of alienation.

The best known example of this "shoot the messenger" phenomenon is Frantz Fanon's criticism of *Je suis martiniquaise* (1948) [*I Am a Martinican Woman* (1997)], in which he excoriates Mayotte Capécia (the name of the novel's protagonist and the pseudonym of the author) for becoming a white man's mistress. Fanon's now-famous attack on *Je suis martiniquaise*, a book that might not have remained in print based solely on its literary merit, has made the novel a touchstone, a symbol of the alienating effects of racism on the colonized. In her discussion of the novel, Condé describes Mayotte's situation as classical alienation: that is, loving a man because his skin is white and he, because of the history of colonial education and aesthetics, appears handsome (*Paroles*, 32). In *Hérémakhonon*, Condé explores the plight of the alienated Antillean *assimileé* through her character Veronica Mercier, self-described as one of those "névrosés de la diaspora" (86) [neurotics of the Diaspora] who travels to Africa, "cherchant à guerir" (86) [seeking a cure (52) for her alienated state. Self-consciously rejecting Mayotte Capécia's reverence for all things white and French, Veronica seeks, instead, to connect with Africa through a sexual relationship with a "nègre [avec] des aïeux" (47) [nigger (with) ancestors (24)], a member of African royalty. However, Veronica discovers that sleeping with a man—even a man who is the "right" color—will not heal her fractured psyche. Rather than achieving the liberation she seeks, Veronica finds herself lapsing into stereotype: like Mayotte she becomes *Marilisse*, a "slave to love" (Pfaff 41; 65).

Historically, the "highly overdetermined"[4] representation of Caribbean women as sexual beings has its roots in the "often ambivalent relationships between black women and white men and the sexual exploitation of the former by the latter" (Andrade 215). Although the obvious sexual violence between master and slave cannot be overstated, as Susan Andrade notes, sometimes, "for black women, liaisons with powerful white men constituted a means by which they might advance themselves, their children, and their families and were therefore not always unwelcome" (215). While in actuality, relatively few women of color sought out white men for social advancement, the resentment these liaisons generated, both from white women and from black men, gave rise to a powerful negative figure in the Antillean literary imagination: *Marilisse*,[5] the complicit whore in Massa's bed whose "charm" was linked to the dark forces of evil and magic. The name is "hissed" at Veronica Mercier at home in Guadeloupe when the community hears that she is dating the son of a prominent mulatto family, and again later when she walks through the West Indian festival in Paris with her white lover, Jean-Michel. Veronica, reacting to the realization that all of her sexual partners have been fair skinned, becomes defensive: "Répétons-le, j'ai aimé ces deux hommes parce que je les aimais. Et que tous ces jeunes mâles noirs que me présentait ma famille me faisaient horreur. Pourquoi ils me faisaient horreur? *Pas parce qu'ils étaient noirs.* Absurde! Je ne suis pas une Mayotte Capécia. Ah non! Pas mon souci, éclaircir la Race. Je le jure..." (55, emphasis in the text) [Once again, I loved these two men because I was in love. All those young black males that my family introduced me to made me shudder. Why? Not because they were black. Ridiculous! I'm no Mayotte Capécia. No! I'm not interested in whitening the race! I swear... (30)]. Here "Mayotte Capécia" functions as a cultural shorthand, one that presumes the reader's familiarity with the characters and conventions of the Antillean literary tradition, which Condé discusses at length in her 1979 study *La Parole des Femmes : Essai sur des romancières des Antilles de langue française* [*Women's Words: Essays on the Novelists of the French Antilles* (my translation)].[6] The theme of the black Antillean woman who, like Mayotte Capécia, seeks to define her identity through a sexual relationship with a non-black is especially pervasive in the novels Condé discusses in this essay.

Mayotte Capécia, the pseudonym for Lucette Combette (*née* Céranus), was born in Martinique in 1916, lived in Paris when she published her two novels, and died there in 1955.[7] *Je suis martini-quaise* and her other work, *La Négresse blanche* [*The White Negress*] are highly autobiographical. Like Capécia, the first-person narrator of *Je suis martiniquaise* is a woman of color who spent her childhood in rural Martinique where she lived with her mother, father, and twin sister. Upon learning that her grandmother was white, young Mayotte says "…je décidais que je ne pourrais aimer qu'un blanc, un blond avec des yeux bleus, un Français" (59) [I decided that I could only love a white man, a blond with blue eyes, a French-man (63)]. During Mayotte's adolescence, her mother dies and her father takes a mistress, a girl not much older than his daughters. Mayotte escapes her father's house and achieves a measure of economic and social independence by becoming a "blanchisseuse' [laundress]. Fanon interprets her choice (rather ham-handedly) as evidence of a subconscious desire to "bleach" her world (*Black Skin*, 45), ignoring Mayotte's continually expressed desire to achieve financial independence through her own labor. Mayotte is proud of the reputation she makes for herself: "Je faisais payer plus cher qu'ailleurs, je travaillais mieux et, comme les gens aiment le linge propre, ils venaient chez moi" (131) [I charged more than others but I did better work, and, since Fort-de-France liked clean linen, they patronized me (108)]. Mayotte has an affair and a child with André, a white French naval officer from the Vichy government during the Second World War, who eventually abandons her and marries a white woman. At the novel's conclusion, Mayotte, isolated and scorned at home in Martinique, escapes to France, where she sadly concludes: "J'aurais voulu me marier, mais avec un blanc. Seule-ment une femme de couleur n'est jamais tout à fait respectable aux yeux d'un blanc. Même s'il l'aime, je le savais" (202) [I would have liked to marry, but with a white man. Only, a colored woman is never quite respectable in the eyes of a white man—even if he loves her, I knew well (153)]. Perhaps she finally begins to awaken to the contradictions of her desire for self-affirmation through marriage to a white man.

Fanon's attack on Capécia's novel is one of the essays published in *Peau noire, masques blancs* (*Black Skin, White Masks*), a collection of his writings in which he says he hopes to destroy the sense of cultural alienation experienced by the colonized bourgeoisie by analyzing it (12). In these essays, written between 1948 and 1952, Fanon addresses the desire on the part of black colonial subjects to inhabit whiteness via a sexual relationship with a white partner as evidence that they who have internalized the colonizers' myths. To illustrate this point, Fanon conducts a "case study" of "Mayotte Capécia" to "see how the Negress behaves with the white man," and René Maran's *Un homme pareil aux autres* (1947) [*A Man Like Any Other* (my translation)] to "try to understand what happens when the man is black and the woman white" (64)."[8] Fanon shows compassion for black men who have become so alienated that an attractive woman must be, by definition, white, yet he refuses to give the same consideration to black women. Fanon's misogynistic dismissal of Capécia's novel ("cut-rate merchandise") has drawn fire from numerous feminist critics.[9] Gwen Bergner, for one, rightly observes that Fanon's critique of Mayotte's choices overlooks the ways in which colonial society "perpetuates racial inequality through structures of sexual difference" (83). Fanon's disregard for the economic benefits of Mayotte's liaison with her white French officer and his readiness to label her a whore and a race traitor seem particularly obtuse in light of his own emphasis on the economic basis of *all* forms of colonialism. What's more, he seems to see black women as individuals making choices, while he sees black men as produced by institutional forces. Commenting on Mayotte's delight in discovering that she had a white grandmother (not so ordinary as having a white grandfather) Fanon states, "[w]hen a white woman accepts a black man there is automatically a romantic aspect. It is a giving, not a seizing" (46). Within the Fanonian race/gender paradigm, white women choose to give themselves, while black women's sexual choices are represented as evidence of having given in to colonial psychosis, to a "black pathology which [Fanon] despises" (Doane 219).

Fanon's preoccupation with color can in part be explained by his upbringing in colonial Martinique in the class to which he would later refer disparagingly as the national bourgeoisie, "a bourgeoisie which is stupidly, contemptibly, cynically bourgeois," having "totally assimilated colonialist thought in its most corrupt form" (162). In his later work, *Les Damnés de la terre* (*The Wretched of the Earth*), Fanon's primary concern will be the economic exploitation of the peasant classes by this newly arrived national bourgeoisie. In *Black Skin, White Masks*, however, it is color prejudice that preoccupies him and limits his analysis, for his study elides the inextricable correlation that exists between skin color and class in the Antilles. Moreover, Fanon's myopic focus on Mayotte's relationship with her white lover, which he denounces as evidence of her "lactification complex" (*Black Skin*, 47), neglects other aspects of the text. Particularly, as Condé notes, Fanon ignores the novel's portrayal of Mayotte's father, "whose irresponsibility and mistreatment of her mother might well be partially responsible for Mayotte's hatred of the black man" ("Order" 131). "The text," Condé continues, "is a precious written testimony…of the mentality of a West Indian girl in those days, [and] of the impossibility for her to build up an aesthetics which would enable her to come to terms with the color of her skin" (131). In contrast to Fanon, Condé here views the protagonist as subject to social forces.

Although *Hérémakhonon* is set in the 1970s, approximately thirty years after Capécia's novel, both Mayotté's and Veronica's lives are circumscribed by the "social pyramid, a vestige of colonialism and slavery that positions a few whites at the top, the mulattos in the middle, and the blacks at the bottom of the socio/economic scale" (Condé, *Paroles* 13). As members of the colored middle class, Veronica and Mayotte exist within a marginal space, a buffer society, created by the *béké* (white colonial) elite to mediate between themselves and the laboring masses. To Veronica, the black bourgeoisie of her childhood was balanced precariously in the social pyramid and could never be free; her identity quest is informed by a need to purge herself of the cultural inferiority complex of her parents' generation: "Ils avaient terriblement peur d'être ce qu'on disait.…Ceux que j'ai aimés, n'avaient pas cette peur-là. Ils étaient libres" (63) [(My parents) were terribly afraid of being what it was said they were…. The people I loved never had that fear. They were free (36)]. Veronica's excuse for having become "a Marilisse with a mulatto" (31)[10] and causing an island scandal that results in her nine-year exile in Paris is her father's obsessive insistence on proper 'form' and that family members be a 'credit to the race.' Veronica's learned sense of inferiority is revealed through her observation that her (previous) lovers have always ridiculed her family, and "en un sens, je les ai choisis pour qu'ils puissent s'en moquer à ma place"(149) [in a way I chose them so that they could do it for me (102)]. Remembering how Jean-Michel, her white Frenchman, "howled" over her sisters and their husbands, Veronica muses, "Qu'est-ce qu'il dirait si je le mettais nez à nez avec Ibrahima Sory? C'est sûr qu'il ne rirait pas" (149) [What would he say if I put him face to face with Ibrahima Sory? He wouldn't laugh, that's for sure (103)]. She confesses to finding Ibrihama Sory, her first African lover, attractive because he has the quality that she prizes, yet knows she sorely lacks: "Il est bien dans sa peau" (89) [He's at ease with himself (56)]. However, the "freedom" that Veronica attributes admiringly to Jean-Marie and Jean-Michel is predicated on their relative positions of superiority (mulatto and white, respectively) in the hated "social pyramid" that Veronica despises but has nonetheless internalized; and Sory's "freedom," while unencumbered by colonial color-politics, derives from his family's complicity with the empire-builders of the nineteenth-century and with the political dictators of the twentieth.

In addition to the psychic alienation experienced by assimilated West Indians who, like Mayotte Capécia, seek to ascend the social pyramid by rejecting blackness, Fanon proposes a second type of alienation: intellectual alienation, arising from the *Négritude* movement's ensuing rejection of Europe and its followers' quest for roots in Africa.[11] Fanon explains, "To many colored intellectuals European culture has a quality of exteriority…. Not wanting to live the part of a poor relative, of an adopted son, of a bastard child, shall he feverishly seek to discover a Negro civilization?" (1967, 230). Although Fanon well understood the anguish that led France's assimilated "bastard children" to seek legitimate origins in Africa, he rejects the notion that such a return is possible, refusing to "exalt the past at the expense of my present and my future" (226). Thus, for Fanon there are two main tragic figures in *Black Skin, White Masks*: "[T]he black who has internalized the myth of the colonizer [and]…the black colonized who turns from Europe and towards Africa in search of an 'authentic' blackness" (Taylor qtd. in Andrade 220). The former, suffering from Condé's "classic alienation," is personified by Mayotte Capécia; the latter, intellectually alienated, is Condé's Veronica Mercier, who, unable to make sense out of her present self travels to Africa "pour essayer de voir ce qu'il y avait avant"(31) [to try and find out what was before (12)]. In *Hérémakhonon* Condé reinscribes the tragic figure of Capécia's Mayotte while responding to the treatment she receives at the hands of Fanon: Condé concurs with Fanon's dismissal of simplistic notions of *Négritude* but disputes his sexist representations of alienated West Indian women.

Fanon claims to know what women of color seek, in spite of declaring that he "knows nothing" about their psychosexuality: "All these frantic women of color in quest of white men are waiting. And one of these days, surely, they will be surprised to find that they do not want to go back, they will dream of a 'wonderful night, a wonderful lover, a white man'" (*Black Skin*, 49). Reversing Fanon's model, which casts the woman of color, via Mayotte Capécia, as a race traitor, Veronica Mercier leaves a white lover behind in Paris to wait for Ibrahima Sory, her aristocratic "nigger with ancestors," the man through whom she hopes to reconcile her divided self and find peace. The novel's title, *Hérémakhonon*, which means 'wait for happiness' in Malinke (figuratively 'welcome house'), is also the name of Sory's compound, where Veronica passes countless hours awaiting her enigmatic lover's return.

Hérémakhonon calls into question Fanon's blanket assumptions about the sexual choices made by women of color. Citing Mayotte's determination to marry a white man, Fanon claims that "every woman in Martinique" hopes to "whiten the race" via a sexual relationship with a light(er)-skinned man because "[i]t is always essential to avoid falling back into the pit of niggerhood" (47). And although Veronica is "sterile" (55),[12] and thus unable to propagate the race in any case, prior to her arrival in Africa, she has slept only with fair-skinned men, so "according to Fanonian logic, Ibrahima Sory, as the darkest and most African of Veronica's sexual partners, is the most appropriate," at least in terms of his color (Andrade 222). However, Veronica's lover is also Minister of Defense, strong-man and heir-apparent to the repressive dictator who rules the unnamed West African country in which the story is set.[13] Veronica, who remains willfully apolitical, rationalizes, "la personne politique d'Ibrahima Sory me laisse indifférente.…Je ne suis pas venue me mêler de leurs querelles, trancher, prendre parti. Je suis venue pour me guérir d'un mal…. Par lui, j'accéderai enfin à la fierté d'être moi-même. Il n'a pas été étampé (71) [The political person of Ibrahima Sory leaves me cold…. I didn't come here to get mixed up in their quarrels and take sides. I came to find a cure…Through him I shall at last be proud of what I am. He wasn't branded (42)]. Hewitt notes that Veronica's relationship with Sory "reproduces on an individual scale her desire *vis-à-vis* Africa in general"(*Tightropes*, 183); that is, her desire to find "une terre non plus peuplée de nègres…mais de Noirs" (89 [a land inhabited by Blacks, not Negroes (56)], an authentic black world with dignity and pride. Veronica's unsuccessful attempt to cure herself of alienation via a sexual relationship with Sory sheds light on the sexist inconsistencies of *Black Skin, White Masks*: Fanon aggressively rejects essentialized notions about a universal African culture as a source of origins and wholeness for alienated West Indian men; yet, when it comes to West Indian women, he falls back on the same essentializing categories (European/Antillean, white/black) to proscribe who is and who is not an appropriate sexual partner, presumably because black *women* are the ones Fanon holds responsible for the "lactification" of the Negro race.

Initially, Sory frees Veronica from the insular, color-obsessed, petit-bourgeois world of her French Antillean childhood because he represents the mythical ancestral Africa with which she wants to connect. However, with Sory, as with her previous lovers Jean-Marie (the mulatto from Guadeloupe) and Jean-Michel (the white Frenchman), Veronica feels like *Marilisse*, a sexual traitor, and she endures the same cut-eye glances and whispered insults to which Mayotte is subjected for "betraying her race" and her country with a white officer in the Vichy government. Mayotte reacts with indifference to a woman's muttered disapproval when she sees Mayotte with her white-skinned infant: "J'entendis une femme dire que j'avais trahi notre race. Eh bien, oui! J'avais peut-être trahi notre race, mais j'en étais fière" (188) [I heard a woman say that I had betrayed our race. Well, yes! I had, perhaps, betrayed our race, but I was proud of it (145)]. In *Hérémakhonon*, Veronica is more sardonic when she walks into her classroom (she officially came to Africa to teach philosophy) after Sory has jailed one of her students, a political dissident, and finds scrawled on the blackboard in red chalk the words "Nous détruirons les Ministres / Leurs Mercedes / Et leurs Putains" (106) [WE SHALL DESTROY THE MINISTERS, THEIR MERCEDES, AND THEIR WHORES (68)]. Unnerved by the incident, Veronica muses, "Si je comprends bien, dans ce pays, faire l'amour revient à faire un choix politique" (106) [If I understand correctly making love in this country comes down to making a political choice (69)], which, of course, is precisely what Fanon argues *vis-à-vis* the woman of color and the *white* man. Veronica chooses to become Sory's lover and to accept the perks that attend the position (villas, cars and drivers, a measure of political freedom), all the while ignoring that these things are an impossibility for the average citizen under his repressive regime. As Gerise Herndon notes, Veronica tries to isolate her sexuality from other elements of her identity (732). Following the blackboard-writing incident Veronica fumes: "[Avec] Jean-Marie: je me faisais Marilisse. Jean-Michel, aussi—surtout. À présent *quoi encore*? Qu'est-ce qu'ils vont inventer pour m'empêcher de faire l'amour en paix?" (109) [With Jean-Marie—I was called *Marilisse*. With Jean-Michel, too—especially Jean-Michel....(and that's why I left [Paris] after all.) But now what? What are they going to invent now to stop me from making love in peace? (71)]. Sex is not all that Veronica really wants or needs, but like *Marilisse,* the submissive, sexually insatiable, politically indifferent, opportunistic "whore,"[14] she rationalizes her unhealthy relationship with Sory. Eventually though, Veronica decides that her "whorishness" is not due to her affair with the white man, but to the fact that "she accepts sexual and material favors from a (black) man engaged in sanctioned murder" (Andrade 222).

Hérémakhonon can be read, as A. James Arnold notes, as a "negative of Alex Haley" (Veronica finds "lots of sex, but no roots" in Africa) (711); but the novel also rejects the popular supposition that people of the Black Diaspora will find wholeness in a return to the Motherland. Indeed, like *Black Skin, White Masks,* the novel rejects any wholesale valorization of that which is "authentically" African (untainted by the effects of the slave trade and colonialism). Trying to determine the basis of her attraction to Sory, Veronica reflects: "J'aime cet homme ou une certaine idée que j'ai besoin, à travers lui, de me faire de l'Afrique? À bien réfléchir aimer c'est toujours se faire une idée....Quelle est cette idée?... Celle d'une Afrique, d'un monde noir, que l'Europe n'aurait pas réduit en caricature d'elle-même"(119) [Do I love this man or a certain idea I have to have of Africa? When you think about it, it's the same thing. Loving a man is the myth you create around him...What is this idea? That of an Africa, of a black world that Europe did not reduce to a caricature of itself (77)]. However, as her protagonist's thoughts indicate, Condé is skeptical of both the man (and by extension, the political leaders of many African countries)[15] and the myth of return to a prelapsarian Africa. When Sory imprisons and later murders Veronica's friend Saliou (a leader of the opposition), she abandons her pose of willful blindness and quits Africa, sadly aware that neither the African past nor a present day African prince will give her the wholeness she seeks. She wonders in the end how she could have made such a mistake: "Je me suis trompée, trompée d'aïeux, voilà tout. J'ai cherché mon salut là où il ne le fallait pas. Parmi les assassins" (244) [My ancestors led me on. What more can I say? I looked for myself in the wrong place. In the arms of an assassin (176)]. Although Sory possesses the legitimate African lineage that Veronica longs for, his complicity with the dictator's exploitative regime makes it impossible for her to reduce her world-view to a simple Europe/Africa opposition. Indeed, Herndon argues that although the Westernized Afro-Caribbean middle class (as represented by Veronica's parents) "is criticized for its hypocrisy," the novel's implicit message is that "the neocolonial power of leaders like Sékou Touré deserves much stronger condemnation" (736). And as Condé explains, "the problem for me is not fighting white people who are bad and evil, but fighting our own people who are bad and evil" (Nunez). Rather than critiquing women's sexual choices, it is important to unearth power structures that allow human rights abuses to go unchecked under the guise of anti-colonialism.

Hérémakhonon is loosely based on Condé's experiences in Guinea under Sékou Touré, but it is not, she insists, fictionalized autobiography: "It was a novel of protest" (Pfaff 40; 63). Although Condé says that she, "like everyone else of [her] generation" (33; 53) was a committed Marxist, after living in Africa and seeing leaders who championed "the great struggle of Africa and suffering mankind" while "actively imposing suffering on their own people," she became disenchanted with African socialism ("Order" 45). Condé says that when she "wrote *Hérémakhonon*, there was an oversimplified militancy in the air, along with a devout faith in African socialism and the mythification of that ideal," convictions she now characterizes as superficial and naïve. "Basically," she continues, "I wanted to express how much I had been wounded by everything I had seen in Africa and to point out how difficult it was to build a nation" (40; 63). Condé's fictionalized post-independence African state aptly illustrates what Fanon describes in his 1961 essay "The Pitfalls of National Consciousness": "Before independence, the leader generally embodies the aspirations of the people for independence, political liberty, and national dignity. But as soon as independence is declared, far from embodying in concrete form the needs of the people in what touches bread, land, and the restoration of the country to the sacred hands of the people, the leader will reveal his inner purpose: to become the general president of that company of profiteers impatient for their returns which constitutes the national bourgeoisie" (166). Indeed, Condé's fictionalized West African country—where babies die of malnutrition, where schoolchildren are menaced by armed soldiers, where adolescent girls and boys prostitute themselves, and where old women beg in the streets while Sory and his associates, dressed in bespoke Mao suits, sweep through the ravaged landscape in a fleet of Mercedes—embodies the post-independence state that Kwame Anthony Appiah characterizes as a kleptocracy (64).

"I'm no Mayotte Capécia": Engaging with Fanon in *Hérémakhonon*

Condé writes in "Order, Disorder, Freedom, and the West Indian Writer" that Antillean women writers "displease, shock, and disturb" because they suggest "that before thinking of a political revolution, West Indian society needs a psychological one" (131). Consequently, their novels have been consigned to obscurity for violating an implicit agreement between West Indian writers and readers to respect a "stereotypical portrayal of themselves and their society" (134). Indeed, Condé's wry observation about the reception of the works of her literary foremothers might be applied to that of her own first novel as well. *Hérémakhonon*'s unflinching portrait of post-independence Africa did not win critical acclaim in the African or the Antillean press; the former pointedly ignored the novel; the latter "massacred" it (Pfaff 32; 52). And although she admits to being stung by the vitriol of some of the attacks (particularly one that compared her to Mayotte Capécia), Condé acknowledges that the novel was written "to provoke, get on people's nerves, irritate, and run counter to everything that was being said and done. It was written to displease…" (32; 52). Reading *Hérémakhonon*, we see that while Condé takes issue with Fanon's sexism, in particular with his wrongheaded attack on Mayotte Capécia, blaming the West Indian woman of color for the "Manichean delirium" of internalized racism, she shares his anguished view of the futility of simplistic notions of *Négritude* and of the tragedy of post-colonial Africa, of the internal and external violence wrought by the slave trade and colonialism, and of the way in which the African people have been betrayed by corrupt political leaders. Ultimately, *Hérémakhonon* is a novel about "disenchantment and pain" (40; 63), an elegy for the dream of "a black world which would speak through one voice, through the univocal voice of its poets and writers" (Condé, "Order" 125). Through her insistence on asking difficult questions and her refusal to accept easy or politically correct answers, Condé has carried out the charge with which Fanon concludes *Black Skin, White Masks* (written nine years before he died at age 36): "My final prayer: O my body, make of me always a man who questions!" (232). Going beyond Fanon in her questions, however, Condé's works show us not only that there is no generic "Man," but also that the master narrative has inscribed black women's bodies with social meaning. Condé never ceases to investigate the implications of that meaning.

Notes

1. Condé refers here to the decimation of indigenous Amerindian populations, especially the Carib and Arawak/Taino people who inhabited the region prior to colonization , as well as the importation and systematic acculturation of Africans who were enslaved.

2. The French term for an educated French subject or citizen, born in another land, but indoctrinated in French cultural values.

3. In his essay "Negritude and the Gods of Equity," Wole Soyinka argues that British colonial subjects, in contrast, were never made to intone sentences such as *my ancestors the Gauls* because "the British... had no intentions of insinuating such ideas of a shared ancestry into the minds of their subjects" (148).

4. See Hortense Spillers evocative article, "Mama's Baby, Papa's Maybe: An American Grammar Book," for a discussion of the multiple overdeterminations of black female sexuality.

5. In one of the many inner monologues that punctuate Condé's text, Veronica recalls the figure of *Marilisse*: "Étant en partance, le sieur Cazeau habitant au Cul-de-Sac a mis en vente une jeune négresse de belle figure prénommée Marilisse, bonne blanchisseuse. On la prendra à l'essai" (39) [Due to his forthcoming departure, Sieur Cazeau, inhabitant of Cul de Sac, has put up for sale a young Negro girl of pleasant features named Marilisse. Good laundress. Can be taken on a trial basis (17)]. A novel by the same name was published in 1903 by Haitian writer Frédéric Marcelin. Interestingly, Marcelin's Marilisse, like Capécia's Mayotte, is a laundress; but far from being the stereotypical pampered mistress of a white man, Marcelin's protagonist, after having been jilted by the (black) father of her child, ends up supporting her entire extended family (male and female) with her labor.

6. Vèvè Clark counts in *Hérémakhonon* more than one hundred and twenty-five allusions (direct and indirect) to "Euro-America and to the African Diaspora as well as to the cultivated and popular arts from both cultures. *Mayotte Capécia* and *Mahalia Jackson* are treated as recognized references sharing a wealth of connotations comparable to *Swann's Way* and the *Douanier Rousseau*" ("Developing... *Hérémakhonon*" 307).

7. See Beatrice Stith Clark's article "The Works of Mayotte Capécia (With Apologies to Frantz Fanon)," as well as her later introduction to her English translation of Capécia's two novels.

8. This statement is rather disingenuous when one considers that in 1952, Fanon married Josie Dublé, a white woman whom he met in Lyon, France.

9. See Susan Andrade, Lizabeth Paravisini-Gebert, Gwen Bergner, and Christiane Makward (*Mayotte*).

10. This particular phrase is used in the English version to fill in an ellipsis in the original: "Il suffoque. Oui je sais, je sais… / -Ce Jean-Michel…" (56) [He suffocates. Yes, I know, I know. Instead of that, I turned myself into a Marilisse with a mulatto who, caught virtually in mid-coitus, has not made up my honor. And now, if that was not enough. / "This Jean-Michel…." (31)].

11. *Négritude*, as first conceived of by its founders, Léopold Senghor, of Senegal; Léon Damas, of French Guiana; and Aimé Césaire, of Martinique, was a means of "get[ting] rid of our borrowed clothing—the clothing of assimilation—and asserting our essential being, namely our [N]egritude…the cultural heritage, the values and particularly the spirit of Negro-African civilization" (Senghor qtd. in Gendzier 40). *Négritude* thus provided a crucial alternative to assimilation; but in its early phase, it still relied on European stereotypes of Africa (considered more passionate and closer to nature) as its point of opposition. Especially in Africa, *Négritude* was often perceived as a romanticized quest for lost origins, and was, in consequence, less influential for African writers and intellectuals than it was for their Antillean counterparts. The ideology of *Négritude* exerted a powerful influence on Fanon's intellectual development. He was particularly affected by Jean Paul Sartre's "*Orphée noir*" (1948), which argues that the goal of *Négritude* must be to transcend itself; its objective, paradoxically, is to create a consciousness which will render it ultimately unnecessary. Sartre's *Négritude* is a means not an end, a negative moment in the Hegelian dialectic that will culminate in the erasure of black and white racism to create a new human synthesis without racial distinctions. Fanon engages with Sartre's essay in *Black Skin, White Masks*, revealing his own ambivalence in the process. On one hand, Fanon is no champion of *Négritude*, which he ridiculed as "the great black mirage," a product of an alienated and disaffected middle class who, failing in their attempts at assimilation into white European culture, fall back on a search for lost roots in a romanticized African past. On the other hand, alienated Martinican that he was, Fanon also recognized the need for this "black mirage," so much so that he considered Sartre's definition of *Négritude* a great disservice. For more information on Negritude, see Lilyan Kesteloot, *Black Writers in French: A Literary History of Negritude*.

12. This passage is not found in the French.

13. Some of the events described in *Hérémakhonon* are based on Condé's experiences in newly independent Guinea, where she lived from 1960 to 1964. At first an admirer of Guinean President Sékou Touré, she later became disenchanted with the dictatorial and oppressive aspects of his regime (see Pfaff 40-41; 63-65).

14. Veronica refers to herself as a whore several times throughout the novel: she recalls the names her father called her: "Intellectuelle de gauche. Putain" (28) [Left-wing intellectual. Whore (9)]; after the students call her a "whore," she flippantly refers to Adama (a white man's mistress) as "ma soeur en putainerie" (108) [my sister in whoredom (70)]; and she admits to Pierre-Gilles that while she, unlike him, does not practice sodomy she does "prostitute to [her] desires what [she's] unable to obtain" (148) (this last passage is not found in the French).

15. When asked in an interview with Elizabeth Nunez about the way the media reports on corruption in Africa, Condé replied that while "one cannot deny the corruption of the régimes there…it should not lead us to conclude that Africa is inferior. It took years for European countries to arrive at democracy. Even now many of them have not achieved it….So why should we be ashamed of the problems of Africa? They are aggravated by neocolonialism, by the lack of education for the people. This situation is the consequence of many years of colonialism, of independence that happened under the worst possible conditions….Africa is trying hard to find solutions. I believe that one day it will."

IN THE FACE OF THE DAUGHTER: FEMINIST PERSPECTIVES ON *MÉTISSAGE* AND GENDER

Gloria Nne Onyeoziri

Is it possible to theorize race and culture without attention to gender? Most postcolonial theorists seem to think so. They have viewed *métissage*[1] more in relation to race and culture than to gender. However, recent critiques of the apparent absence of women's voices in the Caribbean *créolité* movement have led some theorists to consider the possible gender biases reflected in past analyses of *métissage*, most specifically, Frantz Fanon's condemnation of the Martinican novelist Mayotte Capécia as a "neurotic mulatto" woman obsessed with the desire for "lactification" (making a family whiter and whiter over several generations).[2] A discussion of the relationship between *métissage* and gender (such as sexual exploitation, struggles for emancipation and mothering) in novels by Maryse Condé shows that *métissage* remains a useful term of analysis of certain forms of racial and sexual oppression and their continuing influence. In many of Condé's novels, the ironic voice of a third person narrator challenges stereotypes and prejudices in the reasoning of her characters and ultimately of her readers (see, for example, *La Belle Créole,* 2001). In Condé's *La vie scélérate* (1987), however, the relationship between *métissage* and gender manifests itself in the active reconstructing and deconstructing voice of a *métis* [multiracial] female narrator. Condé's perspective suggests that, contrary Fanon's claims, *métissage* is not necessarily a temptation of lactification for black women, but often the sign of a challenge to patriarchal authority and a means of confronting deeply embedded myths of both racial and sexual superiority, as well as utopian visions of imagined harmony.

Literary critics would not find it productive to reinstate any "scientific" or biological basis for "race" as a category of difference within and among population groups. Nevertheless, *métissage* may still be a useful concept to describe racial and sexual stereotypes that constrain individual and collective actions in the context of lived experience; and *"creolization,"* Michael Dash's English translation of the term in Glissant's works may not be a suitable substitute for *métissage* (Lionnet, *Autobiographical Voices* 4 n. 6).[3] Françoise Lionnet makes a case for the usefulness of this term, for example, when she argues that *métissage* should be understood as a practice of resistance to hegemonic cultures because it remains a site of "undecidability and indeterminacy" resulting from cultural mixing around the world (8). For women, the term can thus serve as a source of solidarity when it enables us to demystify "all essentialist glorifications of unitary origins, be they racial, sexual, geographic, or cultural" (9). Lionnet proposes a linguistic and rhetorical approach to *métissage* aimed at exposing "the ideological and fictional nature of our racial categories" (16). Though Lionnet sees liberating potential in *métissage*, Condé treats *métissage* with some scepticism. In her novels, preconceived notions "unitary origins" and "racial purity" or even about *métissage* itself, form basic problems that the ironic narrative voice uses to describe and critique a creolised world that remains racist and sexist, and is seldom redeemed by solidarity among oppressed groups. The advantage of following Lionnet's lead in retaining *métissage* as a productive term is that the subversive and feminist perspective she implies lends itself to an analysis of gender issues, even if the way those gender issues play themselves out in Condé's novels subvert the very notion of solidarity.

The way Condé weaves sexual and racial oppression throughout her narratives obliges us to maintain a historically motivated, race-related sense of the concept of *métissage* in order to understand its dynamics in her works. The historical framework for *métissage* arose when the colonial plantation economy of the West Indies began to function (especially after the decimation of indigenous populations) through slave labour and the African slave trade (Toumson 22). This system posited a colour bar as an absolute border never to be crossed. Otherwise, the definition of the slave as property would lose its clarity if not its validity. *Métissage* was on the one hand a materialization of that line (92-3), performance both of the dichotomy between the races and of sexual fantasies of the forbidden. On the other hand *métissage* was a non-place in the social structure, a mode of existence that could never be acknowledged, at least within the human realm (92).

Condé's novel *La vie scélérate* performs a narrative of *métissage*[4] in the sense that through the act of narrating, the *métis* narrator explores the ways in which her mother and great uncles crossed racial boundaries and thereby put in place the ambiguities she now faces as a woman, a daughter, and an identity-conscious member of a Black family.[5] Claude Elaïse Louis does not identity herself as narrator until well over halfway through the novel, and she presents her narrative as a conventional multi-generational family saga, beginning with a patriarchal founder: "Mon aïeul Albert Louis qui n'était encore l'aïeul de personne, mais un beau nègre d'environ trente-deux ans ..." (13) [My father Albert Louis was not yet the forebear of anyone that day but a handsome Negro of around thirty-two years of age (3)].[6] This "family saga" begins at the moment when Albert Louis, described as a "nègre," first decides to break away from the plantation economy and embark on the adventurous course that will eventually lead to the *embourgeoisement* of his descendants.

By beginning with her ancestor, Claude withholds from her readers not simply her presence as an autodiegetic narrative voice, but also the knowledge of her gender. What's more, she conceals her "mixed-race" origin, and the particularly marginalized nature of her life as the illegitimate, unwanted and forgotten offspring of a relationship between a black woman and the son of an established and respectable *métis* family who had already been promised in marriage to a woman of his own "class." Without immediately revealing her difference, Claude nevertheless establishes both a claim of belonging and the tenuousness of her existence: "Ma propre existence était dans les limbes. Celle de ma mère aussi. Même mon grand-père Jacob, n'avait pas commencé de se tapir dans le ventre de sa mère" (19) [My own existence was still in limbo. That of my mother as well. Even my grandfather Jacob was not yet nesting in his mother's belly (9)]. Once the identity of the first-person narrator is revealed, all these relationships fall into place: that is, a version of this family's history that is not centered on the life and vision of the patriarch, but one that is controlled by a female *métis* voice, the voice of Claude.

In this sense Condé privileges the voice and version of the marginalized Other through the revelation of *métissage*. As Marie-Agnès Sourieau discusses, Claude's subversive narrational act enables her to affirm the creoleness of her family while keeping a precise account of its resistance to that process. "Mais si le *métissage* a une valeur émancipatrice," Sourieau writes, "il s'agit aussi de garder le souvenir de [son] pays dans les mémoires, de lui garder sa voix. C'est le rôle de Claude, «l'enfant de notre demain», énonce Jacob. C'est elle qui, tout en recueillant l'héritage du passé, va rompre avec la stérilité de l'unicité d'origine pour assumer le caractère composite de la culture antillaise" ("La Vie" 122) [But if *métissage* has an emancipating value, it is a matter of keeping the memory of [one's] homeland in people's minds, of preserving its voice. This is the role of Claude, "the child of our tomorrow," says Jacob. It is she who, while piecing together the heritage of the past, will break with the sterility and unicity of origin to assume the composite character of West Indian culture]. *Métissage* thus has value in that it can resuscitate actual family history in spite of attempts to bury 'shameful' elements.

The preoccupation with "unicity of origin," combined with the fear of transgressing the bounds of racial purity, reflect the spatial metaphor of the "color bar" that becomes even more revealing in relation to this novel when translated by Roger Toumson into mythical terms. Toumson focuses on the Cain figure as an important underlying structure in *métissage* mythology. The notion of two brothers—one pure, the other impure, and the racially impure having an unnatural hatred for his half-brother and ultimately the desire to kill him—conveys both the sense of monstrosity and illegitimacy associated with the *métis* and the fear that the "racially pure" person experiences when faced with the image of impurity. As the embodiment of "impurity," the *métis* both confirms and challenges the racial ideology that establishes "purity." The motif of fratricide "réapparaît, plus particulièrement, chez les écrivains caribéens et latino-américains, sous l'espèce de l'antagonisme de deux demi-frères nés d'une même mère mais de pères racialement différenciés" (138-39) [reappears, more particularly, in the works of Caribbean and Latin American writers in the form of antagonism between two half-brothers born of the same mother but of racially differentiated fathers]. This motif appears in various forms in *La vie scélérate*, particularly in Albert's rejection of Bert (Albert's first son from an earlier marriage) from the "official" Louis family when he marries a white woman in France. His father's decision to disown him evokes the banishment of the reprobate Cain.[7]

Albert's philosophy echoes the Cain motif because the patriarch considers himself racially pure and attempts to control or even cut off family members when they cross the color bar. Albert's notions of racial purity stem in part from a reaction to racism: he was so moved by the ideas of Marcus Garvey that he took race pride to absurd extremes. When Albert sees Garvey's claim on a poster in English, translated by the narrator in a footnote—"J'apprendrai au Noir à voir la beauté qui est en lui" (43) [I shall teach the Black Man to see beauty in himself] (34) —it reverberates through the consciousness of several generations as the idea is written, transmitted and remembered. Later in the narrative, Albert sends a letter to Garvey with his son Jacob who has joined a trade mission to New York. Jacob arrives at Garvey's headquarters only to be told the leader has just died, so the letter is never delivered. In it, however, Albert writes: "Je n'ai rien fait de ma vie. Et pourtant comme vous, je suis fier de ma race. Je crois à une race noire pure autant qu'un Blanc qui a du respect pour lui-même croit à une race blanche pure" (119) [I have done nothing with my life. And yet like you, I am proud of my race. I believe in a pure black race as much as a self-respecting white believes in a pure white race (122)]. Claude's interest in her black ancestor is closely related to Albert's recurrent interest in the life and teaching of Marcus Garvey. Although ancestor and descendent share a concern for racial identity and self-affirmation, the patriarch's "Black consciousness" has led him to a denial of the humanity of the only person in his family who is committed to preserving his memory. Perhaps the perception of his uselessness represents Claude's viewpoint more than his own, since she comments: "Je ne possède pas le texte de cette lettre, mais je peux aisément en imaginer le contenu" (ibid.) [I do not have the text of this letter in my possession but can easily imagine its contents (ibid.)]. A narrator determined to document her family's past, uncharacteristically speculative in this case given the meticulous archivist that she is, attributes to her Black ancestor a claim to identity that marks him as a defender of "racial purity." At the same time, she prepares the way for the incongruence that her own presence as his descendant will imply: not only is she *not* "racially pure," she is also aware of the effects on her family and on her life of the patriarch's desire to maintain "racial purity."

When Albert sends Bert to study in France, a family friend raises the question of mixed race marriage: "Même Lamine Senghor qui est marié à une Picarde! Moi, ma femme est comme toi et comme

147

moi: noire! Là commence notre fierté: à la couleur de nos compagnes" (148) [Even Lamine Senghor's married to a woman of Picardy!
Me, my woman is like you and me: black. That's where our pride
begins: with the color of our women (155)]. Not all readers may be
familiar with Lamine Senghor, Senegalese founder of the "Ligue de
défense de la race nègre," but his name resonates with the family
name of the *négritude* poet Léopold Sédar Senghor, whose wife
was also a white woman from France. Bert's marriage to a white
working-class woman and his virtual disappearance from the Louis
family tree adds further irony to the idea of Senghor's name being
associated with racial betrayal: he is known as one of the most
famous proponents of cultural *métissage* as a means of integrating
African culture into world culture. Near the end of the novel when
Albert is long gone and Thécla's "sin" in bearing the mixed-race
Claude has been told, Dieudonné, one of Albert's grandchildren
comments: "Les savants nous prouvent que les races n'existent
pas. Il n'y a que les cultures. Nos parents et nos grands-parents se
sont mobilisés sur une idée fausse qui va mourir d'elle-même. Mais
dans le cas qui nous préoccupe, je crois que notre aïeul, tout paria
et puant qu'il était aux yeux de la petite et moyenne-bourgeoisie
établie, a manifesté des préjugés de classe! Marie n'aurait pas été
une ouvrière d'usine que la face du monde aurait été changée!"
(318) [Scientists say there is no such thing as race. There are only
cultures. Our parents and grandparents mobilized themselves
around an erroneous idea that will die out of its own accord. But
in the present case I believe our forebear, pariah and outcast that
he was in the eyes of the established bourgeoisie, exhibited class
prejudices! If Marie had not been a factory worker the world as
we know it would have been different! (349)]. In attributing these
words to Dieudonné near the end of her narrative, Claude consigns
to history the principle on which her family was founded. She thus
inscribes the critique of her own exclusion in an ironic class analysis. By this logic, the first Albert had failed to recognize his own
marginality: he severed a branch of his own family tree in order to
maintain status of superiority when, in fact, this superiority had
never been accorded to him.

Early in her account of Albert Louis' life, Claude the archivist
reveals her own elitist judgment as the educated descendant of an
intellectually unsophisticated ancestor: "Je possède le journal que
tint mon aïeul assis au milieu des embruns du pont, son encrier
d'encre violette calé sur un tas de cordages. Il ne présente aucune

valeur littéraire. La syntaxe en est lourde et les fautes d'orthographe fréquentes" (59) [I have the journal my ancestor kept, seated in the middle of the ocean-sprayed deck, his inkpot filled with violet ink and propped against a pile of rope. It is of no literary value. The syntax is awkward and the spelling errors frequent (53)]. Once readers know Claude's identity as narrator, we come to understand that she is not just an innocent seeker of origins but a judge of both her patriarchal ancestor and her mother, and ultimately even of herself. When she does reveal her racial origins (while still withholding her gender), she presents her father Denis Latran as a "mulâtre freluquet mais assez beau qui avait passé sur elle sans la voir" (169) [a young whippersnapper of a mulatto but fairly handsome, who walked past without seeing her (179)] and suggests that her mother was attracted to him by the sting of his arrogance and mistook this emotion for love. This observation implies that Claude sees her birth as the product of an act of sexual and racial politics. She owes her existence to the pride of her great-grandfather relived by her mother, who at the same time compromised the family's "purity" out of a sense of racial self-affirmation, for Claude suggests that her mother was attracted to Denis precisely because her invisibility to him as a black woman became an obstacle for her to overcome. It is hardly surprising, then, that Thécla, who in her daughter's eyes lacked a clear sense of racial identity and consciousness, would abandon her *métis* daughter for the first ten years of her life, only to reclaim her when a legitimizing white step-father became available to adopt this child who conceives herself as the product of a contradictory claim to identity.

When Thécla visits Guadeloupe for her mother's funeral, her father Jacob asks on seeing Claude, "A qui cette enfant-là? [Whose child is this?], and Thécla replies, "C'est à moi!" [It's mine]; but Claude herself could read "la honte de ses yeux" (206) [the shame in her eyes (222)]. The shame is partly in Claude's being *hers*, but also partly in the inability or refusal to answer the other half of the question, to name the absent and racially othered father. This absent father remains nonetheless present in the child presented to the last patriarch of a family determined to define itself as Black. This moment's significance as a peripeteia resides neither in the daughter, who in "hiding" her shame still claims her rightful place as an heiress of the Louis family, nor in the question of the grandfather who eventually accepts Claude as a grand-daughter, but in the memory of the narrating subject re-articulating her mother's ambivalent revelation to fit Claude's own vision of her family's destiny. That vision incorporates into the commemoration of "the Black man's struggle," as exemplified by the patriarch, the memory of the intentionally forgotten *métis* family members (Bert, Bébert son of Bert, Aurélia and even Claude herself who came close to being forgotten). They alone can authenticate (because they have known the same racial oppression that founded his struggle) a continuation of the patriarch's quest for self-affirmation; even though, paradoxically, it was that very quest that led him to deny their existence.

But what is behind this rejection of the *métis* child (figuratively or even literally in the case of both Bert and Claude)? Referring to Freud's *Totem and Taboo*, Toumson shows us how the rejection of the *métis* reprobate corresponds to a totemic sexual prohibition. In a slave-colonial plantation culture, he writes "la race et la couleur sont des emblèmes totémiques. Au même titre que la prohibition de l'inceste, la prohibition du mélange racial est un interdit dont le rôle est de garantir le fonctionnement au sein de la société des fratries et des classes" (116) [race and color are totemic emblems. Like the prohibition of incest, the prohibition of racial mixing is an interdiction whose role is to guarantee the successful functioning within society of sibling-groups and of classes]. While the need to limit symbolic dysfunction within the family and society inspires fear of *métissage*, that totemic aspect also implies the desire for what is feared; in the Freudian terms Toumson uses here, fear is the manifestation of a repressed desire.

In attempting to understand her family's history and destiny, Claude confronts not only its rejection of its own *métissage*, but also the need to understand what led several members of the family (including l'oncle Jean, a hero of Guadeloupian cultural and political pride, and Claude's own mother) to transgress racial barriers. As the slave economy started to wind down in the late 19th century and the forms of repression began to change, the monstrous, menacing version of *métissage* began to give way to an ideology of "harmonious synthesis," a means of bringing the races together: "Placé au confluent des races, [le Métis] est investi d'une fonction médiatrice, d'une mission christique....L'histoire idéologique et symbolique du *métissage* est faite de l'alternance et de l'inversion de deux imageries: l'une dysphorique, damnatrice, l'autre euphorique et salvatrice" (94-5) [Placed at the intersection of races, [the *Métis*] is endowed with a mediating function, with a Christlike mission....The ideological history and the symbolism of *métissage* is constructed from the alternation and inversion of two systems of imagery: one dysphoric and damning, the other euphoric and redemptive]. One suspects that Toumson, in his critique of modern versions of *métissage* ideology and in particular the utopianism of the *créolité* movement in the Caribbean,[8] sees a certain degree of continuity between these recent schools of thought and the 19th century romanticized vision of *métissage*.

Integration and "race-mixing" does not necessarily lead to equality. In the Americas since 1492 "les races et les peuples s'y sont métissés mais sans se mélanger: hybrides mais séparés. Les interdits s'y sont accrus, multipliés, aggravés. C'est donc bien parce que l'utopie du mélange des sangs et de la réunion des âmes ne s'est pas réalisée que le *métissage* demeure une «valeur-refuge» d'avenir, un mythe idéologique d'actualité" (24-5) [races and peoples have been crossed without mixing: hybrid but separate. The prohibitions have grown, multiplied and deepened. It is thus by virtue of the fact that the utopia of mixed blood and the joining of souls has not been realized that *métissage* remains a refuge value, a contemporary ideological myth]. Toumson himself, however, implies that *métissage* as a utopian vision remains desirable though elusive. Reading literary texts in view of their authors' beliefs will necessarily involve interpretation of *métissage*—as liberatory or restrictive—*métissage* continues to return in Condé's narrative preoccupations as an insoluble but tantalizing puzzle.

Claude has been playing a sagacious game. Creating a puzzle for herself and her readers, she conceals herself as if to earn her right to act as the historian of a family that almost failed to recognize or even notice her (until her grandfather was approaching death). She now recognizes what her obsessive search for documentation has been suggesting all along: that the writing of a "family saga" was already an illusion. The scarcity of archival material reflected a deeper forgetfulness that was already at the centre of her identity: the central cause of the Louis family's disintegration was the "forgetting" of Albert's firstborn son Bert. Thécla reproduced this act of forgetting by abandoning her own daughter throughout the latter's childhood. Claude's desire to unearth the connection with Bert's offspring may be seen as her response to their similar feeling of being disowned.

This forgetfulness is on the one hand analyzed by Claude as a result of class and sexist oppression,[9] and on the other hand presented as the major motivation for her to reconstruct the record of that oppression in light of her "chance" meeting with Aurélia. Aurelia, the other *métis* great-grandchild of Albert Louis, dares to accuse the recognized branch of murdering her father and grandfather by its act of neglect and passive disowning. This is why, when describing her childhood exile with a white foster family, Claude reflects: "Ainsi donc, je rejoins Bert et Bébert et j'appartiens comme eux à la lignée de ceux sur qui on fit le silence. De là est née, sans doute, instinctive ma solidarité avec eux" (174) [And so I join with Bert and Bébert, and belong as do they to the lineage of those who are never mentioned. From that no doubt comes my instinctive solidarity with them (186)]. Bert was condemned by his father for disobeying a set of un-stated "strict principles" according to which he had been brought up and which Claude describes as follows: "Il ne fallait fréquenter ni les Blancs ni les mulâtres. Les Blancs étant les ennemis naturels et les mulâtres d'odieux bâtards ayant hérité de l'arrogance de leurs pères et oublié qu'ils sortaient de ventres de négresses. Mais surtout, il fallait fuir les autres nègres, car de toute éternité les nègres ont haï leurs semblables et cherché de toutes leurs forces à leur nuire! Il fallait donc vivre seul. Superbement seul" (72) [One was to frequent neither whites nor mulattoes, the whites being natural enemies and the mulattoes despicable bastards who had inherited the arrogance of their fathers and forgotten that they came from the bellies of Negro women. But above all, one was to avoid other Negroes. For from time immemorial Negroes had hated their fellows and sought with all their might to do them harm. Therefore one was to live alone. Superbly alone (69)]. Her words not only represent the beliefs she associates with her ancestor. They also evoke for the reader the weight of the impossible burden placed on Bert by Albert's attempt to realize his dream of racial integrity, which as a consequence makes his son (and perhaps his perceived rival for the love Elaïse his second wife) an incarnation of his own self-hatred.[10]

The sexual implications adhering to the term *métissage* shown in this struggle between Claude and the patriarch (when Claude joins Bert and Bébert as the unnameable relatives who disobey the taboos against miscegenation), also help to focus our attention on the sexual aspect of oppression underpinning many historical transcultural acts and events. Claude's struggle for voice also calls our attention to the absence of women's voices in much of the mainstream discourse of the creoleness movement. James Arnold remarks that "the more inclusive master narrative that guides the identification of crucial historical moments in the emergence of creole culture in *Lettres créoles* is able to engage critically the *métissage*, both cultural and biological, in which the actors are white male *béké*, and black female slaves" (29). Seeing creole culture through the lens of *métissage* forces us to recognize the costs as well as the benefits of cultural contacts—contacts that are often based on the assumption of both sexual and racial inequality.

Through Claude's role as narrator, *La vie scélérate* breaks new ground in the recognition of this dimension of *métissage* in West Indian culture. We have seen two narrative processes that enable Claude to establish her position in relation to the forebear/patriarch with whom her story begins: her gradual and strategic self-revelation; and the reuniting through her of the two branches of the Louis family: the line that remains "pure" (until Claude arrives), and the line that had "compromised itself." In the third and final process, Claude presents her mother Thécla, the lost soul who, paradoxically, seems to have the least reason for being lost. Perhaps the clearest sign in the novel of a shift from a traditional and patriarchal understanding of *métissage* to something closer to a feminist perspective is that the real incarnation of Albert's self-hatred in Claude's own life is not the vaguely mythologized forebear, but her mother. Claude's relationship with Thécla mirrors Albert's relationship with Bert. As Sourieau explains: "Incapable de surmonter son complexe d'infériorité raciale, elle destitue sa fille de son identité, reproduisant la même oblitération que celle qu'Albert avait infligée à son fils Bert" (1997, 214) [Incapable of overcoming her racial inferiority complex, she robs her daughter of her identity, reproducing the same erasure that Albert had inflicted on his son Bert]. Thécla here plays a pivotal role: she acts as a link between the black family of the Louises, a family rooted in Guadeloupian society and history, and a cosmopolitan, creolized existence engaged in a hopeless search for identity. Without this link provided by her mother, Claude's witness would be nothing more than a family saga that would simply end out of pure exhaustion (exhaustion of memory, of recognized offspring or even of the will to share in a collective memory in the first place), for as the family becomes creolized, it thins out and is about to disappear. Aurélia is the last living descendant of Bert; Claude's father Tima never had other children, and her mother Thécla, despite her one husband and six or more lovers, never had a child other than Claude.

Claude, perhaps a little ironically, refers to Thécla's conception by Tima after repeated miscarriages as a "moment de grâce" (109) [moment of grace (107)], because it was her last chance to have a child. Claude sees her mother through this romantic lens while simultaneously perceiving of her as a black woman whose self-image has been shaped by racism. For example, Claude explains her mother's profound hatred for her uncle Jean's French wife Marietta: "Elle croyait lire au fond de ses yeux un mépris qui n'était peut-être qu'au fond d'elle-même" (142) [Deep within Marietta's eyes Thécla thought she read a contempt that was perhaps only deep within herself (148)]. Is it as a *métis* woman or as a detached, unloved daughter that Claude imagines this sense of scorn on the part of Marietta? Does this imagined scorn ultimately arise from the black woman's scorn for herself? Claude insists that her lack of objectivity in talking about Thécla is irremediable: "Elle m'a trop peu aimée pour que je ne lui en tienne pas rigueur" (165) [She loved me far too little for me to forgive her for it (174)]. These stark words reflect Claude's conviction that her own mother cannot love her. Claude's explanation for this lack of love is unconvincing: "Feignant de mépriser l'estime des bourgeois parce qu'elle savait ne jamais pouvoir l'obtenir. Marginale par excès d'ambitions impossibles à satisfaire! Pour moi, ma mère était en toc!" (*ibid.*) [Pretending to disdain the esteem of the bourgeoisie since she knows she could never earn it. An outsider due to an excess of ambitions impossible to satisfy! For me, my mother was a sham! (*ibid.*)]. Yet is Claude's judgment later attenuated by her repetition of Thécla's statement to her after Jean's funeral? "Quand tu es devant moi, ce n'est pas toi, Coco, que je vois. C'est ton père avec son sourire belles dents blanches de garçon bien élevé alors que le dernier coupeur de cannes avait plus d'honnêteté que lui.… Quand je te vois, oui, ce n'est pas de ma faute, c'est tout cela que je vois! Eux, lui!…Nous sommes condamnées à marcher jusqu'au bout de nos vies sans jamais pouvoir nous donner la main!" (274-5) [When you are with me, it's not you I see, Coco. It's your father, with his fine white-toothed, well-brought-up smile, when the lowest cane cutter has more honesty in him that he did.… When I see you, yes, I can't help it, it's all that I see! Them, him!... We are doomed to go on until the end of our lives without ever being able to help each other! (301)].

Sourieau insightfully interprets this passage as a reflection of "the racist ideology that underlies the socio-racial relations of [Guadeloupe]" ("Une écriture," 215). From the narrator's point of view, the mother's confession further demonstrates that racial complexes are only mediated by the face of the *métis*, which is ultimately condemned to invisibility. The dominant male gaze[11] replaces the gazed-upon face of the child waiting for her parent's gesture of acknowledgement. In this way, Claude's mother denies her daughter's self affirmation of self because her mother obsesses over the racial hurt inflicted on her by the child's father, an injury she now associates with the child. This failure confirms sexual as well as racial hegemony. Claude understands the failure, despite her lack of sympathy for her mother, as a permanent impediment to her mother's fulfillment as much as to her own. Claude knows that *métissage* must manifest itself as a physical sign or mask in order to bear witness to this imagined (since Thécla is actually looking into her daughter's face) though real residual sexual power of the male gaze: the memory of a *métis* man looking in superiority at her mother continues to disrupt their relationship as women and as women of color.

Condé's treatment of racial and sexual relations reflects a determined effort to question received ideas—be they the most canonical myths of the colonial experience or archetypes of the anti-colonial struggle—and to bring out the contradictions and paradoxes that all such ideas involve. Condé illustrates such contradictions through the failure of a *métis* narrator like Claude to identify with her mother, ironically because of a *métis* father's disdain. Condé refuses any essentially positive view of *métissage* as a means of overcoming racism. *Métissage* often divides the family, as when Dieudonné's French wife in *La vie scélérate* leads to his alienation from his brothers; or it is alternatively associated with personal ruin, exile and death, as in the case of Albert's first son Bert whose marriage to a white working-class woman seals his abandonment by his patriarchal black father. Condé is nevertheless acutely aware of the persistence of *métissage* in post-colonial sexual and racial relations, with its political implications as an uneven but equally unending power struggle. Enough of a feminist to recognize the need, given this struggle, for solidarity among women, she is too much an iconoclast and too honest to suggest that such solidarity is often possible. At the same time, Condé has underlined the role played by women in the history of *métissage* and put in place subjects reflecting on their own experience of that history. In so doing, however, she does not allow her ironic stance to deny the historical reality of oppression of Black people by the European colonial enterprise: one has only to remember the gaze of a *métis* man's "white" derision that Thécla admits to seeing in the face of her daughter.

Notes

1. [In French, originally defined as (at times forced) race-mixing or hybridization of plants; it has come to mean, briefly, the amalgamation or braiding of diverse cultural components or transculturation that creates a new cultural entity or identity. Eds.]

2. See "The Gendering of Créolité" by James Arnold, as well as Françoise Vergès, who writes in "Métissage, discours masculin et déni de la mère": "Pour la plupart de ces écrivains [de la créolité], le métissage se conjuge [sic] au masculin. Point de femme métisse" (82) [For most of these writers (of the creoleness movement), *métissage* is conjugated in the masculine. There is no *métisse* woman]. Unless otherwise indicated, all English translations are my own.

3. Glissant's more recent texts establish a shift from *métissage* to *creolization*.. In a passage introduced by the question "And why *creolization* and not *métissage*?" (*Introduction à une poétique du divers*, 16-7), Glissant describes *creolization* as *métissage* plus a surplus value which is its unpredictability. Accidents of history subvert systematic schemes of colonial progress toward homogeneous cultures, whereas *métissages* constitute predictable events.

4. In order to emphasize the central role of the narrator, this use of the term "narrative" follows Gérard Genette's canonical definition of *récit*: "Je propose … de nommer *histoire* le signifié ou contenu narratif …, *récit* proprement dit le signifiant, énoncé, discours ou texte narratif lui-même, et *narration* l'acte narratif producteur et, par extension, l'ensemble de la situation réelle ou fictive dans laquelle il prend place" (72) [I propose to call *story* the signified, or the narrative content…, *narrative* proper the signifier, discourse or narrative text itself, and *narration* the productive narrative act, and by extension, the totality of the real or fictional situation in which that act takes place]. Claude's act of narration *as a métisse woman* produces a text that is, as a result, a narrative of *métissage*.

5. In her essay in *Penser la créolité*, Marie-Agnès Sourieau recognizes the importance of this narrational aspect of this novel when she explains how the *métis* woman descendant (Claude) of a black patriarch (*l'aïeul* Albert) takes over the role of narrator (114). In "*La Vie scélérate*: une écriture de l'h/Histoire" she points out that the "roman familial" Claude sets out to write is a common scenario in West Indian literature (208).

6.   The narrator announces more than half-way through the novel, "Moi, Claude Elaïse Louis, je naquis à la sauvette dans une clinique du XVe arrondissement à Paris, la nuit du 3 avril 1960" (179) [I Claude Elaïse Louis, was born in secret in a small private hospital in the fifteenth arrondissement of Paris, on the night of April 23, 1960 (185)].

7.   Played out in historical situations of racial contact, this myth can also reflect, according to Toumson, a "structure familiale racialisée (139) [a racialized family structure]. In this structure, the *paternal* function of the white master as a free, creative genitor and as the ultimate figure of authority both depends upon and signals the absence of the black "genitor."

8.   For example Toumson views *négritude* and *créolité* as "deux lectures complémentaires d'un même *symbolisme dominé*" (75) [two complementary readings of the same symbolism of being dominated]. They correspond "à la transformation par inversion d'un discours politique en un discours apolitique" (76) [to the transformation by inversion of a political discourse into an apolitical discourse]. Thus his choice of the term *métissage* as the basis of his research does not reflect a preference for more old-fashioned terminology but a refusal to see creoleness as a new and progressive stage in an illusionary "evolution" of racial relations.

9.   For example the name of Bert (Albert) commemorated Albert's dream of reproducing himself, so that his decision to torpedo his firstborn's development, send him to Angers and abandon him finally for marrying a working-class white woman, reflects the souring of his dream of "teaching the Black Man to see the beauty in himself." On the other hand, the name of Jacob, the other first-born, commemorates the black American friend murdered by racists and asserts the right of survival and freedom of lack peoples.

10.   This passage is described by Sourieau as the result of traumatic experiences dating back to Albert's original suffering and passed on to his descendants ("une écriture" 212).

11.   That male gaze is also a societal gaze: it is not only Denis, but also his family and his class that Thécla sees looking at her when she looks at Claude. This gaze may be considered patriarchal in the sense that Denis used Thécla as an object and abandoned her for his own social convenience. It is also racial since he would choose a more advantageous marriage with a métis woman. Finally, the effect of this gaze is an example of hegemony because it is Thécla's inability to overcome its influence on her mind, especially in relation to her métis daughter, that contradicts and undermines her commitment to maintaining the respect for her African origins (and Marcus Garvey) she received from her grandfather.

(UP)ROOTING THE FAMILY TREE: GENEALOGY AND SPACE IN MARYSE CONDÉ'S FICTION

Johanna X. K. Garvey

"La passiflorinda donne une fleur mauve et faiblement parfumée qui n'a pas beaucoup de valeur médicinale. Ce sont ces rameaux et surtout ses racines qui en possèdent."

–La Vie scélérate (46)

[The passionflower displays a mauve and lightly perfumed bloom that has little medicinal value. It is the branches and above all the roots that do the healing.]

–Tree of Life (38)

Like many contemporary writers with origins in the Caribbean, Maryse Condé explores identities formed in diaspora—in her case, that created by the African slave trade and forced migration to the Americas and Europe. Her novels often trace such routes in a process that researches lineages and personal histories, as a female character seeks to place herself on the branch of a family tree. This project generally follows a patriarchal logic, however: fathers root the tree, and children are its fruit; wives bear children and then disappear; mothers are neglectful if not altogether absent from their children's lives. As one critic notes of the concept of diaspora, its original meaning "summons up the image of scattered seeds, and we should remember that in Judeo-Christian (and Islamic) cosmology, seeds are metaphorical for the male 'substance' that is traced in genealogical histories.... Diaspora, in its traditional sense, thus refers us to a system of kinship reckoned through men and suggests the questions of legitimacy in paternity that patriarchy generates"

(Helmreich 245). In addition, botanical metaphors are frequently used to link people and places in this process of genealogical exploration and mapping: "The metaphor of diaspora, especially when mapped onto a particular territory, naturalizes historical connections and ideas about territory in a fashion similar to [arboreal metaphors]" (246). In her fiction, Maryse Condé employs similar connections between lineage and territory, mapping diaspora as experienced by a plethora of Caribbean subjects. Consequently, readers benefit from exploring the implications of such concepts as the "family tree": how might an author simultaneously represent and challenge colonial/imperial norms, themselves "rooted" in hetero-patriarchy?

On the surface, Maryse Condé's fiction appears to stand in contrast to the works of a writer like Dionne Brand, where genealogies are partial and often push male progenitors to the sidelines or omit them altogether. Condé's characters repeatedly cling to the notion of a discernable lineage, a path traced backwards through generations to arrive at origins—the doubling of 'routes/roots' that has become a catchphrase in Caribbean studies. Condé structures many of her narratives by conventional depictions of roots, trees, lineages; even the titles of some of her novels (as translated into English) point to her seeming obsession with tracing family lines and seeking origins—*Tree of Life*, for instance, or *The Last of the African Kings*.[1] Many of her fictional works thus envision tracing lineages as her characters delve into the past, for as she says about one of the characters in *La Vie scélérate*, "Henceforth, history must be subordinated to the process of collective or family history" (Pfaff 67; 99). In creating such family histories, Condé may seem to move beyond nation, but not to relinquish "a community apart from the rhetorics of kinship and the naturalized heterosexism and patriarchy that it perpetuates" (Helmreich 247). That is, while each text may rely on irony to critique characters' longing for solid family ties or to undermine their desire for a unified Black identity, Condé's narratives appear to be structured by conventional concepts of genealogy in order to define both relationships between characters and the trajectories they follow in their not-so-nomadic wanderings. In *La Vie scélérate/Tree of Life*, the protagonist Coco is researching and writing her family history, from Guadeloupe to Panama to San Francisco, New York, and Paris; the narrative is structured as a self-conscious telling of both the search and of the family stories it uncovers.[2] Can such a reflexive strategy serve to undermine con-

160

ventional representations of family, uproot the family tree perhaps, and produce more creative, inclusive notions of identity? For some readers, Condé's novels may appear to solidify reductive ways of locating genealogy, for they seem to reaffirm hetero-patriarchal constructions based in colonial and imperial models; but they are more complex than that, and she herself would resist an assessment of her work as rooted in place, time, and family. She contends that wandering is crucial for the creative writer; being a nomad is much more productive than putting down roots (Pfaff 28; 46).[3] Certainly Maryse Condé's novels are wide-ranging and nomadic, each cast of characters representing the African Diaspora from a myriad locations in the Caribbean, the U.S., and Europe, with gestures back to Africa. And in commenting on her works, Condé emphasizes the shared history of these multiple spaces and identities, while also stressing the necessity of living not in the past but the present, as seen in numerous essays in this volume.

Indeed, on closer reading, and when examined as a collective *œuvre*, Condé's fiction illustrates perhaps better than that of other contemporary Caribbean writers the complexities and contradictions, the multiple histories and "fragmented Diversity" (Glissant, *CD* 97) of Antillean identities and spaces.[4] Condé's collection of narratives also bodies forth what Glissant has termed "Relation," when he writes, "We were circling around the thought of Chaos, sensing that the way Chaos itself goes around is the opposite of what is ordinarily understood by 'chaotic' and that it opens onto a new phenomenon: Relation, or totality in evolution, whose order is continually in flux and whose disorder one can imagine forever" (*Poetics of Relation* 133). Glissant suggests that rather than a clearly delineated family tree where relations are straightforward and easily traceable, Caribbean "relation" is messy and chaotic, arising as it does from intersecting routes and intertwining roots. Condé's depictions of Caribbean histories and identities, and of familial connections—and especially of the search to retrace lines and fill in gaps in genealogies—capture these complexities.[5]

An investigation of three of Condé's novels tracing this concern with lineage reveals that a different version of genealogical excavation, recuperation, and projection emerges. Given that this vision remains for the most part hetero-patriarchical, it may not take as radical a form as the "antigenealogy" conceived of by Deleuze and Guattari as "not simply an inversion of existing hierarchies"; but Condé's vision also challenges conventional depictions of genealogy by representing an effort to insert a matrilineage into the family narrative, and thus like their "antigenealogy" envisions "a model of human experience that remains dynamic, chaotic and multiple" (Rohrback 483). Condé's *œuvre* suggests ways to manipulate standard genealogy, and if not to uproot the family tree, to offer creative strategies for confronting the legacies of a history marked by crossings and fissures, upheavals and gaps, the traumatic heritage of the African Diaspora.[6]

Maryse Condé's concern for lineages takes shape beginning with her first novel, *Hérémakhonon* (1976), which follows the Guadeloupean Veronica from her home island to France and then to Africa. While this novel is not one of the primary texts under discussion, the protagonist frequently expresses her belief that Africans enjoy a stronger, more direct link to previous generations, and that an African can trace his family tree and know with certainty who are his ancestors. In contrast, Veronica locates her own roots in the slave trade, "du sperme du blanc égaré dans des vagins des négresses" (38) [a white man's sperm gone astray in some black woman's womb (17)]. She considers herself a "bastard" and mockingly refers to the family tree from which she is attempting cut herself off by journeying to Africa. Her views change over the course of the narrative, however, and eventually she does come to understand that she has made a mistake. "Mes aïeux, je ne les ai pas trouvés" [I didn't find my ancestors], she says. "Trois siècles et demi m'en ont séparée. Ils ne me reconnaissent pas plus que je ne les reconnais. Je n'ai trouvé qu'un homme avec aïeux qui les garde jalousement pour lui seul, qui ne songe pas à les partager avec moi" (193) [Three and a half centuries have separated me from them. They didn't recognize me any more than I recognized them. All I found was a man with ancestors who's guarding them jealously for himself and wouldn't dream of sharing them with me (136)]. Although the protagonist has failed in her quest to unearth roots in Africa as a way of breaking with those in the West Indies, the several references to the Middle Passage and to the concomitant traumas that have left a lasting mark on the Caribbean establish a context for the (re)searching of identity that guides many of Condé's later novels.[7]

Over the course of Condé's *œuvre*, we see a gradual movement away from both Africa and family trees and toward a new view of roots that turns slave ships into maternal bellies pregnant with Antillean generations, West Indian relations. Oceanic spaces will take on greater significance, while the emphasis on patrilineage—

literally and figuratively on *sperm*—is treated with increasing irony. Condé's characters, especially her female protagonists, become passengers on carefully charted voyages who explore the multifaceted meaning of Caribbean identity. In *La vie Scélérate*, a young woman moves toward her own rewriting of family history, recuperating and then discarding the text of a male ancestor as she prepares to compile her own version; in *Les derniers rois mages/The Last of the African Kings*, another young woman disappears into Africa, while her parents cling to illusions of African origin that serve no clear purpose; and in *Desirada*, yet another young woman finally relinquishes her search for an unknown father and embraces the ability to shape her own identity. In these narratives of Caribbean "family trees," Condé fashions and then sheds different costumes in which to clothe the Caribbean subject who seeks selfhood in origins and an identity in untraceable roots. Perhaps the ocean itself, surrounding and shaping the West Indies and covering those lost traces, can become the site of pathways to identity and also to the future.[8]

While *La vie scélérate* (1987) [*Tree of Life* (1992)] begins with the male progenitor and erases his wife, the first-person narrator introduces herself more than halfway through the novel as a female descendant, Claude Elaïse Louis or Coco. Engaged in finding her own identity as she searches for information on her family, she also relies on the writings of her forebear, Albert Louis: "Je possède le journal que tint mon aïeul…La syntaxe en est lourde et les fautes d'orthographe fréquente. Aussi, je ne prendrai pas la petite d'en reproduire des extraits" (60) [I have the journal my ancestor kept.… [The] syntax is awkward and the spelling errors frequent. Therefore I shall not take the trouble to reprint extracts from it (53)]. Though she refers to this ancestral text, she in fact silences Albert's voice, replacing it with her own telling of family histories. As Coco seeks to find her place in the cross-cultural mix, this telling also spans generations and continents; and even if Coco appears to be more conscious of her state as a fatherless child, her frequent reference to "bellies" underscores the role of maternity in her tale. The text itself reminds us that the original "belly" is manifold, for the slave ships that bore ancestors to the Americas are succeeded by generations of women: Theodora, mother of the ancestor Albert; Elaïse, his wife; and Louise, mother to Elaïse. In fact, Coco's full name pays homage to these maternal ancestors even as she herself bemoans the lack of a father. The man who fathered her—one of her mother Thécla's many lovers—abandoned the two in France when Coco was an infant, so Coco believes that she lacks roots and seeks out "des miettes d'information pour les engranger dans le lieu sûr de ma tête" (277) [crumbs of information to store them in the safety of my mind" (293)].

When asked whose child she is, Coco can answer only after her mother Thécla has brought her "home" to Guadeloupe and introduced her to that side of her family: "Dans les premier temps, m'interroger ainsi revenait à me mettre à la question, puisque ma réponse révélait la moitié obscure et béante de mon origine. Père Inconnu. Absent. Fugueur. En cavale. Indifférent. Indigne. A présent, cela m'était bien égal, cette béance à mon flanc!" (331-32) [In earlier times, questioning me that way was tantamount to torturing me, since my answer revealed the dark and untenanted half of my origins. Father Unknown. Absent. Gone away. On the run. Indifferent. Unsuitable. At present it was all the same to me, that gap in my flank! (351)]. Through her mother she has found a lineage, so that now she can say, "Moi, je n'avais plus honte. J'avais planté mon drapeau dans l'île (332) [I, I was no longer ashamed. I had planted my flag on the island (351)], an ironically masculine image. The narrative emphasizes repeatedly the heterosexual and coupled nature of such a definition of self via family and rootedness; as for example when Coco and her young friend Melissa come across a couple in the park having sex: "...nos pieds butèrent sur les racines emmêlées et noueuses d'un caoutchouc.... Voici que touchés par la baguette d'une de ces Carabosses toujours prêtes à errer là où elles ne doivent pas et à jeter leurs mauvais sorts, elles prirent la forme d'un homme et d'une femme, les derniers que notre naïveté se serait attendue à voir dans cette tenue..." (263) [...our feet stumbled over the knotted and tangled roots of a rubber tree.... And now, touched by the magic wand of one of those wicked witches forever ready to stray where they should not and to cast their evil spells, they took the form of a man and a woman, the very last whom our naïveté would have expected to see in that state of dress" (277)]. At every turn, Coco runs up against the heterosexual and coupled nature of roots, which becomes an insistence that one must issue from a recognized union of father and mother. The jeers of children and the scorn expressed by adults about Coco's *illegitimacy* also underscore the value placed on legal paternity, reflected in a set of cultural expectations and judgments that the text both asserts and subverts.

(Up)Rooting the Family Tree: Genealogy and Space in Maryse Condé's Fiction

In a study of genealogy and fiction, Lee Quinby argues that while all genealogy is fiction, all fiction is not genealogical. Her definition of genealogical fiction illuminates what Condé achieves in *La vie scélérate*, and in her works as a whole: "Genealogical fiction focuses on the rogue events, people and places that are excised from conventional historical and literary narratives so as to problematize the founding tenets of accepted ('acceptable') history: the tracing of origin as the singular, miraculous moment from which all meaning and privilege derive; the insistence on continuity and influence; and the disavowal of contingency, accident, and novelty in the dispersion of events that have impacts on our lives. Fiction that is genealogical challenges the will to knowledge that freezes the past by claiming its injustices and cruelties to be ordained or inevitable" (xix).

Indeed, Condé produces such "genealogical fictions" in which she explores the meanings of Caribbeanness for characters who struggle to uncover missing histories by researching on a fictional level what the fiction is exploring on the cultural and political levels. At key moments in *La vie scélérate*, Coco appears ready to emerge as the griotte who will create a new story, as she is clearly destined to be a writer. "Il se préparait ce temps," she says, "où personne ne saurait plus raconter le passé familial, faute de connaissance. Où les vivants n'apparaîtraient plus au jour après d'interminables gestations de ventre en ventre pour se doter d'un capital génétique séculaire. Où le présent ne serait plus que le présent. Et l'individu que l'individu" (343) ["The time would come," she says, "when none would be able to recount the family's past for lack of knowledge. When the living would no longer issue forth endowed with an ancient genetic heritage after interminable pregnancies in one belly or another. When the present would be nothing but the present. And the individual nothing but the individual" (363-64)]. Yet the pull of family is too strong—and the desire for genealogy as constitutive of identity too powerful—for Coco to resist. As she says in the final paragraph of the novel: "Et d'ailleurs saurais-je faire mentir le sang de toute ma lignée—et c'est là l'autre aspect de cette histoire, mon histoire—depuis mon aïeul Albert avec ses belles dents à manger le monde...jusqu'à ma mère, oui, même elle, surtout elle, qui saigna de toutes les défaites et brûla de toutes les désillusions avant de prendre refuge de l'autre côté du monde...(346) [And anyway, how could I deny the blood of my entire ancestry—and this is the other aspect of this story, my story—beginning with my forebear Albert with his fine teeth made for devouring the world.... up to my mother, yes, even she, especially she, who bled from all her failures and was consumed by all her disillusions before taking refuge on the far side of the world (368)]. Coco's words illustrate how powerful this desire for "bloodlines" remains, specifically for the female descendant who aspires to authorship.[9]

Despite this adherence to an ancestry rooted in the male, this lineage ends with Coco as daughter of Thécla, and as a writer who may go on to narrate new stories now that some of the past has been pieced together and set down in words. Coco's narrative—the first-person "I" present from the first page—personifies the proliferation of family across a huge swath of the globe. As she says near the story's end, "Il faudrait que je la raconte [l'histoire] et ce serait mon monument aux morts à moi. Un livre bien différent de ceux ambitieux qu'avait rêvés d'écrire ma mère…. Un livre…qui pèserait quand même son poids de chair et de sang. Histoire des miens" (337-38) [I would have to tell [the story] and it would be a memorial monument of my own. A book quite different from those ambitious ones my mother had dreamed of writing…. A book…heavy with its weight of flesh and blood. The story of my people (357)]. She performs her own (re)mapping of genealogies in the written word and refuses linearity in favor of a chaotic diversity—rhizomatic wanderings rather than limited branchings from a single root. Her story-telling also dis-places the bellies of slave ships as a site of origin and births a potential vision of Caribbean identity.

In a subsequent novel, *Les derniers rois mages* (1992) [*The Last of the African Kings* (1997)], Condé continues to trace family roots throughout the Diaspora—from Abomey in Africa, outwards to Martinique and Guadeloupe, to the Southern U.S. as well as New York City, to France, and back to Benin, via Anita, the young daughter of the central couple. In this novel, however, traced by an ironic narrative hand that refuses to validate history or to value Blackness in and of itself, all paths prove fruitless.[10] The daughter Anita remains at best a shadowy presence, glimpsed sporadically but never the focus of attention in the dueling tales of her parental genealogies.

As in Condé's other novels, ancestry here is multivalenced. Even though the connections to an African lineage are questioned and even mocked, such a tie is the founding pretext for the entire narrative. In the novel's opening scene, Anita's father Spero, husband of the American Debbie, awakens from a nightmare, and

> [il] ouvrit les yeux sur le portrait de son arrière grand-père qu'il avait peint lui-même à 14 ans à partir de la photographie qui depuis trois générations s'étalait sur la cloison de la salle à manger de la maison familiale. Le vieillard avait emmené avec lui dans l'exil [aux Antilles] cinq de ses femmes [et d'autres membres de la famille]. Djéré, le grand-père de Spéro, se trouvait à l'extrême gauche dans les bras de la plus âgée des reines, béat, bâtard apparemment bien-aimé que pourtant la famille avait laissé derrière elle avec quelques objets aussitôt devenus reliques, quand elle était repartie pour l'Afrique. Cet abandon avait bouleversé toute l'existence de Djéré et de ses descendants (13-14).
>
> [his] eyes opened on the portrait of his great-grandfather that he himself had painted at the age of fourteen from the photograph that for three generations had adorned the dining-room of the family home. His great-grandfather had brought with him into exile [in the West Indies] five of the leopard wives [and other family members]. Djéré, Spero's grandfather, was cradled on the far left in the arms of the oldest queen; this blissful, apparently beloved illegitimate son, however, would be left behind by the family together with other relics when they returned to Africa. This abandonment would dramatically affect Djéré's entire existence and that of his descendants. (5)]

Just as Coco in *La vie scélérate* is marked by her "illegitimate" status—the lack of a father—Djéré's "failed ancestry" is passed on to generations of sons; all the while in the U.S., Debbie and her friends blindly revere the connections to African royalty.

Condé's text satirizes, from multiple angles, an attraction to African "roots" and the identities deriving from such fantasized lineages. As Spero himself thinks when considering Anita's decision to work in Benin, "Le passé doit être mis à mort. Sinon, c'est lui qui tue. Est-ce que ce n'était pas toutes ces bêtises d'ancêtre et d'Afrique qui avaient fait de Djéré et de Justin ce qu'ils étaient devenus? Deux Rois Mages, deux ivrognes, risée du morne Verdol? Est-ce que ce n'était pas ce qui faisait le malheur de trop de noirs autour d'eux, tellement occupés à se bâtir d'imaginaires généalogies qu'ils n'avaient plus la force de conquérir à leur tour leur Amérique? Qu'espérait-elle? Qu'attendait-elle de ce voyage jusqu'aux sources du temps d'antan?" (124) [The past must be condemned to death. Otherwise it will become the killer. Wasn't it all that nonsense about an ancestor and Africa that turned Djéré and Justin [Djéré's son] into what they were? Two Wise Men, two drunkards, the laughingstock of the Morne Verdol? Wasn't this the misfortune of too many blacks they knew who were so busy building imaginary family trees that they had lost out on conquering their own America? What was she hoping for? What did she expect from this voyage to the very beginnings of time long ago? (82)]. Such words echo Condé's own statements as she comments with approbation on Spero's philosophy: "The quest is over.... He understands that people must live in the present and confront present-day problems instead of constantly living with their eyes turned toward what went before, toward a more or less mythic time in the past" (Pfaff 95; 139-40). Yet the novel seeks out the fictional past, represented in the twin threads of Anita's parentage, as it interweaves with an historical past to create an imagined community; so while Spero may voice a rejection of history both familial and global, he also seeks to ease his sense of disconnection in the present: "Chez lui? Est-ce que ces mots avaient encore un sens? Après tant et tant d'années d'exil, est-ce qu'une terre est toujours natale? Et est-ce qu'on est toujours natif? On arrive dans le pays et on ne connaît plus ni sa parole ni sa musique. On cherche sans jamais le trouver le *piébwa* de son placenta. Coupé à ras par les promoteurs immobiliers.... Non, il n'avait plus de place nulle part. Lui aussi, comme l'ancêtre, il était en exil" (169-170) [Home? Did these words still have a meaning? After years and years of exile, is any soil still native? And do you still belong? You arrive home and no longer recognize the words or the music. You look but the tree with your placenta is gone. Chopped down by the property developers.... He no longer had any place to turn. He, too, like the ancestor, was in exile (115-116)]. The text complicates visions of home and concepts of identity by underscoring this exilic state while also limning the threads that link the ancient African kingdom of Abomey to the Martinique and Guadeloupe of Spero's forebears, and to Crocker Island off the coast of Charleston where Spero and Debbie have settled.

Throughout the novel, Djéré's notebooks, as well as some of the passages from an omniscient narrator, represent threads that trace back to the African ancestor; and near the end of the narrative we learn that the dead ancestor, no longer in exile, is bored in the land of the dead. He thus seeks to live again and manages to do so. Lodging himself in the body of a newborn African child on 6 January 1980, he becomes the new son. The patriarchal (and heterosexual) genealogy comes full circle and reestablishes itself, while daughters are silenced or eliminated by the narrative: Anita never speaks from Africa, and the new African son's twin sister is stillborn.[11] Silencing thus accompanies a scene of male birthing, in which females are patently erased. As Anne McClintock argues, such a preoccupation with male origins also marks imperialism: "Historically, the male desire for a guaranteed relation to origin—securing, as it does, male property and power—is contradicted by the sexual doubling of origins, by women's visibly active role in producing a child and men's uncertain and fleeting contribution. The insistence on patrimony marks a denial.... The sexual scene of origins…finds an analogy in the imperial scene of discovery.... Hence the imperial fixation on naming, on acts of 'discovery,' baptismal scenes and birthing rituals" (29). In *Les derniers rois mages* we see such a denial, and no clear suggestion of ways to counter the vision of origins as male, family trees as rooted in patrimony. Of course, as numerous critics note, Condé's works are written in an ironic mode, which helps to explain the dis-ease often expressed about her fiction and critics' frustrated attempts to locate and label these texts.[12] Certainly this narrative mocks both any character's belief in the African ancestor and Debbie's blind worship of this version of genealogy. And the story does not end with the rebirth of the (male) ancestor, but with Spero awaiting Debbie's return, thinking of the sea and of death and imagining a watery suicide. He does not choose this ending, however—does not repeat the tragic deaths of the Middle Passage, opting instead to remain on the dock. The concluding lines embrace but do not cross the gap between Spero and Debbie, as her ferry is just pulling away from the mainland: "Enveloppé de pluie, Spéro se releva et revint vers l'abri des voyageurs. De l'autre côté de l'eau, pointillant la noirceur de l'éclat de ses lumières, le ferry avait commencé son voyage de retour vers Crocker Island" (304) [Wrapped in rain, Spero got up and returned to the passenger shelter. On the other side of the water, speckling the darkness with its lights, the ferry had begun its journey back to Crocker Island (210)]. As it ends ambiguously on both sides of the water, the text thus gestures towards the sea itself as point of origin and return in this genealogical fiction.[13]

In speaking of the earlier *La vie scélérate*, Condé has said that she imbued the character of Coco with aspects of her own eldest daughter, so that the author offers self-criticism through Coco's mother Thécla. In creating a daughter-writer who retrieves family history, and in basing the Louis family of this novel on her own, Condé herself becomes the lost mother, looking for the female descendant who will create communities from diaspora. While Condé critiques the search for a romanticized African past, she nevertheless affirms some connections: "I want to stress that the African Diaspora in the West Indies and the Americas has a common history and shares the same heroes, dreams, and aspirations. Members of the African Diaspora should not remain isolated within their national shells. It's not a Pan Africanist ideal per se, but rather a way for diaspora members to claim a common heritage" (Pfaff 69-70; 103). In the more recent novel *Desirada* (1997) [*Desirada* (2000)], origins and genealogy again figure centrally, as the protagonist Marie-Noëlle tries to discover her father's identity and to understand her heritage. Encountering contradictory and incomplete information whenever she listens to versions of her family history, she traces geographies of identity in proliferating paths across the ocean: from Guadeloupe to France to Boston, journeying through her own Atlantic triangle.[14]

Marie-Noëlle's mappings mirror the stories she is told, as well as those she invents, versions of her family history that offer competing truths. Though Marie-Noëlle appears focused on unearthing the identity of the man who impregnated her mother Reynalda at the age of fifteen, the narrative refuses to unveil those paternal origins. Instead, mother and grandmother, as well as numerous surrogate mothers, relate a plethora of stories to Marie-Noëlle and suggest directions her life might take. In *Desirada*, more vividly than in the earlier novels, Condé outlines a different, more encompassing Caribbean genealogy. In this process, the bellies of slave ships replace patrilineage with the history of trauma and family lines too complicated to be represented in arboreal images—or even in those images like the mangrove that some argue is more suited to West Indian identities.[15] As the narrator comments, "Tous les Guadeloupéens sont parents. Premièrement, ils sont pour la plupart sortis du même ventre-négrier, expulsés au même moment, sur les mêmes marchés aux esclaves" (176) [All Guadeloupeans are related to one another. First of all, most of them came out of the belly of the same slave ship, ejected at the same moment on the same auction block (161)]. This statement is not restricted to Guadeloupe; it embraces the entire Caribbean, as Condé's Antillean characters claim home in a wide range of locations.

The image of slave ships as maternal bellies offers a new version of family and a striking challenge to the familiar delineations of the family tree. Narratives of the Caribbean frequently rely on familial relations to represent the diversity of the region, as well as to chart paths backwards to origins in Africa and Europe. Indeed, seeking out one's family would seem a most logical pretext for exploring the diaspora, as it offers a way to trace connection and to illustrate what Glissant terms "a pattern of fragmented Diversity" (*CD* 97).[16] A preoccupation with family in a narrative leads readers to expect relationships, shared histories, memories, stories, and most obviously lineage. In *Desirada*, Marie-Noëlle is gradually forced to understand and accept the fictive nature of such connections. She must also cope with both trauma and loss, experiences that are located in Guadeloupe and in the Caribbean more generally. Reynalda's nightmares and constant need for cleansing, as well as her total rejection of her daughter, shadow the text as a reminder of the original rape of Black women in the slave ships. No matter who Marie-Noelle's biological father may have been, she has emerged from an originary trauma experienced by her mother.[17] As she pursues her investigation of roots, Marie-Noëlle finds a series of fictions surrounding that moment of shock and pain: fictions that vie with one another for credibility and validity until the closing pages. "Désormais, il me faudra tout simplement vivre avec cet inconnu, ce noir derrière moi" (252) [From now on I shall quite simply have to live with the unknown, this area of darkness behind me (231)], she says, in an interesting feminist revision of Athena emerging from the head of Zeus. "Je suis sortie du noir. Je suis sortie mal armée, pas du tout parée pour l'existence de la tête brillante de ma mère" (252) [I came out of the dark. I came straight out of the brilliant head of my mother, totally unprepared and ill-equipped for life] (231). At this point, Marie-Noëlle recognizes that a viable option would be to forget the past and to move on as an individual—or at least as the brilliant creation of the prolific imagination of Maryse Condé herself.

Yet Marie-Noëlle wants to write, and to do so she believes that she must have a father. Working on her dissertation in the U.S., she sees her research as hard labor in cemeteries, ones not beautiful like the ones back on her island: "Comment pouvait-elle écrire? Comment pouvait-elle prendre la plume tant qu'elle ne saurait ni qui elle était ni d'où elle sortait? Bâtarde née d'un père inconnu. Belle identité que celle-là! Tant qu'elle n'aurait pas d'autres indications à inscrire sur son livret de famille, elle ne pourrait rien mener à terme" (220) [How could she write? How could she take up the pen as long as she didn't know who she was or where she came from? Illegitimate child, father unknown. A fine identity that was! As long as she had no other details to record in her family register, she would never make a success of anything (200)]. In contrast, her mother Reynalda, who abandoned her not long after birth and has never nurtured her, is writing the story of her own life. A successful author, Reynalda perhaps represents the path of Condé herself. "Dans le fond, Marie-Noëlle says, "elle est écrivain, ma mère, et elle a bâti sa fiction. Moi qui vis, je dois chercher la vérité autre part. Où? Il faudrait tout réinterpréter, tout recommencer depuis le commencement" (252) [She's basically a writer, my mother, and she has constructed her fiction. I'm living it and must search for the truth elsewhere. Where? It needs a new reading, starting all over again from the beginning (231)]. Interpreted from this angle, this text may offer a new version of genealogy, one that looks not only backwards (to incomplete histories and dead-ends) but to the present with glimpses into the future.

One also senses a partial laying to rest of Guadeloupe as homeland, illustrated most clearly when Marie-Noëlle journeys to visit her grandmother Nina on the island of La Désirade, where she finds Nina living in the cabin on a cliff that she (Marie-Noëlle) has dreamed about incessantly. The grandmother's words at the end of this visit echo for the larger narrative of family and roots, not just Marie-Noëlle's story but that of the Caribbean subject as envisioned by Condé: "Il n'y a pas de place pour toi ici. Tu es une terre rapportée. Ici, chacun depuis la naissance connaît le chemin dans lequel il doit marcher et la place où, à la fin, il faudra qu'il se couche. Ne demande plus rien à ta maman, cette menteuse de premières. Lasse-la avec ses contes à dormir debout. D'ailleurs, ne demande plus rien à personne. Tu as l'instruction. Tu as l'éducation. Tu as ta belle santé. Vis ta vie. / Qu'est-ce qui te manque?" (202-03) [There's no place for you here. Popping up like an outsider. Here everyone knows the path he must tread from the cradle to the grave. Don't ask your maman for anything more, she's a first-rate liar. Leave her be with her fairy tales. In fact, don't ask anyone for anything more. You've got schooling. You've got education. You've got good health. Live your life. What more do you need? (184)]. Just as both mother and grandmother—the maternal and matrilineal—stand as obstacles to the search for paternity, Guadeloupe itself disappoints Marie-Noëlle. She comes to realize that it exists for her more as a legendary site than as the rapidly changing, "modernizing" country she visits after such a long hiatus. Guadeloupe, too, refuses her complete reentry and full identification. As Reynalda's husband Ludovic tells Marie-Noëlle when she tracks him down in France, "nos mythes ont la vie dure. Nous croyons que les liens de parenté sont les plus solides…[mais] nous sommes là à répéter…des choses que la réalité contredit" (277) [our myths are hard to dispel. We believe the ties of parenthood to be the strongest…(but) we are still repeating things that reality contradicts (255)]. And he ends by telling her that she must look to herself, stop "épier par-dessus [son] épaule" (277) [peeking over (her) shoulder (255)] and look to her future instead. Marie-Nöelle's responsibility for creating her own life, for giving birth to her identity, is thrown back on her own shoulders.

Passages near the end of *Desirada* suggest that in Reynalda Condé may be first inscribing and then shedding one reading of identity; at the same time, however, in Reynalda's daughter we can perceive a rejection of the insistence on "legitimacy" and patrilineage. As Marie-Noëlle sets off across Paris in search of yet one more clue to her parentage, she wonders about the usefulness of her quest: "Elle avait essayé toutes les avenus possibles et il ne restait que celle-là, la dernière, ouverte devant elle. Pourtant, depuis quelque temps, elle se posait la question: est-ce qu'elle ne pouvait pas continuer de vivre comme elle le faisait? Sans identité, comme une personne à qui on a volé ses papiers et qui erre à travers le monde? Est-ce qu'ainsi elle n'était pas plus libre? C'est une sale manie de vouloir savoir à tout prix d'où on sort et la goutte de sperme à laquelle on doit la vie" (243) [She had tried every avenue possible, and only this last remaining one stretched out in front of her. Yet for some time now she had asked herself why not go on living as she was. Without an identity, like someone whose papers have been stolen and who drifts aimlessly through the world? Wasn't she freer like that? It's a terrible thing wanting to know at any cost where we come from and tracking down that drop of sperm that gave us life (223)]. At this moment Marie-Noëlle seems to accept uncertainty and even to embrace its freedom; at the same time, because her maternal side does not provide what she seeks she posits identity in terms of biology and the paternal. Yet, unlike Coco who is poised to write the family history tracing back through the male line, and also unlike Anita who disappears into Africa and remains voiceless, Marie-Noëlle initiates a challenge to conventional genealogy in Condé's works.

This daughter ultimately does not want an answer to her parentage—that missing sperm—because "réelle ou imaginaire, cette identité-là avait fini par me plaire. D'une certaine manière, ma monstruosité me rend unique. Grâce à elle, je ne possède ni nationalité ni pays ni langue. Je peux rejeter ces tracasseries qui tracassent tellement les humains. Elle donne aussi une explication à ce qui entoure ma vie. Je comprends et j'accepte qu'autour de moi, il n'y ait jamais eu de place pour un certain bonheur. *Mon chemin est tracé ailleurs*" (281) [I have ended up liking this identity, real or imagined. In some way or another my monstrosity makes me unique. Thanks to it I have no nationality, no country, and no language. I can shrug off all those tiresome bedevilments that bedevil human beings. It also provides an explanation to everything surrounding my life. I can understand and accept that there never was any room in my life for a certain kind of happiness. *My path is traced elsewhere*" (259, my emphasis)]. In these lines, the text gestures toward the complex task of defining Caribbeanness—an identity both real and imagined, a product of colonialism and enslavement and of the myriad attempts to fill in the gaps in that history. The "path traced elsewhere" does not follow a direct lineage back to origins, nor does it lead to the branches of a distinct family tree. Instead, the path of identity Marie-Noëlle claims as her own resembles the indecipherable tracks traced and retraced across watery depths; and the Caribbean islands—defined as they are by the surrounding seas—lie at the center of continual voyaging. Marie-Noëlle thus moves beyond Anita's voiceless disappearing into Africa and Coco's retelling that omits the significance of ships' bellies, for she envisions a new configuration of Caribbean identity. As Glissant notes of those who lost their lives in the course of the Middle Passage, they "*sowed in the depths the seeds of an invisible presence*" (*CD* 66, emphasis in original). He continues: "Submarine roots: that is floating free, not fixed in one position in some primordial spot, but extending in all directions in our world through its network of branches" (67). In *Desirada*, Marie-Noëlle reaches a similar understanding of Caribbean roots, including the revolutionary image of slave ships as maternal bellies, and embeds that vision at the core of her identity.

(Up)Rooting the Family Tree: Genealogy and Space in Maryse Condé's Fiction

Taken together, these three novels by Maryse Condé offer a clear example of the predicament of the Antillean or West Indian in the late twentieth century who seeks to define Caribbean-ness, that is, to define an identity located in the spaces between Africa, Europe, and the Americas. In Condé's works, this search would appear to be both compulsive, irresistible, and necessary, and repetitive, fragmentary, and incomplete. A sense of wholeness or of healing from the multiple traumas does not ultimately come from the roots that so many of her characters obsessively attempt to trace, the origins that both structure their lives and yet elude them. Instead, as Coco and Marie-Noëlle indicate, contemporary daughters can begin to trace a path that is not genealogical, as they turn to writing-as-becoming and claim new spaces in which to shape a new identity. Condé has spoken of Marie-Noëlle in terms of sterility but also selfhood in her focus on the present.[18] Rather than the familiar metaphor of a tree, or even the rhizome hailed by Glissant (in echo of Deleuze and Guattari), perhaps the ocean offers a more useful way to perceive this as-yet unformed vision of identity, spaces over which Condé's characters trace their histories—elsewhere and otherwise.

Notes

1. The original title, *La Vie scélérate*, does not translate literally as "tree of life" but rather as "Life the Perfidious," "The Scoundrel Life" or "This Criminal Life" (all rather awkward phrasings). The translator's choice of English title captures the text's wide branching across the globe as it follows one family's migrations outward from a Caribbean center.

2. On the absence of an originary Caribbean history and the concomitant desire for one, see Andrade, 216.

3. See also "Errance et enracinement dans *La Vie scélérate* de Maryse Condé" by Pascale Bécel (esp. 139). In "Caribbean Insularization of Identities in Maryse Condé's Work: From *En Attendant le Bonheur* to *Les Derniers Rois Mages*," Mireille Rosello argues that quests for roots "imply accepting the representations of territories as 'naturally' dominated (if they are 'small' islands) or powerful (if they are huge continents)" (570). She raises the question of whether Condé's work leads to a vision of a transnational literature (568), and points to the irresolvable question of Caribbean origins (572).

4. For a discussion that challenges the perception that Glissant's theories celebrate diversity, see Hallward, who posits that in *Poétique de la relation*, Glissant "runs into the same problem as does Deleuze:

how to write a philosophy of difference without 'others,' beyond specificity?…Glissant like Deleuze celebrates a difference generated through the specific—in a discourse based on the extinction of the specific" (44). On Glissant and Caribbean dispersion, see Bécel ("Errance et enracinement" 136).

5.   In *The Negotiated Self: The Dynamics of Identity in Francophone Caribbean Narrative*, Anne Malena discusses Condé's avoidance of a unifying discourse on Caribbean identity (74); and in an interview Condé expresses her thoughts about the search for ancestors as follows: "Je pense que tous les colonisés ont ce besoin de chercher leurs aïeux. On vous a toujours menti sur votre histoire, on vous a toujours caché votre histoire ou travesti votre histoire, on ne vous a raconté que l'histoire officielle des vainqueurs, vous avez envie de chercher vos aïeux" (Anagnostopoulos-Hielscher 73) [I think that all colonized peoples have this need to search for their ancestors. You've always been lied to about your history, your history has always been hidden or misrepresented because they only told you the conquerors' official history, so of course you want to seek out the story of your ancestors (Eds.' trans.)].

6.   In Chapter 7 of her study, *The Daughter's Return: African-American and Caribbean Women's Fictions of History*, Rody discusses the trauma of the Middle Passage and a history of dislocations (esp. 183). Although I disagree with Malena's equation of tree and rhizome in *The Negotiated Self* (156), see her article, "The Figure of the Critic in Condé's novels" for a discussion of the image of the tree and Caribbean identity and/versus Glissant's use of Deleuze and Guattari's rhizome metaphor. In "Family and Other Trees," Anthea Morrison describes Condé's work in terms of a progression toward *enracinement* as an antidote to the problem of identity (85), but she does not challenge the image of the tree. In contrast, see Anagnostopoulos-Hielscher, who argues that particularly in her most recent novels, Condé "n'hésite pas à démontrer l'absurdité des discours de la filiation et du mythe fondateur, représentatifs d'une fidélité absolue à une généalogie unique et responsables de l'obsession de la bâtardise qui tourmente l'Antillaise, et qui est inhérente à sa constitution en tant que sujet" (70) [has no problem addressing the absurdity of discourses of filiation and of founding myths that represent an absolute fidelity to a unique genealogy and are responsible for the obsession with illegitimacy that haunts the Caribbean subject, in fact, whose very subjecthood is constituted by this obsession (Eds.' trans.)].

7.   In *Autobiographical Tightropes*, see Hewitt's chapter on this novel, "Mediations of Identity through the Atlantic Triangle: Maryse Condé's *Heremakhonon*" (esp. 175) for a discussion of Antillean identity for Veronica—on one's own and/versus in relation.

8. While Paul Gilroy's theories of the Black Atlantic might be useful here, as I and others have discussed, he does not take into account women's experiences of the "triangle trade" and the African diaspora. See Elizabeth DeLoughrey's "Gendering the Oceanic Voyage," and my own article on exile, memory, and resistance in Dionne Brand's fiction.

9. In "Emancipating the Voice: Maryse Condé's *La Vie scélérate*," Anthea Morrison describes Coco as accepting a problematic genealogy (622); and in "Exile and Homecoming" she discusses Coco's becoming the griotte and telling history, as well as her returning home, without, however, getting at the complexity of this process in the novel. Bécel claims that "Coco finit par revendiquer une sorte d'antigénéalogie qui passe outre son père (absent) et sa mere (sans amour maternel)" (143) [Coco ends up claiming a kind of antigenealogy that goes beyond her father (absent) and her mother (lacking maternal love) (eds.' translation)], and links this assessment to Deleuze and Guatarri's (and Glissant's) elaboration of the rhizome. While I would disagree with this characterization of Coco's achievement, see Bécel's conclusion about the "structure mosaïque" [mosaic structure] of Coco's narrative, which offers a way to join "enracinement et errance" [rootedness and wandering] (147). See also Dominique Licops (esp. 114).

10. On Condé doubting Blackness, see her interviews with Taleb-Khyar (352) and with Clark (esp. 115-16).

11. Hewitt argues in "Condé's Critical Seesaw" that female genealogy is voiced by a male character (Spero) in this text (649), but scenes such as this birth of an African son counter such moves. On the boy's birth near the end of the novel, see Ann Smock's article on the novel, in which she asks, "Is the future indefinitely the resurrection of an exhausted, zombie story, the return of a past which can—since it's always being liquidated in one way or another (since practically everyone is, after his or her own fashion, indifferent to it if not positively anxious *not* to understand it)—never end?" (677).

12. In her article, "The Figure of the Critic in Condé's Novels," Anne Malena looks at the author's refusal of ready-made solutions, and in this discussion Malena connects Condé's use of irony with Myriam Chancy's notion of *culture-lacune* as she describes it in *Searching for Safe Spaces: Afro-Caribbean Women Writers in Exile*.

13. On this inconclusive ending, as well as the use of ocean imagery, see the Smock article cited above (esp. 678). In "Caribbean Insularization of Identities in Maryse Condé's Work" Rosello argues that we should read this novel as "a proliferation of fragments which no one can hope to centralize" (574).

14. Licops notes that in *Desirada* the characters' movement toward cities "s'accompagne d'une re-connaissance de la part inconnaissable de

l'origine, d'une perte de mémoire" (111) [is accompanied by a re-membering of the unknowable part of the origin, by a loss of memory (Eds.' trans.)].

15. In his discussion of the "poetics of the mangrove" in "Looking for Roots among the Mangroves" (459, 463), Hayes sees as an alternative to the patrilineal family tree (471). His argument for seeing an "essential queer[ness]" in Condé's articulation of roots as a mangrove, however, seems overstated (471).

16. In her earlier novel *Traversée de la Mangrove* (1989) [*Crossing the Mangrove* (1995)], a dead man's wake provides another tactic for engaging a multiplicity of characters in relation; but in most of her works Condé appears preoccupied primarily with familial ties.

17. On sexual violence, gaps, and a genealogy of colonialism and neo-colonialism in *Desirada*, see Salvodon's review of the novel (esp. 252).

18. In the McCormick interview Condé discusses this possible sterility (527) and comments that Marie-Noëlle illustrates her own (Condé's) belief that "one has to define one's identity personally" (519). Condé talks about the ending of the novel with Anagnostopoulos-Hielscher in their interview (esp. 73-74), and Licops address it in "Expériences Diasporiques et Migratoires" (115).

Transgressing Boundaries, Challenging Categories

MARYSE CONDÉ, HISTORIAN OF THE BLACK DIASPORA

Laurence M. Porter

Superficial views of Francophone Caribbean literature often contrast Guadeloupe with Martinique through gender polarization, placing female, Guadeloupean novelists such as Maryse Condé, Simone Schwartz-Bart, and Myriam Warner-Vieyra on one side, and the male, Martinican theorists such as Aimé Césaire (*Négritude*), Édouard Glissant (*Antillanité*), Raphaël Confiant and Patrick Chamoiseau (*Créolité*) on the other. By overlooking Condé's extensive publication of textbooks and scholarship about the culture and history of the Caribbean, on the one hand, and the Martinicans' many novels, on the other, we create an artificial diptych, based on the centuries-old assumption that men reason, whereas women emote. From there it takes only a step to fantasize an ontological contrast of feeling to thinking, to claim that female authors from Guadeloupe indulge in subjective, introspective effusions that narcissistically mirror women authors' own gender-bound destiny, whereas male authors from Martinique dominate the domain of abstract rationality, expressed by the successive theoretical discussions that have given Caribbean Francophone literature its most prominent profile over the last three-quarters of a century.[1]

To illustrate the sexualized fantasy of a female Guadeloupe and a male Martinique as it can occur in popular culture, consider the jacket copy of four representative Francophone Caribbean novels—two by Guadeloupean women, and two by Martinican men—each with a woman protagonist. In Maryse Condé's most widely acclaimed novel, copy on the cover of the English translation explains that "it was Tituba's *blind, all-consuming love* of the slave John Indian that led her from safety into slavery, and the bitter, vengeful religion practiced by the good citizens of Salem, Massachusetts. Though protected by the spirits, Tituba could not escape…the lies and accusations of that hysterical time." On the cover of the original version of Simone Schwartz-Bart's widely read novel, we read that the protagonist Télumée Miracle "*a souffert de sa condition de femme*, de Noire et d'exploitée. Pourtant, … *sa volonté de bonheur*, de 'récolter par pleins paniers [the stereotype of woman as gatherer] cette douceur qui tombe du ciel', est la plus forte" [has suffered from her condition of being a woman, a black person, and a victim of exploitation. However,…her will to be happy, to 'gather basketsful of that sweet joy that falls from the sky,' is stronger]. In contrast, Raphaël Confiant's eponymous heroine "Eau de Café" is described as follows: "sorte de *Mère Courage à l'étonnante vitalité et au profond savoir, est un point de ralliement* [pour son village]" [a kind of Mother Courage with astounding vitality and deep wisdom, provides a rallying point]. And Patrick Chamoiseau's Marie-Sophie Laborieux, "devenue l'âme du quartier Texaco…*mène la révolte* contre les mulâtres de la ville, contre les békés qui veulent s'approprier les terres, contre les programmes de développement qui font le temps-béton. « *Je n'avais jamais perçu tant d'autorité profonde irradier de quelqu'un* », the narrator-observer remarks [who has become the soul of the Texaco shantytown…leads the revolt against the urban mulattos, the wealthy whites who are trying to appropriate land for themselves, and the development projects that create the Age of Concrete. "*I had never seen such depths of authority emanating from anyone*"] (emphases added).[2] From this perspective, it appears that Caribbean women writers' female protagonists seek love and submit to history, whereas male Caribbean writers' women protagonists seek leadership and make history. A marketing device aimed at the widest literate audience, jacket copy lacks credibility as a source of scholarly judgment for an educated audience. But as an elemental expression of unsophisticated attitudes, it opens an illuminating window on the history of the naïve reception and representation of texts—a naïveté lurking in everyone's cultural unconscious.

The *Négritude* movement of the 1930s sought to exalt pride in blackness, linking all the communities of black African origin by celebrating their "race" through both lyrical and militant literature.[3] Aimé Cesaire's *Cahier d'un retour au pays natal*, the masterpiece of this movement, combined a vehement assertion of black dignity with intense lyricism and a forbiddingly intellectual, Surrealist complexity, proving that a black person could think more profoundly and write more vigorously than any other commentator on the Francophone scene at that time. Forty years later, Édouard Glissant, in his famous *Le Discours antillais*, preached "Antillanité," a sense of regional identity in the Caribbean and French Guyana that could lead some day to a political federation of the four French overseas "départements" in the area, plus other Caribbean Hispanophone, Anglophone, and Lusophone groups consisting of the descendants of slaves. This dream has never been realized; at length, even Glissant's admiring disciples abandoned it.[4] In the third phase of Caribbean identity politics, these disciples promoted "*Créolité*," intending to rally an oral counterculture among the marginalized, post-colonial subaltern peoples of the region.[5] It opposed "Americanness," "a migrant culture in a splendid [and monolingual] isolation" (Bernabé 92). Ironically, celebrating the ideal of *Créolité* in the essay went hand in hand with abandoning its use in literature: Confiant originally wrote in Creole, until Chamoiseau's example and the international prizes he received persuaded Confiant to embrace formal French for his literary compositions.

Clear and compelling as the male Martinicans' theoretical statements have been, the practical sociopolitical range of their preoccupations has progressively narrowed. Not only does "Créolité" sacrifice the international scope of Négritude, but it also relinquishes the regional political thrust of "Antillanité" in favor of a local, monolingual cultural history and estheticism lexically spiced with creolisms. In practice, the proposed ideal of "diversality" comes down to "becoming Martinican" (Bernabé 114, 111), thus reverting to the relatively limited concerns advanced seventy years ago by Jean Price-Mars. His compendium of traditional Haitian legends, *Ainsi parla l'Oncle* (1928), retreats two paces along a hypothetical causal chain, from political action to the potential ground of such action—black pride—then further still, to recuperate a sense of linguistic and folkloristic origins as the groundwork for ethnic pride in Caribbean blacks. An undertow of melancholic resignation comes into play as *Créolité* becomes a writer's occupation, far less comprehensive than, say, Homi Bhabha's "third space" of cultural *métissage*.[6]

The Guadeloupean master Maryse Condé (1937-) more consistently announces and illustrates Bhabha's ideal. Throughout her long career, and without theoretical fanfare—contrasting with the flamboyant self-promotions by the Martinican writers, effected by manifestoes—she has quietly but urgently woven a comprehensive intercontinental history of the black diaspora and of its origins.[7] Her corpus includes fictional experiences detached from major historical events, as well as dramatized historical reconstructions, textbooks, and abundant scholarship. She traces varied lives from the Caribbean, France, North America, and the great medieval kingdoms of West and Central Africa as facets of an overarching historical and personal vision.

Condé's reconstructions of the past are never triumphalist or deontological. Of her first novel, *Hérémakhonon*, she said "The novel is not a handbook telling you what to do, and none of my books should be considered as such" (Pfaff, 42; 66). Condé claims to know no heroes and explains at length that *Moi, Tituba, sorcière noire de Salem* is "moqueur" [ironic]: "It is also a pastiche of the feminine heroic novel, a parody containing a lot of clichés about…the sacrosanct grandmother…Tituba's return to her island, her relationship with the maroons, and the links to spirits who appear and disappear are ironic elements" (60; 90). Condé playfully puts Hawthorne's Hester from Nathaniel Hawthorne's *The Scarlet Letter* into prison with Tituba so that they can have modern feminist discussions. The ending playfully assembles a covert collage of Hilarion Hilarius' dying words at the end of Jacques-Stéphen Alexis's *Compère Général Soleil*.

Condé's groups are no more heroic than are her protagonists: through stories of displacement, wandering, and diaspora, she portrays the agonizing, centuries-long fragmentation of the black community, whose members cannot return from the Caribbean to France or to Africa without feeling exiled and lost.[8] The fragmentation originating the black diaspora—colonizing invasions—appears in the subtitles of the two volumes of Condé's fictionalized history of the Bambara kingdom of Ségou: "Les murailles de terre" [The earthen battlements] and "La terre en miettes" [The earth crumbles]. The author herself lived in the post-colonial aftermath of slavery and colonization. "Toute ma vie est faite d'une série d'exclusions," she says in an interview. "Je m'en suis très bien sortie. Je ne pourrai pas vivre même sans exclusion" (Blérald-Ndagano 392) [My whole life is constructed from a series of exclusions. I survived them very well. In fact, I couldn't even live with exclusions] —meaning: as a child from a wealthy Caribbean family, who did not know Creole; as a Caribbean woman in Africa, who did not know any of the languages spoken there, and who was not Muslim; as a person of color in France; and as the wife of a white man (Richard Philcox, her

British translator), thus considered "a traitor to her race" when she tried to approach African-Americans.[9]

In Condé's early childhood memories, her identity theme combines assertiveness and resultant unpopularity: "Quand j'étais enfant, [mon père] me gâtait énormément mais quand j'ai commencé à avoir ma propre personnalité, nous étions souvent en désaccord car j'avais un penchant pour la controverse" [When I was a child, my father spoiled me terribly, but when I started to develop an independent personality we often disagreed, because I enjoyed a good argument] (Clark 92). Knowing herself to be exceptional, however, and seeking a representative realism, Condé keeps her identity distinct from that of her often helpless, confused fictional characters: "My characters are often antiheroes, people who are not very sure of themselves and are not very likeable…. I like them because they often correspond to human situations I've encountered" (Pfaff 105; 153).

In Condé's fictions, some departures are involuntary (Tituba sold into slavery, "le dernier roi mage" [the last sorcerer-king] exiled); others are motivated by a flight from a relative, boredom, frustration, or shame, and the destination of the latter is determined by a variety of personal ambitions. Only in Condé's recent works does a desire to renew and strengthen family ties enter the picture: Razyé I in *La Migration des cœurs* seeks his son; Marie-Noëlle in *Desirada* is summoned to Paris ostensibly by her mother (actually, by her step-father), and returns to Guadeloupe for her adoptive mother's funeral. All these departures and destinations are determined by the will of others, by emotional dependence on others, or by material constraints. Even at their freest, the protagonists are driven by a hope of that their experience in the new places they go will transform them without effort on their part.

Condé's depiction of the diaspora lacks the messianic dimensions found in male-authored works such as Alexis's *L'Espace d'un cillement*, Césaire's *Cahier d'un retour au pays natal*, or Roumain's *Gouverneurs de la rosée*. Although the trajectory of Condé's protagonists usually reflects the lingering social subordination of women that she acknowledges in her recent interviews—even when they believe themselves to be autonomous, their desires and intentions are mediated by existing conventions—the extraordinary variety of these characters' fates, unequaled in the Caribbean novel, reflects the inventiveness of the implied author. One of Condé's more recent novels, *La Belle Créole* (Paris: Mercure de France, 2001), exorcises helplessness by transferring it to the young male gardener Dieudonné. Foolishly enslaved by his passion for the rich, blonde, sexually predatory Loraine, after her death he commits suicide by shipwrecking a friend's boat, the eponymous entity whose name represents the illusion of happiness with a woman. Unlike most of Condé's female characters, he never manages to leave Guadeloupe. Her women may be driven; *he* is trapped.

Condé's first novels, *Hérémakhonon* and *Une saison à Rihata*, avowedly reflect how Africa initially focused the novelist's hopes for rediscovering her personal and her ethnic identity. "Pour cela, "Condé observed self-mockingly in her 1998 essay "Où commence et où finit la Caraïbe?,"

> il fallait retourner à l'endroit d'où mes ancêtres étaient venus, y re-pousser racines.... J'ai cru. J'ai obéi, et ce fut mon premier voyage. Ah, mes amis, quel bal masqué que ces années-là.... À peine entamé mon compte à rebours, j'ai découvert une chose. De même que la rivière ne remonte pas vers sa source, de même, le Middle Passage ne se navigue qu'une fois. Qu'est-ce que j'avais à rouler mon corps sous des cieux inconnus ? Je me trompais à chaque coup, je prenais le vrai pour le faux, je confondais le mal avec le bien, je m'apitoyais sur le bourreau au lieu de la victime

> [To achieve that, I had to go back to the place from which my ancestors had come, grow new roots there.... I believed that. I complied, and that was my first journey. Oh, my friends, what a masquerade were those years.... Hardly had I launched into my backward reckoning, when I discovered something. Just as a river can't flow back upstream to its source, the Middle Passage can be navigated only once. What had gotten into me, to make me drift about beneath those unfamiliar skies? I made mistakes at every turn, I took the truth for falsehood, I confused evil with good, and I pitied the executioner instead of the victim]. (112)[10]

These two novels, partially autobiographical (1976, 1981), reflect Condé's personal experience of disillusionment with Francophone African governments after Independence (1958-1960), making her the only prominent Francophone Caribbean writer to criticize them (Blérald-Ngadano 138).[11]

For few writers is it more important to distinguish the protagonists and the implied author from the historical author. Leaving
Guinea and separating from her husband in 1964, the historical
Maryse Condé went to Ghana to work for Kwamé Nkrumah's
socialist state, at the time one of the brightest hopes in Africa. There
she helped create textbooks purged of colonialist ideology, became
fascinated with the remains of the great Ashanti kingdoms (Ségou
was Bambara), and came to understand why African independence was so difficult to consolidate. When Nkrumah fell in 1966,
Condé was imprisoned on suspicion of being a spy for the dictator
Sékou Touré and then expelled from the country. Quite unlike her
protagonists, Condé was a courageous, idealistic fighter, if not a
martyr (Pfaff 13-16; 27-29).

Typical of her balanced views, Condé then promptly became
the only prominent Francophone Caribbean writer to compose a
serious, admiring, elegiac fictionalized history of the great indigenous Central African kingdoms before colonization had been completed. Heavily researched, the two volumes of *Ségou* (Paris: Laffont,
1984-1985) had originally been intended for a French *doctorat d'état*.
Unlike the self-absorbed, politically unaware protagonists of *Hérémakhonon* and *Une saison à Rihata*, Condé herself had met revolutionary leaders such as Malcolm X, Kwame Nkrumah, and Ché Guevara
when they came to Ghana to give lectures to students. As she tells
Pfaff, "In Ghana I started to reflect more deeply on Africa, its reality
and myths, the future and problems of socialism. I had very good
friends among African militants in exile in Ghana" (14; 27).[12] After
her own protracted stay in Africa, Condé no longer seeks to live
there herself—much less to intervene politically—but she periodically writes nostalgic evocations of the grand African past, notably
in *Les Derniers Rois Mages* (the Ashanti Empire) and in *La Colonie
du nouveau monde* (ancient Egypt). Ironically, the success of *Ségou*
(300,000 copies were sold initially) determined Condé to return to
Guadeloupe, to focus her writing on her native region, and to devote
herself to local causes, including independence: "I am an *indépen-
dantiste*. I am a militant supporter of Guadeloupe's independence
though I am convinced I'll never live to see it" (65; 97).[13]

Condé's novels evolve from texts dominated by the viewpoint
of one young female to polyphonic works where many divergent
viewpoints representing persons of various ages and of both
genders appear. From a subjective viewpoint, Condé's novels trace
how she became skeptical about Panafricanism, Socialism, and

187

Revolution.[14] But the dramatization of individual failures in these works achieves success because through their very accumulation, their image of blacks in the diaspora comes to transcend any single identity. When Condé depicts several successive generations within the same work, each will remain mysterious to the next. Autonomy can be realized, Condé believes, only if the quest for defining one's identity through the past remains frustrated.

Condé adopts a *locus classicus* of the identity quest when she reverses the telescope, devoting a novel to the community trying to understand the Stranger instead of vice-versa. I refer to the amalgam of disparate memories of Francis Sancher shared among those attending his wake in *La Traversée de la mangrove*. The twenty-some commentators in the discussion cannot define Sancher, but their very effort draws them together. Thus they evoke the international ethnic *communitas* of the black diaspora freed from conformism or compulsion, frustrated in the past but not limited in the future, once the false hope of a Promised Land has been abandoned.

Starting with *Ségou*, Condé increasingly writes *romans-fleuves* that trace family history through several generations: *La Vie Scélérate, Les Derniers Rois Mages, La Migration des Cœurs, Desirada*.[15] But the succession of several generations in her text is an empty signifier. Depending on the context, it may connote unity and common effort, or else fragmentation and dispersion that contrast a desirable past with an agonizing present. Although the personal history of the survivor of the last generation can suggest maturation and hope for the future, Condé depicts collective history as something endured, not constructed. History is a disruption; these stories, taken singly, present frustrated or at best unfinished quests for identity. Indeed, these latter works heighten the general tone of alienation by depicting certain key characters as strangers and outcasts in their own lands. *Ségou* (1984-1985) treats the cultural alienation of Africans in Africa. Leaving their native Bambara town of Ségou to attend the Koranic school in Timbuktu, young Tiékoro Traoré and his brother Siga become curiosities, mocked and scorned after having been honored as sons of notables at home. To be accepted, they must remove all outward signs of their true ethnic identity, even their tribal names. In *La Vie scélérate* (1987), Albert Louis, the French-speaking Guadeloupean, fails to integrate himself into the English-speaking Guadeloupean community of Gâtun. Finally, *La Migration des cœurs* (1995) denounces the irremediable internal exile of victims of color prejudice who fail to find happiness by "marrying up" or by having affairs with persons of lighter skin in order to heighten their self-esteem or to "blanchir la race." Throughout Condé's novels, she dramatizes the isolation and estrangement of certain characters by multiplying allusions to, reports of, and citations from malicious gossip (Blérald-Ndagano 257-58).

Only by considering most of Condé's fictions as a group, as composing a trans-familial, transnational *roman fleuve*, can one recognize how she has surpassed her more aggressive peers. Thanks to her achievements, Guadeloupe, traditionally considered more "African," "black," passive, and backward than Martinique, emerges as a leader in reestablishing awareness of black culture, history, and traditions. With all due respect to the jacket copy cited above, the fictional characters of the male Martinican writers usually consist of male seekers and female objects (Chamoiseau's heroine Marie-Sophie Laborieux is an exception, but a male expatriate revolutionary for Haiti must teach her to write well, and sympathetic males must protect her community from within and without, while the imposing figure of Aimé Césaire looms in the background as a potential *deus ex machinâ*). The gender of Condé's protagonists shifts from male to female and back as we explore her works. She adopts a black standpoint that transcends conventional gender roles, while frankly enumerating one failed quest after another—travel from the Caribbean to North America in the seventeenth or the twentieth century; a move from Paris to Africa and a powerful dictator-lover; attempted recuperation of one's African heritage while remaining in the Western hemisphere. She deliberately depicts flawed, incomplete characters, rather than exemplary, idealized figures.[16] She refuses the facile solutions of the happy ending or heroic martyrdom; her most memorable characters recall Camus's Sisyphus, happy or resigned to the inconclusive, arduous striving that is his doom.

The novel *Desirada* (1997), especially, recapitulates Condé's imaginative effort of diasporic reconstruction. The story begins on La Désirade, an island some eight miles east of Guadeloupe. The title suggests an epic of desire. That desire belongs primarily to Marie-Noëlle, the last of her direct line—and apparently not destined to have children—as she searches for her family origins. Her family offers little help. Her mother, Reynalda, wants only to forget Guadeloupe. She had tried to commit suicide after becoming pregnant by an unknown father when she was fifteen. Shortly after Marie-Noëlle's baptism, Reynalda gives her up to her godmother

Ranelise, a benevolent restaurateur, and leaves for Paris to make something of herself, sending only a yearly card. Ranelise keeps Marie-Noëlle but neglects to adopt her formally. Therefore, when the child turns ten, despite her godmother's and her own dread and disarray, she must go join her mother in Paris, where she has been summoned. Marie-Noëlle tries to reconstruct an identity for herself through imaginary memories of her birth and baptism, having lost her sense of self after the abrupt ending of her enchanted childhood with the loving Ranelise. From members of her family, Marie-Noëlle eventually hears three contradictory stories about her mother Reynalda. At length, her dour, taciturn mother Reynalda volunteers a brief account of her own life. She always came in first in her class, and her vocal gifts so impressed the bishop that he arranged for her tuition to be paid at the school in La Pointe, the major town on Guadeloupe. She stayed with an Italian jeweler, Gian Carlo Coppini, with whom her mother Nina had sex every night.

A freestanding flashback in Part I describes another version—one elaborated by Marie-Noëlle's speculative daydreams—of Reynalda's experience at La Pointe at age 10. In this second version, Reynalda finds a kindly teacher who supports her, but she refuses to tell this teacher about her life with Gian Carlo Coppini, with whom she, not her mother, had sex every night.

After secondary school, followed by nearly three years of treatment at a TB sanitarium in Vence, Marie-Noëlle seeks identity vicariously by accepting the marriage proposal of a black jazz musician, Stanley, who plans to go work in the United States. Ironically, Marie-Noëlle can create new family roots, in marriage, only by uprooting herself from Paris. As for Stanley, he uses the artistic capital of his ethnicity—the reputation that blacks have as jazz musicians—to escape his origins and find celebrity in a promised land.

Condé's descriptions of the black communities in Paris and in Boston show that a common ethnic origin does not necessarily produce harmony. In the suburb of Savigny-sur-Orge, Africans, Caribbeans, and Réunionais live close together, but the latter two groups avoid the quarrelsome Africans (36).

In Boston meanwhile, Marie-Noëlle finds a position caring for a 5-year-old girl and teaching her French. The girl's mother Anthea is a wealthy black bourgeois intellectual who teaches at Harvard. Anthea has overcome the embarrassment of having devoted her doctoral dissertation to Jane Austen by becoming the world's leading authority on slave narratives. She treats Marie-Noëlle as her adopted African daughter Molara's sister (thus merging the U.S., the Caribbean, and Africa), and subsidizes Marie-Noëlle's training and her career.

Part II begins by erasing Marie-Noëlle's imaginative reconstruction of her own past in the Caribbean. At her loving adoptive mother Ranelise's funeral in Guadeloupe, she scandalizes the villagers by being unsociable. Marie-Noëlle doesn't weep over Ranelise; instead, she drinks heavily. Bitter thoughts of her mother's neglect absorb her, and she has recurring nightmares about vainly seeking her father, about her husband and lover leaving, and about a bare shack on a high rocky plateau. Gian Carlo and most of the members of his family have died; his daughters have returned to Milan. Marie-Noëlle interrogates Aristide Delmonico, the husband of one of them, Fiorella, but he mocks her quest: "Comme cela, elle était venue à la recherche de sa famille? (Il riait.) A la recherche de son identité? (Il riait plus fort.) L'identité, ce n'est pas un vêtement égaré que l'on retrouve et que l'on endosse avec plus ou moins de grâce. Elle pourrait faire ce qu'elle voulait, elle ne serait plus jamais une vraie Guadeloupéenne" [So, just like that, she'd come to seek her family? (He laughed.) To seek her identity? (He laughed louder.) Identity isn't a lost article of clothing that you find again and slip on, more or less gracefully. Whatever she tried, never again could she be a true Guadeloupean] (172). As her quest for family history stalls, Marie-Noëlle must resign herself to seeking her grandmother, whom she imagines alternately as a devil or an angel. She visits la Désirade; curious islanders follow her.

Here the implied author seems to contradict the theme "you can't go home again." She observes "Tous les Guadeloupéens sont parents. Premièrement, ils sont pour la plupart sortis du même ventre-négrier, expulsés au même moment, sur les mêmes marchés aux esclaves. Deuxièment, dans les plantations, des liens se sont noués entre ceux-là et les autres, promiscueux, proches comme des incestes" [All Guadeloupeans are related. In the first place, most of them came out of the same bilge of a slave ship, expelled at the same time, to land in the same slave markets. In the second place, on the plantations, they bonded with the other slaves, promiscuously, incestuously close] (176). But what the implied author suggests is that one can find identity with a group only by sharing its members' fate. To have left Guadeloupe—or to have had one's parents leave it—for a better life elsewhere breaks the bonds of solidarity. An episodic return to rediscover one's originary identity must be egotistical; preoccupation with the self and its relationship to the past cuts one off from possible friendships with those available in the present.

On La Désirade, Marie-Noëlle reencounters the shack in her nightmare—it is her grandmother's. She introduces herself to the old woman as the daughter of Reynalda and of Gian Carlo: "C'était la première fois qu'elle déclinait sa généalogie, qu'elle nommait au grand jour le nom de ceux qui l'avaient engendrée. Et c'était comme si enfin, elle prenait possession d'elle-même et qu'elle marquât sa trace sur la terre" [It was the first time she had recited her genealogy, that she openly spoke the names of her parents. At it was as if she were finally taking possession of herself, and tracing her mark on the land] (180). But instead of reacting with shame, remorse, or anger, Nina stares and then bursts out laughing raucously. Nina explains: "Si j'ai un conseil à te donner, c'est d'oublier tout cela et de retourner là d'où tu es sortie, en Amérique. Il n'y a pas de place pour toi ici. Tu es une terre rapportée. Ici, chacun depuis la naissance connaît le chemin dans lequel il doit marcher et la place où, à la fin, il faudra qu'il se couche.... ne demande plus rien à personne. Tu as l'instruction. Tu as l'éducation. Tu as ta belle santé. Vis ta vie. Qu'est-ce qui te manque ?" [If I have any advice for you, it's that you forget all that stuff and go back where you came from, to America. There's no place for you here. You're foreign soil. Here, from the moment of birth, everyone knows what path he must take, and where to be buried at the end.... Don't bother people with your questions any more. You've got an education. You've got a good upbringing. You have your good health. Live your life. What more do you need?] (202-203). Identity must be consensual; it depends on recognition.

The contradictions and *blocages* [obstacles] encountered during Marie-Noëlle's search for identity demystify that search for us. When Marie-Noëlle returns to Roxbury, Guadeloupe seems unreal. Her students' attitudes contribute only to making it seem more so: "Pour tous, la Guadeloupe, c'était la Californie en mille fois mieux. Un endroit paradisiaque" [They all thought Guadeloupe was a glorified California. A paradise] (218). As they err on the side of romanticism, providing her with an unwittingly ironic corrective by exaggerating her original hopes concerning her native land, from Paris her stepbrother Garvey (whose name reflects the dream of establishing a free black state in Africa) provides a corrective on the side of realism, of emotional detachment. "Il visiterait ... surtout, la Caraïbe, silo où tant de races s'étaient fécondés avant de partir ensemencer le monde. Qu'elle ne s'y trompe pas ! Il ne s'agissait surtout pas d'une sempiternelle-quête-de-l'identité. Il était un Européen.... Il n'y avait en lui ni nostalgie d'un temps longtemps mythifié, ni d'un beau pays natal à reconquérir" [He planned to visit, above all, the Caribbean, that silo where so many races had multiplied before setting off to seed themselves throughout the world. But she shouldn't misunderstand! The issue was, least of all, a never-ending-identity-quest. He was a European. He felt no nostalgia for an era that had long since turned into myth, and no desire to win back a beautiful homeland] (231).

When Marie-Noëlle returns to Paris, she also visits Mme Duparc, for whom Reynalda had worked when she was 15, and hears a third story different from both previous ones. Mme Duparc confirms that Reynalda was completely ungrateful, and uninterested in her daughter. Mme Duparc had brought Marie-Noëlle's mother to Paris at her own expense, after having been approached by her relative, the bishop of Guadeloupe. Reynalda's story of having received a grant from the administration of the Départements d'Outre-Mer must have derived from her desire to be considered completely independent. Once again, Marie-Noëlle's search encounters a *blocage*; but reflecting privately, Marie-Noëlle realizes that the praise of her mother's voice, and the promise of a singer's career, must have come from Gian Carlo as a strategy for seduction, and that Nina may have been unaware that her daughter was her rival in adultery (256).

Invited by her stepfather Ludovic to speak about America to an immigrants' mutual aid society, La Main Ouverte, Marie-Noëlle avoids discussing her empty life. She hides behind "une fable digne d'un congressiste républicain, faite de clichés ramassés ici et là et à laquelle elle-même ne croyait pas" [a tall tale worthy of a Republican congressman, made of clichés picked up here and there, a tale that even she couldn't believe] (264). But she is rapidly unmasked by naively materialistic questions and by the audience's inquiries about her husband and her family. Unlike her forebears, who manage to shield their idealized self-image from examination, Marie-Noëlle endures a beneficent humiliation. She will have to start her life anew.

Then Ludovic tells her his own story. It was he who had asked Reynalda to bring Marie-Noëlle to Paris, thinking that his wife would love her daughter once she saw her. But parental love often is a myth. When Marie-Noëlle propositions her stepfather, he refuses, recognizing her motivation as a wish for revenge on her mother. Like Nina, Ludovic says to Marie-Noëlle: "Si j'ai un conseil pour toi, c'est d'aller enfin de l'avant. Reynalda te donne l'exemple. Elle te prouve que le passé, même le plus douloureux, finit par mourir et que la passion réalise les ambitions qui semblent aux autres les plus extravagantes" [If I have any advice for you, it's to get moving, finally. Reynalda is setting you an example. She's proving to you that the past, even at its most painful, finally dies, and that passion can realize those ambitions that seem the most unrealistic to others.] A double humiliation for the rejected daughter. "D'ailleurs, qu'est-ce que nous pouvons construire quand nous parlons de nous-mêmes ? ... Laisse-moi là où je suis. Il te reste à découvrir ton Amérique" [Anyway, what can we construct by speaking of ourselves? Let me be. You still have to discover your America], Ludovic concludes (278).

Back in Boston, Marie-Noëlle feels weak, convalescent. Ludovic had told her she had no goals, but she realizes she does have one—being happy. She will remain silent until she has learned how to invent lives. As Condé explains in her 1999 interview with Blérald-Ndagano, Marie-Noëlle must learn to realize "[que] l'on fera partie d'un monde dans lequel on n'a pas d'identité précise, dans lequel on n'a pas de nationalité précise ... Et pourtant, il faudra qu'elle vive"[she'll become part of a world where she has no specific identity, no specific nationality. But she still has to live] (394-95). Marie-Noëlle exemplifies and involuntarily models the *prise de conscience* that, in Condé's view, all people of color must ideally achieve. Maryse Condé sums up her own novels thus: as *Hérémakhonon* deconstructed the heroic myth of black Africa devised by the Négritude movement, *Desirada* contests the narrow Creole framework advocated by Chamoiseau, Confiant, and Bernabé in their influential *Éloge de la Créolité* (Blérald-Ngadano 397).[17]

Whereas Condé's fictions, inspired by but distinct from her own life, blended *from the beginning* the recuperation of black identity through fictionalized historiography (*Ségou*) and literary and cultural history, Marie-Noëlle comes *belatedly* to the work of self-recuperation through "inventing lives" (writing fiction), having renounced the historical quest—personal or otherwise. Like Marcel

Proust's anonymous narrator in *À la recherche du temps perdu*, at the ending of her novel, she reaches the point where Condé had begun.[18] To pursue her vocation, Condé acknowledges repeatedly that she must always remain a stranger.

Although a literary figure of surpassing importance, Condé is not unique. Compare Simone Schwartz-Bart's *Ti-Jean l'horizon* in 1979. Schwartz-Bart tells of a mythic figure who returns to Africa only to be rejected because of his slave ancestors. After France also proves unsatisfactory, he returns to Guadeloupe. Unlike Césaire, however—whose *Cahier d'un retour* affirms black pride by inciting his people to rise above their condition of shame and subjugation in Martinique, and whose continual allusions to Lautréamont, Rimbaud, Apollinaire, and the Surrealists take episodic breaks from the work of redeeming Martinique to bask in the lofty intellectuality of the Métropole—Schwartz-Bart affirms Guadeloupe as a culture with intrinsic value. Contrast this attitude with the quasi-autobiographical novel sequences by writers such as Jean-Louis Baghio'o or Joseph Zobel: they achieve assimilation to French culture through educational striving in the Caribbean, then travel to France only to find themselves in a dead end, estranged from both their host culture and their own.

Male Francophone Caribbean authors have often encountered difficulties when they attempted to renew themselves. Seeking a foundational identity first in their ethnicity ("Négritude"), then in geography ("Antillanité"), and finally in language ("Créolité"), they have constructed fictive histories that compensate for historical defeats, only to fall into anticlimax with autobiographical sequels depicting assimilation, in Paris, to Metropolitan France and its cultural values, even after having depicted the failure of such assimilation in the Caribbean. Condé, in contrast, systematically exposes the myth of a possible happy assimilation anywhere: in a return to Africa (*Hérémakhonon*), in the United States (*Moi, Tituba, sorcière noire de Salem*), or in the Islands (*Traversée de la Mangrove*). The heroine of *Desirada* recuperates her past from the tales of two previous generations, only to realize at last that she must overcome her fixation on her ancestors in order to learn to live in the present. Condé's synthetic vision achieves an overarching, open-ended diasporic consciousness that imposes no conditions for membership, and that perpetually renews itself through its steady expansion. Her *œuvre* stands astride all four lands—Africa, the Caribbean, France, and the United States. And this *œuvre*, which one might characterize with a non-hierarchical organization of fragments, a "verbal quilt," [19] or better yet, the French "*patchwork*" (quilting), is still in progress.

Perhaps Condé has written no single work as brilliant as Chamoiseau's *Texaco*, which won France's most prestigious literary prize for fiction, the Goncourt—but the sum of her works has achieved a more imposing overview of the history of black African and black diasporic civilizations than has any other Caribbean writer's body of work. Each novel resembles a facet of a crystal, not all of whose reflections can be seen at once. The surpassing scope and variety of her production entitle Condé to be considered the leading fictive historian of the black diaspora. The stakes are high: "If we are more aware of our heritage and of everything we can share, exchange, and say, we will be stronger in the sort of cultural struggle in which we have been losers so far...so as to have something with which to respond to the White world, which constantly hammers us with its values" (Pfaff 99).[20] A manifesto directs us down only one path; Condé, instead, opens a world of cultural treasures, among which we may freely choose.

Notes

1.	Opposing "The Gendering of Créolité" (oral presentation, October 1993, Colloquium on "Repenser la Créolité," the University of Virginia), A. James Arnold explained how the masculinizing of these dominant theories has relegated Caribbean women's literature to the background.

2.	Maryse Condé, *I, Tituba, Black Witch of Salem*; Simone Schwartz-Bart, *Pluie et vent sur Télumée Miracle*; Raphaël Confiant, *Eau de Café*; Patrick Chamoiseau, *Texaco*. All French to English translations above and hereafter are mine unless otherwise noted.

3.	This celebration of the "Black race" was essentially the attitude of Maryse Condé's parents. Because they were unaware of their rich African heritage, however, and blindly Francophile, their prideful self-image was alienated from the beginning. See Condé's autobiography, *Le Cœur à rire et à pleurer: Contes vrais de mon enfance*, ch. 1, "Portrait de famille" (11-19). They also lacked solidarity with their own servants: their self-esteem required that they modify the hierarchy of whites / mulattoes / blacks by dividing the last group into rich and poor, so that they would not stand on the lowest rung of society, and they prized their mastery of French, their elegant dress, and their professional status, in emulation of the Metropolitan whites (see ch. 3, "La Lutte des classes," 27-32). Any reminders of their slave ancestry were too painful to be discussed or even acknowledged (see ch. 5, "Leçon d'histoire," 39-44).

4. See Celia M. Britton, *Édouard Glissant and Postcolonial Theory: Strategies of Language and Resistance*; Roger Elbion, "*Mahagony*, quelle langue?"; and Edouard Glissant, *Le Discours antillais* and *Traité du tout-monde*.

5. Jean Bernabé, Patrick Chamoiseau, and Raphaël Confiant, *Éloge de la créolité / In Praise of Creoleness. Édition bilingue.*

6. See Homi K. Bhabha, *The Location of Culture* (index, s.v. "hybridity").

7. Compare Christopher Miller: "What is striking in this body of work [*Hérémakhonon, Une Saison à Rihata, Ségou*, and *Moi, Tituba, sorcière noire de Salem*], when looked at as a whole, is Condé's concerted effort to *reweave* the broken threads of the diaspora through the exploration of history" (179). Condé's urgency shows through clearly in a recent interview with Nick Nesbitt: "À la Guadeloupe et à la Martinique, c'est un fait que la mémoire est plus que raturée. On a complète-ment oblitéré tout ce qui rappelait l'action que les ancêtres avaient pu mener.... La situation de l'histoire des Antilles est déjà signée, entérinée, enterrée" (225 n32) [In Guadeloupe and Martinique, it's true that memory is more than simply crossed out. Everything has been completely obliterated about what actions our ancestors might have taken.... History in the West Indies is already signed, sealed, and delivered (Eds.' trans.)]

8. "You can't return to your people once you've left them," as Condé explains, is also a central motif of *La Vie scélérate* (Pfaff 42; 66). Joseph Zobel's *La Rue Cases-Nègres* and Patrick Chamoiseau's *Chemin d'école* amply demonstrate that privileged Caribbean persons of color in his and Condé's generation were thoroughly alienated from their own culture by their experience in schools whose syllabus was firmly dic-tated by Metropolitan France.

9. On the tortuous relationship between Condé's self-image and her Caribbean homeland, see the Vèvè A. Clark interview (1989), and Leah D. Hewitt, *Autobiographical Tightropes* (1990, 5,8, 161-90, 199-201). On her inner relationship to Africa, see Jonathan Ngate, "Maryse Condé and Africa: The Making of a Recalcitrant Daughter."

10. In her interview with Vèvè A. Clark (100-101), Condé explains that *Hérémakhonon* was inspired by Sékou Touré's suppression of dissi-dent intellectuals in Guinea during 1962.

11. Cp. Hewitt 1990, 5 and 190). In a 1984 interview entitled "Condé, Afrique, un continent difficile" (*Notre Librairie* 74, April-June), Condé generalized: "Pendant un temps, les Antillais ont cru que leur quête d'identité passait par l'Afrique. C'est ce que nous avaient dit des écrivains comme Césaire et d'autres de sa génération; l'Afrique était pour eux la grande matrice de la race noire et tout enfant issu de

cette matrice devait pour se connaître, fatalement, se rattacher à elle. En fin de compte, je pense que c'est un piège.… La quête d'identité d'un Antillais peut très bien se résoudre sans passer, surtout physiquement, par l'Afrique" (22) [For a time, Caribbean blacks thought that their identity quest led through Africa. That's what Césaire and other writers of his generation had told us; for them Africa was the great womb of the black race, and every child born from that womb inevitably had to reconnect to it in order to achieve self-knowledge. When all is said and done, I think that's a trap.… A Caribbean person's identity question can be resolved quite effectively without passing— physically, especially—through Africa]. In *Lettres Créoles…*, Patrick Chamoiseau and Raphaël Confiant generously acknowledge Condé's pioneering demystification of Africa in her early novels (152).

12. Elsewhere Condé explained "le Mali, la région de Ségou, m'ont donné un profond bonheur, une sorte d'éblouissement, qui était un contact presque physique avec ce que le passé africain avait pu être.… [*Ségou*] était un hommage à une terre qui m'a révélé une dimension de mon passé que je ne connaissais pas" (Jacquey, 57) [The Segou region in Mali gave me profound happiness, a sort of ecstasy, an almost physical contact with what the African past could have been.… *Ségou* was a homage to a land that revealed to me a dimension of my past I had not known (Eds.' trans.)].

13. She believes, however, that Mitterrand's Leftist government in France from 1981 through 1995 completely drained off and consumed the revolutionary energies of advocates for Antillean independence (Blérald-Ngadano 385-87). Condé expresses her support for Guadeloupe's independence through political activism rather than in her literature; and unlike Chamoiseau or Confiant, she uses little Creole language or Creole-inflected French in her work. See Ama Mazama, "Langue et problématique de la langue dans l'œuvre de Maryse Condé."

14. Condé's identity quest in her essays follows a path opposite to that of the novels. For her as for many writers, thought in essays evolves over time from generalization to confession, whereas thought in fictions evolves from (disguised and distorted) confession to generalization. In "Éloge de Saint-John Perse," an essay about her decade of residence and work in Africa, she states, "panafricanisme, socialisme, révolution s'étaient révélés…comme autant de notions devenues mensongères" (22) [Panafricanism, socialism, revolution turned out to be lies].

15. An undeservedly obscure example of that genre by a male Caribbean Francophone writer is Jean-Louis Baghio'o's *Le Flamboyant à fleurs bleues*, which begins with several generations of black buccaneers. Condé wrote an admiring, important preface.

16. In Alice Walker's "womanism" Condé finds the closest parallels to her view of what a woman's role in society should be: a refusal to renounce any aspect of her personality, or any role she wishes in society. Excepting Tituba in the wholly invented final scenes of *Moi, Tituba, sorcière noire de Salem*, however, Condé does not depict female political leaders such as we find in Jacques-Stéphen Alexis, Jean-Louis Baghio'o, or Jacques Roumain. In an interview with Blérald-Ndagano, Condé says : "Les femmes, chez moi … ont toutes des opinions politiques, des opinions sociales. Elles ont la conviction que dans la vie, elles doivent travailler pour la collectivité. Je ne pense pas qu'elles aient le désir de jouer un rôle de premier plan qui serait un rôle politique, puisque dans la réalité, les femmes antillaises … viennent très rarement sur le devant de la scène pour jouer un rôle politique. On laisse cela aux hommes" (383) [At home in Guadeloupe, women all have political and social opinions. They believe that they should work for the good of the collective. I don't think they have the desire to play a leadership role in politics because, in fact, West Indian women rarely come forward to play a political role. They leave that to the men (Eds.' trans.)]. I am heavily indebted to Blérald-Ndagano's rich, excellent dissertation throughout this study. It is a mine of information.

17. The repetition compulsion reveals which topics hold the greatest importance for individual writers. Condé's most recent novel, *Histoire de la femme cannibale*, reworks *Desirada*. Thanks to Anne-Katell Jaffrezic, who is writing a dissertation on the identity quest in Francophone Caribbean women's fiction and film, for this reference.

18. On Condé's reminiscences of Proust, particularly in *Le Cœur à rire et à pleurer: Contes vrais de mon enfance*, see Nesbitt, *Voicing Memory* 196-99.

19. See Rachel Blau DuPlessis, "For the Etruscans" (278).

20. And she adds, "…I laugh at myself [as I do at African American leaders who wish to rediscover a mythic Africa]. My quest is over. It ended with *Ségou*…. People have to understand one day that the quest must end and that they should live in the present" (quoted and summarized from Pfaff 98-100; 144-46]). Nesbitt, *Voicing Memory* 199-202) brilliantly discusses Condé's recent, apparently triumphalist play *An tan revolisyon: Elle court, elle court la liberté* (Basse-Terre: Le Conseil Régional de la Guadeloupe, 1989) as an ironic pastiche. The subtitle's allusion to the children's game "Il court, il court, le furet" (compare the veiled citation of the 17th-century Québécois folksong "À la claire fontaine" in the title *Le cœur à rire et à pleurer*) reinforces his arguments. See also Vèvè A. Clark, "Developing Diaspora Literacy and *Maroon* Consciousness" and "Developing Diaspora Literacy. Allusion in Maryse Condé's *Hérémakhonon*," in Davies and Fido, eds.

MONSTROUS READINGS: TRANS-GRESSION AND THE FANTASTIC IN CÉLANIRE COU-COUPÉ

Dawn Fulton

Is Célanire Pinceau a female Caribbean Frankenstein?[1] Condé is certainly not enigmatic about the potential connection between the heroine of her 2000 novel *Célanire cou-coupé* and Mary Shelley's creature, for the doctor who reattaches Célanire's severed head to her body and brings her back to life does so in explicit emulation of his "hero" Victor Frankenstein. Even without this direct reference, the resonance between these two texts would be difficult to overlook: Célanire is a scientifically impossible creature spurned by her maker, who goes out into the world striking fear and horror in those she encounters in an apparent quest for vengeance. Like Frankenstein's creature, Célanire represents a social monstrosity to the extent that she is positioned outside the familiar world, presenting a challenge to that world and disturbing its boundaries. As an outsider, the character thus affords the possibility of interrogating the social and cultural codes that exclude her, functioning in many ways as the very embodiment of the fears and anxieties particular to her historical context. Condé revises Shelley's creation, however, with a character who confronts a very different set of circumstances from those lived by Frankenstein's monster. As her heroine travels from Guadeloupe to France, the Ivory Coast, and Peru in her apparent pursuit of vengeance, Condé outlines a myriad of cross-cultural circumstances in the early part of the twentieth century, suggesting through Célanire what might have been rejected as monstrous or aberrant in such contexts. The fantastic genre of the novel suggests that the ways in which Condé revises the physical form of Shelley's creature are equally important, and that these revisions of the classic monster ultimately provide a revealing commentary on the notion of cultural hybridity.

The first few moments of Célanire's life establish her affiliation with the monstrous on both moral and physical levels: as a newborn she is found in the street in Guadeloupe, the victim of an attempted human sacrifice ordered by a desperate politician hoping to save his career. This "inhuman" crime is followed by the "unnatural" operation that saves her, as Dr. Jean Pinceau spends seven hours reconstructing the body of this tiny infant, who, upon her arrival on his operating table, had lost all of her blood and was "clinically dead" (106). Having recently read with fascinated interest Shelley's *Frankenstein*, Dr. Pinceau sets himself to his task with heady enthusiasm: "Je devais raccorder les artères, les veines, les nerfs, les tendons tranchés....Après, j'ai recousu les chairs. J'ai greffé sur la couture en dents de scie qui garrottait le petit cou une bande de peau prélevée sur la cuisse....Il me fallait du sang pour irriguer tout cela. J'ai transfusé celui de deux poulets que j'ai envoyé Ofusan quérir en vitesse. Tout le temps, je sentais qu'enfin j'étais l'émule de mon héros Victor Frankenstein et cela me cravachait. Moi aussi, j'égalais le Créateur et, quand l'enfant s'est mise à éternuer et à pleurer, je me suis senti éperdu d'orgueil"(117) [I had to reconnect the severed arteries, veins, nerves, and tendons...Then, I sutured the flesh. I grafted a strip of skin taken from her thigh onto the jagged suture that twisted around her neck...I needed blood to irrigate my work. I transfused the blood from two chickens that I sent Ofusan to fetch as fast as she could. The whole time I felt that here I was at last emulating my hero Victor Frankenstein, and it spurred me on. I too was equal to the Creator, and when the child began to sneeze and cry I was overcome with pride (107)]. Like Victor Frankenstein, Pinceau is intoxicated by his own power at this moment of creation, and like the Swiss doctor he too is suddenly horrified by the sight of the creature he has brought to life. Although he adopts Célanire and gives her his name, he remains unable to feel any affection for her, and is instead repulsed by her existence and especially by the scar around her neck, a constant reminder of his unnatural act.

The introduction of Célanire as an adult in the opening pages of the novel replicates this element of difference that marks her. Although her monstrous scar is concealed beneath an ever-present scarf, she is nonetheless someone who stands apart from the rest, someone who never escapes notice. The initial description of her is given through the eyes of Father Huchard as she arrives with other missionaries in the Ivory Coast in 1901, having completed her religious education in Paris. For Huchard, this woman is clearly out of the ordinary: "C'est que simplement l'oblat n'était pas ordinaire. Elle ne parlait guère. Elle ne semblait pas curieuse, excitée comme ses compagnes, impatientes de commencer leur apostolat. En plus, sa couleur la mettait à part, cette peau noire qui l'habillait comme un vêtement de grand deuil. Elle n'était pas franchement négresse. Plutôt métisse d'on ne savait combien de races. Elle ne portait pas l'habit religieux, n'ayant pas prononcé de vœux…(14) [It was simply the fact she stood out from the others. She hardly spoke. She did not seem curious or excited like her traveling companions, who were eager to begin their missionary work. What's more, her color set her apart, that dark skin that clothed her like a garment of deep mourning. Her features were not strictly black – rather, a hybrid of goodness knows how many races. She did not wear religious garb, since she had not yet taken her vows... (1)]. Huchard also, of course, notices the scarf around her neck, but as we see here, the "uncommon" quality of Célanire extends beyond this specific physical difference: as an object of the gaze, the heroine troubles conventional boundaries on multiple levels. Indeed, Célanire's situation at the novel's opening is emblematic of her position at the crossroads of a number of cultural, geographical, religious, and racial allegiances: she is a Guadeloupean woman in Africa, a Christian missionary who has not taken her vows, a person of mixed race in European clothing and with a European education. Her "monstrosity" thus arises in part from her refusal to remain within any given social boundary.

In a significant departure from the Frankenstein model, however, the creature in Condé's text is strikingly beautiful. Rather than inspiring universal horror and being categorically rejected from human society, as is the case for Shelley's monster, Célanire incites fascination as well as fear, holding a seductive power over men and women alike. Her beauty does little to normalize her, however; instead her mysterious sexuality is aligned with sorcery, as characters wonder if she has bewitched those who appear to have lost themselves under her influence. Condé thus suggests here a striking connection between Célanire's monstrosity and female sexuality; Célanire becomes a kind of Medusa figure, dangerous to those who dare to look at her, especially if their gaze is returned. While her admirers compare her eyes to stars, diamonds, and other precious stones, they are also frightened by their light: "leur éclat était insoutenable" (142) [it was difficult to sustain the look in those gleaming eyes of hers (131)]. Dr. Pinceau, furthermore, compares Célanire's scar to female genitals, describing it as "obscène, violacée comme un sexe infibulé" (119) [obscene...purplish as an infibulated labium (109)]. The doctor's horror at his creation thus evokes a Freudian castration anxiety, an anxiety reinforced later in Célanire's story by the mysterious deaths that accompany her on her journey, as two of the men who die are castrated.[2] Célanire would seem to represent the very embodiment of female sexual power, seen as dangerous and unnatural by others, and, in this instance, doubled by the presence of a monstrous scar.

In this context, however, the fact that Célanire can—and does—choose to conceal her scar cannot be underestimated. For if, as Chris Baldick has underlined in regard to *Frankenstein*, the moral function of the monster is primarily to render *visible* the results of aberration or unreason,[3] how then can we define a monster capable of hiding the primary sign of her unnaturalness at will? Indeed, for those who gaze upon Célanire, the anxiety she elicits is rarely produced by the scar itself, but rather by the fact that her neck is covered, making observers wonder what she is hiding; they are troubled not by the sight of something unnatural, but rather by the uneasy sense that something unfamiliar or threatening *could* be concealed behind her scarf. Célanire thus retains a certain amount of control over her own unnatural status: it is she who determines whether or not the physical markings of her monstrosity will be shown, and thus she who maintains the state of interpretive uncertainty in the other.

This control is an important aspect of Célanire's monstrosity, since it is not only as a physical being that she provokes anxiety, but as an active participant in the social circles she enters. Instead of conforming to the conventions of each of these settings, Célanire uses the power gained from various interpretive facets of her identity—her beauty, her religious faith, her European schooling—to claim spaces of her own and then to disturb the existing boundaries of convention. Indeed, transgression seems to be her primary motivation: each of her choices indicates a refusal of social norms, a troubling of the limits of acceptable sanctioned behavior. Célanire's specialty is the scandal, the blatant violation of familiar codes of conduct. Her actions thus contribute to the suspicion and disapproval she inspires in others, but this perception results from a conscious choice to rebel. Like the control she maintains over the visibility of her own body, Célanire's participation in her social worlds allows her to define her transgressions according to her own terms.

Among her principal transgressions is the advancement of women's education and independence: upon her arrival in the Ivory Coast, Célanire (thanks to the sudden and, according to some, all too convenient death of the former director) takes over the Foyer des métis, and transforms it into a haven for women, where girls can take classes alongside their male peers, and where young women can find protection from abusive husbands or from the practice of female excision. She also determines that the Foyer will provide a more nurturing home for orphans, insisting on their education and careful attention to their health. As the land surrounding the Foyer is cultivated, Célanire almost literally transforms the place into a garden paradise for her harbored women and children, a world apart from their previous lives of abuse, subservience, or neglect.

The Foyer thus becomes a quintessential space of transgression. By separating married women from their families and offering them an education equal to that of men, Célanire disrupts the Muslim social order to which they belong. She is unambiguous about the ramifications of her project, explaining to one character that her efforts stem from a desire to correct the errors of African society as she sees them: "A son avis, il n'y avait qu'une ombre à cette belle civilisation: le traitement des femmes" (34) [In her opinion there was only one dark side to the beauty of its civilization: the treatment of women (24)]. Her project is thus aligned with the intentional editing (and therefore disruption) of the cultural norms of the region. Meanwhile the physical work she does on the land is also viewed with suspicion: "Ses projets concernant le Foyer étaient inquiétants, car les terres entourant le Foyer n'étaient pas sans maître. Elles appartenaient aux Ebriés" (28) [Her plans for the Home were troubling, for the land around it did in fact belong to someone. It belonged to the Ebriés (18)]. No act of hers can be neutral, since the land, the space she occupies is not a blank page: in every domain she enters there is a pre-existing order she disturbs. Here in Adjame-Santey she manifestly disregards the indigenous codes of ownership and tradition, replacing them with her own "monstrous" vision of society. Added to this complexity is of course the fact that she is transforming these social orders in the name of the French state and as a member of a Christian mission. Despite her proclaimed devotion to African culture, then, she is nonetheless performing these cultural and religious transgressions as an outsider.

Célanire's presence in Adjame-Santey and later in Guadeloupe represents a threat not only because she promotes the liberation and education of women, but also because she blatantly violates sexual taboos. The two projects are in fact closely linked, since it soon becomes apparent that at the Foyer in Adjame-Santey Célanire has also founded a brothel, with the specific goal of encouraging interracial love. In her mind, the solution to colonialism is to be found in the intimate relationship between the African woman and the European man: "Est-ce qu'un colon qui avait serré une négresse dans ses bras restait le même?... Le Foyer des métis serait le lieu de rencontre qui manquait, l'endroit privilégié où naîtrait, croîtrait, se multiplierait l'amour entre les races. C'était cela sa vocation" (51) [Once the colonizer had clasped a black woman in his arms, could he ever be the same again?... The Home for Half-Castes would be that meeting place that was sorely lacking, a privileged place where love between the races would fructify, grow, and multiply. That was its vocation (41)]. Through her Foyer Célanire thus institutionalizes sexual practices that until her arrival had remained unacknowledged, silenced by social convention. Beyond the disruption caused by the visibility of these transgressions and the intentionality of her project, Célanire also leaves her mark on the economic system in Adjame-Santey. The African women receive gifts from their French partners that, in combination with the education they complete, allow them to substantially shift their social status: "Ainsi, relativement fortunées, sachant lire et écrire elles firent de beaux mariages et contribuèrent à la naissance d'une véritable aristocratie dans le pays" (90) [Relatively well off, therefore, knowing how to read and write, they married into good families and helped form a veritable aristocracy in the country (80)]. Célanire's project fundamentally transforms the economic system of exchange in the region, giving rise not only to a changed relationship between the races, but also to a new social class.

The heroine's own sexuality of course participates in this particular transgression, as she has an affair with and eventually marries the French colonial officer Thomas de Brabant in a direct violation of his own personal interdiction of physical intimacy with African women. According to several reports from those working at the Foyer, she is also sexually involved with two women: Mme Desrussie, the widow of the mysteriously deceased director of the Foyer, and Tanella, an African woman accused of murdering the king's uncle in a refusal of his sexual advances. Célanire provokes further disturbance by allowing this intimacy to be publicly legible: one of the instructors at the Foyer recounts that Célanire and Tanella "buvaient du champagne dans la même coupe jusqu'à être complètement grisées. Une fois les visiteurs partis, elles s'enfermaient dans la même chambre. Si Tanella était timide, Célanire était très hardie. Même en public, c'étaient des 'ma cocotte' et des 'ma chérie doudou' qui n'arrêtaient pas et des caresses sans équivoque" (84) [drank champagne from the same glass until they were completely intoxicated. Once the visitors had left, they locked themselves in the same room. If Tanella was shy, Célanire was excessively bold. Even in public it was a never-ending serenade of "my pet" and "my little darling" and unequivocal caresses (74)]. Again, Célanire's transgressive acts are doubly so in that she *chooses* to make them visible as such, maintaining control over the social perception of her actions. Later, in Guadeloupe, she once again uses institutionalization as a means of reinforcing the visibility of supposedly unnatural behavior. Through her relationship with a lesbian separatist and founder of a women's association, she designates a space for this association which will allow women to live in isolation from men: "Sous leur impulsion, l'inoffensif îlet Fajoux…était transformé en Lesbos" (176) [At their initiative, the innocent little island of Fajoux…was transformed into Lesbos (165)]. The surrounding Guadeloupean society reacts, not surprisingly, with a mixture of shock and fear: "Les pêcheurs, choqués par ces accouplements qui se faisaient presque sous leurs nez, se dépêchèrent de relever leurs filets et le poisson commença à manquer en Grande-Terre" (176) [The fishermen, shocked by the copulation going on almost under their noses, quickly hauled in their nets, and it wasn't long before there was a shortage of fish in Grande-Terre (166)]. As in Africa, Célanire's initiative, specifically because of its transgressive nature, engages a transformation of the landscape and causes a fundamental shift in the systems of economic exchange in the region.

Condé's creature, then, is monstrous not only because of her unknown origins, her unnatural re-creation, and her hideous scar, but also because she represents transgression in her acts—in the space she occupies, the partners she chooses, the politics she enacts, the institutions she builds. In each of the religious, cultural, and spiritual spheres she encounters, she exposes the limits of socially sanctioned behavior by violating those limits. Just as Victor Frankenstein's creature can be seen as the manifestation of a range of contemporary social anxieties, from Enlightenment science to maternity to revolutionary upheaval in France, Célanire exposes the fears and concerns particular to the various worlds she enters.[4] Unlike Shelley's monster, however, she is in control of her own monstrosity, and thus can to a certain extent manipulate her public through an understanding of their anxieties.

Public perception is central to Célanire's experience. As we have seen, her transgressions are twofold, in that she disrupts the limits of social convention and then forces that society to confront her disruptive acts by making them visible. To return to the image of her scar, however, it is important to remember that the *concealment* of transgression can be equally disruptive: in fact, Célanire is perhaps all the more threatening because those around her are not entirely sure who she is or what her true motivations are. Versions and explanations conflict; first-hand accounts of her behavior meld into rumor and exaggeration; and interpretation vacillates with shifts in audience. By maintaining this aura of mystery, Célanire keeps her public suspended in a constant state of interpretive uncertainty, and it is perhaps in this sense that she is most "monstrous," since she refuses even the interpretive proscriptions of a society constantly thwarted in its attempts to fix her identity.

In this context the genre with which Condé chose to tell Célanire's story merits closer consideration. The novel is designated a *"roman fantastique,"* signaling a narrative form well suited to echo Shelley's classic. But beyond the thematic link to the monster's creation, the genre mirrors the conception of this heroine in crucial ways: even in its most general definition, the fantastic narrative elicits the collision of various worlds, of the real and the unreal, the known and the unknown, the natural and the supernatural. It is thus first and foremost a transgressive genre, in that it depends upon the departure from the familiar, the escape from the normative. Linked to the fantasy, it suggests the breaking of social codes and the crumbling of boundaries between the possible and the impossible.[5] Inherent in this collision of worlds is also the encounter with the other—the alien, the demon, the monster, the sorcerer, the mythical creature. The newly formed narrative world of the fantastic thus inscribes multiple modes of understanding and communication; the fabric of the fantastic is necessarily a patchwork one, combining various and conflicting perceptions of reality and suggesting a context in which such perceptions might coexist. In this sense, the fantastic can itself be seen as a "monstrous" narrative: much like Frankenstein's creature, it is an entity constructed from the suturing of materials from disparate sources.[6] Condé's novel too follows this model, not only because of the element of the supernatural but also due to its diverse cultural lexicons and multiple spheres of reference. The conflicting worlds inhabited by Célanire produce fragments of information that shift constantly and refuse to cohere around any single vision of reality. The narrative is thus "monstrous" in that it does not represent a coherent whole through the lens of any particular interpretive context.

There is, however, an important substantial (in the literal sense) difference between Shelley's creature and Condé's: for Célanire as a physical being is not a patchwork of disparate human body parts but a *single* human body severed in two and then reattached. In fact, the splitting of her body is (just barely) incomplete, as when she is discovered in the street her head "hangs by a thread": "sa tête ne tenait qu'à un fil" (116). Presumably it is this fragile remaining connection between body and head that allows Jean Pinceau to perform his miraculous operation. We need not interpret this detail as "naturalizing" the event in any way: the revival of Célanire's bloodless body (not to mention the replacement of her human blood with that of a chicken) ensures the potential incursion of the unnatural. But it is important to note this critical morphological difference between the classic creature and Condé's heroine: the result of Jean Pinceau's labor is, while monstrous and incoherent, the (re)assemblage of parts from a single human body.

If we return to the question of form, then, the discursive function of Célanire's reassembled body is instructive. For, as we have seen, the circumstances of Célanire's re-creation mean that she can, if she chooses, *appear* to be a scientifically coherent physical form; she can appear to belong to the natural world, with only the mysterious scarf as a disturbing suggestion of other possibilities. Her monstrosity thus does not have to be immediately apparent, but will emerge depending on how she is seen by others. Similarly, the fantastic as a genre functions crucially on interpretation: the categories navigated by the fantastic—of realism and fantasy, of possible and impossible, of known and unknown—are categories established by the reader. Depending on such factors as cultural or historical background, religious belief, gender, age, sexuality, and individual experience, a given reader will be equipped with his or her particular conception of the "natural" or the "real," and will recognize the fantastic as a disruption of that specific set of codes.[7] In *Célanire cou-coupé*, by invoking such systems of understanding as animism, Christianity, Islamic faith, and Western science, Condé allows for a culturally diverse lexicon in order to produce a potentially limitless number of "monstrous" narratives, both of Célanire herself and of events in the novel. The text thus insists on a multicultural reading, an interpretive participation in its monstrosity.

What is striking about Condé's novel is that these various possible interpretations of events coexist simultaneously. Multiple accounts of a single series of events are offered side by side, conferring no priority of the rational over the irrational, the secular over the sacred, the known over the unknown. In particular, the numerous deaths that coincide disconcertingly with Célanire's presence produce heightened interpretive tension in the novel, as each one of them has a number of possible explanations, none of which is confirmed within the narrative. The body of Thomas de Brabant's French wife Charlotte, for example, is discovered deep in the forest, destroyed almost beyond recognition: "Le spectacle était terrible. On aurait dit que des fauves, mangeurs de chair humaine et buveurs de sang frais, avaient eu affaire à elle. Aux alentours du corps, la terre était labourée en tranchées. Pourtant, aucun lion n'était signalé dans la région" (62) [The sight was horrible. It was as if wild beasts, eaters of human flesh and drinkers of fresh blood, had done her in. All around the body the earth had been clawed into ruts. Yet no lion had been reported in the region (52)]. As evidenced by this citation, the passage describing the discovery of Charlotte's body emphasizes the limits of the possible that, through the lens of the natural, the rational, the scientific, appear to have been severely tested. The hypothesis of an attack by wild animals as the means of death is undermined by the lack of concrete evidence; meanwhile it seems implausible that the less than sturdy Charlotte could have walked alone across the kilometers of dangerous terrain between the forest and her home. General opinion in the community proposes that Célanire is guilty of this murder, yet while the Europeans attempt to find a scientific explanation for how the crime was carried out, the African population sees Charlotte's death as further proof that Célanire is a "cheval," a carrier of evil spirits seeking vengeance on the living and certain to strike again. The novel offers no resolution to this conflict and, as the deaths associated with Célanire multiply, preserves the status of Célanire's culpability as a suggestion, but never as definitive. The conflicting readings of these events thus maintain an unsettling coexistence in the narrative, each representing the impossibility of the others but forced to occupy the same discursive space.

Given this interpretive instability, Condé's novel corresponds to the more strict definition of the fantastic genre elaborated by Tzvetan Todorov in his *Introduction à la littérature fantastique*. Here the fantastic is not simply a genre that allows for departures from the real or the familiar, but one that is characterized above all by the simultaneity of two conflicting worlds, and by the resulting uncertainty on the part of the reader: "The fantastic is that hesitation experienced by a person who knows only the laws of nature, confronting an apparently supernatural event" (Todorov 1973, 25).[8] Once the reader chooses between the natural and the supernatural, the narrative is no longer a fantastic one. The two (or, in the case of Condé's novel, multiple) possible interpretations must carry equal discursive weight throughout the narrative, must conflict with one another without canceling each other out. The effectiveness of the fantastic narrative as elaborated by Todorov thus rests in the power of suggestion, rather than in the power of conviction: "'*I nearly reached the point of believing*': that is the formula which sums up the sprit of the fantastic. Either total faith or total incredulity would lead us beyond the fantastic: it is hesitation which sustains its life" (Todorov, 31). The reader of the fantastic can and should wonder, but must never be certain.

Much as the physical composition of Frankenstein's creature imitates the patchwork construction of Shelley's novel, Célanire's body provides a striking evocation of the fantastic narrative in this strict definition. Even without the piece of cloth to obscure her scar, the "natural" reading of Célanire's body is disturbingly coincident with the "unnatural" one: she is at once whole and divided, at once a living creature and a physical impossibility, at once known and unknown. Unlike Frankenstein's project, Dr. Pinceau's work represents an effort to recover a pre-existing form: Célanire's body thus refers back to the real, even as its scar points to its distance from the natural world. Like the fantastic narrative, then, this heroine's form is a simultaneous suggestion of two conflicting worlds, and her scar is the sign of that disturbance.[9] The anxiety produced by the sight of Célanire, even or perhaps especially when her scar is covered, marks a sudden awareness of the unknown. Célanire, like the fantastic narrative, thus represents at the same time a body existing wholly in the familiar world and the suggestion, necessarily inconclusive, of an unfamiliar one.

Condé's novel in fact evokes such troubled distinctions at various points in the narrative, particularly with reference to the popular knowledge of native communities in the Ivory Coast and in Peru. A reaction to the first mysterious death in Adjame-Santey, for example, proclaims that "aucune mort n'est naturelle" (18) [there is no such thing as a natural death (7)], thus putting the very category of the natural into question. Indeed, the notion of a natural death implies that it is an event that can be understood and known, while in fact death may be one of the most obvious examples of the ubiquitous unknown. Meanwhile in Peru a violent death yields the following comment: "Dans nos pays où l'imagination est souveraine, la curiosité populaire ne se satisfait pas de mystères. Chaque chose doit avoir une explication, de préférence surnaturelle" (224) [In our countries, where imagination reigns supreme, popular curiosity is not satisfied with a mystery. Everything has to have an explanation, preferably supernatural (215)]. Here the idea of the supernatural as a way to elucidate a mysterious event redefines the concept of the explanation as a de-mystifying, rational process: instead of being reasoned away, the supernatural *is* the explanation for the unknown. Like Célanire's scar, these passages evoke a division between two worlds even as they suture them together again, insisting on the arbitrary quality of such distinctions.

In the closing pages of the novel, Célanire seems to have completed a significant chapter in her journey: if she has indeed been pursuing her enemies, the last of their injustices has perhaps been avenged. "'Je n'ai plus rien à faire ici'" (233) [I have nothing more to do here (223)], she announces, and demands that her husband take her back to Guadeloupe. Greatly transformed after recovering from a nearly fatal illness, and seemingly drained of her previous thirst for revenge, she claims that she needs a new purpose, "une nouvelle raison de vivre" (238) [a new reason for living (228)]. Once in Guadeloupe, this newly formed ambition is made clear, as Célanire appears unexpectedly in her husband's bedroom, dressed in silk and lace and telling him she wants a child. "—S'il te plaît!" [—Please!] she pleads, "C'est tout ce que je peux être à présent: une bonne mère" (242) [All I can do now is be a good mother (232)].

Célanire's new reason for living, then, is procreation. With this dramatic conclusion, Condé would seem in a single gesture to recuperate a number of the monsters haunting Shelley's classic narrative: Célanire's claim is an assertion of female creativity, of birth, and of motherhood—a motherhood specifically characterized as "good," and thus an implied revision of the orphan's fate so frequently evoked in *Frankenstein*. But in the cross-cultural contexts of Condé's novel, it seems especially telling that Célanire also revives another monster destroyed in Shelley's narrative: the creature's bride. For Victor Frankenstein's refusal to allow his female creature to live arises out of a phobia of procreation; the thought of "a race of devils...propagated upon the earth" (Shelley, 144) gives him pause and prevents him from granting the creature's demand. The repression of this new species represented by the destruction of the female is thus categorically refused by Célanire's final words: Condé's creature *will* reproduce herself, she will create a new race of monsters.

In the context of Condé's novel, of course, the "race" of monsters spawned by Célanire would be monstrous in part because of their *race*: the product of her union with Thomas de Brabant would be interracial, or worse, racially indeterminate, thus realizing a primary colonial phobia. Again, Célanire's affirmation recuperates Frankenstein's censored material, since the geographical setting of the doctor's anxiety points to a colonial preoccupation hovering also in the shadows of Shelley's novel: in Frankenstein's imagination, it is in the New World that the creature and his bride would have released their race of devils upon an unsuspecting earth.[10] In Condé's novel, the colonial nightmare made real is miscegenation: Célanire's creation will violate the boundaries of race, power, and culture upon which the colonial system depends. Furthermore her child will represent the unknown, an invisible link to her monstrous mother and her mother's own undetermined origins. Célanire's creative act will thus expose the fundamental anxiety of race as a potential unknown.

In the final pages of her fantastic narrative, then, Condé would seem to propose a highly nuanced vision of hybridity. The child, like her mother, will belong at once to the natural and the unnatural, will be at once familiar and unfamiliar. If the foremost sign of the child's monstrosity is his or her mixed race, then that monstrosity must be read in the strictest sense of the fantastic not as an assemblage of multiple parts, but as a simultaneously whole and discontinuous being. The multiracial child is not, after all, the accumulation of different races, but a coexistence. The racial affiliations that contribute to his or her being are not visible as separate or separable parts, but instead must be apprehended as a whole, giving only the imprecise suggestion of otherness. In this sense the disturbance of social codes provoked by Célanire's and Thomas' offspring also troubles the very categories of race: by expressing the simultaneity of racial difference, Célanire's imagined progeny implies that the "parts" of which s/he will be composed are themselves arbitrary categories. Just as the fantastic destabilizes the distinction between the natural and the unnatural, the known and the unknown, the creature that exists as a simultaneous reference to multiple origins throws into question the very possibility of establishing racial divisions. Since the individual races that presumably produced the child are not visible as such, the child's existence destroys their viability as distinct categories. Célanire's final monstrous act is thus to expose the fundamental anxiety of race as a fear of the unknown, and to suggest further that the notion of hybridity, whether racial or cultural, cannot be thought as the sum of a series of parts, but represents rather a monstrous simultaneity of unknown worlds.

Notes

1. I refer here primarily to the creature brought to life by Victor Frankenstein, rather than to the doctor himself, although in using the doctor's name to designate his creation I do wish to preserve some of the identity confusion between the two characters amply elaborated by numerous critics. See in particular Berman (56), Reichardt (138), and Baldick's analysis of the various distortions of the Frankenstein myth (3-9).

2. On the links between the creature's gaze in *Frankenstein* and the Freudian model of the Medusa figure, see Salotto (194-96).

3. Baldick proposes this reading of the Frankenstein myth through Foucault's etymological definition of the monster as a being or object to be *shown* (*monstrare*) in order to *warn* (*monere*) humanity of the potential consequences of vice or unreasoned behavior (10ff).

4. See for example Ellen Moers' reading of *Frankenstein* as a "birth myth" (92), Fred Botting's analysis of the inscription of the French Revolution in Shelley's text, or Chris Baldick's reading of the "mad scientist" anxiety (141-42).

5. Roger Caillois discusses the fantastic as a rupture of narrative coherence in his *Anthologie du fantastique*. On the function of the fantasy in *Frankenstein*, see Rosemary Jackson's essay in *Aspects of Fantasy*.

6. The conception of Shelley's novel as a monstrous narrative, first suggested by the author herself in her introduction to the 1831 edition of the novel with a reference to her "hideous progeny" (25), has been taken up by a number of critics. Fred Botting, for example, has described the novel as "an 'assemblage' of fragments, a disunified text that subverts the possibility and implications of textual and semantic coherence" (27), while Eleanor Salotto proposes that Shelley's text falls into the monstrous inasmuch as it is an autobiographical text, the self-representation of a multiple subject; see also Baldick (30-33).

7. On this aspect of the fantastic, see Morse's introduction to *The Fantastic in World Literature and the Arts* (1-3).

8. Todorov's definition of the genre has not, of course, escaped criticism (see for example Brooke-Rose, Lem, and Sandor), but his emphasis on the *simultaneity* of conflicting interpretations captures an essential component of Condé's narrative.

9. In his work on myths and the fantastic, Andras Sandor uses the image of the scar to evoke the confusing simultaneity of the genre: "The fantastic suggests a scar that cannot be smoothed out, a scar that cannot heal" (349).

10. As Helena Woodard has proposed, this reproduction of the Other is the ultimate colonial fear, "a colonial power's worst nightmare: Caliban's threat to Miranda to people the world with 'little Calibans'" (26).

OEDIPUS AND OEDIPA ACCORDING TO CONDÉ (ALIASES: DIEUDONNÉ AND ROSÉLIE)

Christiane Makward, with Anne Oszwald

Caribbean Oedipus, Black Oedipa—do they exist, like Black Orpheus and Black Venus? Like many of its type, an essay entitled *Oedipe africain* demonstrated the habit of analysts to compile case studies but, disappointingly, in this instance, the patients are psychotic rather than neurotic. They hardly illustrate dramatic relationships to the maternal principle or the parental couple, and they are not afforded restructuring through language, communicating mostly through interpreters. While Africanists would generally not question the solidly patriarchal structure of most African societies, African daughters such as Calixthe Beyala with *Le petit prince de Belleville* (1992) and now Marie NDiaye with *Papa doit manger* (2002) have brazenly shaken the clay-footed colossus. It is tempting to follow Lydie Moudileno in the opening of her remarkable reading of Maryse Condé's *Desirada* (1997). The critic recalls a noted feature of Caribbean cultures: "Largement marquée par la démission des pères, la fiction francophone antillaise nous a habitués aux quêtes identitaires dans lesquelles l'espace maternel est toujours crucial à la formulation des subjectivités modernes" ("Le rire," 1151) [Widely imprinted by the fathers' failure, Francophone Caribbean fiction has made familiar to us identity quests where maternal space is always crucial to the articulation of modern subjectivities].[1] Maternal presence figures prominently in fiction as in Caribbean life.

A 1987 work by French psychiatrist, Jacques André, *L'inceste focal dans la famille noire antillaise* builds upon the extensive socio-psychological literature on gender roles in African-American societies (epitomized in the title *My Mother Who Fathered Me* by E. Clarke).

The Caribbean model is shown to be a matriarchal structure. The mother stands as the ultimate authority figure, and she tends to stay her position by compensating with endemic pluripaternity and *de facto* polygamy. In this system, *mother* as "the master-post" is the only non-interchangeable, non-disposable female: "En régime matrifocal, partir n'est pas mourir. La maisonnée est un espace que l'on quitte pour ne cesser d'y revenir" (371) [In a matrifocal system, out of sight is not out of mind. The (mother's) house is a space you leave to return to endlessly]. Although not matriarchal in the sense of having social power, Caribbean culture clearly rests on matriarchy within the home.

Younger Franco-Caribbean women writers rest their own perspectives toward the problematic family on the general consensus that the mother remains the focus, the supporting beam or *poto-mitan* of societal fabric. The status quo hardly seems endangered. Women are deemed to overvalue and spoil their men and their sons, as if to redeem some unspeakable guilt.[2] But as girls are exposed to new models, and no longer doomed to unwanted pregnancies, they can explore new forms of subjecthood and exorcise ancient, mother-induced blinders. Daughterly resistance is the focus of Gisèle Pineau's 2002 novel, *Chair piment*, but earlier on, in *L'espérance-macadam* (1996) for example, the daughter destroyed the ancient order at the risk of being killed by her own mother.[3]

There probably is not a single text by Maryse Condé that does not modulate in some manner the fantasy known as *regressus ad uterum*, the wish to return to the womb, one step removed from the wish to have never been born, the death wish. As common symptoms of a protagonist's mild or acute anxiety, aspects of this fantasy range from discreet similes—a crab scuttling back to its hole in the sand—to an existential musing that occurs in *Histoire de la femme cannibale*: " ... vous ne voulez pas rentrer en Guadeloupe? / - Elle aussi disait 'rentrer.' Rentrer dans l'île comme dans le ventre de sa mère. Le malheur est qu'une fois expulsé on ne peut plus y rentrer. Retourner s'y blottir. Personne n'a jamais vu un nouveau-né qui se refait foetus. Le cordon ombilical est coupé. Le placenta enterré. On doit marcher crochu marcher quand même jusqu'au bout de l'existence" (246) ["... you don't want to return to Guadeloupe?" / - She said "return." Re-turn, re-enter the island like the mother's womb. The trouble is, once ejected, it's impossible to reenter. To return to nest there. No one has ever seen a newborn that regresses to foetus. The umbilical cord is cut. The placenta buried. One must trek crooked and trek all the same to the other end of existence]. Condé's more attentive readers have long noticed characters' guilt regarding a dead mother, or nostalgia to visit her graveside. This leitmotif appeared in the 1972 play *Dieu nous l'a donné*. Recent auto-biographical texts have shed full light on its link to Condé's own experience. Behind the skepticism she underlined on the father figure in Franco-Caribbean women's novels (in *La parole des femmes*) there lies a personal trauma. Paternal retribution struck when, having disgraced herself as a less than studious student in Paris, she was neither brought home nor informed of her mother's death for several months.[4]

Separation from the mother—that specifically delicate task for the developing young female, as was established by Simone de Beauvoir's and Nancy Chodorow's famed essays[5] —is the real task facing Condé's latest protagonists, the "cannibal woman" and the misfit, mixed-up Dieudonné, who are both excessive mother-lovers. In this critical reading, it is productive to examine how Condé's most recent novels, *La Belle Créole* (2001) and *Histoire de la femme cannibale* (2003*)* constitute a diptych where the same Oedipal attachment to the mother is foregrounded, on either side of the gender divide. These books fully develop a recurring, here-tofore subtle topic. With Condé's seemingly inexhaustible talent for tale-spinning and fabulation, the murder of the father—that crucial component of the Oedipus myth—had already received a particularly elaborate, iconoclastic development in the 2000 fiction, *Célanire cou-coupé*, labelled "roman fantastique" for good reasons [*Who Slashed Celanire's Throat? A Fantastical Tale*]. The quest in this case was to identify, to find, and to destroy the biological father. As indicated elsewhere,[6] Célanire's struggle with her father is terminal for him but nearly fatal for her too: the primordial combat is eerily lyrical, without comic relief, contrary to the bulk of this fanciful, often hilarious novel. It is the major episode in the narrative that truly justifies the critical label of "fantastic" or "marvelous realism" claimed by the subtitle.

Creative writers in French have always exploited the homonymy of *la mer* [the sea] and *la mère* [the mother]. Poets, novelists, songwrit-ers have connected the terms through countless metaphors around amniotic fluid (euphemised as "les eaux"), the womb, paradise lost, fusion, milk, soothing waves and rocking boats. So it seems legiti-mate to embark on a psycho-critical voyage to read Maryse Condé's *La Belle Créole*, a novel partly built around these symbols, and also including unabashed components of the Oedipus myth. The title refers to an aging sailboat, the favourite shelter of the (well-named) orphaned protagonist Dieudonné [Godgiven], raised in ignorance of his father's identity.

Throughout the novel, various motifs are spun in spider-web fashion, to connect the protagonist Dieudonné to maternal symbols: his late mother Marine, whose name needs no comment, the sea itself, the boat, as well as his aging mistress Loraine, whom he kills (rather) accidentally. Loraine's first name may be an antithetical reference to the least 'marine' but dearly 'French' region on the German border (Alsace-Lorraine); more likely—for the quality of her voice, her fair hair, and such—it evokes the actress Lauren Bacall. At an advanced stage of alcoholism, this Loraine is anything but a 'dry' character. Many surges of a melancholic desire to regress to the womb, to return to the sea, to swim in "Loraine's waters," punctuate the narrative. In the second half of a disorderly yet ordered narrative (numbered chapters, plot conducted in a fragmented spiral), Dieudonné is also seized by the urge to kill his father, having finally learned that the sarcastically named Milo Vertueux had abandoned Marine before the boy's birth (a trauma experienced by the author herself in her student years). The conspicuous Oedipal structure is embedded in a richly detailed, very contemporary Guadeloupean context. Tradition—fear of darkness, family law of silence, leitmotif of the "infernal" dogs—plays its part; but the narrative gives primacy to the current social frescoe: contemporary mobility for the haves or jet-setters, vagrancy for the have-nots, squatters and boat-people, and rampant political unrest.

Dieudonné's confused feelings regarding motherhood, fatherhood, and love peak in bouts of parricidal impulse and unrecognised homosexual desire. His quest for the mother's exclusive love (Loraine stands as the perfect love object, that is the lover and substitute mother) constitutes the private, psychological drama in this novel, purportedly a rewriting of *Lady Chatterley's Lover*, whose author, D. H. Lawrence, also penned, lest we forget, *Sons and Lovers*. However, other readings will certainly show that this may be the most political and 'creolist' novel written by Condé in recent years, since the narrative is strictly limited to her native island. The reality described and the passions, however, will appear very familiar to denizens of the world aware of the paramount clash of the powerless and the powerful, a clash that knows no ethnicity, gender, or religion.

Oedipus and Oedipa According to Condé: (Aliases: Dieudonné and Rosélie)

The novel opens on Dieudonné's acquittal for the murder of a rich, ill-famed *béké* employer, his faithless lover Loraine. Details will slowly trickle in but the reader is at once informed of the protagonist's "orphan" status. His lawyer rhetorically vows to be the uncle, father and grandfather Dieudonné never had (21). As in *Desirada*, the grandmother figure here is a none too nurturing presence. The mother's given name, Marine, first appears in connection with hurricane Hugo, which branded Dieudonné's memory at age ten. Their house being very fragile, Marine had found shelter in Fanniéta's solid, concrete apartment. Dieudonné proves incapable of taking his turn in the collective rape of a girl, taking place during the passage of Hugo (an intertextual compliment to Pineau's *Macadam Dreams*?). The boy is labelled "Makoumè" (24) [faggot] by the gang, Condé informing us that nine months later a baby girl was born to the victim, who named her Huguette. The young mother will never breathe a word about the "origins" of her pregnancy, but most irrationally she bears a special grudge towards Dieudonné.

We also learn that Dieudonné is subject to "fits" eventually declared "genetic": "Maladie génétique? En clair, cela veut dire maladie qu'on est incapable de guérir" (23) [Genetic disease? In clear language, it means a disease that can't be cured]. This unusual definition exemplifies Condé's humor and her tight control of narrative: for now, there must be erasure of the "origins" and the genitor question, for Dieudonné as for baby Huguette. As part of this opening, we find out how Marine, working to repair the roof of her fragile dwelling, had crashed down at her son's feet and become paralysed. The mother-child role now reversed, she survived a few years, in Dieudonné's devoted, silent care: "C'est dans le silence que, des années durant, il avait pris soin de sa mère. On lui avait percé un trou dans la gorge par où sortait un filet de voix sourd, caillouteux. Elle ne s'en servait jamais, commandant son garçon par regards et par signes, le remerciant de la même façon" (33) [It was in silence that, for years, he had taken care of his mother. A hole had been pierced in her throat to let out her husky, jerky voice. She never used it, ordering her son with glances and signs, thanking him in the same way]. In case we missed the message, public rumor goes: "Dieudonné avait adoré Marine. Durant son long calvaire, il avait été un fils sans reproche, la nourrissant à la cuillère, la baignant, la frictionnant, l'habillant, lui faisant faire ses besoins sans dégoût. À sa mort, qui avait été un soulagement pour toute la famille, on avait cru qu'il deviendrait fou. Il avait disparu au beau mitan de la veillée.... Des heures plus tard, ils l'avaient retrouvé errant sur des rochers en bordure de mer" (158) [Dieudonné had adored his mother. Through her long martyrdom, he had been an exemplary son, spoon-feeding her, bathing her, rubbing her, dressing her, helping with her bodily functions without disgust. When she died—which was a relief for the whole family—they thought he would lose his mind. He had left right in the middle of the wake.... Hours later they found him wandering among rocks along the sea]. Clearly the sea lies in the place of the mother. Dieudonné finds a shelter that combines the virtues of a symbolic womb, such as the sea and the boat, and the actual nurturing powers of an ageing woman: Loraine as substitute mother.

As she will later explore with the character of Rosélie in *Histoire de la femme cannibale*, Condé creates with Dieudonné a derelict, non-malicious, selfless figure, prone to love and care to a rare degree. Before his mother's accident, Marine's friendly bosses and owners of *La Belle Créole* had "adopted" and integrated the boy into their happy family. So, he knows what paradise tastes like: "des palmes aux talons, [ils] lui apprenaient à caracoler dans le ventre de la mer" (26) [with fins on his feet, (they) taught him to romp around the womb of the sea]. There is an explicit link between Dieudonné's physical ailment and his mental discomfort: his headaches and occasional nervous fits remind us of Proust's and Gide's childhood psychosomatic troubles.

The boy's condition worsens notably after his protectors' departure—they leave their boat behind—and after his mother's death, naturally. Illegal drugs are found to soothe his anguish, but their effect is soon surpassed by his love for Loraine, a portly, fifty-plus beauty, the age of his own mother: "Inutile de dire qu'une fois Dieudonné au service de Loraine, ses maux de tête s'envolèrent. À croire que ses regards, son odeur, ses rares sourires, toute sa personne composaient une drogue plus magique que le crack, plus puissante que tous les remèdes" (70) [Needless to say, once Dieudonné was in Loraine's service, his headaches vanished. As if her glances, her smell, her rare smiles, her entire person composed a drug more magical than crack, more powerful than any medicine]. For nearly a year, Loraine is the mother figure *par excellence*, performing the Oedipus/Jocasta complex we read in a situation where the protagonists themselves only see love (Dieudonné), or brash self-indulgence (Loraine reputedly has "collected" Black gigolos).

Oedipus and Oedipa According to Condé: (Aliases: Dieudonné and Rosélie)

From Dieudonné's standpoint, this is a 'true love' story: the narrative voice insists on the quality of the devotion Dieudonné shows to Loraine. More caring, healing, and 'mothering' take place than material gains or sexual intimacy. This relationship—sex aside—duplicates his tender care and unconditional love for Marine:

> Quand commença-t-il à l'entourer de soins?...Il prit l'habitude de dormir léger, léger comme une mère dont l'enfant est fiévreux, car ses nuits étaient peuplées de mauvais rêves, toujours les mêmes, de douleurs, toujours les mêmes…. Et, la servant ainsi, il croyait servir Marine ressuscitée. Il se sentait revenu au temps où sa mère vivait encore, prostrée dans son fauteuil, pareille à une momie, ne communiquant avec lui que par ses regards toujours lumineux à force de tendresse…. Il comprit vite qu'elle était aussi seule sur terre que Marine. (60-61)

> [When did he start pampering her?...He took to sleeping light, as light as a mother whose child has a fever, because his nights were full of bad dreams, always the same ones, full of pains, always the same ones…. And, serving her in this way, he thought he was serving Marine risen from the dead. He felt he was back to the time when his mother was still alive, prostrated in her armchair, like a mummy,[7] communicating with him only through eyes always bright with tenderness…. He quickly understood that she was as lonely on earth as Marine].

He thus adopts a maternal role to symbolically resuscitate Marine.

But Loraine does not love him as his mother did. She uses him for comfort when needed and discards him when drawn elsewhere, to the wrong 'object' in classic Racinian style, leaving Dieudonné devastated: "Elle s'avançait, trébuchant, s'appuyant sur le bras de Luc alors que, pensait-il, elle ne pouvait s'appuyer que sur le sien…. S'était-il trompé en croyant qu'elle avait besoin de lui, autant qu'autrefois Marine avait besoin de lui ?" (78) [She was stumbling along, leaning on Luc's arm when, he thought, she could only lean on his…. Did he fool himself by believing that she needed him as much as Marine had, earlier?]. The superimposition of Loraine and Marine is repeatedly conveyed in Dieudonné's thoughts, and it is related to ambiguous feelings about Luc: desiring to be in Luc's place, as Loraine's love object, and feeling uplifted by Luc's attentions, desiring to become him, to fuse with the radiant young artist.

These are what Condé would call "cannibalistic" impulses that torture the protagonist and are not controlled by him.[8]

Luc's appearance on the (Oedipal) scene brings on a third fall from grace. After the Cohens' departure and Marine's demise, the harmless, gentle protagonist is now callously chased away: "Alors elle s'était mise à hurler…: - Je m'en fous. En tout cas, disparais…. La veille, il avait planté pour elle des alamandas bleus, si rares à acclimater. Malgré cela, elle le jetait dehors ainsi qu'un chien. Avait-il mérité qu'elle le maltraite pareillement? Des larmes roulèrent sur ses joues. Seule, Loraine avait le génie de lui mettre les yeux en eau. (112) [Then she started yelling…: - I don't care. In any case, get lost…. The day before he had planted blue alamandas for her, the ones so tricky to grow here. Did he deserve such mistreatment from her? Tears rolled down his cheeks. Only Loraine knew how to turn his eyes to water]. Thus, Loraine's house becomes another lost paradise, propelling Dieudonné in search of a new shelter: "La pluie, épuisée par ses accès de violence, s'était calmée. Elle l'enveloppa tiède aux épaules…. Rejeté, exclu, il s'assit dans le jardin. Dans la noirceur, l'ylang-ylang embaumait le bonheur perdu" (77) [The rain, spent in its violent fits, had calmed down. It set a warm wrap around his shoulders…. Rejected, excluded, he sat down in the garden. In the darkness, the scent of the ylang-ylang gave out a fragrance of happiness lost]. This imagined Eden signals another attempt to return to the comfort of the womb.

Dieudonné then reconnects with a previous paradise, the Cohen's family boat, *La Belle Créole* of times before his mother's accident: "Il alla se réfugier à *La Belle Créole* où, hormis son bref passage avec Lili [Loraine's dog], il n'avait pas mis les pieds depuis des mois et se heurta à Boris, qui s'abritait du mauvais temps" (73) [He took refuge on *La Belle Créole* where, apart from his brief visit with Lili, he had not set foot for months, and he bumped into Boris, seeking shelter from the bad weather]. The leitmotif of the boat as shelter and private space is central to the story. It is compared to a woman's body, the space of his desire to go back to the womb and stop suffering: "Dieudonné retrouva *La Belle Créole* comme une femme aimée dont il aurait été séparé pendant longtemps" (208) [Dieudonné recovered *La Belle Créole* like a loved woman he would have been separated from for a long time]. The Creole myth of the seductive *manman d'lo* is subjacent here: Dieudonné is in love with the sea and the boat, as if with a prow siren. Internal voices denounce his unusual passion: " - Quitte ce bateau. Les hommes ne sont pas des poissons pour rester dans l'eau" (165-6) ["Leave that boat. Men are not fish to live in water"].

The metaphor goes further, as Dieudonné, whose nostalgia is the prenatal fusion experienced in Marine's womb, fits "naturally" in the rocking boat in the water, and loves swimming, with erotic connotations and associations with Loraine: "...la mer pouvait se comparer à un cheval de rodéo, cabrée, gonflée, parcourue de lames qui désarçonnaient.... Lui, si elle l'avait voulu, ne se serait pas éloigné d'elle en ces heures de liesse universelle (217) [...the sea could be compared to a rodeo horse, skittish, pumped up, seized by waves that threw off the rider.... If only she had wanted, he would not be away from her at this time of universal celebration]. Concurrent equine imagery applies to the boat and the sea: Condé works with the myth of *Manman d'lo*, turning old Neptune into the 'Queen of the Fish' or super-siren (or sea-mare) in a flamboyant sally: "Pendant qu'il s'affairait, on aurait cru que *La Belle Créole* comprenait ses intentions. Elle tressaillait, vibrait...piaffait, humait l'air...Doucement, il détacha *La Belle Créole* du quai, la sentit frémir, la flatta comme un cheval dont on entend ménager la fougue.... Brusquement, tout fut comme avant" (229-30) [It was as if *La Belle Créole* understood his intentions. She quivered, she vibrated,...she stomped, and sniffed the air.... Softly, he untied *La Belle Créole* from the pier, he felt her shuddering, patted her like a horse whose fire must be tempered.... Suddenly, everything was like before]. Thus, Dieudonné rides off, not into the sunset but down under, into the marine realm, a blue space that will fill his eyes forever (244).

His ultimate vision again superimposes the love of Loraine, the sea, and his mother as the text glides over various feminine pronouns (*elle, celle*):

> Il suffirait que le vent se lève...pour qu'il soit emporté vers le pays d'où l'on ne revient jamais. N'est-ce pas ce qu'il voulait? Ce qu'il désirait de toutes ses forces? Il n'avait rien à faire sur une terre où elle n'était plus.... Elle était morte figée dans la violence, peut-être dans la haine. Alors, il allait rejoindre celle qui ne l'avait jamais rudoyé ni méprisé, celle qui ne s'était jamais trompée sur son compte. Elle le prendrait contre elle et il suffoquerait dans ses bras. Peut-être, dans l'inconnu qui l'attendait, retrouverait-il Marine (243).

> [All that was needed was a rising breeze...to be taken away to the land of no return. Wasn't it what he wanted?

225

What he desired with all his will? He had no business in a world she had left.... She had died frozen in violence, in hate perhaps. So, he would return to the one who had never roughed him up nor spurned him, the one who was never mistaken about him. That mistress would press him against her and he would be stifled in her arms. Perhaps, in the unknown world awaiting him, he would find Marine].

Enveloped, smothered, lost, he imagines a blessed oblivion.

In *La Belle Créole* Condé creates an empathetic illustration of the archetype we can name Caribbean Oedipus. Though not devoid of irony, it shows how personal history repeats itself and fits into History. Dieudonné kills Loraine 'accidentally' (she is drunk, they struggle, her gun goes off), but also because she has insulted 'the Race' through the individual victim. Having claimed that her 'Godgiven' gift is Luc—not Dieudonné, a less than nothing piece of rot—she trespasses: "Il te manque la trique dont tu garderas éternellement le souvenir" (224) [What you are missing is the stick you'll never forget through eternity]. Condé's novel suggests how tragically normal it is for a man raised without a father to have no paternal 'instinct,' no desire to attach himself durably to a female other than a mother figure. In such a world, female solidarity can function, as long as the hierarchy is clear. The narrator is not completely cynical about it. Carla encounters such a community when she goes with Inis to Maraval, where her single mother lives with her divorced sister and her daughters: "Là, dans cette commune rurale...elle se retrouvait parmi les femmes sans hommes dont la vie s'honorait de tâches sans éclat: cuisiner, élever des enfants, tenir une maison.... À chaque fois [Carla] se demandait si là ne résidait pas l'essentiel du bonheur; si sa quête du parfait compagnon n'était pas irréaliste" (198) [In that rural community...she stood as one of those women without a man, whose life was graced by humble tasks: to cook, to raise children, to run a household.... Each time, Carla wondered if the essence of happiness was not there, if her search for the perfect partner was not unrealistic].

Dieudonné's story ends with a display of paternal guilt at the memorial service: his body has not been found, only the boat. Vertueux's wife has waged moral war on him since they heard about his son's trial and acquittal: "...ils ne virent pas Milo Vertueux, agenouillé au dernier rang, la tête entre les mains. Sa femme l'avait persuadé que tout était arrivé par sa faute" (253) [...they did not see

Milo Vertueux on his knees in the back row, his head in his hands. His wife had convinced him that everything was his fault]. Adding irony to this vindictive note, Dieudonné's own, unacknowledged baby son is also present, in Ana's arms, an earthly replica of the absent father. This tableau satisfies the Oedipal drive to parricide—Vertueux's atonement in this case—the definitive fusion with the motherly waters: the hero is lost "en mer"; and with him, the possible continuation of the male curse.

In her restaging of the Oedipal tie to the mother—in modern terms, an unsatisfactory or underdeveloped sense of selfhood—Condé includes her deconstruction of gender in a minor but explicit mode. We saw how Dieudonné was tagged "faggot" by older boys in a rape scene. Earlier still, he had been seduced by a pedophile and kept it a dark secret, with a tremendous sense of shame (114-15). As the drama builds up, Luc arrives to embody the modern, triumphant bisexual artist. A cynical liberator, Luc destroys Dieudonné's happiness by seducing him and damaging his love for Loraine. Homosexual desire is perceived as life threatening; it is at first violently rejected by Dieudonné, but eventually the young man senses the 'naturalness' of desire with less awe. After the New Year's celebrations, some hard drinking, and an outing at the beach among beautiful, naked young people (216), he recovers himself, only making love to "his favorite mistress," the sea.

Although Luc's interest has now opened a window for Dieudonné—escape from the island, from bondage to Loraine, and perhaps from vagrancy—his sexual energy is deliberately 'feminized' by the narrator. Dieudonné is atypically indifferent to sex as such. We see him pass up casual encounters (136) but make love to Loraine out of tenderness and devotion. He becomes a murderer and a genitor by accident, sleeping with Ana only once (99). And Condé credits her protagonist with mothering skills akin to family instincts: "Depuis qu'il avait perdu Rébecca [sic] Cohen, Dieudonné avait toujours rêvé d'une petite soeur. Enfant, il épiait le ventre de Marine. Désespérément plat et pour cause. Sa mère, il le savait, ne faisait pas l'amour. Pourtant, au lieu d'apprécier cette chasteté, il aurait souhaité la voir constamment engrossée" (129) [Since he had lost Rebecca Cohen, Dieudonné had always dreamed of a little sister. As a child, he would watch Marine's belly. It remained desperately flat, with good reason. He knew his mother did not make love. But instead of appreciating such chastity, he wished to see her constantly pregnant]. Unlikely perhaps, and certainly unsuited to our basic claim about an Oedipal bond, these 'feminizing' touches to Dieudonné's portrait encapsulate the novelist's flair (superior intelligence) regarding gender stereotyping and sexual orientation.

Three decades ago, as the question of 'difference' became a major focus for philosophical reflection, 'sexual politics' a familiar concept, and sexual orientation a crucial legal issue, prominent psychoanalysts were exploring the spectrum of psychological bisexuality, with Christian David's *La Bisexualité psychique* as a major contribution to the field, and a classic reference. While Condé's own exploration of sexual ambiguity is marginal but noticeable in *La Belle Créole*, as seen above, it is patently playful in *Célanire cou coupé*, and it becomes 'the purloined letter' of the plot, unspotted but central to *Histoire de la femme cannibale*. In this novel, the dominant point of view is Rosélie's; she is a fifty-year-old painter from Guadeloupe, now living in South Africa and recently bereft of her white male companion of twenty years. Her musings and reminiscences intermingle with ongoing developments that pertain to detective fiction, as is often the case with Condé. The murder will be resolved in the end; meanwhile, Rosélie is deeply depressed, and more than ever estranged from her environment, an affluent white district of Capetown. She is fortunately in the able care of a substitute mother figure, Dido, a sort of *da* (dry nurse) who loves discussing the morning newspaper with her over coffee.

A wonderful addition to Condé's rich gallery of landless, well-travelled, and disoriented protagonists, Rosélie considers her given name "absurd" (13). It was made up by her mother, like a "mantra" of the parental couple. It is not the motherly half ("Rose") that carries the absurdity but the conjugation of the two. Readers will remember that Rose-Aimée was the given name of the Haitian restavek-turned-boat-girl in Condé's *Haiti chérie/ Rêves amers* (1991/2001). In "Rosélie," the father rhymes intertextually with Télumée's Elie (romantic, then crazed, alcoholic companion, and batterer) in Simone Schwarz-Bart's celebrated *Bridge of Beyond* (1972). This "absurd" name encapsulates the impossible dream with which Rosélie grapples periodically, as she falls in love and is abandonned or must lose her love object.

The protagonist as an artist is not new in Condé's *œuvre*, but Rosélie is the first fully developed character of a female artist. Luc the painter, and art dealer Loraine were minor references on a theme Condé already treated substantially in *Les derniers rois mages* (1992). Lydie Moudileno has deftly shown in "Portrait of the Artist as a

Dreamer" that the character of Spéro voiced Condé's impatience with the "devoir de mémoire" or debt to the Race, the limitations imposed on the Black artist. Spéro is distressed—nightmares about crabs invading his body are one symptom—because he let himself "be trapped in the notion of a political engagement through art, thus repressing his own creative impulse": he has become "nothing but a counterfeiter" (631). Spéro, like the writer Sancher in *Traversée de la Mangrove* (1989), changes the community by representing it, while his own self-awareness remains unfinished, with freedom of self-expression usually denied him by the community. In contrast to previous novels, the artist's identity quest is fully treated in *Histoire de la femme cannibale*. It can arguably be designated the 'real' story of the title, whereas the enigma and resolution of her partner's murder provide the surface plot line.

This novel is dedicated to "Richard" (Philcox, Condé's husband) with thanks (on the left page) to Michel Rovélas, the painter of several "variations" on the theme of cannibalism.[9] An educated reader will expect multi-leveled signification and s/he will not be disappointed. In the daily news, which her servant-friend Dido[10] reads with her, Rosélie the painter-protagonist has discovered a 'real' cannibal woman, a woman not so haphazardly called "Fiéla," accused of having somehow processed and rather methodically eaten her husband. At some point, Rosélie will refer to herself, in self-deprecation, as a "descendant of cannibals" (107).

Rosélie's identity quest moves between her identification with Fiéla and her various reflections on art. The artist's responsibility is explicitly discussed in a conversation between the protagonist and a black militant artist, after Rosélie delivers, exceptionally and painfully, an academic talk about Black creativity (201-207). She is stunned when faced with the question: "Est-ce que vous n'êtes pas fière d'être noire ?" (205) [Aren't you proud to be Black?]. Her perceived failure to convey any message to her audience only consolidates her choice of silence, or insignificant verbal communication. The revealing model, Fiéla the cannibal, will remain strictly speechless (like Jane Campion's protagonist in *The Piano*).

Since childhood, Rosélie has allowed herself a single "language": painting. But what exactly does she paint? A lover taking a quick tour of her studio emerges in shock: "Mon Dieu, c'est le cabinet de Barbe-Bleue! (132) [My God, this is Bluebeard's closet]. With rare exceptions, such as a seascape in "une infinité de variations de gris" (192) [infinite variations of grey] that sold instantly, Rosélie has always painted horrible things with a special fondness for red and earth tones, and brush strokes and lines suggesting viscera and blood. And she hates fish, while Stephen, her white Franco-British companion, loves going out with fishermen and sailors (188). We learn that Rosélie already painted impressive 'horrors' as a child (which she never was: "Moi je n'ai jamais été un enfant," 13). A flashback provides an occasion for Condé to flaunt her playful outrageousness as she lets us hear the schoolmistress:

> La maîtresse de dessin surtout se plaignait: "Il faut voir ses compositions libres. Des horreurs. L'autre jour, elle a dessiné une femme, jambes écartées d'où coulait une fontaine de sang. J'ai crié: "Bon Dieu, c'est quoi ça?" Elle m'a répondu: "C'est un viol." J'ai demandé, en colère: "Tu as déjà vu des viols, toi? Ces qualités de choses-là ne se font pas dans notre pays." Elle m'a répondu: "Moi, on me viole tous les jours." Et quand j'ai crié en rage: "Ne dis pas des choses comme ça! Qui te viole?" Elle m'a répondu tout tranquillement: "Mon papa, ma maman, tout le monde (160).

> [The art teacher especially complained: "You should see her free compositions. Dreadful stuff. The other day, she drew a woman with legs apart and a fountain of blood flowing. I screamed: "Good God, what's that?" She answered: "It's a rape." I was incensed: "You've already seen rapes? That sort of thing does not happen in our country." She replied: "I am raped every single day." And when I cried in rage: "Don't say things like that! Who rapes you?" She replied calmly: "My dad, my mom, everybody."]

As if the next paragraph were unrelated (it heads a new chapter), there follows a direct question to Fiéla (Rosélie's alter ego, the speechless cannibal woman in jail) who, like the painter, does not think, or rather, does not verbalize her mental life.

For Rosélie, "rien" and negative constructions are the backbone of her minimalist syntax: "Rien, je n'en pense rien. Je n'en pense rien puisque je n'y connais rien. Je ne connais rien à rien. Je ne sais que peindre" (57) [Nothing, I don't think anything about it. I don't think anything about it because I don't know anything about it. I know nothing about anything. I only know to paint]. "Nothing" is her initial response to painful queries. The question to Fiéla that opens this chapter ("...que lui reproche-t-on?" [why do people badmouth him?]) is a question to herself: why do people badmouth Stephen, shot three months earlier? It will remain unanswered until the last chapter, but it triggers a sweeping tribute to Stephen and to the quality of his love, since he often declared to Rosélie that she was a "cadeau extraordinaire, trop précieux pour moi, comme ceux que ma grand-mère me faisait dans le temps" (161) [an extraordinary present, much too precious for me, like the ones my grandmother used to give me in the old days]. And he goes on and on, adding: "Si je te perds, mon existence redeviendra ce qu'elle était avant toi: une désolation. Je n'avais rien à moi. Je vivais au travers d'autres hommes. Comme un Indien Tupinamba, je dévorais leur foie, leur rate, leur coeur. Mais ces âcres festins me laissaient plus morose encore. Repu, je réalisais mon indignité. Tu m'as tout donné" (161) [If I lose you, my life will go back to what it was before you: a wasteland. I had no life of my own. I lived through other men. Like a Tupinamba Indian, I'd devour their liver, their spleen, their heart. But those bitter feasts left me more joyless still. Once full, I measured my worthlessness. You've given me everything]. Beyond Stephen's noteworthy association of his grandmother with Rosélie (seen as the perfect substitute mother), his loving tirade, as she recalls it, serves as a shield or censorship, like the negative constructions that characterize her passivity. No, she will not answer the question: why don't they like Stephen?

In this crucial passage we come to realize that the cannibalism fantasy is a metaphor for a variety of relations perceived as out of control, engulfing or devouring. It is also superimposed on the childhood metaphor of being raped. There is blood, violence, anguish, dismemberment in people's 'inner cinema,' in their fantasies and nightmares, in Rosélie's painting, and often in the characters' 'real lives' as imagined by novelists. Ultimate violence happens outside the symbolic realm, in 'real' life and death: Condé does remind her readers of the memorable French case involving a Japanese man. Fiéla—whose name evokes the gall and the liver—enacts the 'real life' (or the mythical) level of resentment and vengeance. After years of chewing on her pain, this betrayed, silent wife, acted it out: she cooked her husband, as Calixthe Beyala's recent novel suggests: *Comment cuisiner son mari à l'Africaine* (2000). Traditional children's literature is of course full of devouring horror tales; so are 'gory' thrillers, while the old Greeks had invented Medea.

Thus, Condé renews our awareness that the 'oral' and the mouth are fundamental. Cannibalizing life is the law of art, including the self in auto-fictions. So is the modern feeling of 'being devoured up' by life's constraints, hence the success of techniques to retrieve a sense of selfhood in 'well-being.' How does cannibalism illustrate a painful Oedipal knot that must be resolved for the subject to be free? Rosélie, our "Black Oedipa," has been somewhat functional in her life but forever haunted by a deep sense of failure on all counts: talent, physical appearance, intelligence, social graces (her "invisibility" is a leitmotif), linguistic skills, material and intellectual independence. In essence, Stephen—a very articulate professor of English literature—rescued her from incipient prostitution in a godforsaken African town, twenty years earlier (25-27). A stranger everywhere, Rosélie's selfhood counts only two building blocks: compulsion to paint, refusal of motherhood. She declined to marry Stephen to spare her sense of duty to the Race, and to alleviate her chronic "white man's black bobo" discomfort. We learn how Rosélie and Stephen were in perfect agreement not to have children, another variation on "cannibalism," as seen in the description of her friend's children as "trois braillards affamés pareils à des vautours qui se repaissaient du foie et des entrailles de leur mère" (189) [three starved, wailing mouths who feasted like vultures on their mother's liver and entrails]. Now "abandoned" by Stephen, Rosélie must generate income, but she has always shrunk from promoting her painting. Somehow, of course, her paintings are her (unloved) children.

Her "godmother" Dido manages her new career as healer. Common sense holds that healing sessions pay off much better than peddling horrific art. So a new force looms in Rosélie's psyche, a forerunner of "ce qu'elle ne posséderait jamais...la confiance en soi " (223) [what she would never possess...self-confidence]. Because it is a 'given,' and a cliché about marginalized women in general and the Caribbean woman in particular, 'healing' has been displaced by painting in Rosélie's development (besides, Condé has already delivered a famous healer called Tituba). But Rosélie knows she has "the gift," revealed to her by her mother as patient one : "Les dons de Rosélie s'étaient manifestés très tôt. A six ans, il lui suffisait d'appuyer ses menottes sur les paupières de Rose dont le corps avait sérieusement commencé à ballonner et qui, en conséquence ne fermait plus l'oeil, tourmentée par les absences d'Elie. Du coup, la malheureuse dormait, paisible, comme un bébé jusqu'à neuf heures du matin" (28) [Rosélie's gifts showed up very early. At age six, all she had to do was lay her little hands on Rose's eyelids: her body had started ballooning seriously and so she could not sleep anymore, tormented as she was by Elie's absences. But then, the wretch could sleep peacefully, like a baby, until nine]. Rosélie's gift serves as a source of livelihood that is just as temporary as the relief she was able to give to her mother.

The narrator cannot summon images strong enough to convey Rosélie's awe at her mother's prolonged martyrdom, a fateful, horrifying, unexplained, monstrous obesity that caused her to lose her lovely voice, her mobility, her life. A curse is suspected, and a link to Elie's philandering or to Rose's father's even more heinous crimes (80). Rose's custom-made coffin is squarely Gulliverian (four meters by four) for her five hundred fifty-plus pounds. This surreal mother had doted over her single daughter and largely stifled her with love and the need thereof; such is the key of Rosélie's insecurity. Rose's monstrous "whale-like" body haunts the painter's soul, the mother is overwhelming, omnipresent, the plethoric image of mental anguish and love betrayed. The daughter resisted engulfment by growing tall and thin, by spurning food (her *da* would cook blood—curdled and fried—to prevent anemia). Once grown, Rosélie left home and stayed away ; but she always compulsively symbolized her mother's slow death through her unusual art: "Pourquoi toujours des sujets si horribles? Corps démembrés, moignons, yeux crevés, rates, foies éclatés. / J'aime l'horreur. Je crois que dans une vie antérieure j'ai fait partie d'une portée de vampires. Mes canines longues et pointues ont perforé le sein de ma mère" (58) [Why always such horrible themes? Dismembered bodies, stumps, pierced eyes, spleens and livers busted. / I love horror. I think that in another life I was born in a litter of vampires. My long and sharp eye-teeth have pierced my mother's breast]. This novel is indeed a tale of *Corps-à-corps avec la mère*, to paraphrase Irigaray's title, and even of 'corps-à-corps avec le corps [mort] de la mère,' a case of mother-daughter 'body-to-corpse' combat.

A room of her own was never the problem for Rosélie; at times she even touched fulfilment, although creating was usually the prelude to berating her creations (126). A favorite tune for her is the song "Sometimes, I feel like a motherless child...." As she comes near closure and rebirth, the artist still spurns her canvases, sour daughters ignored by their mother: "Est-ce que nous ne comptons plus pour toi? Tu sembles l'ignorer, nous sommes le sang qui te donne la force, le sang qui irrigue ton coeur et chacun de tes membres. Si tu ne peins plus, tu ne vis plus" (277) [Don't we count for you any longer? You don't seem to realize we are the blood giving you strength, the blood irrigating your heart and each one of your limbs. If you don't paint, you don't live any more]. But there was "the gift," revived by Dido. Eventually, the narrator and the reader—and obscurely, the protagonist—are enabled to relate it to the daughterly crime, and to the guilt. At work massaging an insomniac patient, or a raped young girl, Rosélie is said to "receive" or take in the internal chaos of the other. "Chaque fois qu'elle pansait des blessures, elle songeait aux deux êtres qu'elle n'avait pas soulagés. Sa mère qu'elle adorait" (78) [Each time she nursed wounds, she thought of the two beings she had failed to take care of. A mother she adored]. After more sad memories of Rose float by, Rosélie shares a crucial thought (in the narrator's free indirect style): "Car la seconde personne à qui elle n'avait jamais offert la paix de l'âme, c'était elle-même. A réfléchir, ce n'est pas pour surprendre. Le cancérologue ne soigne pas son cancer" (80) [And the second person she had never provided peace of mind for was herself. Not surprising, come to think of it. The cancer specialist does not treat his own cancer]. Eventually, Rose's quiet martyrdom colaesces with Fiéla's mute suffering in Rosélie's own anguish: the "cannibal woman" will eventually commit suicide (sentenced to fifteen years because her husband's "good name" was dismantled as imposture).

Rosélie feels guilty for having done nothing to help Fiéla. In another situation, she watches an Afrikaner woman on her deathbed, clinging to life until her son arrives, and as if again filled with guilt, Rosélie recalls her mother: "Rose avait fini ses jours pareillement: seule dans une maison trop grande, négligée par son mari, désertée par son unique enfant. Au fond de leurs yeux se lisait un identique récit de solitude et d'abandon, comme si c'était le lot des mères et des épouses" (103) [Rose's days had ended in the same way: alone in a huge house, neglected by her husband, deserted by her only child. The same tale of solitude and abondonment could be read deep in their eyes, the fate of wives and mothers, as it were]. The full 'confession' of Rosélie's betrayal of her mother finally unfolds in the text (166-69), heralding the protagonist's closure of the mourning process. To avoid seeing the monstrous mother's body, there was a five-day fugue in Paris, including suicidal drinking and a sexual encounter. Unlike the author, and like the Afrikaner's son, Rosélie did arrive "home" in extremis, only to read dereliction in the mother's ultimate glance: "Rose reposait sur son lit, les yeux à demi ouverts. / A l'entrée de Rosélie, ils s'élargirent, la fixèrent, décochant ces dards, ces flèches qui allaient se vriller dans son coeur, son esprit, son âme, en toute saison, carême comme hivernage, à toute heure, jour et nuit, puis ils chavirèrent, et s'éteignirent. / A jamais" (169) [Rose was lying on her bed, her eyes half opened. / As Rosélie walked in, they widened, riveted on her, shooting the darts, the arrows which would tunnel through her heart, her brain, her soul in all seasons, through Lent's drought and summer's rains, at all hours, day and night. Then they keeled and went out. / Forever]. At this point in the narrative, Rosélie has faced (confessed to herself and the reader) the full extent of what haunts her, and she can now start nourishing her self.

Thanks to Dido's managing skills, healing provided is healing received, and Rosélie is actually rebuilding herself. One patient becomes an appreciated lover, though he will gently let her down in due course. Even more importantly, one day, a young patient gone mute, the victim of a vicious rape, presents to her what must be kept secret from the child's mother: "dessins lumineux" (145) [luminous drawings]. The girl confides that she will become a painter, like Rosélie. Thus, Rosélie has given birth to an artist and rebirth to her self. Step after hesitant step and avoidance moves, Rosélie finally uncovers the extent of her delusion and the meaning of her psyche's fault. It is identical to Rose's fault, 'eternal Eve's fault': to place the highest value on love and companionship, to seek identity outside the self. She acknowledges that the self-destructiveness which has driven Fiéla to actual cannibalism, and Rose to insulation through obesity, can be conquered through creativity. For three months, she had been unable to paint. The novel's closure, a promising end, shows Rosélie's new style of painting: resuming her usual palette of colors "elle sentait se réveiller en elle l'impatiente clameur de ses entrailles se préparant à l'enfantement" (317) [below, she could feel the impatient call of her belly preparing to give birth]. This time, the painting will not evoke the threatening mother's flesh, nor Fiéla's crime of absorption and digestion, but a large pair of eyes, the icon of power, awareness and selfhood. Rosélie has begun forgiving herself and believing in her own powers: Black Oedipa need not destroy herself nor tear out her eyes to see the internal light.

In extremis, the novel yields a positive message, not so common in Condé's work. We have observed this same message in other major women writers: Germaine de Staël or Colette come to mind. But for a contemporary, intellectual readership, Condé projects the drama of defective individuation from the mother, whose other face is the delusive "investment" of unreliable love objects. The identity quest was at the core of Condé's first novel, as Thomas Spear recalled: "Véronica wanders from one man to another [and one continent to another], seeking everywhere but within herself the answer to her soul-searching" (725). It remains at the heart of her formidable voyage in literature. The two recent novels we have read jointly constitute a masterful diptych on the gender divide, dealing with what Frantz Fanon diagnosed in René Maran's *Batouala* (1921) as the "abandonment neurosis." Both protagonists suffer from a sense of isolation and dependance on a maternal figure that painfully dominates their psyche ; but Black Oedipus fails where Black Oedipa prevails: severing the hold of the Mother's body and its multifarious masks. The real world of young adults, enthralled by the *Matrix*,[11] undecided between reality and virtuality, and confusing 'literature' with 'fiction,' has a long way to go. Playing lucidly with psychoanalytical motifs, Condé seriously questions contemporary myths such as belonging and being rooted, guilt in exile, and nomadism. Most recently, she takes a tough look at popular wisdom on interracial couples, bisexuality, and the "nature" of "love." Even if we can associate a confidence[12] with a fictional image, our post-Freudian Maryse Condé exerts full control over her protagonists' problems: (they are) not hers.

Notes

1. This and subsequent English translations of French citations are our own unless otherwise indicated.

2. See Maryse Condé's interview with Barbara Lewis (550), and the Makward interview with Gisèle Pineau (1206).

3. See Makward, "Presque un siècle de différence amoureuse: Simone Schwarz-Bart (1972), Gisèle Pineau (1996)."

4. Many thanks to Ann Scarboro: the "Teacher's Guidelines" of her 2003 video interview of Maryse Condé (Mosaic Media) first alerted me to Condé's revealing autobiographical essay in the Gale database: *Contemporary Authors Online*, Gale, 2002.

5. Respectively *Le deuxième sexe* (Paris: Gallimard, 1949) Part IV, Chapter 1, "Enfance" ("Childhood"), and *The Reproduction of Mothering; Psychoanalysis and the Sociology of Gender* (Berkeley, CA, University of California Press, 1978).

6. See Makward: "Célanire Superwoman, ou les nouvelles impertinences de Maryse Condé."

Oedipus and Oedipa According to Condé: (Aliases: Dieudonné and Rosélie)

7 . "Mummy" stands for mummified person here and not for "mother"; the homonyms are an interesting coincidence.

8. This association is born out in the text : "En le voyant, Dieudonné, qui n'avait jamais envié personne, fut possédé d'un désir qu'il ne put contrôler: être cet inconnu, se glisser à l'intérieur de sa peau, vivre à son souffle, suspendu aux battements de son cœur.… Une douleur qu'il n'avait pas ressentie depuis longtemps lui enserrait la tête, l'estomac, le cœur aussi" (72-73) [Seeing him, Dieudonné, who had never envied anybody, was overwhelmed by a desire that he could not control: to be this stranger, to slide inside his skin, to live through his breath, clinging to his heart's beats.… A pain that he had not felt for a long time crushed his head, his stomach and his heart too].

9. Our sincere thanks to Marianne Bosshard who shared impressions as well as a snapshot of the Rovélas painting owned by Maryse Condé, throwing light on various motifs in the book. On Condé's tongue-in-cheek vindication of cannibalism, see her interview with Lydie Moudileno, where the author declares: "J'utilise le mot [cannibale] parce que je suis antillaise et que nous sommes en principe descendants des cannibales. Christophe Colomb a découvert des peuples qui étaient des cannibales. On est passé de Carib à cannibale. Je vous renvoie pour cela à Glissant. Le 'cannibale' est revendiqué comme ancêtre littéraire.… Et Suzanne Césaire, en Martinique, qui écrit en 1942 que 'La poésie antillaise sera cannibale ou ne sera pas'" (122) [I use the word because I am Caribbean and in principle we are descendants of cannibals. Christopher Columbus discovered people who were cannibals. We went from 'Cannibal' to 'Carib'. I'll refer you to Glissant on this point. The 'cannibal' is reclaimed as a literary ancestor.… And Suzanne Césaire, of Martinique, wrote in 1942: "Caribbean poetry will be cannibalistic or it will not be"].

10. Dido, in the French popular echolalia, is a big-eater: "Et Didon, dit-on, dina du dos d'un dodu dindon" [Dido, they say, dined off the backside of a fat he-turkey].

11. Condé makes countless cross-cultural references (Assia Djebar, Seamus Heaney, Kofi Annan, United Colors of Benneton, etc.) and mentions the actor of the original *Matrix* savior-hero: Keanu Reeves. Needless to say, we wonder about the unconscious implications of having designated "matrix" the ultimate evil power.

12. See in particular the violent confrontation of mother and daughter, resolved in tears and an intimate embrace, closing the segment "A nous la liberté?" in *Le coeur à rire et à pleurer; Contes vrais de mon enfance*: "Je glissai la main entre ses seins qui avaient allaité huit enfants, à présent inutiles, flétris, et je passai toute la nuit, elle agrippée à moi, moi roulée en boule contre son flanc, dans son odeur d'âge et d'arnica, dans sa chaleur. / C'est cette étreinte-là dont je veux garder le souve-

nir" (136) [I laid my hand between her breasts, they had fed eight children but were now useless and shriveled, and I spent the whole night that way, she was clinging to me, I was a ball rolled against her flanks, in her scent of old age and arnica, in her warmth. / That is the embrace I want to preserve in my memory]. We could also refer to her interview with Ann Scarboro, where Condé states about her mother: "I would not say she was difficult. I would say my mother was very complex. She was the first black woman of her generation to become the principal of a school. So I would say that she had a kind of hardness at the professional level. She was ahead of her time. She was what one would call today a career woman. She thought that a woman found herself in work; a woman should prove to everyone what she was capable of doing" (courtesy of Ann Scarboro, Mosaic Media).

Problematizing Postcolonial Histories

HISTORY'S THEFT AND MEMORY'S RETURN IN MARYSE CONDÉ

Katherine Elkins

Maryse Condé's writing is clearly situated in the Francoph-one Caribbean tradition that is suspicious of History, for as Bernabé, Chamoiseau and Confiant argue in *Eloge de la créolite*, any kind of historical methodology in relation to the Caribbean only returns to to "la Chronique coloniale"—as they refer to recorded history of colonialism. One of the tasks of writing, therefore, is "la mise au jour de la mémoire vraie" [updating true memory] (38).[1] Our history, they write, is not totally accessible to historians: "Notre Chronique est dessous les dates, dessous les faits réper-toriés: *nous sommes Paroles sous l'écriture*. Seule la connaissance poé-tique, la connaissance romanesque, la connaissance littéraire, bref, la connaissance artistique, pourra nous déceler, nous percevoir, nous ramener évanescents aux réanimations de la conscience [Our chronicle is behind the dates, behind the known facts: *we are the Words behind writing*. Only poetic knowledge, fictional knowledge, literary knowledge, in short, artistic knowledge can discover us, understand us, and bring us, evanscent, back to the resuscitation of consciousness] (38, emphasis in the original). True memory, in other words, finds its truth in an artistic realm that bypasses colo-nial history.

Édouard Glissant goes further: he suggests in *Poétique de la rela-tion* that an obsession with history is itself informed by western notions of identity and proposes that the *intention historique* should be replaced by an *intention poétique* (132). The Caribbean writer, moreover, should embrace wandering and a search for others. For Glissant, uprooting can allow for identity construction to take place, and errancy is beneficial when it is experienced as a search for the Other[2]; often, he claims, it is even possible to find oneself by taking up the problem of the Other. It is for this reason that, citing Deleuze and Guattari, he posits the "rhizome" as an alternative to the notion of roots (23). The rhizome, in contrast to the root, enters into precisely this relation with the Other.

Condé's writing reflects much of this same skepticism of history, as well as a continued emphasis on exile and errancy as solutions to the legacy of colonialism and slavery. Like Glissant when he writes that the Caribbean writer's experience of time is aggravated by the void, what he calls "the final sentence of a plantation," Condé views Guadeloupe as resonating with this sentence, appearing to her, she says, as a void, "le néant." To be Antillean does not mean filling this void with the facts of one's own lost history—this would be, in the words of Glissant, to indulge in the dangerous "longing for history"[3] that he describes in *Poétique de la relation*. Instead, the only solution is to wander, always in search of others' stories. As Condé writes in her study of Césaire's *Cahier d'un retour au pays natal*: " Être un Antillais finalement, je ne sais toujours pas très bien ce que cela veut dire.... Est-ce qu'un écrivain doit avoir un pays natal? Est-ce qu'un écrivain doit avoir une identité définie? Est-ce qu'un écrivain ne pourrait pas être constamment errant, constamment à *la recherche des autres hommes*?" (23) [To be an Antillean in the end, I don't really know what that means.... Should a writer have a homeland? Should a writer have a definite identity? Couldn't a writer be constantly wandering, constantly in search of others?][4].

This search for others' stories is the focus of Condé's fictional work *Nanna-ya*, a story that also addresses quite explicitly the relation between history and memory and takes Glissant's notions of errancy and the rhizome one step further. Instead of evoking a nostalgia for history, she portrays its theft and reworking by what she calls "memory." Where Glissant argues for replacing history with poetry, Condé proposes a poetics that continues to engage with history by stealing from it. Condé, in other words, proposes a subversive approach to the problem of history that stems from her knowledge as a writer: writing always involves "stealing" much of one's material from elsewhere, and history should not be exempt from this activity.

Her story *Nanna-ya* begins with the character George, who as a young child tries to alleviate a sense of not quite belonging—a rootlessness that Condé embraces. In contrast to Condé's own strategy, however, George searches for his own story by fantasizing a genealogical link to a local mythic figure, a local legend named Tacky, leader of a slave uprising. As a child George dreams about Tacky, and as an adult George takes on the project of documenting and writing *l'Histoire de Tacky*, or *The History of Tacky*. No doubt George imagines that this "History" would give him a sense of who he is in the present, but instead, the past takes over, edging out the present entirely as George immerses himself more and more deeply in writing the past, expanding the document to almost 1000 pages. This past binds him all the more tightly by weakening his own connections to the present. Indeed, he says the time he spends on the project seems to hold no importance in comparison with the greatness of the history he is writing. His own self is thus gradually eclipsed by his history of another. While he sees his history as a method of redemption, of proving to those around him that he is not merely a "un égoïste, un homme sans qualitiés"(157) [a self-centered man with no redeeming qualities (90)], it actually draws him further and further away from his present goal and from connecting to those around him. In fact, his *Histoire* seems to put him into conflict both with the demands of the present and with those closest to him. It becomes representative of his strife with his wife, whom he blames for the fact that he is the man he has become.

George is descended from slaves, but his wife is descended from the Maroons, West Indians who fled to the hills to avoid enslavement. One of George's goals, however, is to show that the Maroons themselves aided the English. He wishes to show that even they do not have a past untainted by oppression and slavery. His history, in other words, focuses increasingly on proving that his wife's ancestors were not champions of freedom. He even speculates that it might have been a Maroon who pulled the trigger on his hero, Tacky. It is not too difficult to see this speculation as indicative of the strife between George and his wife. At the same time, writing the history also leads to a literal betrayal of his wife, as he begins an affair with the local librarian, Joyce, a London-born woman whose father is Jamaican and whose mother is English. Joyce leaves London and returns to Jamaica only when she, perhaps a little like George, senses she does not quite belong.

George responds to this sense of not belonging by trying to make Tacky's story his own. As Condé's story suggests, however, it is highly suspect that the two men are even related, so George, in effect, is stealing Tacky's story. Moreover, George is unable to acknowledge the theft as theft because he is so blinded by his effort to link himself to the past. His own story remains one of alienation: George goes in search of his own history and his own story, but instead loses himself entirely in another's, much like the historians whose "méthodologie ne leur donne accès qu'à la Chronique coloniale" [methodology restricts them to the sole colonial chronicle] (38).

In contrast to George, Joyce does not search out her own roots, nor does she look for a history of her ancestors. Joyce, like Condé's Antillean writer-wanderer, wanders into this story and takes it as her own. George gives Joyce his manuscript to type and she steals it. This theft of a history allows her to edit an unshapely mass of historical facts into a story that is also *her* story written from a first-person perspective. Her writing puts the self back in the center of the history, turning a third-person, objective history into a first-person, subjective story. Because it is not her own, she has no fear of rewriting it and replacing the third person with the first person, even replacing 'fact' with fiction. Joyce, in other words, is able to do what George is not: turn this history into her own personal tale. She rewrites history in the first person as fictionalized memory. While George goes looking for himself and always finds another, Joyce goes looking for another's story — George's — and finds her own.

Obviously, Joyce's character presents moral problems: she takes George's life work and disappears. This theft leaves George devastated at the end of the novel. In her interview with Condé, Françoise Pfaff remarks on just this point: "I find it regrettable that, being the daughter of a Jamaican man and an Englishwoman, she travels from England to search for her ancestors in Jamaica and ends up having to steal them, literally and symbolically, through this manuscript" (57-58; 87). Pfaff objects to the way in which Joyce steals another's story rather than finding her own, and clearly, this element of the narrative is disturbing. But one could also argue that history has always been stolen, albeit usually by the victors. Perhaps, Condé suggests, no other method exists. While one could find this theft troubling, one could also see it as necessarily subversive: instead of a refusal of history, Condé proposes a necessary theft that must always be unsanctioned and irreverent. Within the narrative, moreover, Joyce's theft of history and her re-writing of it in a fictional, first-person narrative has restorative properties. At the end of *Nanna-ya* George's wife tells him that his story served only to hurt both himself and those around him: "Cette Histoire de Tacky, tu t'en servais pour faire mal. A moi. Aux autres. Et finalement, tu te faisais du mal à toi-même" (123) [That (hi)story[5] of Tacky, you were using it to cause pain. To me. To others. And in the end, you were hurting yourself as well (113)]. It is the theft of the history that has restored George to *his* present, to his family, to his wife, and to himself. George's wife has the last word in Condé's novella, or two words that she repeats for emphasis: "À présent..." she says, "À présent." These last words are a reminder of the need to return to the present, to focus on the "now" rather than stay chained to a past. Ending as it does with these words, the novella becomes an invocation to search for one's stories in the present, perhaps even in another's story—the very suggestion that Condé makes in her study of Césaire cited above.

Perhaps we may follow Condé's trajectory even further. What if the theft of history represents Condé's response to the potential dilemma of the alienation that arises from the way the master narrative 'writes' individuals. Given that history, the master narrative of a collective past, does not belong to any of us individually, our history must be stolen. George mistakenly tries to turn his own story and his own past into a myth, but by attempting to make his story cohere in this way, he ends up with a history burdened by a stultifying weight of the master narrative. Joyce's theft allows her to cut, embellish and fictionalize the story. It is noteworthy that her theft allows her to reverse the process of alienation begun by George when he attempts to write his story by focusing on the legend of Tacky. When Joyce steals George's story and rewrites it in the first person as though it were her own, she reverses George's earlier gesture of alienation whereby he lost himself in another's story. There's as much of myself in the story, she claims, as there is of Tacky. Perhaps there is even more.

We can explore the possibility that memory returns what history has stolen by examining this notion of alienation as it appears in Condé's autobiographical work, *Le coeur à rire et à pleurer* [*Tales From the Heart*]. In analyzing these autobiographical reflections on alienation, a fictional reversal in storytelling clearly emerges as the only solution. If history in the form of slavery and the Middle Passage is, for Condé, at least partially responsible for a sense of not belonging, the theft of history in a fictionalized story allows for a return of stolen property. The return is not to a lost past but to a self situated as an "I" at the center of the imaginative process of storytelling.

Condé's autobiographical work begins with a childhood memory of alienation and expulsion that occurs while the family is vacationing in Paris. Condé tells of the first time—obviously significant given her later wanderings—that she considers not responding to a call to return home. While playing in the street in Paris, she and her brother are called home. Her brother encourages her not to respond to the call. Ignore them, he says, since "Papa et maman sont une paire d'aliénés"(14) [Papa and Maman are a pair of alienated individuals (6)]. "Aliénés?" she asks? What does that mean? She doesn't dare ask him, but instead tries to align this new and strange name with those most familiar to her. The young Condé must try to determine the meaning of this new word "aliéné," and she concludes that it seems to indicate disease, contagion, even possible death. Exposure to alienation is also, one suspects, her first lesson in mortality, the first time she senses that life, like her view of her parents, moves in only one direction, and that no return to an earlier time is possible. Linking the realization that her parents are alienated to the first time that she considers not responding to the call to come home only reinforces the lesson that the circular journey is always a false one: there is no return home.

Condé's confrontation with the word "alienated" also leads to her first attempt to connect words with the people around her—an echo, perhaps, of the act of writing. As she tries to integrate this unknown work into her knowledge of her parents, she concludes, "À minuit, à force de coller tous les indices entre eux, je finis par bâtir un semblant de théorie. Une personne qui cherche à être ce qu'elle ne peut pas être parce qu'elle n'aime pas être ce qu'elle est" (16) [At midnight, after piecing all the clues together, I came up with a vague theory. An alienated person is someone who is trying to be what he can't be because he does not like what he is (7)]. Condé describes Guadeloupe as a void, a nothingness. In both cases—whether writing about the people around her or writing about her homeland—she must construct a theory, an understanding, in place of missing information.

Condé's definition of alienation here would seem to describe George quite well. George attempts to be what he is not (a descendent of Tacky) because he does not want to be what he is (a descendent of slaves). He searches for a new self in myth. The young Condé, by contrast, searches for herself in the space opened up by demystification and disenchantment—from the knowledge of what it might mean to be alienated. An unclear present that comes in

246

the form of a new, strange word, is what allows her to construct her theory, indeed even her own sense of self. She decides not to be alienated, not to try to be what she is not: "À deux heures du matin, au moment de prendre sommeil, je me fis le serment confus de ne jamais devenir une aliénée" (16) [At two in the morning, just as I was dropping off, I swore in a confused sort of way never to become alienated (7)]. Her own conception of self arises precisely in this space of negativity.

Condé thus begins the story of her childhood with an event out of which she willfully constructs her own identity. But her construction of identity depends on more than lived experience and conscious will, for there is also a communal past that haunts her in a much more dangerous fashion, shaping her life in ways she at first does not understand. Her parents, she tells us, praised all things occidental; but one suspects that this praise required burying certain cultural or ethnic memories of a history that continued to weigh on their present.

In a second remembered moment, Maryse's interactions with a playmate are informed by a history of which she had until then remained ignorant; and Condé recounts the incident in a chapter significantly entitled "Leçon d'histoire" or "History Lesson. On the ritual evening walks with her parents as a young girl, Maryse befriends a young white girl with whom she plays every evening. Their play, however, enacts a master-slave dynamic. The white girl rides her like a beast of burden and continually hits her. Eventually Maryse objects, and the white girl responds, "Je dois te donner des coups parce que tu es une négresse" (42) [I have to hit you because you're black (56)]. When Maryse asks her parents about this, her mother's evasion and her father's terse words, "On nous donnait des coups dans le temps" (44) [They used to beat us a long time ago (57)], convince her that there is a lost, silent past—a secret—which, although inaccessible to her in a conscious way, nonetheless somehow shapes her present. She writes that she became aware of a secret hidden in her past, a painful, shameful secret that would be inconvenient, maybe even dangerous, to know. Her parents had buried this secret in the depths of their memory.

After her confrontation with the white girl, Maryse never sees her again at the usual spot. Although the author concludes that what she remembers as a real event may have been a fictionalization of her own mind (44), the act of writing this story reveals a past that had been inaccessible to the conscious mind. Condé's search for other people's stories, and her telling them through writing, is perhaps a solution to the danger of being haunted by this history lesson, a lesson that comes in the form of a deeply buried memory of slavery. The young Maryse does not follow her parents' path of storing this 'secret' deep within the self. She will speak, ask questions, and tell stories.

Near the end of Condé's autobiographical narrative, she relates the story of a vacation meant to be a "cure" for her mother. Once again, the experience highlights the difference between her parents' denial of the past through a suppression of memories and her own method of connecting past to present through storytelling. Traveling to a part of Guadeloupe with which they are unfamiliar, the family makes the mistake of renting a house in a mulatto section of town where they are ignored and excluded because of their dark skin. This exclusion upsets her parents, who desire inclusion, so, Condé writes, her mother "enterra ce souvenir au fin fond de sa mémoire et ne s'exprima là-dessus que par soupirs, mimiques et hochements de tête" (110-11) [buried this experience deep in her memory and any reminder came out as a series of sighs, gesticulations and shaking of the head (120)]. Her mother represses the memory; and yet, like Maryse's history lesson, this memory shapes her mother's present in a physical, tangible form. No matter how silent she may remain about her 'exile,' the memory will speak itself in bodily gestures. Young Maryse, on the other hand, is thrilled by being exiled in her own land (108). As a child, exile affords her two advantages: she discovers unknown people and places, and she enjoys anonymity as an ignored observer. Her exile is also the source of endless tales that she recounts to her friend, Yvelise (111). The adult author continues to turn her own exile to advantage: it forms the negative experience upon which she will construct her own stories of other people and places, her own storytelling.

In this light, we might reevaluate Condé's stated preference for wandering and the search for others, as she explains in her interview with Pfaff, "Then you realize that you must continue wandering. I believe now that it's this wandering that engenders creativity. In the final analysis, it is very bad to put down roots. You must be errant and multifaceted, inside and out. Nomadic" (28; 46). Condé is fully aware that there is no going back to the past or to oneself. Her response as a writer will be to affirm her memory of exile, perhaps even memory as exile, so that she may tell stories of other people and places. Wandering can only take place in the present, in other places, in other people.

In this same interview with Pfaff, Condé also explains her reasons for not living full time in Guadeloupe, reasons that center on maintaining an ability to create: "When you are outside the country, you mythicize it, which is normal. You imagine things and visualize a sort of paradise with lush nature and friendly people. *You invent a lot and create something deep down within yourself.* But when you come back home, you are faced with the country's reality. *You look for what you thought you left behind and don't find it.* You quickly become disappointed and frustrated" (28, my emphasis; 46). Return in any true sense is not possible. And even if you do return, you do not find what you thought you left behind. In Guadeloupe, Condé is simultaneously too suffocatingly close to her physical past, and too imaginatively far away. In contrast, physical distance and imaginative proximity through writing allow for the construction of stories. Exile allows her to recreate in her imagination a story that replaces a past she can never return to. Fabulation, rather than a search for lost time, is the only response to memory as exile. This fabulation, moreover, constructs something in the emptiness of the self.

In this way, it is also understandable why Condé chooses to relinquish Césaire's goals of representing one's own particular Caribbean community. Instead, she often writes of other communities, whether a small New England village in *Moi, Tituba, sorcière noire de Salem*, or an African community in *Segou*. Where is Maryse Condé in these stories? She is present in the same way that Joyce is present in her rewriting of George's story. Writing others' pasts and stories allows her to create a tale of her own, often speaking from the first person.

To the imposing and suffocating distance of a history that, as in the case of George, brings only a stultifying weight, Condé thus proposes what could be termed a 'disorder of memory' that allows for the construction of a self in the present at its very center. Using the fragments of a disordered memory, as Condé does in "History Lesson" and Joyce in *Nanna-Ya*, the writer is able to reconstruct a semi-fictional past in the place of a history that leaves no room for the self precisely because it eclipses the individual who exists in the present. The disorder of memory, moreover, allows the melding of one's personal story with a collective past in a way that is restorative rather than debilitating, as in the case of her parents.

One can be haunted by the presence of one's own unspoken past, or one can search for the stories of others and creatively write the past into existence in the present. The latter is Condé's solution. Her writing allows her to bridge the distance created by a past that is unknown, and her exile allows her to maintain the space of a wandering subject. Returning to *Nanna-ya*, we can see even more clearly the similarities between the fictional Joyce and the writer Condé. As a bi-racial woman, Joyce is an outsider who cannot truly "return" to her roots in Jamaica, nor can she feel completely at home in England. This position in-between allows her to rewrite history, which alleviates a community—George's entire family—from the weight of the past that George has been bringing to bear on their lives in the present. She rewrites another's story as her own, situating herself, as Condé does, within others' stories. Joyce's imagination constructs something with the past through a process of cutting out whole sections and turning a weighty historical tome into a single, cohesive story with her own "I" situated at its center. If history has stolen one's past, the response is to steal back from history. Moreover, by turning what she has stolen from George's history of Tacky into memory, Joyce undoes the work of alienation. This is not a simple return to the past; it is a wandering, a theft, a reappropriation by which another's story is rewritten as one's own.

Is the task of Condé as a postcolonial francophone writer the theft of the manuscript and even, perhaps, the theft of history? As a Guadeloupean, Condé is also an outsider to this tale about Jamaica. Perhaps literature is always the theft of another's history, both to relieve the other's burden and to return it remembered as a personal tale of memory. Condé cuts and embellishes like her female protagonist, rewriting history in order to simultaneously steal the past and return it, remembered, as truly her own. In this instance, therefore, imagination and memory are more important than a history composed only of "facts." Perhaps this is why a character says in *Nanna-ya*, "C'est peut-être cela la seule hérédité veritable! L'imagination!"(172) [That may well be the only real heredity! The imagination! (103)]. Heredity's gift does not, as George imagines, lie in the historical details of a mythical past; it lies in the way the past can make itself felt in slightly changed form in the present, in a re-told, re-membered form. History is not absent from Maryse Condé's project; but the only true gift of the past lies in the work of an imagination that steals from history and turns history into memory without losing focus on the present. In this way, *Nanna-ya* exhibits the interplay between memory and history that Condé herself describes: "The interplay between history and memory…is also in the postmodernist tradition. Historical facts authenticate a purely fictional narrative, which proceeds to subvert them, since what is essential is not history but fiction" (Pfaff 69; 103). What is essential in *Nanna-ya* is not the *History of Tacky* but its memorial transformation into personal narrative. Historical facts may authenticate a fictional narrative, but this narrative then subverts history by returning, in the present and as one's own fiction, what history has stolen.

Notes

1. Citations from this work are taken from the bilingual edition.
2. See especially Chapter 1, *Poétique de la relation*. In "Looking for Roots Among the Mangroves" Jarrod Hayes discusses the mangrove as a critique of roots.
3. Michael Dash translates Glissant's phrase "désiré historique" as a "longing for history" or a "longing for the ideal of history" (ctd. in Lionnet 1995, 76, note 19).
4. Unless otherwise indicated, all translations are my own.
5. The French term *histoire* has the double connotation of 'history' and 'story,' which shows precisely the kind of fluidity between the two terms that Maryse Condé manipulates. Whereas the translator of *Nanna-ya* chooses to call George's work the *Story of Tacky*, however, I would suggest that "History" is more appropriate: while the French term is undoubtedly ambiguous, George's work exhibits all of the negative effects of a colonial 'history' as a opposed to the creative, poetic reworking of Joyce's "Story."

MARYSE CONDÉ CREOLIZES THE CANON IN *LA MIGRATION DES CŒURS*

Maria Cristina Fumagalli

Maryse Condé's *La migration des cœurs* (1995), translated into English as *Windward Heights* by Richard Philcox in 1998, transposes Emily Brontë's *Wuthering Heights* into a Caribbean universe, adapting and transforming it as if it were a musical variation on a previous theme.[1] Set in Cuba, Guadeloupe, Marie-Galante and Dominica, the novel recounts the life of almost three generations of Guadeloupeans at the turn of the century and offers its readers both an account of and a meditation on the process of creolization in Guadeloupean society and in the Caribbean as a whole.

Condé's novel begins in Cuba in 1898, a watershed in Cuba's history. As Brontë did before her, Condé remains very specific about dates; but rather than opening in 1801 (as *Wuthering Heights* does), she sets *La migration des cœurs* in the second half of the nineteenth century, changing the chronology to suit Caribbean history. In 1898, Cuba was in full turmoil and had been for a while. A new separatist insurrection, led by José Martí, Antonio Maceo and Máximo Gómez, had begun on February 24, 1895, and the skillful use of guerrilla tactics made this revolt very difficult to quell for the Spanish forces. By 1895, the Cuban sugar industry had collapsed, leaving the countryside full of unemployed sugar workers ready for revolt. In the meantime, the progressive abolition of slavery (reaching completion in 1886) called for a drastic reorganization of the social system.

Despite the fact that by the beginning of 1898 both José Martí and Antonio Maceo had been killed by Spanish forces, in *La migration des cœurs*, José de Cépéro, "lieutenant général des armées nationals, chef supérieur politique de la province de La Havane, gouverneur militaire de celle-ci et capitaine général de l'île de Cuba" (12) [lieutenant general of the armed forces, political head and military governor of the province of Havana and captain general of the island of Cuba (5)] reminds us that their deaths had changed nothing: the battle for independence was as fierce as before (if not fiercer) (13, 5). Meanwhile, however, the United States was growing increasingly worried about the Cuban situation: ultimately, they could not tolerate Spain ceding sovereignty to the Cubans. At the end of Part One Chapter Three, Doña Stéfania Fonséca, the young widow of a rich tobacco planter, voices the fears (or wishes) of many Cubans at the time: "José Marti est mort pour rien. Bientôt Cuba sera une colonie de l'Amérique. Ses soldats sont déjà dans le port n'attendent qu'une occasion pour se jeter sur nous" (22) [José Martí has died for nothing. Soon Cuba will be a colony of America. Her soldiers are already in the port, awaiting the moment to hurl themselves upon us! (15)]. Doña Stéfania is referring to the arrival of the battleship *Maine* in Havana in January 1898. Shortly afterwards, on the night of February 15, the *Maine* exploded and 258 men were killed in the blast. In Part One of the novel, we are shown how, immediately after the event, people started making all sorts of conjectures: "Accident? Attentat? Perpétré par qui? Dans quel but? En tous cas, deux cent soixante marins étaient morts, et les États-Unis d'Amérique réclaiment vengeance. Ils parlaient déjà de déclarer la guerre à l'Espagne… Quel allait être l'avenir de Cuba?" (30) [Accident? Attack? Perpetrated by whom? And why? Whatever the case, two hundred and sixty sailors were dead and the United States of America was calling for revenge. There was already talk of declaring war on Spain… What lay in store for Cuba? (23)]. The chapter ends with these questions and the book offers no answers to them in the following pages.

As a matter of fact, the causes of the explosion of the *Maine*, which has been frequently blamed as the trigger for the Spanish-Cuban-American War, are still to be determined. What is known, however, is that the U.S. government blamed Spain while Spain rejected all accusations and advanced the explanation of an internal explosion. Shortly afterwards, in April 1898, taking advantage of the wave of emotional outrage that the death of so many U.S. soldiers had caused in his country, the then President of the United States, William McKinley, requested of Congress the authority to intervene militarily in Cuba, transforming the "Cuban war of liberation into a U.S. war of conquest" (Pérez 94).[2] Therefore, the fact that the novel begins by "zooming in" on this particularly crucial historical moment, allows Condé to present us simultaneously with two different "histories" of the island (and of the Caribbean as a whole): a history of colonial and neo-colonial exploitation and domination, and a history of political insurgency and resistance.

Cultural resistance is especially foregrounded: Condé's novel opens on a specific day of the year, the Epiphany, or the Día de Reyes, with the description of a procession that used to take place on that day. As Nicolás Guillén writes in his diary, the Día des Reyes was a very important date for colonial Cuba because the white masters would allow their black slaves "to feel as though at home in their own land and sing and dance in the warmth of their own family and their tribe and worship their gods and again be subjects of their king" (Augier vol. I, 212-13 qtd. in Benítez-Rojo 296). Moreover, in his work on the Afro-Cuban celebration of the Día de Reyes, Fernardo Ortiz reports that through the streets of Havana, a group of dancing and singing black slaves carried on their backs a huge, artificial serpent which represented both "the death of the snake and the celebration of his characteristics" (41 qtd. in Benítez-Rojo 297). According to Benítez-Rojo, the procession was originally a way of "channelling the violence of the white against the black through the death of a scapegoat. In reality, the snake-killing dance was an exorcism of slavery. At the same time, it tried to conjure away the danger of the Negro's sociocultural dissolution as an African entity within the violent contexts of plantation society" (298).[3]

In *La migration des cœurs* our attention is first drawn to Melchior, who leads the procession carrying the banner of his God, Chango. Melchior, we soon discover, "n'était pas une personne ordinaire. C'était un *babalawo*, grand prêtre de la *santería*, fils d'un *omo-koloba* qui, dans la pompe de son rang, avait rejoint Chango quelques annés plus tôt (13) [was no ordinary mortal [but] a *babalawo*, a high priest of *santería*, son of the *omo-koloba*, who, with the pomp due to his rank, had departed this life several years before to join Chango (5)]. A few pages later, we learn that "tout *babalawo* qu'il était, Melchior était un bon Catholic" (21) [for however much a *babalawo* he might be, Melchior was nevertheless a staunch Catholic (14)]. At the end of the procession, Melchior enters the cathedral, heads for the chapel of Santa Barbara and kneels in front of the statue of the virgin saint whose image, however, "était présente dans tous les temples de la santería. On la représentait en jeune fille yoruba, le front auréolé de cheveux crépus, les pommettes striées de balafres, assise à dos de cheval et serrant contre sa poitrine un régime de plantains, qui étaient la nourriture favorite de Chango" (14) [could be seen in every temple dedicated to *santería*, depicted as a young Yoruba girl, her forehead haloed in frizzy hair, her cheekbones scored with scars, seated on a horse, clutching against her breast a bunch of plantains, Chango's favourite food (6)]. As Benítez-Rojo explains, the *Shango* (or Chango) cult draws on some "sixty gods or great spirits": more than thirty of these are African deities (mostly Yoruba), about twenty are of Catholic origin and three Indoameri-can; two came from India with indentured servants, and one from China (158). The overall significance of the procession, rather than in the plot itself, resides in the promiscuous character of this cos-mogony, in its cross-cultural potential for social resistance offered by diverse cultural matrices, in its representation and celebration of creolization in action. This religious practice is in fact a genuine cul-tural offshoot of that violent but creative friction of diverse peoples of assorted races with different gods, cultures and languages who, forced into plantations, colonialism, indentureship and economic exploitation in general, had to adapt to a new environment and to one another in a context of extreme degradation. In Condé's account of the Epiphany procession the crucial element of the sacrifice of the snake/scapegoat does not take place; however, the chapter does contain two allusions to sacrificial rituals and snakes (14, 7; 21, 14). As a result, the violence endemic to post-slavery society is not exorcized but is somehow free to find its way and claim its victims throughout the novel.

From a strictly narrative point of view, the account of the pro-cession is intriguing precisely because it is irrelevant to the rest of the plot. Its appearance is not even justified by what we might call "faithfulness to the source-text": neither the procession nor the whole section "Cuba" in the first part of the novel has any equiva-lent in *Wuthering Heights*. Cuba, in fact, is the place where Razyé, the Caribbean Heathcliff, escapes after learning that his beloved Cathy would never marry him. Razyé's time in Cuba constitutes the counterpart for the famous (or infamous) three mysterious years that Heathcliff spends making a fortune while he is away from Cathy and from *Wuthering Heights*. Recently, a few critics have been formulating interesting theories about these three years. Accord-ing to Marina Warner, the novelist Angela Carter speculated that

Heathcliff was "a black child, or half-black child – Brontë insistently calls him 'swarthy'." Carter hypothesizes that the mysterious fortune that made Heathcliff feel damned might have been the fruit of his work for the British slavers in Africa (3-4). As a matter of fact, by the early 18th century, London, Bristol and Liverpool had developed into prosperous slave ports sending manufactured goods to Africa in return for human cargo: as a result, during the 19th century, a black community began to establish itself in Liverpool (Martin 144-45). Of course, it is impossible to prove or disprove Carter's theory. Nevertheless, it seems to be well in keeping with the historical period in which the novel was set and, most importantly for the purpose of our discussion, it "chimes" with *La migration des cœurs*. In *La migration des cœurs*, there is no mystery: Condé decides to let Razyé tell us all about his life in Cuba and what happened to him after he was put in prison there:

> …un beau matin…des juges féroces m'ont proposé:
>
> – Que préfères-tu? Mourir en prison ou bien garder la vie en tuant d'autres hommes?
>
> Illogique, j'ai préféré la deuxième solution.… [Je] suis monté dans la forêt, la *manigua*, pour traquer les partisans et ceux qui les soutenaient. C'est-à-dire tous les paysans…. Tous les jours…j'incendiais des villages, je torturais des femmes et des enfants, je massacrais du bétail. Parfois…je tombais nez à nez avec des nègres tout nus qui se cachaient là, ne sachant pas que l'esclavage était fini. Ils ne savaient plus l'espagnol et étaient revenues aux langages de l'Afrique. Ceux-là, je les tuais quand même, mais avec mauvais coeur. (119)
>
> [One morning…ruthless judges…offered me a deal: "Choose! Either you die in prison or else you save your skin by killing other men." Illogically, I chose the second solution.… I climbed up to the forest, the *manigua*, to hunt down the rebels and their supporters. In other words, all the peasant folk.… Every day… I set fire to villages, I tortured women and children, I slaughtered cattle. Sometimes,… I came face to face with men, hiding naked in the forest, not knowing that slavery was over. They could no longer speak Spanish and had returned to the languages of Africa. I killed them even so, but felt bad about it. (116)]

Heathcliff's ambiguous status in *Wuthering Heights* –"hero or demon?" (Eagleton 100)—is thus "transferred" onto Razyé who, back on his native island after slaughtering former black slaves in Cuba, puts "la Guadeloupe à feu et à sang" (336) [Guadeloupe to fire and the sword (348)] and becomes a popular figurehead for the black insurgents.

La *migration des cœurs* and *Wuthering Heights* are both roughly divisible into two parts: what comes before Cathy's death and Heathcliff/Razyé's revenge following it. After Cathy's death, as we will see, Condé's book becomes more and more independent from Brontë's narrative and more focused on Caribbean reality. Condé exploits and explodes the narrative structure of *Wuthering Heights* and substitutes two narrators (Nellie Dean and Mr Lockwood) with more than ten narrators of different sex, class, race, and cultural background in order to record more faithfully the social, racial, and cultural complexity and diversity of the Caribbean and to promote a heterogeneous and inclusive concept of creolization.

Social realities, according to Terry Eagleton, also lie at the heart of *Wuthering Heights*. In *Myths of Power*, he claims that "the crux of *Wuthering Heights* must be conceded even by the most remorselessly mythological and mystical of critics to be a social one. In a crucial act of self-betrayal and bad faith, Catherine rejects Heathcliff as a suitor because he is socially inferior to Linton; and it is from this that the train of destruction follows" (101). According to Eagleton, Mr. Earnshaw—the man who "finds" and adopts the orphan Heathcliff—represents the disappearing yeomanry in late eighteenth century England, while the power of the landed gentry is embodied by his neighbours, the Lintons (105).[4]

In *La migration des cœurs* the class/race conflict present in *Wuthering Heights* is radicalized, and so is Razyé's personal revenge against those who humiliated him and prevented his union with Cathy. Condé replaces the Lintons with the aristocratic *béké* de Linsseuil family, and Razyé is adopted by Hubert Gagneur, a mulatto offspring of a black slave and a *béké* (from whom he inherited the property of Windward Heights). Gagneur's wife, Irminette Boisgris, was a fatherless mulatto too. Before dying (as in *Wuthering Heights*) she gave her husband two children, Cathy and Justin (Hindley), profoundly different both in temperament and in "colour." Justin is described as "triste et taciturne. [Avec une peau] claire, assez claire pour qu'il se gagne à la force du poignet une place dans la société des Blancs" (25) [sad and taciturn [with fair skin] fair enough for him to earn a place for himself in white folk's company through sheer hard work (18)]. Cathy, on the other hand, is "autoritaire, violente, toujours prête à répliquer, sournoise,…de la couleur du sirop qu'on vient de sortir du feu et qu'on refroidit au plein air, les cheveux noirs comme des fils de nuit et les yeux verts (26, 25) [bossy, headstrong, always ready to answer back, and artful,…the colour of hot syrup left to cool in the open air, with black hair like threads of night and green eyes (19)]. From the very beginning of Condé's novel, therefore, we start becoming acquainted with some of the "one hundred and twenty eight different degrees of pigmentation" established by the French colonizers in an attempt to distinguish between the children of mixed race relations (Ashcroft, *Key Concepts* 142).

In nineteenth century Guadeloupe the mulattos (Condé's Gagneurs) were a class of people who lived in terror of "*négrification*" and in constant search of "*blanchiment*" (Bangou, 100) [whitening (my translation)]. But they were above all a class on the move, forever trying to climb the social ladder at a time of great socio-economic instability. Doctor Bellisle, a dark-skinned mulatto in *La migration des cœurs*, thus comments on some of the alterations in the social structure of the island: "Ils les connaissait tellement. Ces békés à présent sans un sou, méprisant tous les gens à peau plus foncée que la leur, mais bien obligés de faire semblant, vu leur nouvelle condition (134) [He knew these white Creoles like the back of his hand, not a cent to their name, despising anyone with a darker skin, but forced into making pretences given their new state of affairs (130)].[5] This "new state of affairs" was strictly connected with the fact that in the latter half of the nineteenth century sugar producers had to compete against the technologically developed European beet sugar industry.

At the turn of the century the mulattos were not the only group "on the move" whose political and economic advancement constituted a threat for the white élite. In 1898, led by Hégésippe Légitimus, the Socialists of the "Parti des Noirs" had become the first political party in Guadeloupe. In Henri Bangou's words, the "Parti des Noirs" was "totally in control of the island" and "Légitimus, leader of this party, was the mayor of Pointe-à-Pitre."[6] It is not surprising, therefore, that at the time allegations were made against him and his party members concerning the fires that destroyed some of the cane-fields on the island. In Condé's novel, Aymeric de Linsseuil is forced to sell part of his property to the *Crédit Foncier*

Colonial, but his financial ruin is actually blamed on the arson attack on his cane-fields (154-56; 152-54).[7] Condé's narrator suggests that Razyé might have been responsible for this disaster: Razyé himself speaks of his desire for vengence: "Je vais me venger, et d'une façon éclatante… mon histoire passera dans celle de ce pays" (110) [I shall take my revenge…. And my story will go down in the history of this country (106)]. The narrator also adds that he had just joined forces with the black Socialist leader Jean-Hilaire Endomius, "député-maire de La Pointe" (117) [assemblyman and mayor of La Pointe (114)], whose men were (allegedly) held responsible for setting fire to other *békés'* cane-fields (150; 152).

An "indirect" or "unofficial" implication of the "Parti des Noirs" in the arson attacks of the time is difficult to assess. *Le Courrier de la Guadeloupe*, a newspaper owned by the *béké* Ernest Souques, land owner and proprietor of numerous sugar factories and, according to Christian Schnakenbourg "l'anti-Légitimus" (qtd in Thiébaut 200), launched a campaign against the so-called "incendiaries noirs" ("black arsonists") which was aimed at obtaining a reinforcement of law and order on the island and creating a psychosis of fire (Thiébaut 62). In 1900 the case against Légitimus and his supporters was dismissed for lack of evidence (Lara 329), and, according to Légitimus, Guadeloupe's cane-fields were actually set alight by his political enemies who had the precise intention to accuse him and his supporters in order to discredit them in front of the electors.[8] Nevertheless, one of the explanations advanced for some of the fires was insurance fraud and, overall, they seem to have been either "accidental" or "acts of personal revenge" (Thiébaut 27).[9] By foregrounding an interconnection of "personal" and "political" motives behind the arson attacks on the cane-fields, Condé's narrator invites us to meditate on how historical "narratives" were (are) strategically produced. At the same time, the narrator offers a variety of accounts of these events in the text: "Certaines affirmaient avoir croisé des cavaliers noirs, portraits crachés des hommes de main de Jean-Hilaire Endomius. D'autres soutenaient avoir vu, de leurs yeux vu, vers les dix heures du soir, le ciel lâcher une boule de feu qui d'un seul coup avait embrasé les cannes" (155) [Some claimed to have seen a pack of black horsemen, the spitting image of Jean-Hilaire Endomius's henchmen. Others swore that they had seen…a ball of fire fall from the sky…that set the cane-fields alight (154)]. In so doing, the narrator undermines the distinction between fact and fiction, history and story.

Maryse Condé Creolizes the Canon in *La migration des cœurs*

When the financial and political success of other groups in society was seriously threatening the superiority and economic privilege of the white élite at the end of the century, there was an exacerbation of the already prevalent racist ideology, discrimination, and oppression. In *La migration des cœurs,* during the celebration of the marriage between the *béké* Aymeric de Linsseuil and the mulatto Cathy Gagneur, the collective grumble of the black people observing the multitude of *békés* gathered for the occasion reminds us that in the Guadeloupe of the 1880s the abolition of slavery had not improved Black people's economic conditions at all: "Voilà bientôt cinquante ans que l'esclavage des nègres est soi-disant fini, et pourtant ils ne trouvent que la misère au fond du *kiwi* de leur vie" (55-56) [It's been almost fifty years since slavery's supposed to be over and yet the blacks only find misery at the bottom of life's bowl (49)]. On the same occasion, Condé's narrator introduces us to the secret racist views of some of the most prominent *békés* of Guadeloupe: "Est-ce que c'était la fin du monde que s'annonçait? Est-ce que, les unes après les autres, les familles allaient s'allier à des mulâtres comme les Linsseuil le faisaient aujourd'hui? Ou pire encore, à des nègres? Et, qui sait, un jour, à des Zindiens? Est-ce que la Guadeloupe allait devenir un vaste *manjé-kochon* où on ne distinguerait plus ni les couleurs ni les origines? Plûtot mourir" (56) [Was this a sign of the end of the world? Were families, one after the other, going to marry into mulatto families like the de Linsseuils were doing today? Or worse still into black families? And who knows, one day into Indian families? Was Guadeloupe going to become one vast pig-swill where you couldn't tell one colour or origin from the next? Rather be dead (49)]. It is not surprising therefore, that despite being a product of mixed liaisons, Catherine Gagneur/de Linsseuil will never be able to act as a "bridge" between the two dominant racial groups on the island. She is instead induced to believe that she must choose which side of the non-existent bridge between the two corresponding cultures ("Africa" and "Europe"/ "Savagery" and "Civilization") she wants to belong to.

Cathy earlier confided to Nelly Raboteur that she could never marry Razyé because "ce serait trop dégradant. Ce serait recommencer à vivre comme nos ancêtres, les sauvages d'Afrique!" (20) [it would be too degrading. It would be like starting to live all over again like our ancestors, the savages in Africa! (13)]. As Henri Bangou explains, in Guadeloupe the mulattos were trying "to get as close as possible to the békés but, above all, to distinguish themselves from the *uneducated* and *barbarian* Africans."[10] It is significant to note that in *Wuthering Heights* Cathy is "forced" to stay at Thrushcross Grange (and therefore turn into a "lady") because of the wound caused by the Lintons' dog's bite, while in *La migration des cœurs* Cathy, who has *not* been bitten by a dog, accepts Huberte de Linsseuil's invitation to stay at Belles-Feuilles plantation (and therefore to "whiten" herself) "avec ravissement,…comme si elle ne savait pas qu'ils ne la lui pardonneraient jamais" (35) [with delight,…as if she did not know that they would never forgive her for what she was (29)].[11] When anticipating her life as the wife of the *béké* Aymeric de Linseuil, she dreams of listening to Mozart, dancing the *quadrille*, and speaking French with educated people (37; 30-31).

In order to become a de Linsseuil, Cathy undergoes a process of acculturation (absorption of *béké* culture) which, despite the fact that her husband Aymeric "adores" her, is never completed by inter-mixture and reciprocal enrichment between *béké* culture and Creole culture, but rather by her complete deculturation. As a result, both Creole culture and language are suppressed. For example, when Aymeric teaches his wife the French/Latin names of animals and trees his attitude is rigidly prescriptive and he is not in the least bit interested in learning their Creole counterparts from her: "Ne dis pas *kongolio*. C'est de l'iule qu'il s'agit. Ne dis pas *manzé Marie*. C'est sensitive, son nom" (98) [Don't say *kongolio*. Say myriapod. Don't say *manzè Marie*. Say sensitive plant or mimosa pudica (94)]. At the peak of her desperation, Cathy, tries to reverse her misery (to no avail) by reclaiming her black heritage back shortly before her death: "… je me demande si la religion chrétienne n'est pas une religion de Blancs faite pour les Blancs; si elle est bonne pour nous autres, qui avons du sang d'Africain dans les veins. Est-ce qu'il ne devrait pas y avoir une religion pour chaque race, chaque people de la terre?" (86) [… I've wondered whether the Christian religion is not a white folks' religion made for white folks; whether it's right for us who have African blood in our veins. Shouldn't there be a religion for every race, every people on this earth? (81)]. Only too late does Cathy begin to accept the African part of her origins.

In *Wuthering Heights* Catherine dies because she "trades her authentic selfhood for social privilege" (Eagleton 101): as a member of the declining yeomanry, her own survival (and the survival of yeomanry as a whole) requires that she turn her back both on her class values and on her personal principles and that she consort with, or rather, submit to the morals and standards of the landed gentry, the Lintons. Similarly, in *La migration des cœurs* Cathy loses her reason and dies because she is deprived of the right to maintain her identity as "Creole," an identity that would exceed the Manichean dynamic of racial discourse and delegitimize what Kathleen Balutansky and Marie-Agnès Sourieau define as "Europe's obsession with linear origins, and especially with 'being' as a stable category of integrity and purity" (3). In this regard, it is noteworthy that despite being identified with "blackness" and "Africa" by those around him, the text alerts us to the fact that Razyé's own origins are far from "linear" or "stable." Not only was he found (at least according to Hubert Gagneur's story) "nu comme un ver…en plein milieu des *razyés*. [Son] nom vient de là" (17) [as naked as the day [he] was born, on the barren heath and cliff—the *razyés*—hence [his] name (9)], but on his first entrance in the novel he is thus described: "Il était tout de noir vêtu à la mode française, depuis ses bottes de cuir solidement lacées jusqu'à son chapeau de feutre à bord rond ourlé d'un gros-grain. Sa peau aussi était noire, de ce noir brillant que l'on appelle ashanti, et ses cheveux entortillés en boucles comme ceux d'un *bata-zindien*" (15) [He was dressed all in black in the French fashion, from his tightly-laced leather boots to his felt hat sewn with a large hem stitch. His skin too was black, that shiny black they call Ashanti, and his hair hung in curls like those of an Indian half-caste, the Bata-Zindien (7)]. The description of Rayze's physical appearance signposts his "creolised" identity.

Cultural creolization is the foundation of Guadeloupe's history. In 1854 Guadeloupe, slavery was "replaced" by immigration, usually under indenture arrangements, and most of the immigrants were Indians.[12] Razyé, therefore, might have been the offspring of a clandestine mixed black/indian couple, a hypothesis reinforced by the fact that, when he first arrives at L'Engoulvent, Nellie Raboteur describes him as "négre ou *bata-zindien*" (28) [a little black boy or Indian half-caste (21)]. The creolized nature of Razyé's origin is further sustained in Nellie's tale when she compares him at one point to "Otaheite, le héros indien que l'on voit dans les livres des images" (30) [Otaheite, the Indian hero you see in picture books]. In a conversation with him she speculates that "peut-être que vos ancêtres étaient des princes et des princesses" [perhaps your ancestors were princes and princesses? (30)] and asks: "Qui sait ce qu'étaient nos parents avant d'être emmenés ici en esclavages?" [Who knows what our parents were before we were brought here as slaves? (30)]. For Eagleton, Heathcliff's independence from blood-ties frees him from social customs. In *La migration des cœurs* Razyé's unclear origin positions him outside racial and social conventions, thus making him a threat to these same conventions and what they stand for. He could be creole like Cathy and Justin; he could even be the natural son of their father, thus anticipating the incestuous fate of Razyé II and Cathy II. In order to neutralize the menace, Razyé's racial identity is polarized and postulated as essentially black/African by those who are most threatened by him. Significantly, it is Justin who first gives Razyé this kind of stable racial identity. Walking in on Razyé and Cathy feeding one another Jamaican plums in a state of apparently innocent sensuality and hilarity, Justin "se précipita vers sa soeur et, d'une seule calotte, il l'envoya rouler à terre. En même temps, il reprit son créole qu'il abandonnait depuis peu et hurla: '*Kimafooutyesa*! Ma fille, qu'est-ce que tu veux? Un ventre à crédit? Et avec un nègre encore!'" (33) [rushed over to his sister and with one cuff sent her sprawling to the ground. At the same time he revived his Creole that he had been neglecting somewhat and shouted: "Kimafooutyesa! Ti-ma-fi, sé on vant a krédi, ou vlé poté ban mwen? E épi yon nèg anko?" (26)]. Justin is worried that his sister, rather than being preoccupied with "whitening" her blood, might instead end up pregnant by a "nègre"/"nèg," and therefore he forbids Razyé from entering the house from this point on in the story. What renders Razyé's story truly tragic, however, is the fact that it is his beloved Cathy who, in what Eagleton would define as "a crucial act of self-betrayal and bad faith" (101), sanctions Justin's *négrification* of Razyé when she claims to Nelly that she cannot marry him because he reminds her of "nos ancêtres, les sauvages d'Afrique!" (20) [our ancestors, the savages in Africa!] (13). The text does not let this simple opposition remain, however; the narrator points out that Razyé, the "nègre"/"nèg," is confined by Justin "aux travaux des champs avec les Zindiens" (33) [to the fields with the Indians (26)].

Eagleton's description of the initial relationship between Cathy and Heathcliff in *Wuthering Heights* as "a paradigm of human possibilities" characterized by "loving equality" (103) could just as easily apply to Condé's Cathy and Razyé. They both speak Creole (no other languages are spoken at L'Engoulvent before Hubert Gagneur's death and Justin's decision to go to school) and share everything (including the bed). As Catherine and Heathcliff before them, Cathy and Razyé inhabit a "primordial moment of pre-social harmony, before the fall into history and [racial] oppression"

(Eagleton 109). Razyé and Cathy's relationship carries on after Justin's banishment of Razyé; but it comes to an end when Cathy is befriended – or better, tolerated – by the island's békés and is "allowed" to join the high society of Guadeloupe following Justin's marriage with the white Creole Marie-France La Rinardière. In both *Wuthering Heights* and *La migration des cœurs*, society negates this "ideal," alternative, pre-social and pre-racialized world.

In *La migration des cœurs*, Cathy is married to Aymeric de Linsseuil, but the daughter she bears is fathered by Razyé. The birth of Cathy (II) coincides with her mother's death. Although no one seems to suspect her parentage, the narrator explains that this child's difference was noted: "À la différence de ses frères, un hâle déjà foncé l'obscurcissait, comme si elle était remontée dans le temps à la recherche d'une généalogie oubliée. Cela lui préparait un bel avenir! On ferait la moue, on comparerait, on dirait: 'Comme elle est brune!'"(92) [Unlike her brothers her skin had already darkened, as if she had gone back in time in search of a lost family-tree. This forbode a fine future for her! They would make faces and comparisons and declare: 'How dark she is!' (87)]. Indeed, when Razyé sees Cathy for the last time, just hours before her death and the birth of Cathy II, he is unaware that Cathy is carrying his child. After Cathy's death, Aymeric de Linsseuil brings the child up as if she were his own daughter; despite his daughter's dark skin colour, he never suspects (or pretends he never suspects) that his wife has been unfaithful to him.

At Belles-Feuilles, the Linsseuils' estate, Cathy II grows up enjoying, paradoxically, all the privileges of a *béké* while developing a real adoration for her white "father" Aymeric and completely absorbing his Englightenment ideals (45; 37) and his culture. Cathy II knows the Latin names of all the different types of mangroves because this is what her father taught her, and when "elle s'efforçait de parler créole…ceux qui étaient présents entendaient bien que ce n'était pas sa langue maternelle, que c'était le bon français qui avait l'habitude de sortir de sa bouche et qui se battait pour en prendre le chemin" (223) [she tried to speak Creole…those present could hear it was not her mother tongue and that it was proper French that was used to coming out of her mouth and was desperately trying to gain the upper hand (225)]. However, Cathy II never managed to feel at ease among the de Linsseuils for whom she was a constant source of embarrassment. After her beloved father's death she moves to the small isle of Marie-Galante, twenty-six kilometres South-East of Guadeloupe, to be a school teacher and live on her own.

At the same moment that Cathy II is born, Irmine de Linsseuil, Cathy's sister in law and Razyé's *béké* wife, gives birth to a son who "était, en plus clair, le portrait tout craché de Razyé" (105) [was the very image of Razyé, but a lighter skinned version (101)]. Once grown-up, these two children (who, of course, are unaware that they are half-brother and sister) meet in Marie-Galante where Razyé II too had "escaped" from his family. Their first conversation articulates very clearly the clash of values of different social groups in Guadeloupean/Caribbean society and deserves to be quoted at length. Not only do the two speakers, both dark-skinned, share the same father; almost paradoxically, Razyé II is the one with a white biological parent, which allows Condé to demonstrate how Caribbean society was (and still is) too complex for the cultural differences among its people to be measured by a simplistic racial criterion. The two first meet when Razyé II (or better, First-born Sobrimol, as Razyé II has renamed himself) decides to start a new life and approaches the village schoolmistress (that is Cathy II), to ask her if she could give him some private instruction in order to help him to get a school diploma. Cathy II replies that she is not sure to be up to the task, but Razyé "reassures" and simultaneously challenges her by referring to the way in which she had celebrated the carnival with her pupils:

> - Vous etês capable de transformer des petit-fils d'esclaves en marquis. Cela veut dire que vous etês capable de tout ce que vous voulez.

> Elle sentit qu'il se moquait et répondit d'un ton défensif:

> - C'était pour jouer. Le carnaval est un jeu.

> Il haussa les épaules.

> - Vous auriez pu jouer à autre chose. À ressusciter leurs ancêtres Moudongues ou nègres marrons, par exemple… Est-ce que vous connaissez l'histoire de ce morceau de terre et de ces gens qui vous paraissent tellement inoffensifs, *pa vré* ?…Je vous emmènerai à la mare au Punch ou bien au morne Tarteson, là où il y a quelques années la foule a tenu tête aux gendarmes. Et vous saurez qui sont vraiment les gens de Marie-Galante… .

- Je sais que nous connaissons des temps très difficiles. Tout le beau travail qu'avait fait M. Schoelcher n'a servi à rien. Les anciens esclaves ne respectent pas Dieu et ne veulent pas travailler ...

À ces mots, il se mit en colère et s'écria:

- Vous parlez comme les esclavagistes! Et puis cessez de nous rebattre les oreilles avec M. Schoelcher, M. Schoelcher ... On dirait que les esclaves n'ont rien fait pour gagner leur liberté. (230-31).

["You can change grandsons of slaves into marquises," he said. "So you are capable of doing anything you want."

She felt he was poking fun at her and replied on the defensive: "That was for fun. The carnival is an amusement."

He shrugged his shoulders.

"You could have played at other things. Dressing them up as Mandingo ancestors or Maroons, for example...Do you know the story of this piece of land?...And of this people who seem so harmless to you?...I'll take you to the Punchbowl Pond or else Tartenson Heights, where a few years back the crowd stood up to the gendarmes. And you'll see who the people of Marie-Galante really are... "

"I know we are going through difficult times. All Monsieur Schoelcher's fine work has led to nothing. The former slaves respect neither God nor work."

On hearing these words, he flew into a temper.

"You talk like the slave-owners," he cried. "And stop going on about Monsieur Schoelcher, Monsieur Schoelcher. You'd think the slaves did nothing to win their freedom." (233-34)].

Razyé II's words seem to have an effect on Cathy II. The reader learns that "brusquement, elle voyait tout le ridicule de sa conduite. Quelle idée l'avait prise d'avoir poudré à frimas les têtes grenées de ses petits nègres?" (231) [all at once she realized how ridiculous her behaviour had been. What had got into her to powder the peppercorn heads of her little children like hoar frost? (234)]. Cathy II seems to be in the process of realizing that her actions are both a consequence and a sad re-enactment of the process of "blanchiment" or "lactification" — to use Frantz Fanon's term — imposed on her by the de Linsseuils. Hence, she resolves that "il fallait découvrir qui elle était réellement. Des Moudongues, des nègres marrons, elle avait, certes, entendu parler, mais toujours de façon négative… Histoires de vol and de viols, de massacres et de tueries à la machette" (234) [she had to discover who she really was. Mandingos, Maroons, she had certainly heard of them, but always in a negative fashion… Stories of rape and robbery, massacres and murder (237)]. Cathy's resolution comes to naught, however, imprisoned as she is in the "manicheism delirium" (Dide and Guiraud 164 qtd in Fanon, *Black Skin* 183) that pairs Good with White and Evil with Black.

Shortly after her encounter with Razyé II, Cathy II meets Razyé, the man she hates the most in the world because she considers him responsible for the financial downfall and death of her beloved father Aymeric. The consequences of this confrontation are utterly disquieting for Cathy II, who vehemently desires the death of Razyé to the point that she feels almost ready to kill him: "… devant celui qui avait assassiné son papa à coups de grèves et des révoltes d'ouvriers agricoles…elle n'avait qu'une seule envie: s'emparer du couteau de cuisine et le lui planter dans le dos. Comme une négresse marronne qui taillade à coups de machette le maître qui l'a violée" (256) [… face to face with the man who had murdered her father through a series of strikes and riots…she had only one desire: to grab the kitchen knife and stick it in his back. Like a woman of the Maroons hacking with a cutlass at the master who had raped her (262)]. When she confesses her sins to Father Dupuytren, Cathy II can't help but associating what is "wicked, sloppy, malicious, instinctual" (Fanon 192) in herself with her black ancestry, which re-enacts her mother's belief that her lower emotions and the "dark" side of her soul are her black/African side, as she says early in the novel: "C'est comme s'il y avait en moi deux Cathy, et cela a toujours été ainsi depuis que je suis toute petite. Une Cathy qui débarque directement d'Afrique avec tous ses vices. Une autre Cathy qui est le portrait de son aïeule blanche, pure, pieuse, aimant l'ordre et la mesure" (48) [It's as if there were two Cathys inside me…. One Cathy who's come straight from Africa, vices and all. The other Cathy who is the very image of her white ancestor, pure, dutiful, fond of order and moderation] (40). As a result, like the "Negro" in Fanon's *Black Skin, White Mask*, and as her mulatto mother before her, Cathy II, "is forever in combat with [her] own image" (Fanon 194).

Cathy II, who will never be able to get rid of her "white mask," remains alienated from a very substantial part of her real self for most of her life: despite the fact that she becomes Razyé II's wife, she continues to sign her diary as Cathy de Linsseuil. At the same time, when the fishwife Ada befriends her during a particularly difficult time, Cathy II tells her "j'aurais tellement aimé être ton enfant. Sortie de ton ventre à toi, négresse simple et vaillante, les deux pieds dans la réalité (316) [I wish I were your child. Out of the womb of a hardy, stout-hearted woman like yourself with both feet on the ground (326)]. Cathy II describes her own mother to Ada as having "la tête farcie de rêves et d'envies" and asks "Où est-ce que cela l'a menée?" (316) [her head stuffed with dreams and longings. Where did that get her? (326)]. Like her mother, Cathy II is a Creole character who, paradoxically, feels comfortable either identifying with the *békés* de Linsseuils (albeit in the secrecy of her diary) or with black people such as Ada, but who is never actually capable of accepting her true Creole self.

In the course of Condé's novel, Cathy II and Razyé II (who never confesses to Cathy II who his father really is) fall in love, get married and move to Roseau, in Dominica, still unaware that they are actually brother and sister.[13] History repeats itself as the birth of their daughter Anthuria coincides with the death of her mother. He decides to return with his daughter to his family in Guadeloupe, only to discover that his father Razyé is dead and that his mother, the *béké* Irmine de Linsseuil, is trying to turn his siblings into *békés* by sending his brothers to "un collège de jésuites à Bordeaux" [a Jesuit school in Bordeaux] and his sister Cassandra to a "pension-nat des soeurs à Versailles" (330) [the nuns' boarding school in Versailles (341)]. Razyé II realizes that he does not want this kind of life for himself or for his daughter, and covering Cathy Gagneur's personal route in reverse, he decides to move to Windward Heights with the baby.

Razyé II's choice carries significant symbolic weight, especially if we read the ending of the family's saga in Condé's novel with *Wuthering Heights* in mind. At the end of Brontë's novel, Hareton — son of Hindley Earnshaw and legitimate successor of the patriarch Hareton Earnshaw who founded Wuthering Heights in 1500 — manages to repossess the property that Heathcliff had taken away from his father. Wuthering Heights, though, will remain uninhab-ited because Hareton and his wife, Catherine Linton/Heathcliff/Earnshaw, have decided to live at Thrushcross Grange, the Lintons' estate. The conflict between landed gentry and yeomanry, that according to Eagleton informs Brontë's novel, seems therefore to be won by the landed gentry as both Wuthering Heights and Hareton appear to be assimilated by the Lintons and Thrushcross Grange. However, Brontë's conclusion to the novel sanctions the victory of Thrushcross Grange only up to a certain point. After the death of both his parents, Hareton grew up at Wuthering Heights with Heathcliff as surrogate father, and despite Catherine's *mission civilisatrice* (the refined daughter of Edgar Linton teaches him manners and how to read and write), he continues to represent a "Heathcliff-like robustness" the Grange must learn to come to terms with (Eagleton 120).[14]

In *La migration des cœurs* Condé capitalizes on the ambiguity of Bronte's ending. Razyé II refuses to be assimilated by the *béké* world that his mother Irmine de Linsseuil is recreating for herself in La Pointe (a replica of Belles-Feuilles) and moves to L'Engoulvent, a property that used to belong to the mulatto Hubert Gagneur and a place where only Creole used to be spoken. However, although he does not make any effort to repair the house infested by rats, bats, termites and iguanas, Razyé II does not let the estate decay as Hubert Gagneur and his father did when they were in charge of it; like the would-be *béké* Justin Gagneur before him, he hires some workers to clear the "*razyés* et [les] *banglins* qui couvraient la savane autour de la maison et à planter en légumes" [thornbushes that covered the savanna around the house and plant it with vegetables (345-346)].[15] This new world that he creates for his daughter, therefore, results from the interaction and adaptation of different outlooks on life, outlooks that up to that moment had been considered incommensurable.

The title of the last section of *La migration des cœurs*, "Retour à l'Engoulvent" [Return to l'Engoulvent],[16] is slightly deceptive: unlike Razyé II who had lived there as a baby, Anthuria had never been to Windward Heights/L'Engoulvent before. Indeed, Razyé soon learns that Windward Heights (like Wuthering Heights) is haunted by its own past and its burdens. A visit to the graveyard of the property confirms Razyé II's suspicions about his father and Cathy II's mother and instills in his mind a new tormenting thought about his daughter: might she be, therefore, the fruit of an incestuous relationship? From the moment this question "slips" into his heart, Razyé II, contrary to his father who was obsessed with the past, becomes obsessed with the future and with what will become of his daughter. He refuses to believe that her future will be marred by her past – "une si belle enfant ne pouvait pas être maudite" (337) [such a lovely child could not be cursed (348)] –but he is so concerned about her that he "ne prenait plus aucun soin de sa personne, et son odeur traînait derrière lui comme la fumée d'un train de cannes à sucre" (337) [no longer [takes] care of himself and his smell [trails] behind him like the smoke from a sugar-cane train (348)].

Like *Wuthering Heights*, *La migration des cœurs* has no conventional happy ending, but Condé's novel leaves the ending more open because the fate of Anthuria remains unclear. Will she succeed in piecing together a Creole identity capable of making sense out of the violent contradictions, the pain and the hope, and the love and the hatred that are intertwined in her personal history, and, more generally, in the history of Caribbean people? Several images that lead back to the Epiphany procession in the opening chapter offer some clues. First we learn that to prepare himself for death, Razyé had adorned his room ritualistically with "des dizaines de bougies allumées sur un autel devant des images bariolées et païennes, des flacons, des calebasses, des clous et des objets de fer-blanc éclaraient la pièce comme en plein jour" (265) [dozens of candles burning on an altar with gaudy, pagan images, flasks, calabashes, nails and tin objects [that] lit up the room like daylight (271)]. And once his death comes, it is as mystifying as his origin: his wife Irmine finds Razyé dead, "couché par terre...la chemise deboutonnée sur son torse velu. Son corps ne portait aucune trace de blessure" (267) [lying on the floor his shirt unbuttoned...no trace of wound...on his body (272)]. The sacrificial and mysterious overtones of Razyé's demise, coupled with the fact that a snake is actually mentioned by his children on the same night of his death (264; 271), allow us to conjecture that the "snake," the "scapegoat" that was missing from the procession on the Día des Reyes in Cuba has finally been slain, "channelling" and "conjuring away" racial violence (at least provisionally and symbolically).

Moreover, if *nomen est omen*, Anthuria seems to have been bestowed by her mother with a name capable of counteracting, and in more than one way, the child's (alleged) "curse." First of all, Anthuria has not been given a "replica" name like both her parents (Cathy II and Razyé II), a sign that in spite of being the offspring of an incestuous relationship, she is bound to make a new start. "Anthuria" derives from anthurium, a plant well-known for its beauty and showy foliage and indigenous to tropical America. It is a "Creole" plant, if we take "Creole" to mean what it means to Condé when she reminds us that "Loreto Todd, in *Pidgins and Creoles* (24), gives the meaning…of the Spanish word *criollo*, Fr. *créole*, as 'native to the locality, country.'"[17] Strictly speaking there are no "natives" (or only a handful of them) in the Caribbean, but Condé appropriates Todd's definition of Creole to promote her all-embracing, non race-based notion of creolization: it includes not only the whites but also the Africans born on the plantations and all the other ethnicities of the Caribbean and their descendants (including the diasporic ones).[18] Housing the "inclusive" urge that has grown in Caribbean literature in the past thirty years, *La migration des cœurs* posits Caribbean identity as something to invent—both in the current sense of "creating" and in the Latin sense of "finding"—"a production which is never complete" (Hall, "Cultural Identity" 392). As Stuart Hall has pointed out, Caribbean identity "is not an essence but a *positioning* . . .; a matter of 'becoming' as well as of 'being'"; as such it belongs to the future as much as to the past and does not simply imply the rediscovery of a lost and elusive past but also the creative and imaginative "re-telling" of that past (392-395). In Condé's novel the past is literally "buried" at Windward Heights, or at the bottom of the sea where Cathy II's secret diary lies—before reaching Guadeloupe, Razyé II/First-Born has thrown it amid the waves *without* reading it— and the future needs to be invented.

Condé, in fact, does not limit herself to relegate an alternative way of life to the "realms of myth and metaphysics" (Eagleton 120). *La migration des cœurs* gives us some hope in a possible—albeit gradual, painful and uncertain—realization of what, borrowing Eagleton words for the last time, we can term the Caribbean "ideal" (120), that is, the transformative and creative potential of creolization as a process. After all, Anthuria seems "well placed" to succeed in her search for her Creole identity: she inhabits the *new* Windward Heights thus finding herself in a new space "at the crossroads of forgetting and remembering, of an elusive past to be re-imagined and an uncertain future" (Balutansky and Sourieau 9).[19] In other words, she is in a "position" (both metaphorically and not) that might allow her to set in motion the "creativity" implicit in the very etymon of the word "Creole"[20] so that she might be prompted to do what Yanick Lahens suggests all Caribbean people should do: "Without trying to get rid of our history…and instead of tirelessly seeking to stick back together the broken pieces of our identity, why not use this multiplicity precisely to invent the future that…we represent?" (156). In Rayzé II's words: "une si belle enfant ne pouvait pas être maudite" [such a lovely child [can]not be cursed].

Notes

I would like to thank *The British Academy* for an overseas conference grant that enabled me to present a paper based on this essay at "The Caribbean Unbound," Franklin College, Lugano (Switzerland), and Dr. Maurice Lee, editor of the *Journal of Caribbean Literatures*, for giving me permission to include in this chapter extracts from my article entitled "Maryse Condé's *La Migration des Coeurs*, Jean Rhys's *Wide Sargasso Sea* and (the Possibility of) Creolization," first published in the *Journal of Caribbean Literatures*, vol. 3. no. 2 (pp.65-88), © 1997.

1. For this image I am indebted to Maryse Condé herself who used it to explain the relationship between her text and Brontë's during a reading in London in May 1998.

2. For another perspective on these events, see Jules Robert Benjamin, *The United States and Cuba* (3, 5).

3. The Africanized carnival of the Día de Reyes was prohibited in 1880, the year slavery was abolished in Cuba; however, according to Benítez-Rojo, the Negroes of Havana put their dances into the whites carnival (299). The procession described in *La migration des cœurs* actually takes place *after* the abolition of slavery in Cuba.

4. See Eagleton (117).

5. It is noteworthy that the family name Linsseuil recalls *linceul*, French for "shroud," which might point to the soon-to-come demise of this family and the social order they stand for while "Gagneur" ("winner" in French) could stand in for the economic "rise" of the mulatto class.

6. "En 1898 le Parti du people," Bangou writes, "le parti des Noirs était maître incontesté de l'île...Légitimus, chef de ce parti, était maître de Pointe-à-Pitre" (117). All English translations are my own unless otherwise indicated.

7. As Don R. Hoy informs us in "Changing Agricultural Land Use on Guadeloupe, French West Indies," when the conditions of the Guadeloupean cane producers worsened through competition with beet sugar producers, the French Government established the *Crédit Foncier Colonial* as a way to support cane growers by giving them low-interest loans (285). As farmers reneged on their loans, the bank took possession of their canefields and other prize land, which was then sold cheaply to French companies (285).

8. See especially his letter dated 21 March 1901 and cited in Bangou (118).

9 . See, for example, the fire which destroyed a shop in Petit-Canal and the case of Julia Florimond who set fire to her lover's house for revenge (Thiébaut 29 and 40 respectively).

10. "...de se rapprocher du Blanc mais surtout...se distinguer de l'Africain *inculte* et *barbare*" (100).

11. Belles-Feuilles is the Caribbean counterpart of *Wuthering Heights'* Thrushcross Grange, while Windward Heights (*L'Engoulvent* in the original) is the Caribbean Wuthering Heights.

12. According to Eric Williams, Guadeloupe's immigration statistics read as follows from 1854 to 1877: Indians, 42,595; Africans, 6600; Chinese, 500; Madeirans, 413; Europeans, 379; Annamites from Cochin China, 272 (349).

13. The island of Dominica, renowned for its two languages—French creole, English—and birthplace of Jean Rhys, author of *Wide Sargasso Sea*—(the well-known rewriting of Charlotte Bronte's *Jane Eyre*)—provides a further bridge between the French-speaking Condé and the English literary tradition represented by Emily Brontë.

14. Of course the relationship between the schoolmistress Cathy II and her pupil Razyé II is modelled on the one that Brontë establishes between the educated Catherine and the uncouth Hareton.

15. The fact that in the French original Razyé II eliminates "*razyés*" rather than "thornbushes" is obviously much more poignant in this context.

16. It goes without saying that Condé's title for this chapter, "Retour au pays natal" [Return To My Native Land], and even more the title of the preceding chapter—"Retour à l'Engoulvent" [Return to l'Engoulvent], echo and gesture towards Aimé Césaire's *Cahier d'un retour au pays natal* [*Return to My Native Land*].

17. It is noteworthy that at Justin-Marie's wake Aymeric Linsseuil and his second wife Marie bring "des gerbes de lis et d'anthuriums" (206) [bunches of white lilies and anthuriums (207)]. Since the white lily is the well-known symbol of France, the anthurium could be seen as the symbol of the "Creole" world.

18. Amongst the multiplicity of tales that constitute *La migration des cœurs*, in fact, one also finds the tales of Sanjita, whose parents arrived in Guadeloupe from Calcutta in 1868, and of her daughter Etiennise (157-167 and 168-177; 155-165 and 166-176 respectively).

19. Interestingly, the words that Balutansky and Sourieau employ to situate creolization in the Caribbean universe in their "Introduction" to *Caribbean Creolization* are equally appropriate to describe the position that Anthuria (who, in a way, represents cultural creolization) occupies at the end of the novel.

20. "The word 'Creole'...appears to have originated from a combination of the two Spanish words 'criar' (*to create, to imagine,* to establish, to found, to settle), and 'colon' (a colonist, a founder, a settler) into 'criollo': a committed settler, one identified with the area of settlement, one native to the settlement though not ancestrally indigenous to it" (Brathwaite 10).

REWRITING THE POSTCOLONIAL: MARYSE CONDÉ'S *LA MIGRATION DES CŒURS*

Carine M. Mardorossian

Maryse Condé's rewriting of Emily Brontë's Victorian novel renames Wuthering Heights "L'Engoulvent" and locates it in La Guadeloupe in the last years of the nineteenth-century. The Caribbean rejoinder begins with Razyé's (Heathcliff's counterpart's) return from Cuba after a three-year exile and goes on to tell the story of his revenge on his rival and the latter's descendants. Whereas in Brontë's *Wuthering Heights* (1848) this rivalry is predominantly represented in terms of a class conflict, it is overlaid in Condé's novel with a racial dimension that forcefully illustrates the intertwined racial and class hierarchies of Caribbean societies. As a black Creole of unmixed African ancestry, Razyé is a member of the lowest class, while at the other end of the social spectrum, his rival the white planter (or *béké*) Aymeric de Linsseuil owns twenty-percent of Grande-Terre's lands. The object of their obsession, Cathy Gagneur, belongs to the mulatto or "colored" class who gained their freedom during slavery and aspire to the same status as the *békés*. Throughout the novel, what remains remarkably consistent with the original is Razyé's unrelenting passion for his childhood love and his unrepentant cruelty towards everyone else. What is radically different is the second generation's fate, since the young lovers in *La migration des cœurs* do not get to experience the domestic bliss that concludes *Wuthering Heights*: the second Catherine, Cathy II, dies in childbirth like her mother after realizing that the man whose child she is having is her own half-brother. Furthermore, Condé explodes the double narration of *Wuthering Heights* into a multitude of narrators whose first-person "récits" alternate with the third person narration. Most of her narrators are black creoles who are at the bottom of the social hierarchy, i.e. servants, ex-slaves, nannies (called *mabos*), housekeepers, fishermen, obeah men (*babalawos*), or helpers. They meet the protagonists in passing and give their own version of events without, however, subordinating their own experiences to that of the protagonists.

Synopses of literary rewritings such as this introductory paragraph are sooner or later bound to invoke the relationship between the postcolonial rewriting and its source-text. It is indeed simply impossible to do justice to the newer text's complexities without highlighting the parallels and differences between the two narratives. In this case, however, such a comparative plot summary is somewhat misleading insofar as this essay does not in fact offer an analysis of Maryse Condé's rewriting in relation to its source-text but to the larger context of postcolonial revisionism.[1] Ever since the publication of *The Empire Writes Back* (1989), the first sustained theoretical investigation of postcolonial literatures, literary rewritings of the English and European canons have been treated as paradigmatic instances of the postcolonial project. Their revisionary thrust has been seen as exemplary of the field as a whole, since postcolonialism in all its guises has always been concerned with replacing colonialist images of difference with alternative and empowering representations from the margins. Jean Rhys's *Wide Sargasso Sea*, the Caribbean rewriting of the other Brontë masterpiece, exemplifies these standard practices insofar it was explicitly written to correct *Jane Eyre*'s imperialism. By contrast, *La migration des cœurs* is not so much a rewriting of Emily Brontë's novel as it is a rewriting of the assumptions and tropes that motivate analyses of postcolonial rewritings. The revered maneuvers of postcolonial revisionism that this novel interrogates are the interlinked issues of history, resistance, and agency.

REWRITING HISTORY AS MEMORY

In their influential *In Praise of Creoleness*, the Martinican writers Bernabé, Chamoiseau, and Confiant emphasize the importance of collective memory to Antillean and postslavery cultures where the only account of the past is otherwise restricted to the colonial chronicle. In light of the "non-history" that defines the New World (to use Édouard Glissant's term), the Creole cultures of the Antilles have had to turn to their storytellers, folktales, and landscapes to bring about the "resuscitation of [Caribbean] consciousness"

(Bernabé et al., 99). Only the acceptance of creoleness through these indirect but vital channels, the Créolistes insist, "will allow us to invest *these impenetrable areas of silence where screams were lost*" (99 [emphasis in the original]).

In promoting collective memory as the means of resurrecting the lost history of the Caribbean, the writers of this manifesto seek to move beyond the "anti-colonial literary militantism" (100) that defines many progressive approaches to postcolonial cultures and to develop a relational paradigm that challenges rather than merely inverts the terms of colonialist binaries such as self/other, black/white, etc.: " Through this kind of vision, we return to the magma that characterizes us. It also frees us of anticolonialist literary militantism so that we will not examine ourselves in order to find a singular ideology, an apodictic truth, or the ten commandments of a table of laws,…but rather because we want to know ourselves, bare in our flaws, in our barks and pulps" (100). *La migration des cœurs*'s representational politics resonates with these declarations insofar as Condé too is invested in undermining orthodoxies, whether of a colonial or postcolonial kind. And she too seeks to challenge the totalizing nature of Western values and history through memory. As she explained in an interview with Barbara Lewis, "if you write a history of Guadeloupe, you are going to talk about the War and the Second World War. You are going to explain the problems of immigration, how many people went to live in France, and so on. If you ask people what is important, they may never mention these things. They are going to mention the hurricane of 1928 or 1989" (549). Similarly, *La migration des cœurs* dramatizes not official history but what Condé calls "the tiny events which have more importance to people than the big events" (549), the "memory" or "mind of the people…. It is something which may be very minute, very unimportant, but it can change a whole life. Memory may be something very trivial, very banal. But not to the person who lives that life" (548-9). These statements help explain why an elaborate and linear historical narrative is often absent from Maryse Condé's fiction. And *La migration des cœurs* is no exception. The novel comprises "little pieces of incomplete narratives, little islands of knowledge spread over many different places, under many different forms" (Rosello, "Caribbean Insularization" 572-73); it is up to the reader to fill in the blanks and reconstitute the historical background.[2] The narrator "is not even interested in centralizing a combination of all the incomplete tales" (573).

For instance, the few historical events that are explicitly referenced in the narrative seem paradoxically inconsequential to character or plot development. The explosion of the battleship U.S.S. Maine off the coast of Havana is a case in point. Historically, the warship U.S.S. Maine which President McKinley had ordered to Havana to evacuate American citizens and property blew up on February 15, 1898, resulting in the loss of two hundred and sixty-six lives. Claiming that Spain had masterminded the explosion, the United States declared war and after a swift victory, occupied Cuba and annexed Puerto Rico and Guam. This historical event is ultimately what precipitated the United States' intervention in the Spanish-Cuban conflict and correlatively, the onset of neocolonialism. Yet, despite the crucial role it played in Caribbean history, it is only significant in *La migration des cœurs* insofar as it coincides with Razyé's departure from Cuba. In fact, when the news of the explosion reaches the boat that is taking the protagonist back to Guadeloupe, it only briefly interrupts the account with which the current narrator Nelly Raboteur is entertaining the female passengers.[3] Nelly's listeners speculate momentarily about the United States' reaction and Cuba's fate before the shocking news drops out of the narrative altogether. The next chapter is entitled "Le récit de Nelly Raboteur (suite)" and proceeds with what was really preoccupying the passengers, namely Nelly's chronicle of the enigmatic Razyé's personal background. The book never answers the question Razyé had formulated onshore at the sight of the Maine, namely "what are the United States up to?," and readers have to fall back on their own knowledge of Caribbean history to understand the consequences of the tragedy. Razyé's own inquiry into these political affairs is revealed to be just a passing thought rather than a question whose answer he has any interest in determining.

The novel's anti-linear approach to history combined with its characters' striking indifference to its "convulsions" should not, however, mislead us to ascribe to Condé herself a cavalier relation to historical and political events. The focus on memory does not occur at the expense of history. It simply makes it impossible to examine history independently of memory. The characters' indifference to the "big events" that get mentioned in passing does not exemplify a brand of ahistorical individualism whereby their fate is of their own making and the context a mere background against which their agency plays itself out. Rather, the historical, industrial and social changes that shook Guadeloupe at the onset of neocolonialism are shown to affect the characters' lives in ways they themselves do not suspect. Just as *Wuthering Heights's* buried relation to history ultimately reveals a complex engagement with hybridity and Englishness,[4] the patched representation of historical events in *La migration des cœurs* urges us to question not history's relevance but the ways in which it comes to mean and matter in people's lives. History is no longer merely an objective backdrop that is impervious to the way it is lived, told, or remembered.

The explosion of the Maine epitomizes Condé's interrogation of conventional historiography in this novel.[5] Significantly, the narrator announces the news of the tragedy by juxtaposing two pieces of information, namely that the cause of the destruction remained unexplained—"Accident? Terrorism? Perpetré par qui? Dans quel but?" (30) [Accident? Terrorism? Perpetrated by whom? And why? (23)]—and that the United States was already talking about declaring war on Spain to take revenge: "Ils parlaient déjà de déclarer la guerre à l'Espagne" (30) [There was already talk of declaring war on Spain (23)]. By implying that the culprit and the punishment are determined before any conclusive and incriminating evidence was found (and none was ever found), the text draws attention not to history as an unvarying background against which fictional incidents gain meaning but as a discursive event that requires ideological scrutiny. The contrast between unsolved mystery and premature decision emphasizes that the past is not a transparent reality accessible to all but an entity that is 'narrated' to serve particular interests. Dona Stefania's earlier statement, that "bientôt Cuba sera une colonie de l'Amérique" (22) [soon Cuba will be a colony of America (15)], comes back to haunt us and suggests that the underlying cause of the war had less to do with the Maine than with the North Americans' desire to chase Spain out of Cuba. As Tom Miller explains about the historical episode, "although its fate came to represent our entry into the Spanish-American War, it has become clear to historians that had the Maine not exploded, some other reason would have catapulted us [Americans] into the struggle for supremacy in Cuba" (55).

Thus, the historical fact with which Condé opens her rewriting marks the impossibility of separating the facticity of history from its ideological use and abuse. It disrupts the authority of historical narratives all the more so since the causes attributed to the Maine's sinking have only emerged over the last hundred years. The ultimate truth, we are told on the centennial commemoration of the sinking, has to this day remained elusive (T. Miller 56).[6] This episode also illustrates Condé's reconceptualization of the practice of "postcolonial rewriting" itself since the actual historical events referenced in her novel speak more to contemporary neocolonial relations than about past colonial ones. What matters is not revising the past so much as reading the present. At our own historical juncture when the United States government has made all kinds of unfounded allegations to convince its constituency of the urgency of a preemptive war against Iraq, such focus on the discursive nature of history takes on a prophetic dimension. The power dynamics with which the novel opens are unfortunately as relevant to our present as to its Guadeloupean past. No wonder that Razyé's question "What is America up to now?" should remain unanswered, since we are still in the process of finding that out.

A crucial historical episode in the novel that similarly illustrates its complex relationship to conventional historiography is that of the labor unrests that shook Guadeloupe in 1898-99. Like the explosion of the U.S.S. Maine, the ideological ramifications of these events have stirred quite a controversy amongst historians. Scholars are debating the degree to which the burnings of crops that raged in Guadeloupe at the time were in fact politically motivated. On the one hand, some historians argue that the fires were the workers' response to the poverty that ensued from radical changes in cane production. They symbolize, in other words, lower-class resistance to labor exploitation. On the other hand, Foucaultian critics like Claude Thiébaut argue that most of these fires were only motivated by personal vendettas; therefore, what had political and historical import was not the burning of crops but its ideological appropriation by the Guadeloupean and French press. Condé's novel intervenes in this debate by collapsing these two historiographic explanations, highlighting instead the imbrication of the political with the personal, and of history with memory. Individuals are shown to have unpredictable and often inconsonant relation to the events that shape their lives.

From 1860s onwards, Guadeloupe, along with other Caribbean islands that were economically dependent on the sugar industry, had to radically change its production methods in order to compete with two emerging rivals in the world economy: the European-produced beet-sugar that had been flooding the markets and the spread of cane cultivation in other tropical areas (India, Mauritius, Java, the Philippines and Réunion, Brazil and Louisiana). To make up for the resulting fall in prices, planters in the Caribbean had to increase production and did so by replacing their old sugar mills with "centrales" or gigantic factories. These modern industrial plantations benefited from the rapid developments in science and technology and used new machinery to process twice the amount of sugar from the same quantity of cane as the outdated mill. This industrialization and consolidation process did not occur, however, without negatively impacting the already precarious situation of the field workers. The need for cane cutters was only seasonal and left the laborers unemployed for several months of the year. Plantation owners also resorted to wage reductions to try and make Guadeloupean cane prices competitive. The deputy-mayor Endomius explicitly evokes this context in the novel when he states: "Peu à peu, les usines ont remplacé les habitations-sucreries du temps longtemps. Ces usines traitent les cannes d'un groupement de planteurs qui leur sont liés par contrat. Du point de vue des patrons, cela signifie une productivité accrue, abaissement des coûts. En réalité, cela veut dire simplement pour nos travailleurs agricoles: pauperization plus grande" (122) [The factories have gradually replaced the old sugar-mills. These factories process the cane from a cooperative of planters who are under contract to them. From the owners' point of view, this means increased productivity and lower costs. For the workers, it simply means widespread impoverishment (119)].

It is in this climate of labor discontent that the "Parti Noir" emerged in May 1898, and that its leader Hégésippe Légitimus (whose fictional counterpart in *La migration des cœurs* is in fact Endomius) was elected president of the Conseil Général [the regional council] of La Guadeloupe. Légitimus was an eloquent orator whose fiery injunctions were often condemned as powerful incitations to violent action. He used his own newspaper *Le Peuple* to exhort the black underclass to rebel against their oppressors and "to set the Antilles alight [embraser les Antilles]": "Puisque, malgré toutes nos protestations les plus légitimes, on ne veut nous faire ni droit, ni justice, il ne nous reste plus qu'à nous défendre.... Nous crions à nos frères et soeurs: achetez donc des revolvers, mesdames et messieurs et brûlez-leur la gueule" (qtd. in Thiébaut 35) [They refuse to give us either rights or justice, despite our most legitimate protests, and leave us no choice but to defend ourselves.... We screamed to our brothers and sisters: ladies and gentlemen, go out and buy revolvers and burn their faces off (eds.' trans.)]. And as the contemporary headlines in Guadeloupe and in France attest, Guadeloupe did indeed have its share of man-made fires in the last two years of the nineteenth-century. What remains a point of contention, however, is the degree to which Légitimus was directly or indirectly responsible for them.

According to the historian Claude Thiébaut, the fires in 1898-1899 Guadeloupe, far from symbolizing the workers' effective means of fighting exploitation, were in fact nonpolitical incidents ideologically deployed by the ruling class to consolidate class boundaries. What was noteworthy about these incidents, Thiébaut argues, was not the number or proportion of the fires so much as the extensive coverage they got in the press. In Foucaultian fashion, Thiébaut thus reframes the question and asks not who did it and why, but "why such a press campaign, and why at that precise time?" (51).[7] He also points out that there were no more fires now than before the blacks got access to political representation in the Conseil Général. In other words, by exaggerating the situation in the media and pointing to a socialist plot, the "grands blancs" were, Thiébaut explains, instigating a conspiracy of their own. They were trying to influence public opinion both in Guadeloupe and in the *métropole* to reform the political structure and the laws of the Republic which, to their mind, were giving power to the section of the population that was ruining the island, namely the blacks. Throughout 1899, the dominant class of whites campaigned to modify the Constitution on the grounds that universal suffrage gave power to uncouth savages. They longed for the "harmonious" times before the French Revolution when political power was distributed based on economic power. Not surprisingly, when the new political and legislative order they were calling for did not materialize, these "blancs-pays" turned to the United States for the fulfillment of their dream. They were hoping that, given the rampant racism in the United States, an American annexation of their island would help re-establish the racial boundaries that French egalitarian ideals had contributed to eroding. Once the U.S. had forsaken the Monroe doctrine by intervening in the Cuban war, it was plausible to assume that the annexation of Guadeloupe would be next on this new colonial power's agenda and would help curb the rise of the radical "Parti Noir" (Thiébaut 88-89).

In *La migration des cœurs*, echoes of Thiébaut's theory of a white colonial conspiracy can be felt in Justin-Marie's claim that "le nom de Razyé est dans tous les journaux sans exception. La Guadeloupe entière a peur de lui. Il travaille pour les socialistes…. Il va tuer les Blancs depuis le premier jusqu'au dernier" (170) [Razyé's name is in every paper, without exception. He is terrorizing the whole of Guadeloupe. He works for the Socialists.... He is going to kill the white folks down to the very last of them (168)]. The press is shown to be overwhelmingly invested in publicizing the fires as a socialist ploy to ruin the planter class. At the same time, however, the main instigator Razyé's involvement also supports the explanation that far from being politically motivated, the fires were actually caused by vengeful neighbors who started them for personal reasons. Indeed, he only joined the socialist effort in order to ruin his rival. In other words, while Thiébaut emphasizes the *békés'* ideological appropriation of localized acts as a means of furthering their racist agenda, *La migration des cœurs* represents both the individual appropriation of political activity for personal reasons and the socialist exploitation of personal animosity for political purposes. What this fraught political context reveals is the extent to which the torching of canefields is a discursive ploy various actors can and do appropriate for their own ends rather than the unproblematic symbol of resistance it represents for much postcolonial criticism. The fact that even at their most destructive, the fires do not threaten the power structure so much as expedite the arrival of neocolonialism only further emphasizes the necessity of revisiting our attachment to a binary notion of resistance.

RESISTING AGENCY

Celebrations of subaltern acts of insurgency and their unsettling effects abound in postcolonialism, all the more so since colonial discourse tends to represent its others as passive and malleable beings who cannot make their own history. Revolts and crop burnings in particular have become powerful symbols of postcolonial resistance and evidence of the very historical subjectivity that colonial texts deny the colonized. By contrast, *La migration des cœurs* reveals not subaltern resistance so much as the postcolonialism's over-investment in creating liberationist cultural codes at all cost. Specifically, Condé deconstructs complacent views of agency and resistance by problematizing militant opposition precisely through her representation of the burning of canefields and plantation estates. Her representation of the black lower class subverts the expectations raised not only by colonial stereotypes but also by anti-colonial discourse. Indeed, her politicized rebel challenges the empowering representation of revolutionary heroes we have come to expect from revisionary postcolonial texts. Instead, she locates her story at a time (1898) when it is ironically the fires' successful ruining of the targeted planters that gets reappropriated by the dominant hierarchy,

As *La migration des cœurs* interweaves historical material such as Légitimus' "Parti Nègre" with Razyé's private predicament, it challenges traditional historiography's focus on landmark events and glorified heroes as catalysts of change. The novel emphasizes instead the fraught but intricate relations between the individual and the collective, the personal and the political, the private and the public, and exposes the ideological processes through which historical "convulsions" like wars and revolutions get disentangled from the webs of individual life and sanitized to write History.[8] Razyé's involvement with a radical organization for social justice forces us to reconsider the motivations of the black heroes and leaders who have historically been hailed as liberators of the people, or inversely, as martyrs for the cause. Razyé is utterly dominated by selfish interests and concerns, yet other characters perceive him as a powerful agent in a significant social movement.[9] After all, as the paternalist priest at Petit-Canal puts it, he is "coupable d'avoir troublé la paix sociale et d'avoir semé des idées de vengeance dans les âmes d'enfant des anciens esclaves" (273) [guilty of having stirred up social unrest and planted the seeds of revenge in the childlike souls of the former slaves (280)]. Similarly, the leader of the "Parti Nègre" Endomius, whose speech and presence ignite *mabo* Sandrine's political consciousness and cause her to go into a trance from excitement,[10] is revealed as an ambitious man who does not hesitate to compromise his principles in order to reach his goal. He too wants to ruin the planters, and despite his claim that education and politics are the only way the black majority will redress power imbalances, it is Razyé's physical strength and violent tactics on which he counts to achieve his ends. What is more, he recruits Razyé even though he knows of the atrocities his new acolyte committed during the 1895-8 Civil War in Cuba. In fact, Endomius does not even flinch at hearing Razyé matter-of-factly recall fighting for the Spanish and the loyalists and killing not only peasants who were struggling for their country's freedom but runaway slaves in hiding who did not know that slavery was over (119). Throughout the novel, Razyé's confessions leave the reader wondering "how many really ordinary [and reprehensible] human beings...are the actual bases of great national and religious movements, [and] just how substantial a part mere chance and erratic behavior have in such movements" (Bruner & Bruner 12-13).

While Razyé's interests and experiences link him to the laborers whose political alliance he has joined, his acts do not stand for 'authentic' expressions of his social position. His vendetta against Aymeric is only incidentally mapped onto the struggle of the black labor force against the white *békés*' control of the economy, and he couldn't care less about any connection he may have with the workers because of the oppression they share based on their social and racial identity. In other words, although the novel brings to light the differential power structures inscribed on the population, it also challenges an identity politics that anchors political opposition in one's racial difference and assumes that one's identity and social position will determine how one acts.[11] The irony, of course, is that it should be Razyé's active participation in a *political* struggle that undermines such models of identity politics and its attendant notion of black solidarity. In this respect, the representation of blackness in the novel echoes Paul Gilroy's notion of the black Atlantic insofar as it repudiates "the racialised figurations of kinship and connectedness that have appeared in the political discourses through which blacks in the Western world have worked to answer the brutal potency of white supremacy" (25). As in the rest of Condé's *oeuvre*, the category of race is scrutinized but not fetishized.[12] Its validity as an explanation of difference is exposed at the same time as its effects are highlighted. Instead of a politics of solidarity based on essential identities, she offers a world where personal affinities constantly violate and expose ideological boundaries set between races and classes.

The novel thus forces us to readjust our readings of Caribbean social and racial relations. Through rebels who are not quite rebels and mimics who are not quite mimics, *La migration des cœurs* does not only write over *Wuthering Heights* but also over one of the major preoccupations of postcolonial studies for the last decade or so, namely the agency of the oppressed. By invoking historical contexts, the novel dramatizes the complexities that arise from our efforts to resuscitate the subaltern's voice/self. On the one hand, the narrative structure provides the perspectives of oppressed people; while on the other hand, the narrative itself problematizes notions of voice and agency by highlighting their complicity with colonialist strategies. Acts of resistance in this narrative do not occur on behalf of an essential subaltern subject entirely separate from the dominant discourse. Instead, they draw attention to the subject-position of the marginalized in a context where neocolonial forces have not only replaced old colonial ties but problematized any notion of the subaltern as "historical subject and agent of an oppositional discourse" (Parry 38).

Razyé's torching of the canefields in *La migration des cœurs* forcefully problematizes the notion that a counter-narrative or history simply entails making the subalterns the subjects of their own histories. Indeed, fictional attempts at representing the subaltern's resistance and agency through unproblematized historical references might ultimately obscure certain realities of the new regimes of power that have replaced colonial authorities. Instead, Condé reveals, history itself is part of a narrative that needs scrutiny. In 1899 Guadeloupe, i.e. the year marking the onset of neocolonialism, the burning of crops does not operate as celebrated emblems of black agency and freedom. Although it is true that the fires in the novel do speed up the ruin of planters like Aymeric, they are also ultimately shown to be ineffectual against the dominance of the big corporations that have already taken over the islands' economy. Indeed, by 1897 the Caribbean cane sugar industry could only be saved by a colossal influx of capital that was far beyond a planter like Aymeric's reach, so Razyé's final torching campaign does not actually ruin him. It only deals the final blow to an already ebbing and bankrupt dynasty. Both the old planter class and the exploited laborers are thus revealed as pawns in a neocolonial game; and the absentee winners are the metropolitan-based companies that at the end of the nineteenth-century stepped in and bought up Guadeloupe's sugar plantations.

In their manifesto *In Praise of Creoleness*, the authors call for a Caribbean poetics that "look[s] for our truths" (Bernabé et al. 101) in order to enhance the collective ability to fight neocolonialism. To this end, they encourage the celebration of the "bursts of our rebellions" and of the "opaque resistance of Maroons allied in their disobedience" (98). The authors urge writers and readers to resurrect these "insignificant heroes, anonymous heroes...who are forgotten by the colonial chronicle" and "have nothing in common with the Western or French heroes" (101). Yet the masculinist notions of heroism and agency with which they offer to replace the Western myths are themselves revealed as just that, myths. What the critic Strachan argues about novelists such as Michelle Cliff and Paule Marshall is also true of the *créolistes*: "These writers have written eloquently about the need for buried truths to be unearthed and for certain myths to be destroyed. It seems counterproductive to offer new myths in their place" (255). In both her criticism and her fiction, Condé takes issue with the assumption that literature should provide Caribbean peoples with an idealized image of themselves and their islands. While the manifesto decrees that literature should recover the dignity of Caribbean realities from their debased rendition in white texts, Condé objects to any process of recovery that glosses over the vulgar and immoral aspects of Antillean societies. Whereas Bernabé, Chamoiseau and Confiant ask for a representation of the Caribbean space and its people that accepts without judging, she asks for both acceptance and judgment. She reminds us that being a rebel is not necessarily about (heroic) agency, nor is being a victim a sign of one's submissive temperament. Such an aesthetics of the reprehensible is clearly a timely contribution to postcolonial criticism, precisely because it checks the impulse of readers too well trained to see justice, freedom, and happiness as an avatar of the strong and the just. Condé's troubling and troubled characters remind us instead that liberty and fairness are not a function of character; they are inalienable rights to which even the basest amongst us are entitled.

Notes

1. For a comparative analysis, see Mardorossian, "Cannibalizing the Victorians: Maryse Condé's *La migration des cœurs*."
2. The interjection of exact historical facts and their interweaving with fictional truths is a staplé feature of Condé's work. Her novel *La vie scélérate* [*Tree of Life*] (1992), for instance, includes watershed events such as the First World War (where, we are reminded, sixteen-hundred and seventy-three Guadeloupeans died for "la patrie"), the construction of the Panama Canal by West Indian laborers, and the death of Malcolm X (Pfaff 103; 69).
3. "Raboter" means to plane down, which is literally what the conformist Nelly and Ellen Dean cannot help but do to the events they narrate. Indeed, like her nineteenth-century counterpart, Nelly Raboteur has assimilated the values of her upper class white female audience, and her tale shows it.
4. See Meyer's analysis of *Wuthering Heights* in her book *Imperialism at Home* (1996).

Carine M. Mardorossian

5. [For further discussion of Condé's use of the explosion of the Maine and of the role of history in the novel, see Maria-Christina Fumagalli's essay in this volume. Eds.]

6. For instance, the two inquiries made in 1898 by Spain and by a United States naval court reached diametrically opposed conclusions: the U.S. argued that a mine sank the ship while the Spanish inspectors blamed the explosion on an internal source. The Cubans, on the other hand, believed that the US had blown up the ship themselves so as to get into the war. In more recent articles, Hugh Thomas and Tom Miller endorse the view that the self-igniting coal the Maine was carrying was in fact responsible for the explosion.

7. His impressive archival research unveils that while the two white-owned newspapers *Le Courrier de la Guadeloupe* and *L'Indépendant de la Guadeloupe* published article upon article imputing responsibility for the "irresistible march of the fires" to the black socialists and magnifying the extent of the damages incurred, the governor of Guadeloupe Morrachini's impartial account was quite different. Morrachini gathered statistics that showed the fires to be either accidental or, when intentional, individualized acts of revenge against a neighbor rather than a socialist conspiracy.

8. The kind of approach to history the novel challenges is epitomized, for instance, by Paul Hamilton's preface to his book *Historicism* (1996) where he cites Ernst Robert Curtius' *European Literature and the Latin Middle Ages* (1979). While Hamilton's main point is to promote a historicist perspective whereby historical context is important to the interpretation of texts of any kind, he does not challenge Curtius' assumptions that the "protagonists of progress" are "isolated" individuals reacting to the context, or that they all happen to be ungendered male subjects. The "protagonists of progress in historical understanding" (Curtius, qtd. in Hamilton 1996, 1) are thus strikingly reminiscent of the protagonists of masculinist history whose pre-eminence feminists and postcolonial critics have exposed as patriarchal bias.

9. In *Ségou* (1984), the characterization of Tiékoro, a Bambara who converts to Islam despite his family's wishes, undergoes a similar treatment. While his murder turns him into a martyr and a hero in his own people's eyes, readers have a hard time sharing such feeling of awe for someone to whose personal motivations and doubts we had access.

10. Unlike his historical counterpart Légitimus, Endomius is the deputy-mayor in *La migration des cœurs*, yet he assumes qualities of the real life Légitimus whose speeches were known for their eloquence.

11. For a critique of identity politics, see Lawrence Grossberg's *We Gotta Get out of This Place* (364-96). As Grossberg points out, the problem

with identity politics is its rationalist assumption that "people act based on a calculation of their interests (376)." See also the studies by Pratibha Parmar and Wendy Brown].

12. See Wa Nyatetu-Waigwa's "From Liminality to a Home of her Own?..." for an elaboration of this point in relation to Condé's earlier novels.

BIBLIOGRAPHY

WORKS BY CONDÉ

Novels/Short Stories/Children's Stories

Histoire de la femme cannibale. Paris: Mercure de France, 2003.

La Planète Orbis. Illustrations by Letizia Galli. Pointe-au-Pitre: Jasor, 2002.

La Belle Créole. Paris: Mercure de France, 2001.

Célanire cou-coupé. Paris: Laffont, 2000. Published in English as *Who Slashed Celanire's Throat?* Trans. Richard Philcox. New York: Atria Books, 2004.

Desirada. Paris: Laffont, 1997. Published in English as *Desirada*. Trans. Richard Philcox. New York: Soho Press, 2000.

Le coeur à rire et à pleurer: Contes vrais de mon enfance. Paris: Robert Laffont (Pocket Paperback), 1999/2001. Published in English as *Tales from the Heart*. Trans. Richard Philcox. New York: Soho Press, 2001.

Revers amers. Paris: Bayard, 2001.

La migration des coeurs. Paris: Robert Laffont, 1995. *Windward Heights*. Trans. Richard Philcox. London: Faber & Faber, 1998.

Les derniers rois mages. Paris: Mercure de France, 1992 [Gallimard, 1995]. Published in English as *The Last of the African Kings*. Trans. Richard Philcox. Lincoln: Univ. Nebraska Press, 1997.

La colonie du nouveau monde. Paris: Robert Laffont, 1993.

Haïti chérie. Paris: Bayard, 1991.

Hugo le terrible. Paris: Sépia, 1990

Traversée de la Mangrove. Paris: Mercure de France, 1989. Published in English as *Crossing the Mangrove*. Trans. Richard Philcox. New York: Anchor, 1995.

La vie scélérate. Paris: Seghers, 1987. Published in English as *Tree of Life: A Novel of the Caribbean*. Trans. Victoria Reiter. New York: Ballantine Books, 1992.

Moi, Tituba, sorcière… Noire de Salem. Paris: Folio 1986 [Mercure de France, 1986]. Published in English as *I, Tituba, Black Witch of Salem*. Trans. Richard Philcox. Charlottesville: Univ. Press of Virginia, 1992 [Ballantine Books 1994].

Pays mêlé. Paris: Hatier, 1985. Published in English as *Land of many colors and Nanna-ya*. Trans. Nicole Ball; introduction by Leyla Ezdinli. Lincoln: Univ. of Nebraska Press, 1999.

Ségou: La terre en miettes. Paris: Robert Laffont, 1985. Published in English as *The Children of Segu*. Trans. Linda Coverdale. New York: Viking Penguin, 1989; Ballantine, 1990.

Ségou: Les murailles de terre. Paris: Robert Laffont, 1984. Published in English as *Segu*. Trans. Barbara Bray. New York: Viking Penguin, 1987; Ballantine, 1988.

Une saison à Rihata. Paris: Robert Laffont, 1981. Published in English as *A Season in Rihata*. Trans. Richard Philcox. London: Heinemann, 1988.

Hérémakhonon. Paris: Union Générale d'Editions, Collection 10/18, 1976. Republished with the title *En Attendant le bonheur (Hérémakhonon)*. Paris: Robert Seghers, 1988; repr. Robert Laffont, 1997. Published in English as *Heremakhonon*. Trans. Richard Philcox. Washington D.C.: Three Continents Press, 1996. [Boulder: Lynne Rienner, 2000].

Anthologies

Anthologie de la littérature africaine d'expression française. Ghana Institute of Languages, 1966.

La Poésie antillaise. Paris: Fernand Nathan, 1977.

Le Roman antillais. 2 volumes. Paris: Fernand Nathan, 1977.

Nouvelles d'Amérique. Edited with Lise Gauvin. Paris: l'Hexagone, 1998.

Selected Literary/Cultural Criticism by Condé

"Autobiographical Essay." Gale Database. *Contemporary Authors Online*. Gale: 2002.

"Les 'Black-British' Donnent L'Exemple?/Are the Black British Setting the Example?" With translation by Richard Philcox. *Black Renaissance/Renaissance Noire* 2, no. 3 (winter 1999/2000): 108-21.

Cahier d'un retour au pays natal: Césaire: analyse critique. Paris: Hatier, 1978.

Césaire, Profil d'une œuvre. Paris: Hatier, 1978.

La Civilisation du Bossale: réflexions sur la littérature orale de la Guadeloupe et de la Martinique. Paris: Harmattan, 1978.

"Créolité without the Creole Language?" In *Caribbean Creolization: Reflections on the Cultural Dynamics of Language, Literature, and Identity*,

Bibliography

edited by Balutansky and Sourieau, 101-109. Gainesville/Barbados: Univ. of Florida Press/West Indies Univ. Press, 1998.

De Christophe Colomb à Fidel Castro: l'Histoire des Caraïbes 1492-1969. Trans. Maryse Condé and Richard Philcox. Paris: Présence Africaine, 1975. Originally published as *The History of the Caribbean 1942-1969*, Eric Eustache Williams. New York: Harper & Row, 1971.

"Eloge de Saint-John Perse," 22 *Europe* (Nov.-Dec. 1995): 20-25.

"Femme, Terre Natale" (essai sur Gisèle Pineau). In *Parallèles: Anthologie de la nouvelle féminine de langue française*, edited by M. Cottenet-Hage and J.-Ph. Imbert, 253-60. Québec: L'Instant Même, 1996.

Guadeloupe. Paris: Vilo/Richer, Hoa Qui, 1988.

L'Héritage de Caliban, essais sur la littérature antillaise francophone. Pointe-à-Pitre: Jasor, 1992. Published in English as *Caliban's Legacy. The Literature of Guadeloupe and Martinique*. Special Issue of *Callaloo* 15, no. 1 (winter 1992).

"Héros et Cannibales." *Portulan* 99 (Novembre 2000): 43-52.

"Noir, C'est Noir" (préface). *Regards Noirs*. Paris: Harmattan, 1996.

"Nèg pas bon." In *Othello: New Essays by Black Writers*, edited by Mythili Kaul. Washington, D.C.: Howard Univ. Press, 1997.

"O Brave New World." Keynote address at the joint meeting of the Comparative Literature Association and the African Literature Association, Austin, Texas, March 1998. *Research in African Literatures* 29, no. 3 (fall 1998): 1-7. Available: http://www.awigp.com/default.asp?numcat=conde3

"Order, disorder, freedom, and the West Indian Writer." *Yale French Studies* 83, no. 2 (1993): 121-135.

"Où commence et où finit la Caraïbe?" *Magazine Littéraire* 369 (October 1998): 112-13.

La parole des femmes: Essai sur des romancières des Antilles de langue français. Paris: L'Harmattan, 1979.

"Pan-Africanism, Feminism and Culture." In *Imagining Home: Class, Culture and Nationalism in the African Diaspora*, edited by Lemelle and Kelley, 55-65. London and New York: Verso, 1994.

Penser la créolité. Edited with Madeleine Cottenet-Hage. Paris: Karthala, 1995.

"The Role of the Writer." *World Literature Today* 67, no. 4 (1993): 697-99.

"Tracés de la Littérature Antillaise/Sketching a Literature from the French Antilles. With translation by Richard Philcox." *Black Renaissance/Renaissance Noire* 1, no. 1 (fall 1996): 138-63.

"Unheard Voice: Suzanne Césaire and the Construct of a Caribbean Identity." In *Winds of Change: The Transforming Voices of Caribbean Women Writers and Scholars*, edited by Adele Newson and Linda Strong-Leek. New York: Peter Lang, 1998.

"The Voyager In, The Voyager Out." Autrement, "La Guadeloupe." *Collection Monde* hors série 123 (Jan. 2001): 250-59.

SELECTED INTERVIEWS WITH MARYSE CONDÉ

Anagnostopoulos-Hielscher, Maria. "Parcours identitaires de la femme antillaise: Un Entretien avec Maryse Condé." *Etudes Francophones* 14, no. 2 (1999): 67-91.

Apter, Emily. "Crossover Texts/Creole Tongues. A Conversation with Maryse Condé." *Public Culture* 13, no. 1 (Special Issue, *Translation in a Global Market*) (winter 2001): 89-95.

Clark, Vèvè. "Je me suis reconciliée avec mon île, Une interview de Maryse Condé." *Callaloo* 12:1 (1989): 87-133.

"Condé, Afrique, un continent difficile." *Notre Librairie* 74 (April-June 1984).

Fratta, Carla. "Entrevue avec Maryse Condé, écrivain guadeloupéen." *Caribana* 1 (1990): 85-92.

Jacquey, Marie-Clotilde Jacquey. "*Ségou* est-il un roman malien? Entretiens avec Maryse Condé," *Notre Librairie* 84 (juillet-septembre 1986): 57.

Lewis, Barbara. "No Silence: An Interview with Maryse Condé." *Callaloo* 18, 5 (1995): 543-50.

McCormick, Robert H., Jr. "*Desirada*—A New Conception of Identity: An Interview With Maryse Condé." *World Literature Today* 74, no. 3 (2000): 519-30.

Moudileno, Lydie. "Moi, Maryse Condé, libre d'être moi-même" ("I, Maryse Condé, Free to Be Myself"), in *Women in French Studies 2002; Tenth Year Anniversary Volume*: 121-26.

Nunez, Elizabeth. "Marysé Condé: Grand dame of Caribbean literature." *Unesco Courier* (Nov. 2000): http//www.unesco.org/courier/2000_11/uk/dires.htm

Scarboro, Ann Armstrong. Interview with Maryse Condé. In Afterword to *I, Tituba, Black Witch of Salem*. Trans. Robert Philcox. Foreword by Angela Davis. Charlottesville: Univ. Press of Virginia, 1992, 198-213.

-----, and Susan Wilcox, producers. *Maryse Condé Speaks from the Heart*: Interview, Reading, "Teacher's Guidelines" (VHS). Mosaic Media, 2003.

Sourieau, Marie-Agnès. "Entretien avec Maryse Condé: De l'identité culturelle." *French Review: Journal of the American Association of Teachers of French* 72, no. 6 (May 1999): 1091-98.

Taleb-Khyar, Mohamed B. "An Interview With Maryse Condé and Rita Dove." *Callaloo* 14.2 (1991): 347-66.

Bibliography

WORKS CITED AND OTHER RELATED CRITICAL STUDIES

Alexander, Simone A. James. *Mother Imagery in the Novels of Afro-Caribbean Women*. Columbia and London: Univ. of Missouri Press, 2001.

Allsop, Richard, ed. *Dictionary of Caribbean English Usage*. Oxford: Oxford UP,1996.

Andrade, Susan Z. "The Nigger of the Narcissist: History, Sexuality and Intertextuality in Maryse Condé's *Heremakhonon.*" *Callaloo* 16, no. 1 (1993): 213-226.

André, Jacques. *L'Inceste focal dans la famille noire antillaise*. Paris: PUF, 1987.

Araujo, Nara. *L'Œuvre de Maryse Condé: A propos d'une écrivaine politiquement incorrecte. Actes du Colloque sur l'œuvre de Maryse Condé, organisé par le Salon du Livre de la ville de Pointe-à-Pitre (Guadeloupe, 14-18 mars 1995)*. Paris: Harmattan, 1996.

Appiah, Kwame Anthony. *In My Father's House: Africa in the Philosophy of Culture*. London: Metheum, 1992.

Arnold, A. James. "The Gendering of Créolité." In *Penser la créolité*, edited by M. Condé and Cottenet-Hage, 21-40. Paris: Karthala, 1995.

-----. "The Novelist as Critic." *World Literature Today* 67, no. 4 (1993): 711-16.

Ashcroft, Bill, Griffith, Gareths, and Tiffin, Helen, eds. *Key Concepts in Post-Colonial Studies*. London: Routledge, 1998.

-----. *The Post-colonial Studies Reader*. New York: Routledge 1995.

Augier, Angel. *Nicolás Guillén: Notas para un estudio biográfico-crítico*. 2 vols. 2nd ed. Santa Clara, Cuba: Universidad Central de las Villas, 1965.

Baghio, Jean-Louis. *Le Flamboyant à fleurs bleues*. Paris: Calmann-Lévy, 1973. Introduction by Maryse Condé.

Baldick, Chris. *In Frankenstein's Shadow: Myth, Monstrosity, and Nineteenth-century Writing*. Oxford: Clarendon Press, 1987.

Balutansky, Kathleen M., and Sourieau, Marie-Agnès eds. Introduction to *Caribbean Creolization: Reflections on the Cultural Dynamics of Language, Literature, and Identity*, 1-11. Gainesville/Barbados: Univ. of Florida Press/West Indies Univ. Press, 1998.

Bangou, Henri. *La Guadeloupe 1848-1939; ou, les aspect de la colonisation après l'abolition del'esclavage* (vol.2). Aurillac: Editions du Centre, 1963.

Barbour, Sarah E. "Maryse Condé and Her Readers: Hesitating Between Irony and the Desire to be Serious in *Moi, Tituba, sorcière...Noire de Salem.*" *Studies in Twentieth Century Literature* 28, no. 2 (summer 2004): 329-51.

-----. "Maryse Condé's Narrative Spectrum." In *Changing Currents: Anglophone, Francophone, and Hispanophone Literary and Cultural Criticism*, edited by Emily Allen Williams. Trenton, NJ: Africa World Press (forthcoming).

Beach, Cecilia. "The Motherland in the Plays of Maryse Condé." In *The Mother in/and French Literature*, edited by Buford Norman, introduction, Nancy Lane, 195-208. Amsterdam, Netherlands: Rodopi, 2000.

Bécel, Pascale. "Errance et enracinement dans *La Vie scélérate* de Maryse Condé." *Etudes Francophones* 13, no. 1 (1998): 135-49.

-----. "*Moi, Tituba Sorciere …Noire De Salem* As a Tale of Petite Marronée." *Callaloo* 18 no. 3 (1995): 608-15.

Benítez-Rojo, Antonio. *The Repeating Island: The Caribbean and the Postmodern Perspective.* Trans. James E. Maraniss. 2nd ed. Durham: Duke, 1996. Originally published as *La isla que se repite: el Caribe y la perspectiva posmoderna.* Hanover: Ediciones del Norte, 1965.

Benjamin, Jules Robert. *The United States and Cuba: Hegemony and Development, 1880-1934.* Pittsburgh: Univ. of Pittsburgh Press, 1974.

Bergner, G. "Who is that masked woman? or, The role of gender in Fanon's *Black skin, white masks*," *PMLA* 110, no. 1 (1995): 75-88.

Berman, Jeffrey. *Narcissism and the Novel.* New York: New York University Press, 1990.

Bernabé, Jean. "Contribution à l'étude de la diglossie littéraire: le cas de *Pluie et vent sur Télumée Miracle*." *Textes, Etudes et Documents* #2 (1979): 103-30.

-----, Patrick Chamoiseau, and Raphaël Confiant, *Éloge de la créolité / In Praise of Creoleness. Édition bilingue.* Paris: Gallimard, 1993 [1990].

Bernstein, Lisa. "Demythifying the Witch's Identity As Social Critique in Maryse Condé's *I, Tituba, Black Witch of Salem*." *Social Identities* 3, no. 1 (1997): 12 pp. Online.EBSCOhost. 5 Oct. 2001. http://mariner.gsu.edu/cgi-bin/Galileo.cgi

Bhabha, Homi K. *The Location of Culture.* London: Routledge, 1994.

Blérald-Ndagano, Monique. *L'Œuvre romanesque de Maryse Condé: féminisme, quête de l'ailleurs, quête de l'autre.* Villeneuve d'Ascq: Presses Universitaires du Septentrion, 2000.

Botting, Fred. "Reflections of excess: *Frankenstein*, the French Revolution and monstrosity." In *Reflections of Revolution: Images of Romanticism*, edited by Alison Yarrington and Kelvin Everest, 26-38. London: Routledge, 1993.

Brathwaite, Edward Kamau. *Contradictory Omens: Cultural Diversity and Integration in the Caribbean.* Mona: Savacou, 1974.

Braxton, Joanne M. *Black Women Writing Autobiography: Tradition within a Tradition.* Philadelphia: Temple Univ. Press, 1989.

Breslaw, Elaine G. *Tituba, Reluctant Witch of Salem: Devilish Indians and Puritan Fantasies.* New York: New York Univ. Press, 1996.

Brittan, Alice. "B-b-british Objects: Possession, Naming and Translation in David Malouf's *Remembering Babylon*," *PMLA*, 11 7, no. 5 (October 2002): 1158-71.

Bibliography

Britton, Celia M. *Édouard Glissant and Postcolonial Theory: Strategies of Language and Resistance*. Charlottesville, VA: The Univ. Press of Virginia, 1999.

Brodzki, Bella and Celeste Schenk, eds. *Life/Lines: Theorizing Women's Autobiography*. Ithaca: Cornell University Press, 1988.

Bronté, Emily. *Wuthering Heights*. Ed. Linda H. Peterson. Boston: Bedford Books of St. Martin's Press, 1992.

Brooke-Rose, Christine. *A Rhetoric of the Unreal: Studies in Narrative and Structure, Especially of the Fantastic*. Cambridge: Cambridge University Press, 1981.

Brown, Ann G., and Maryanne E. Gooze. *International Women's Writing: Landscape of Identity*. Westport: Greenwood Press, 1995.

Brown, Wendy. "Feminist Hesitations, Postmodern Exposures." *differences* 3 no. 1 (1991): 63-84.

Bruner, Charlotte, and David Bruner. "Buchi Emecheta and Maryse Condé: Contemporary Writing from Africa and the Caribbean." *World Literature Today* 59, no. 1 (1985): 9-14.

Caillois, Roger. *Anthologie du fantastique*. Vol. 1. Paris: Gallimard, 1966.

Capécia, M.. *Je suis Martiniquaise*. Paris: Corréa, 1948. *I am a Martinican woman / The white negress: Two novelettes of the 1940's by Mayotte Capécia*. Translated and Foreward by Beatrice Stith Clark. Pueblo, Colorado: Passeggiata Press, 1997.

Césaire, Aimé. *Cahier d'un retour au pays natal*. Paris: Présence Africaine, 1983 [1956].

-----. "Et les chiens se taisaient…" in *Les Armes miraculeuses*. Paris: Gallimard, 1970.

Chamoiseau, Patrick. *Chemin d'école*. Paris: Gallimard, 1994.

-----. *Solibo Magnifique*. Paris: Gallimard, 1988.

-----. *Texaco*. Paris: Gallimard, 1992.

----- and Confiant, Raphael. *Lettres Créoles. Tracées antillaises et continentales de la littérature. Martinique, Guadeloupe, Guyane, Haïti, 1635-1975*. Paris: Hatier 1991.

Chancy, Myriam J. A. *Searching for Safe Spaces: Afro-Caribbean Women Writers in Exile*. Philadelphia: Temple Univ. Press, 1997.

Chodorow, Nancy. *The Reproduction of Mothering; Psychoanalysis and the Sociology of Gender*. Berkeley, CA, Univ. of California Press, 1978.

Clark, Vèvè A. "Developing Diaspora Literacy: Allusion in Maryse Condé's *Hérémakhonon*." In *Out of the Kumbla: Caribbean Women and Literature*, edited by Carole Boyce-Davies and Elaine Savory Fido, 303-319. Trenton, NJ: Africa World Press, 1990.

-----. "Developing Diaspora Literacy and *Marasa* Consciousness." In *Comparative American Identities: Race, Sex, and Nationality in the Modern*

Text, edited by Hortense J. Spillers, 40-61. New York, NY: Routledge, 1991.

Collins, Patricia. *Black Feminist Thought*. New York: Routledge 2000.

Confiant, Raphaël. *Eau de Café*. Paris: Grasset, 1991.

Cottenet-Hage, Madeleine, and Lydie Moudileno, eds. *Maryse Condé: Une nomade inconvenante: Mélanges offerts à Maryse Condé*. Guadeloupe & Paris: Ibis Rouge, 2002.

Danticat, Edwidge. *The Farming of Bones*. New York: Soho Press, 1998.

Dash, Michael J. *Edouard Glissant*, Cambridge, Melbourne, New York: Cambridge University Press, 1995.

David, Christian. *La bisexualité psychique*. Paris: Payot (c. 1975; 1992), 1997.

Davies, Carole Boyce, and Elaine Savory Fido, eds. *Out of the Kumbla: Caribbean Women and Literature*. Trenton, NJ: African World Press 1990.

Degras, Priska. "Maryse Condé: l'écriture de l'Histoire," *L'Esprit Créateur*, 33, no. 2 (summer 1991): 73-81,

Delas, Daniel. *Aimé Césaire ou «le verbe parturiant»*. Paris: Hachette (Hachette supérieure), 1992.

DeLoughrey, Elizabeth. "Gendering the Oceanic Voyage: Trespassing the (Black) Atlantic and Caribbean." *Thamyris* 5, no. 2 (1998): 205-31.

De Souza, Pascale. "When Anancy meets the Desaragnes: an arachnean reading of *The Bridge of Beyond*." *MaComère* 3 (2000):57-68.

Dide, Maurice, and Guiraud, Paul. *Psychiatrie de médecin praticien*. Paris: Masson, 1922.

Doane, M.A. "Dark continents: Epistemologies of racial and sexual difference in psychoanalysis and the cinema." In *Femmes fatales*, 209-48. New York: Routledge, 1991.

Dukats, Mara L. "The Hybrid Terrain of Literary Imagination: Maryse Condé's Black Witch of Salem, Nathaniel Hawthorne's Hester Prynne, and Aime Cesaire's Heroic Poetic Voice." *College Literature* 22, no. 1 (1995): 12 pp. Online. *EBSCOhost* 6 Nov. 2001.http://neptune.libs.uga.edu/cgi-bin/galileo.cgi

DuPlessis, Rachel Blau. "For the Etruscans." In *The New Feminist Criticism*, edited by Elaine Showalter, 271-91. New York: Pantheon, 1985.

Eagleton, Terry. *Myths of Power: A Marxist Study of the Brontës*. London: Macmillan, 1975.

Elbion, Roger. "*Mahagony*, quelle langue?" *Carbet* 10 (1990): 117-41

Fanon, Frantz *Black Skin, White Masks*. Trans. Charles Lam Markmann. New York: Grove Weidenfeld, 1967 [London: Pluto, 1986]. Originally published as *Peau noire, masques blancs*. Paris: Seuil, 1952.

-----. *The Wretched of the Earth*. Trans. Constance Farrington. New York: Grove Press, 1968. Originally published as *Les Damnés de la terre*. Paris: Maspero, 1961 [Présence Africaine: 1963].

Bibliography

Flannigan, Arthur. "Reading Below the Belt: Sex and Sexuality in Françoise Ega and Maryse Condé." *The French Review* 62, no. 2 (1988): 300-12.

Fumagalli, Maria Cristina. "Maryse Condé's *La Migration des Coeurs*, Jean Rhys's *Wide Sargasso Sea* and (the Possibility of) Creolization." *Journal of Caribbean Literatures* 3 (1997): 65-88.

Gaensbauer, Deborah B. "Protean Truths: History as Performance in Maryse Condé's *An Tan Revolisyon.*" *French Review* 76, no. 6 (May 2003): 1139-1150.

Garvey, Johanna X. K. "'The Place She Miss': Exile, Memory, and Resistance in Dionne Brand's Fiction." *Callaloo* 26, no. 2 (2003): 486-503.

Gates, Henry Louis Gates, Jr. "Writing 'Race' and the Difference It Makes." In *"Race, Writing, and Difference*, 1-20. Chicago, IL: Univ. of Chicago P, 1986.

Gendzier, I. *Frantz Fanon: A Critical Study*. New York: Pantheon Books, 1973.

Genette, G. *Figures III*. Paris: Seuil, 1972.

Gikandi, Simon. *Writing in Limbo: Modernism and Caribbean Literature.* Ithaca: Cornell Univ. Press, 1992.

Gilroy, Paul. "Route Work: the Black Atlantic and the Politics of Exile." In *The Post-Colonial Question: Common Skies, Divides Horizons*, edited by Iain Chambers and Lidia Curti, 17-30. New York: Routledge, 1996.

Glissant, Edouard. *Caribbean Discourse: Selected Essays*. Trans. J. Michael Dash. Charlottesville: Univ. Press of Virginia, 1989.

-----. *Le Discours antillais*. Paris: Seuil, 1981. [Folio, 1997.]

-----. *L'intention poétique*, Paris: Seuil, 1969

-----. *Introduction à une poétique du divers*. Montréal: PUM, 1995.

-----. *Poetics of Relation*. Trans. Betsy Wing. Ann Arbor: Univ. Michigan Press, 1997. Originally published as *Poétique de la relation*. Paris: Gallimard, 1990.

-----. *Traité du tout-monde*. Paris: Gallimard, 1997.

Grossberg, Lawrence. *We Gotta Get Out of this Place: Popular Conservatism and Postmodern Culture*. New York: Routledge, 1992.

Gyssels, Kathleen. *Filles de Solitude. Essai sur l'identité antillaise dans les [auto]biographies fictives de Simone et André Schwarz-Bart*. Paris: L'Harmattan, Coll. Critique littéraire, 1996.

-----. *Sages sorcières? Révision de la mauvaise mère dans Beloved (Toni Morrison), Praisesong for the Widow (Paule Marshall) et Moi, Tituba sorcière noire de Salem (Maryse Condé)*. New York: Lanham Univ. Press of America, 2001.

Haigh, Sam, ed. *An Introduction to Caribbean Francophone Writing: Guadeloupe and Martinique*. NY/Oxford, UK: Berg, 1999.

Hall, Stuart. "Culture, Globalization and the World System." In *Culture, Globalization and the World System*, edited by Anthony D. King, 19-39. London: Macmillan, 1991.

-----. "Cultural Identity and Diaspora." In *Colonial Discourse and Post-Colonial Theory: A Reader*, edited by Patrick Williams and Laura Chrisman, 392-403. New York: Harvester, 1994. Originally published in *Identity: Community, culture, difference*, edited by J. Rutherford, 222-37. London: Lawrence & Wishart, 1990.

Hallward, Peter. "Edouard Glissant between the Singular and the Specific." *The Yale Journal of Criticism* 11, no. 2 (1998): 441-464.

Hamilton, Paul. *Historicism*. New York: Routledge, 1996.

Hawthorne, Nathaniel. *The Scarlet Letter*. *Hawthorne: Fanshawe, The Scarlet Letter, The House of Seven Gables, The Blithedale Romance, The Marble Faun*. Ed. Millicent Bell. New York: Library of America, 1983.

Hayes, Jarrod. "Looking for Roots Among the Mangroves." *Centennial Review* 42, no. 3 (1998): 459-74.

Helmreich, Stefan. "Kinship, Nation, and Paul Gilroy's Concept of Diaspora." *Diaspora* 2, no. 2 (1992): 243-49.

Herndon, Gerise. "Gender construction and Neocolonialism," *World Literature Today* 18, no. 3 (1993): 731-36.

Hesse, Barnor. "Forgotten like a Bad Dream: Atlantic Slavery and the Ethics of Postcolonial Memory." In *Relocating Postcolonialism*, edited by David T. Goldberg and Ato Quayson, 143-73. Oxford, UK: Blackwell Publishing, 2002.

Hewitt, Leah D. *Autobiographical Tightropes: Simone de Beauvoir, Nathalie Sarraute, Marguerite Duras, Monique Wittig and Maryse Condé*. Lincoln: Univ. of Nebraska Press, 1990.

-----. "Condé's Critical Seesaw." *Callaloo* 18, 3 (1995): 641-651.

-----. "The Critical F(r)ictions of Maryse Condé: Afterword." In *The Last of the African Kings*, by Maryse Condé, Trans. Richard Philcox, 211-16. London/Lincoln: Univ. of Nebraska Press, 1998.

-----. "Mediations of Identity through the Atlantic Triangle: Maryse Condé's *Heremakhonon*." *Autobiographical Tightropes*, 161-90. Lincoln: Univ. of Nebraska Press, 1990.

-----. "Transmigrations in Maryse Condé's True Tales." In *French Prose in 2000*, edited by Michael Bishop and Christopher Elson, 75-82. Amsterdam, Netherlands: Rodopi, 2002.

Hoy, Don R. "Changing Agricultural Land Use on Guadeloupe, French Indies" in *Peoples and Cultures of the Caribbean*, ed. by Michael Horowitz (Garden City, New York: The Natural History Press, 1971): 267-290

Hulme, Peter. "Columbus and the Cannibals." In *The Post-colonial Studies Reader*, edited by Bill Ashcroft, Gareth Griffiths, Helen Tiffin, 365-

Bibliography

69. New York: Routledge, 1995. Reprinted from *Colonial Encounters: Europe and the Native Caribbean 1492-1797*. London and New York: Methuen, 1986.

Jackson, Rosemary. "Narcissism and Beyond: A Psychoanalytic Reading of *Frankenstein* and Fantasies of the Double." In *Aspects of Fantasy*, edited by William Coyle, 43-53. New York: Greenwood Press, 1986.

Jurney, Florence Ramond. "Voix sexualisée au féminin dans *Moi, Tituba sorcière* de Maryse Condé." *French Review* 76, no. 6 (May 2003): 1151-60.

Kadish, Doris Y., ed. *Slavery in the Caribbean Francophone World, Distant Voices, Forgotten Acts, Forged Identities*. Athens: Georgia Univ. Press, 2000.

-----. "*Tituba* et sa traduction." In *L'Œuvre de Maryse Condé*, edited by Arujo, 231-248. Paris: L'Harmattan, 1996.

-----, and Françoise Massardier-Kenney. "Traduire Maryse Condé: entretien avec Richard Philcox." *The French Review* 69, no. 5 (April 1996): 749-762.

Kasongo, Kapanga. "La doublure culturelle de l'héroïne dans *Moi, Tituba* de Maryse Condé." *Etudes créoles* 17 no. 2 (1994) 61-74.

Kemedjio, Cilas. "The Curse of Writing: Genealogical Strata of a Disillusion: Orality, Islam-Writing, and Identities in the Stage of Becoming in Maryse Condé's *Ségou*." *Research in African Literatures* 27, no. 4 (winter 1996): 124-44.

-----. *De la Négritude à la Créolité; Édouard Glissant, Maryse Condé et la malédiction de la théorie*. Hamburg: Lit Verlag, 1999.

-----. "Les enfants de Ségou: Murailles en miettes, identités en dérive." In *L'Œuvre de Maryse Condé*, edited by Lydie Moudileno, 23-44. Paris: L'Harmattan, 1996.

Kesteloot, Lilyan. *Black Writers in French: A Literary History of Negritude*, trans. Ellen Conroy Kennedy. Philadelphia: Temple Univ. Press, 1974. Revised edition with new preface by the author, Howard Univ. Press, 1991.

Lahens, Yanick. Afterword to *Caribbean Creolization*, edited by Balutansky and Sourieau, 155-164. Gainesville/Barbados: Univ. of Florida Press/West Indies Univ. Press, 1998.

Lara, Oruno. *La Guadeloupe dans l'histoire*. Paris: L'Harmattan, 1979.

Lem, Stanislaw. *Microworlds: Writings on Science Fiction and Fantasy*. Edited by Franz Rottensteiner. New York: Harcourt, 1984.

Lemelle, Sidney J., and Robin D. G. Kelley, eds. *Imagining Home: Class, Culture and Nationalism in the African Diaspora*. London and New York: Verso, 1994.

Lequin, Lucie, and Catherine Mavrikakis, eds. *La Francophonie sans frontière, une nouvelle cartographie de l'imaginaire au féminin*. Montréal: L'Harmattan, 2002.

Licops, Dominique. "Expériences Diasporiques et Migratoires des Villes dans *La Vie scélérate* et *Desirada* de Maryse Condé." *Nottingham French Studies* 39, no. 1 (spring 2000): 110-20.

Lionnet, Françoise. *Autobiographical Voices. Race, Gender, Self-Portraiture*. London/Ithaca: Cornell University Press, 1989.

-----. "Logiques Métisses." In *Postcolonial Subjects: Francophone Women Writers*, edited by Mary Jean Matthews Green et al., 321-43. Minneapolis: Univ. of Minnesota, 1996.

-----. *Postcolonial Representations: Women, Literature, Identity*. Ithaca & London: Cornell Univ. Press, 1995.

-----. "Traversée de la mangrove de Maryse Condé: vers un nouvel humanisme antillais."*French Review* 66, no. 3 (February 1993): 475-486.

Loncke, Joycelynn. "The Image of the Woman in Caribbean Literature with Special Response to *Pan Beat* and *Hérémakhonon*." *Bim* 64 (1978): 272-81.

Madsen, Deborah L. "A for Abolition: Hawthorne's Bond-servant and the Shadow of Slavery." *Journal of American Studies* 25, no. 2 (August 1991) 255-59.

Makward, Christiane. "Célanire Superwoman, ou les nouvelles impertinences de Maryse Condé." In *Femmes et écritures de la transgression*, edited by Hafid Gafaiti and Armelle Crouzières, 17-40. Paris: L'Harmattan, 2003.

-----. "Entretien avec Gisèle Pineau" *The French Review* 76.6 (May 2003): 1202-15.

-----. "La Grande Marronne du Tout-Monde." In *Maryse Condé: Une nomade inconvenante*, edited by Araujo, 167-71. Guadeloupe: Ibis Rouge, 2002.

-----. *Mayotte Capécia ou l'aliénation selon Fanon*. Paris: Karthala, 1999.

-----. "Presque un siècle de différence amoureuse: Simone Schwarz-Bart (1972), Gisèle Pineau (1996)." *Nottingham French Studies* 40, no. 1 (Spring 2001): 41-51.

-----, and Ilona Johnson. "La longue marche des Franco-Antillaises: Fictions autobiographiques de Mayotte Capécia et Françoise Ega." In *Elles écrivent des Antilles*, 309-21. Edited by S. Rinne et J. Vitiello. Paris: L'Harmattan, 1997.

Malena, Anne. "Le Dialogisme au feminin dans l'oeuvre romanesque de Maryse Condé." In *La Francophonie sans frontière, une nouvelle cartographie de l'imaginaire au féminin*, edited by Lequin and Mavrikakis, 274-60. Montréal: L'Harmattan, 2002.

Bibliography

-----. "The Figure of the Critic in Condé's Novels: The Use of Irony for Dialogism." *MaComère* 3 (2000): 94-106.

-----. *The Negotiated Self: The Dynamics of Identity in Francophone Caribbean Narrative.* New York: Peter Lang, 1999.

-----, and Pascale De Souza, eds. "The Caribbean that isn't: rifts and disjunctions." *The Journal of Caribbean Literatures* 3, no. 1 (1996).

-----, and Pascale De Souza, eds. "The Caribbean that is: exploring intertextualities" *The Journal of Caribbean Literatures* 3, no. 2, 1997.

Manzor-Coats, Lilian. "Of Witches and Other things: Maryse Condé's Challenges to Feminist Discourse." *World Literature Today* 67, no 4 (fall 1993): 737-47.

Mardorossian, Carine M. "Cannibalizing the Victorians: Maryse Condé's *Windward Heights.*" In *Changing Currents: Anglophone, Francophone, and Hispanophone Literary and Cultural Criticism,* edited by Emily Allen Williams. Trenton, NJ: Africa World Press (forthcoming).

Martin, S.I. *Britain's Slave Trade.* London: Channel 4 Books/Macmillan, 1999.

Martinus Arion, Frank. "The Victory of Concubines and the Nannies." In *Caribbean Creolization,* edited by Balutansky and Sourieau, 110-117, Gainesville/Barbados: Univ. of Florida Press/West Indies Univ. Press, 1998.

Massardier-Kenney, Françoise. "La question de la traduction plurielle ou les traducteurs de Maryse Condé." In *L'Œuvre de Maryse Condé,* edited by Arujo, 249-58. Paris: L'Harmattan, 1996.

Mathieu-Castellani, Gisèle. *La Scène judiciaire de l'autobiographie.* Paris: Presse Universitaire de France (Coll. Ecriture), 1996.

Mazama, Ama. "Langue et problématique de la langue dans l'œuvre de Maryse Condé." In *Langue et identité créole en Guadeloupe, une perspective afro-centrique,* edited by Mazama, 71-84. Pointe-à-Pitre, Guadeloupe: Jasor, 1997.

McClintock, Anne. *Imperial Leather: Race, Gender and Sexuality in the Colonial Context.* New York: Routledge, 1995.

McCormick, Robert H., Jr. "Return Passages: Maryse Condé Brings Tituba Back to Barbados." In *Black Imagination and the Middle Passage,* edited by Henry Louis Gates, Jr. and Carl Pedersen, 271-81. Oxford, England: Oxford Univ. Press, 1999.

Mekkawi, Mohamed. "Maryse Condé: Novelist, Playwright, Critic, Teacher; An Introductory Bio-bibliography." Washington, D.C.: Howard University Libraries, April 1991; revised September 1992. Available at: http://www.founders.howard.edu/conde.htm

Meyer, Susan L. *Imperialism at Home: Race and Victorian Women's Fiction.* Ithaca: Cornell Univ. Press, 1996.

Miller, Christopher, "After Negation: Africa in Two Novels by Maryse Condé." In *Postcolonial Subjects: Francophone Women Writers*, edited by Mary Jean Green et al., 173-85. Minneapolis: Univ. of Minnesota, 1996.

Miller, Tom. "Remember the Maine." *Smithsonian* (February 1998): 46-60.

Mitsch, Ruthmarie H. "Maryse Condé's Mangroves." *Research in African Literatures* 28, no. 4 (winter 1997): 54-71.

Moers, Ellen. *Literary Women.* New York: Doubleday, 1976.

Mordecai, P. and B. Wilson, eds. *Her true-true name.* London: Heinemann, 1989.

Morrison, Anthea. "Emancipating the Voice: Maryse Condé's *La vie scélérate.*" *Callaloo* 18 no. 3 (1995): 616-25.

-----. "Exile and Homecoming: Maryse Condé's *La vie scélérate.*" In *The Woman, The Writer and Caribbean Society: Essays on Literature and Culture*, edited by Helen Pyne-Timothy, 176-86. Los Angeles: Center for African American Studies, UCLA, 1998.

-----. "Family and Other Trees: The Question of Identity in the Work of Maryse Conde and Simone Schwartz-Bart." In *The Woman, The Writer and Caribbean Society: Essays on Literature and Culture*, edited by Helen Pyne-Timothy, 80-90. Los Angeles: Center for African American Studies, UCLA, 1998.

Morrison, Toni. Ed. *The Black Book.* Comp. Middleton Harris et al. New York: Random House, 1974.

-----. "Memory, Creation and Writing." *Thought* 59 (1984): 385-90.

-----. *Playing in the Dark. Whiteness and the Literary Imagination.* Cambridge: Harvard Univ. Press, 1992.

Morse, Donald E., ed. *The Fantastic in World Literature and the Arts.* New York: Greenwood Press, 1987.

Moses, Wilson J. "Sex, Salem, and Slave Trials: Ritual Drama and Ceremony of Innocence." In *Black Columbia. Defining Moments in African American Literature and Culture*, edited by Werner Sollors and Maria Dietrich, 64-76. London/Cambridge: Harvard Univ. Press, 1994.

Moss, Jane. "Postmodernizing the Salem Witchcraze: Maryse Condé's *I, Tituba, Black Witch of Salem.*" *Colby Quarterly* 35, no. 1 (March 1999): 5-17.

Moudileno, Lydie. "Les écrivains de Maryse Condé: face à la filiation et à l'affiliation." In *L'Écrivain antillais au miroir de sa littérature*, 141-71. Paris: Karthala, 1997.

-----. Maryse Condé and the Fight Against Prejudice: Making Room for the Haïtian Neighbor." *Thamyris: Mythmaking from Past to Present* 5, no. 3 (autumn 1998): 239-53.

-----. *L'Œuvre de Maryse Condé.* Paris: Harmattan, 1995.

-----. "Portrait of the Artist as a Dreamer." *Callaloo* 18, no. 3 (1995): 626-40.

Bibliography

-----. "Le rire de la grand-mère: Insolence et sérénité dans *Désirada* de Maryse Condé." *The French Review* 76, no. 6 (May 2003): 1151-60.

Mudimbé-Boyi, Elisabeth. "Giving Voice to Tituba: The Death of the Author." *World Literature Today* 67, no. 4 (autumn 1993): 751-56.

Munley, Ellen W. "Mapping the Mangrove: Empathy and Survival in *Traversée de la Mangrove*." *Callaloo* 15.1 (winter 1992): 156-66.

Nesbitt, Nick. "Négritude." *Encarta Africa*. Edited by Henry Louis Gates, Jr. and Kwame Anthony Appiah. CD-Rom. Redmond, WA: Microsoft, 1999. Also available at: http://www.geocities.com/africanwriters/origins.html

-----. *Voicing Memory: History and Subjectivity in French Caribbean Literature.* Charlottesville, VA: Univ. of Virginia Press, 2003.

Ngal, Georges. *Aimé Césaire: Un homme à la recherche d'une patrie.* Paris: Présence Africaine (Second Edition), 1994.

Ngate, Jonathan. "Maryse Condé and Africa: The Making of a Recalcitrant Daughter." *A Current Bibliography on African Affairs* 19, no. 1 (1986-87): 5-20.

Niranjana, Tejaswini. *Siting Translation: History, Post-structuralism, and the Colonial Context.* Univ. of California Press, 1992.

Noakes, Beverley Ormerod. "Money, Race and Cultural Identity in the Work of Maryse Condé." *Essays in French Literature (EFL)* 37 (Nov. 2000): 126-43.

Nwankwo, Chimalum. "'I is': Morrison, the Past, and Africa." In *Of Dreams Deferred, Dead or Alive. African Perspectives on African American Writers*, edited by Femi Ojo-Ade, 171-80. Westport: Greenwood Press, 1996.

N'Zengo Tayo, Marie-José. "Children in Haïtian Popular Migration as Seen by Maryse Condé and Edwidge Danticat." In *Winds of Change: The Transforming Voices of Caribbean Women Writers and Scholars*, edited by Adele Newson and Linda Strong-Leek, 93-100. New York: Peter Lang, 1998.

O'Callaghan, Evelyn. *Woman Version: Theoretical Approaches to West Indian Fiction by Women.* London: Macmillan, 1993.

Onyeoziri, Gloria Nne. "L'Ironie et le fantastique dans *Traversée de la mangrove* de Maryse Condé." In *Nouvelles écritures francophones. Vers un nouveau baroque?* edited by Jean Cléo Godin, 404-19. Montréal: Presses de l'Université de Montréal, 2001.

Ortigues, Edmond, and Marie-Cécile. *Oedipe africain.* Paris: Plon, 1966.

Ortiz, Fernando. *La antigua fiesta afrocubana del Día de Reyes.* Havana: Ministerio de Relaciones Exteriores, 1960.

Pouchet-Paquet, Sandra. *Caribbean Autobiograph. Cultural Identity and Self-Representation.* Madison: Wisconsin Univ. Press, 2002.

Paravisini-Gebert, L. "Feminism, race, and difference in the works of Mayotte Capécia, Michelle Lacrosil, and Jacqueline Manicom." *Callaloo* 15, no. 1 (1992): 66-74.

Parmar, Pratibha. "Other Kinds of Dreams." *Feminist Review* 31 (1989): 55-66.

Palcy, Euzhan, director. *Aimé Césaire: une voix pour l'histoire/A Voice for History*. VHS: 1994.

Parry, Benita. "Problems in Current Theories of Colonial Discourse." *Oxford Literary Review* 9 (1987): 27-58.

Pérez, Louis A.Jr. *Cuba and the United States: Ties of Singular Intimacy*. 2nd ed. Athens & London: The Univ. of Georgia Press, 1990.

Perret, Delphine. *La Créolité. Espace de création*. Cayenne: Editions Ibis Rouge, 2001.

Peterson, Carla L. Le Surnaturel dans *Moi, Tituba* de Maryse Condé et *Beloved* de Toni Morrison." In *L'Oeuvre de Maryse Condé. Questions et réponses à propos d'une écrivaine politiquement incorrecte*, edited by Nara Araujo, 91-104. Paris: L'Harmattan, 1996.

Pfaff, Françoise. *Conversations with Maryse Condé*. Lincoln and London: Univ. of Nebraska Press, 1996. Translation by the author of *Entretiens avec Maryse Condé*. Paris: Karthala, 1993.

Phillips, Caryl ed. *Extravagant Strangers. A Literature of Belonging*. New York: Vintage 1997.

Philcox, Richard. Preface. *The Last of the African Kings*. trans. Richard Philcox. Lincoln: Univ. Nebraska Press, 1997.

-----. "Traduire *Traversée de la Mangrove*." In *L'Œuvre de Maryse Condé*, edited by Nara Araujo, 221-230. Paris: L'Harmattan, 1996.

Pineau, Gisèle and Abraham, Marie ed. *Femmes des Antilles, traces et voix*. Paris: Stock, 1996.

Praeger, Michèle. "Maryse Condé: mythes et contre-mythes." In *L'Œeuvre de Maryse Condé*, edited by Araujo, 205-16. Paris: L'Harmattan, 1996.

Quinby, Lee, ed. *Genealogy & Literature*. Minneapolis: Univ. of Minnesota Press, 1995.

Ramsay, Raylene. "The Ambivalent Narrator: Hybridity and Multiple Address as Modernity in Maryse Condé and Mariama Bâ." *Journal of the Australasian Universities Language and Literature Association* 90 (No. 1998): 63-83.

Reichardt, Jasia. "Artificial Life and the Myth of Frankenstein." In *Frankenstein, Creation and Monstrosity*, edited by Stephen Bann, 136-57. London: Reaktion, 1994.

Rhys, Jean. *Wide Sargasso Sea*. London: André Deutsch, 1966. Introd. Wyndham, Francis. Harmondsworth Eng.: Penguin, 1968.

Rody, Caroline. *The Daughter's Return: African-American and Caribbean Women's Fictions of History*. New York: Oxford Univ. Press, 2001.

Bibliography

Rohrbach, Augusta. "To Be Continued: Double Identity, Multiplicity and Antigenealogy as Narrative Strategies in Pauline Hopkins' Magazine Fiction." *Callaloo* 22, no. 2 (1999): 483-98.

Roof, Maria. "Maryse Condé and Isabel Allende: Family Saga Novels." *World Literature Today*, no. 2 (spring 1996): 283-88.

Rosello, Mireille. "Caribbean Insularization of Identities in Maryse Condé's Work: From *En Attendant le Bonheur* to *Les Derniers Rois Mages*." *Callaloo* 18, no. 3 (1995): 565-78.

-----. "One More Sea to Cross: Exile and Intertextuality in Aimé Césaire's *Cahier d'un retour au pays natal*." *Yale French Studies* 83 (1993): 175-95.

Salotto, Eleanor. "*Frankenstein* and Dis(re)membered Identity." *The Journal of Narrative Technique* 24, no. 3 (1994): 190-211.

Salvodon, M. Attignol. "Conflicting Origins: Memory in the Invention of Guadeloupian Genealogy." (Review of Maryse Condé, *Desirada*) *Callaloo* 22, no. 1 (1999): 249-52.

Sandor, Andras. "Myths and the Fantastic." *New Literary History* 22, no. 2 (1991): 339-58.

Scarboro, Ann Armstrong. Afterword to *I, Tituba, Black Witch of Salem*. Trans. Robert Philcox. Foreword by Angela Davis. Charlottesville: Univ. Press of Virginia, 1992, 187-225.

-----, and Susan Wilcox, producers. *Maryse Condé Speaks from the Heart*: Interview, Reading, "Teacher's Guidelines" (VHS). Mosaic Media, 2003.

Schwarz-Bart, Simone. *Pluie et vent sur Télumée Miracle*. Paris: Seuil, 1972. *The Bridge of Beyond*. Trans. Barbara Bray. London: Victor Gollancz, 1975.

Shelley, Mary. *Frankenstein*. Edited by Johanna M. Smith. New York: Bedford/St. Martin's Press, 2000.

Shelton, Marie-Denise. "Condé: The Politics of Gender and Identity." *World Literature Today* 67, no. 4 (autumn 1993): 717-22.

Smith, Arlette. "Maryse Condé's *Hérémakhonon*: A Triangular Structure of Alienation." *College Language Association Journal* 32, no. 1 (1988): 45-54.

-----. "The Semiotics of Exile in Maryse Condé's Fictional Works." *Callaloo* 14,no. 2 (1991): 381-88.

Smith, Michelle. "Reading in Circles: Sexuality and/as History in *I, Tituba*". *Callaloo*,18, no. 3 (1995): 602-607.

Smock, Ann. "Maryse Condé's *Les derniers rois mages*." *Callaloo* 18, no. 3 (1995): 668-80.

Snitgen, Jeanne. "History, Identity and the Constitution of the Female Subject: Maryse Condé's Tituba." *Matatu* 3, no. 6 (1989): 55-73.

Soestwohner, Bettina. "Uprooting Antillean Identity: Maryse Condé's *La Colonie de nouveau monde*." *Callaloo* 18, no. 3 (1995): 690-706.

Sourieau, M.-A. "*La Vie scélérate* de Maryse Condé: Métissage narratif et héritage métis." In *Penser la créolité*, edited by Condé and Cottenet-Hage, 113-25. Paris: Karthala, 1995.

-----. "*La Vie scélérate*: une écriture de l'h/Histoire." In *Elles écrivent des Antilles (Haïti, Guadeloupe, Martinique)*, edited by S. Rinne & J. Vitiello, 207-22. Paris: L'Harmattan, 1997.

Soyinka, Wole. "Negritude and the Gods of Equity." In *The Burden of Memory, the Muse of Forgiveness*. New York: Oxford Univ. Press, 1998: 145-94.

Spear, Thomas. "Île en île--Maryse Condé." Department of Languages and Literatures. Lehman College of City University of New York. http://www.lehman.cuny.edu/ile.en.ile/paroles/conde.html

-----. "Individual Quests and Collective History." *World Literature Today* 67, no. 4 (autumn 1993): 723-30.

Spillers, Hortense. "Mama's Baby, Papa's Maybe: An American Grammar Book." *Diacritics* 17, no. 2 (1987): 65-81.

Stith-Clark, Beatrice. "The Works of Mayotte Capécia (With Apologies to Frantz Fanon)." *CLA Journal* 16, no. 4 (1973): 415-25.

Strachan, Ian Gregory. *Paradise and Plantation: Tourism and Culture in the Anglophone Caribbean*. Charlottesville: U of Virginia P, 2002.

Suk, Jeannie. *Postcolonial Paradoxes in French Caribbean Writing. Césaire, Glissant, Condé*. Oxford: Oxford Univ. Press, 2001.

Tate, Claudia, ed. *Black Women Writers at Work*. New York: Continuum, 1983.

Thiébaut, Claude. *Guadeloupe 1899: Année de Tous les Dangers*. Paris: L'Harmattan, 1989.

Thomas, Helen. *Romanticism and Slave Narratives, Transatlantic Testimonies*. Cambridge: Cambridge Univ. Press, 2000.

Thomas, Hugh. "Remember the Maine?" *The New York Times Review of Books* (April 1998): 10-14.

Thomas, Viola G. "Maryse Condé." *Belles Lettres* 11, no. 1 (Jan. 1996): 20-22.

Todorov, Tzvetan. *The Fantastic: A Structural Approach to a Literary Genre*. Trans. Richard Howard. London: Case Western Reserve University, 1973.

Toumson, R. *Mythologie du métissage*. Paris: PUF, 1998.

Vergès, F. "Métissage, discours masculin et déni de la mère." In *Penser la créolité*, edited by Condé and Cottenet-Hage, 69-83. Paris: Karthala, 1995.

Vreeland, Catherine. "Caribbean Persephones: Motherlessness in Buchi Emecheta and Maryse Condé. *Kobe Jogakuin Daigaku Kenkyujo-Yakuin/ Kobe College Studies* 48, no. 3, 142 (2002): 27-35.

Bibliography

Wa Nyatetu-Waigwa, Wangari. "From Liminality to a Home of her Own?: The Quest Motif in Maryse Condé's Fiction." *Callaloo* 18, no. 3 (1995): 551-64.

Walcott, Derek. "Names" in *Sea Grapes*. London: J. Cape, 1976.

Warner, Marina. "*Indigo*: Mapping the Waters" (1994). *Études Britanniques Contemporaines* n. 5. Montpellier: Presses universitaires de Montpellier. 20 April 2003. http://ebc.chez.tiscali.fr/ebc51.html

Wilson, Elizabeth. "'Le voyage et l'espace clos'—Island and Journey as Metaphor: Aspects of Woman's Experience in the Works of Francophone Caribbean Women Novelists." In *Out of the Kumbla: Caribbean Women and Literature*, edited by Boyce-Davies and Fido, 45-57. Trenton, NJ: Africa World Press, 1990.

Williams, Eric. *From Columbus to Castro: The History of the Caribbean 1492-1969*. London: André Deutsch, 1970.

Wilson, Betty. Introduction to *Juletane* by Myriam Warner-Vieyra, Trans. Betty Wilson, v-xv. Oxford, UK: Heinemann, 1987. Originally published as *Juletane*, Paris: Présence Africaine, 1982.

Wilson-Tagoe, Nana. "Configurations of History in the Writing of West Indian Women." In *Historical Thought and Literary Representation in West Indian Literature*, 223-52. Gainesville: Univ. Presses of Florida, 1998.

Wolff, Rebecca. "Maryse Condé." *Bomb* 68 (summer 1999): 74-80.

Woodard, Helena. "The Two Marys (Prince and Shelley) on the Textual Meeting Ground of Race, Gender, and Genre." In *Recovered Writers/ Recovered Texts: Race, Class, and Gender in Black Women's Literature*, edited by Dolan Hubbard, 15-30. Knoxville: Univ. of Tennessee Press, 1997.

Young, Robert J.C. *Colonial Desire: Hybridity in Theory, Culture and Race*. London: Routledge, 1995.

Zimra, C. "Righting the Calabash: Writing History in the Female Francophone Narrative." In *Out of the Kumbla: Caribbean Women and Literature*, edited by Boyce-Davies and Fido, 143-60. Trenton, NJ: Africa World Press, 1990.

NOTES ON CONTRIBUTORS

Sarah E. Barbour, Associate Professor of French in the Department of Romance Languages at Wake Forest University, has published a book-length study of the novels of Nathalie Sarraute and articles on the works of Marguerite Duras, Sidonie Colette, and Maryse Condé, and on using film in the classroom.

Pascale De Souza, coordinator of the French Program at SAIS/Johns Hopkins and editor of three special issues on the Caribbean, has published some 30 essays on Francophone Literature and recently edited "Oceanic Dialogues: from the Black Atlantic to the Indo-Pacific" (*International Journal of Francophone Studies*).

Katherine Elkins is the Andrew W. Mellon Assistant Professor of IPHS (Humanities) at Kenyon College. In addition to her interest in Maryse Condé, she has written on memory in Baudelaire and has just completed a book on Proust.

Dawn Fulton is an Assistant Professor of French at Smith College. Her essays on literature from the French Caribbean have appeared in such journals as *Callaloo*, *The French Review*, and *The Romantic Review*. She is currently completing a book manuscript on episte-mology in the novels of Maryse Condé.

Maria Cristina Fumagalli, Lecturer in the Department of Literature, Film and Theatre Studies at the University of Essex, UK, has published a book-length study on Seamus Heaney and Derek Walcott, and essays and book chapters on Erna Brodber, Marlene Nourbese

Philip, Maryse Condé, M.P. Shiel, Jean Rhys, Grace Nichols and Perry Henzell's *The Harder They Come*.

Johanna X. K. Garvey teaches at Fairfield University, where she is Chair of the English Department. She has published articles and book chapters on twentieth-century literature and is completing a study titled "'To Pull the Sides of the Sea Together': Caribbean Women Writing Diaspora," in which one chapter focuses on the fiction of Maryse Condé.

Kathleen Gyssels teaches Francophone Caribbean literature and publishes on Caribbean and African American literature in comparative perspective at the University of Antwerp, where she directs a research group on postcolonial literatures. Her publications in French and English discuss major voices of the African diaspora such as Simone and André Schwarz-Bart, Toni Morrison, Maryse Condé and Paule Marshall.

Gerise Herndon, Associate Professor of English, directs the Women's Studies program at Nebraska Wesleyan University where she also teaches international cinema and postcolonial literatures. She has published articles on Euzhan Palcy's films and on novels by Condé, Schwarz-Bart, and Jamaica Kincaid, in addition to essays on whiteness and feminist pedagogy.

Christiane Makward, Professor of French and Women's Studies at Penn State University, has published translations and articles on Francophone and contemporary French women writers. Her books include the autobiography of Corinna Bille, an essay on Mayotte Capécia and a *Dictionnaire littéraire des femmes de langue française* (http//www.personal.psu.edu/faculty/c/j/cjm9/).

Carine Mardorossian, Associate Professor of English and Women's Studies at the State University of New York, Buffalo, has just published a book entitled *Reclaiming Difference: Caribbean Women Rewrite Postcolonialism*. Her articles have appeared in *Callaloo, The Journal of Caribbean Literatures, Modern Language Studies, Signs*, and *Hypatia*.

Victoria Bridges Moussaron, Maître de conférences at the Université de Lille III, teaches translation and literature. She has published essays on Falconer, Mallarmé and Poe, and Colette, as well as translations of Paul de Man on Nietzsche, Irving Wohlfahrt on Benjamin, Michel Deguy's poetry and his essay "Au Sujet de Shoah."

Notes on Contributors

Serigne Ndiaye is the Resident Director of the Council on International Educational Exchange (CIEE) in Dakar. His research and teaching focus on African and Caribbean Literature and Culture, and postcolonial theory. He has taught at Emory University and SUNY-Albany, where he held a Fulbright scholarship.

Gloria Nne Onyeoziri, Associate Professor, University of British Columbia, has published *La parole poétique d'Aimé Césaire* (1992) and is completing a study of irony in African literary discourse. Many of her articles focus on African and Caribbean women writers, including Simone Schwarz-Bart, Maryse Condé, Calixthe Beyala.

Anne Oszwald joined the French Department at Penn State as a doctoral candidate after teaching in Glasgow, Scotland, and is completing research on Boris Vian. Her current doctoral research is on political irony, power and forms of creolisation in Francophone fiction with emphasis on Condé, Confiant, Kourouma and Maillet.

Laurence M. Porter teaches French and Critical Theory at Michigan State University. He has published fourteen books and received the Distinguished Faculty Award and NEH Senior Fellowship. He serves on the editorial boards of *The French Review, Nineteenth-Century French Studies, Studies in Twentieth Century Literature,* and *Women in French Studies.*

Richard Philcox, who frequently addresses the issues of translating Caribbean literature in general and Condé's works in particular, has translated eight of Maryse Condé's fictional works into English, in addition to her autobiographical *Le coeur à rire et à pleurer; Contes vrais de mon enfance* and several of her essays.

Jennifer Sparrow is Assistant Professor of English at Medgar Evers College, City University of New York where she teaches courses in Caribbean literature, American literature, and composition. Her essays on Caribbean literature have appeared in edited volumes and scholarly journals including *Wadabagei* and *MaComère.*

Jennifer Thomas is a doctoral candidate in the Women's Studies Department at Emory University. Her research examines the theme of madness in literature by women of the Anglophone Caribbean and Africa. Prior to embarking on her Ph.D. career, she taught at SUNY Purchase and Manhattan College.

INDEX

NAMES

André, Jacques 67, 131, 217
Arnold, A. James 137, 152

Balutansky, Kathleen 263, 272
Bassnett-McGuire, Susan 36
Beauvoir, Simone de 219
Belafonte, Harry 36
Benjamin, Walter 36
Benoist, Marie Guillemin 70
Bergner, Gwen 132
Bernabé, Jean 6, 25, 241, 276, 287
Bernstein, Lisa 89, 90, 95, 96
Beyala, Calixthe 217, 231
Bhabha, Homi 19, 75
Baldick, Chris 204
Brand, Dionne 160, 278
Brathwaite, Kamau 63
Brittan, Alice 70
Brontë, Emily 25, 34, 37, 253, 257, 258, 269, 270, 275, 276

Capécia, Mayotte 128-131, 134, 139
Césaire, Aimé 6, 17, 18, 21, 108, 181, 195
Chamoiseau, Patrick 6, 52, 181, 194, 276
Chauvet, Marie 78

Chodorow, Nancy 219
Clark, Vèvè 6
Cliff, Michelle 172, 286
Condé, Mamadou 4
Condé, Maryse
  Fictional Works:
  La Belle Créole 24, 143, 186, 219, 222, 224-226
  Le cœur à rire et à pleurer [*Tales from the Heart*] 25, 26, 245
  Célanire cou-coupé 10, 24, 78, 201, 210, 219
  La colonie du nouveau monde 187
  Les derniers rois mages, [*The Last of the African Kings*] 20, 23, 163, 166, 169, 187, 188, 228
  Desirada 23, 24, 35, 78, 163, 170, 171, 173, 174, 185, 188, 189, 194, 195, 217, 221
  Dieu nous l'a donné 219
  Haiti chérie/ Rêves amers 228
  Hérémakhon 5
  Histoire de la femme cannibale 24, 228, 229
  Moi, Tituba sorcière…Noire de Salem [*I, Tituba, Black Witch of Salem*] 6, 22, 43-52, 55, 64, 66, 68, 70-72, 76, 79, 81, 184, 195, 249
  La migration des cœurs [*Windward Heights*] 19, 25, 36, 188,

253, 255, 257, 259, 261, 263, 265, 270-272, 277-283, 285, 286

Nanny-ya [Nanna-ya] 25

Une saison à Rhiata [A Season in Rhiata] 6

Ségou 6, 184, 187, 188, 194

Traversée de la Mangrove [Crossing the Mangrove] 6, 7, 43, 44, 50, 52, 56, 188, 195

La vie scélérate [Tree of Life] 23, 143, 145, 153, 155, 160, 163, 165, 167, 169, 188

Anthologies and criticism:

Cahier d'un retour au pays natal 6, 107, 182, 185

Césaire 6, 17, 18, 21, 108, 181, 195

La civilisation du Bossale: Réflexions sur la littérature orale de la Guadeloupe et de la Martinique 6

La parole des femmes: Essai sur des romancières des Antilles de langue française 219

La poésie antillaise 6

Le roman antillais 6

"O Brave New World" 13, 14

Order, Disorder, Freedom, and the West Indian Writer 129, 139

"The Role of the Writer" 8

global perspective 16

"pleasure of displeasing" 8

Confiant, Raphaël 6, 78, 181, 183, 194, 241, 276, 287

Danticat, Edwidge 13, 39, 40

Dash, Michael 144

David, Christian 228

Davis, Angela Y. 47

Djebar, Assia 81

Douglass, Frederick 71

Du Bois, W.E.B. 71

Dukats, Mara L. 73, 97

Eagleton, Terry 258, 262-265, 269, 270, 272

Fanon, Frantz 16, 23, 122, 127-129, 131-139, 236, 268

Freud, Sigmund 17

Garvey, Marcus 14, 24, 147, 157, 159, 160, 162, 164, 166, 168, 170, 172, 174, 192

Gates, Henry Louis, Jr. 47

Gilroy, Paul 285

Gontran-Damas, Léon 17

Glissant, Édouard 21, 25, 55, 63, 64, 87, 88, 90, 91, 94, 98, 103, 124, 128, 161, 171, 174, 175, 181, 183, 241, 242

Harrison, Tony 35

Hawthorne, Nathaniel 67, 98, 100, 101

Hewitt, Leah 11, 12, 81, 108-111, 114, 127, 135

Holiday, Billie 103

Johnson, Charles 47

Légitimus, Hégésippe 259, 260, 281, 282

Lionnet, Françoise 7, 144

Malena, Anne 81

Manzor-Coats, Lillian 13, 43, 45, 47, 73

Mars, Jean Price 183

Marshall, Paule 286

Morrison, Anthea 190

Morrison, Toni 68, 71, 89

Mukherjee, Bharati 68

Index

NDiaye, Marie 18, 23, 107, 108, 110, 112, 114, 116, 118, 120, 122, 124, 217
Niranjana, Tejaswini 59
Nkrumah, Kwamé 187
Nunez, Elizabeth 3, 14, 138
Nyatetu-Waigwa, Wa 124

Ortiz, Fernando 255

Pfaff, Françoise 3, 4, 7-9, 12, 13, 15, 18, 65, 81, 107, 108, 121, 128, 129, 138, 139, 160, 161, 168, 170, 184, 185, 187, 196, 244, 248, 249, 251
Philcox, Richard 5, 6, 20, 21, 33, 34, 36, 38, 39, 41, 42, 57, 184, 229, 253
Pineau, Gisèle 218, 221

Quinby, Lee 165

Racine 35
Rhys, Jean 64
Robin, Régine 81
Rosello, Mireille 277
Rovélas, Michel 229

Scarboro, Ann 44, 47, 48, 65, 66, 88
Schwarz-Bart, Simone 55, 56, 67
Senghor, Léopold Sédar 17, 147, 148
Shakespeare 33
Shelley, Mary 213
Smith, Michelle 92
Snitgen, Jeanne 99, 101, 102
Sourieau, Marie-Agnès 145, 146, 153, 154, 157, 263, 272

Taleb-Khyar, Mohamed B. 119
Thiébaut, Claude 260, 280-283
Todorov, Tzvetan 211
Toumson, Roger 144, 146, 150, 151, 157

Voulzy, Laurent 36

Walcott, Derek 63, 64, 67, 79, 80
Walker, Alice 8, 12, 101
Wilson, Elizabeth 91, 124, 127, 128

SUBJECTS

Africa
  and myth 137, 194, 195
  return to 195
African religion, see Religion
African Socialism 138
African-American literature, see Literature
Agency 55, 91, 119, 276, 278, 283, 285-287
Alienation 128, 129, 131, 134, 135, 155, 188, 244-246, 250
American literature, see Literature
Ancestors 16, 23, 24, 100, 107, 109, 112, 114, 115, 122, 129, 135, 137, 162, 163, 186, 195, 243, 244, 261, 263, 264, 267
  search for 107, 109
Anti-colonialism 138
Anti-hero 185
Antillanité (Caribbeanness) 18, 19, 181
Antilles, see West Indies
Assimilation 17, 75, 127, 128, 195
Audience 8, 12, 33, 40, 43, 44, 55, 77, 182, 208, 229
Autobiography 11, 64, 66-68, 79-81, 138
  ex-slave 65
  fictional 65-67

Barbados 14, 34, 37, 48, 67, 69-71, 74, 79, 90, 91

317

Béké (Colonial White popoulation) 128, 133, 153, 221, 258, 260-262, 265, 266, 269, 270, 275

Black Atlantic 14, 285

Black Pride movement 9

Cannibalism 19, 22, 229, 231, 232, 235

   see also Translation

Canon 22, 25, 98, 100, 103, 253, 255, 257, 259, 261, 263, 265, 267, 269, 271

   literary 98

Caribbean literature 40, 70, 81, 181

Caribbean, Francophone (French-speaking) 7, 11, 12, 25, 26, 39, 127-129, 181, 183, 186, 187, 195, 217, 241, 250

Caribbeanness, see *Antillanité*

Characters 9-15, 21, 22, 24, 36, 42, 43, 49, 54, 55, 81, 93, 98, 99, 118, 119, 130, 143, 160, 161, 163, 165, 171, 175, 185, 186, 188, 189, 203, 284, 287

Class 4, 13, 99, 132, 133, 137, 148, 151, 155, 157, 190, 206, 258, 259, 262, 275, 280, 282, 283, 286

Colonial language, see Language

Colonialism 15, 17, 91, 94, 101, 103, 132, 133, 137-139, 174, 206, 241, 242, 256

Counter-narrative, see Narrative

Creole 6, 13, 14, 20, 25, 40-43, 49, 50, 53, 54, 56-59, 75, 153, 183, 184, 194, 224, 262, 264, 265, 269-272, 275, 276

   culture 153, 262

   language (Bajan; French; Haitien) 48, 49, 63

Creolisms 41-43, 49, 183

Créolité (Creoleness) 6, 7, 18, 19, 146, 152, 157, 181, 194, 276, 277, 286

Creolization 18, 50, 54, 56, 59, 74, 76, 253, 256, 258, 263, 272

Cuba 253-258, 271, 275, 278, 279, 284

   history of 253, 254

Culture 4, 5, 18, 20-22, 27, 31, 36-38, 42, 43, 49, 64, 68, 71, 74, 75, 77, 78, 99, 122, 127, 128, 134, 135, 143, 146, 148, 150, 153, 181, 183, 189, 195, 205, 213, 218, 262, 265

   dominant 36

Death wish 218

Diaspora

   African/Black 9, 14, 15, 19, 22, 24, 26, 65, 79, 90, 99, 102, 137, 161, 162, 170, 181, 183-185, 187-189, 191, 193, 195

   Jewish 90

"Diaspora literacy" 15

Discourse 11, 54, 65, 70, 71, 87-89, 92, 101, 107, 111, 114, 117, 119, 152, 157, 263, 283, 286

Discrimination 10, 72, 261

Diversity 21, 59, 97, 102, 123, 171, 258

English, see Language

Ethnicity 15, 18, 195, 220

European literature, see Literature

Exile 15, 133, 152, 155, 167, 168, 187, 188, 236, 242, 248-250, 275

Family 8, 15, 23, 36, 96, 113-115, 128, 130, 133, 143, 145-153, 155, 157, 159-175, 184, 185, 188-191, 193, 218, 220, 222, 224, 227, 245, 246, 248, 255, 258, 266, 269

Family tree, see Genealogies

Index

Fantastic 24, 78, 201, 203, 205, 207-211, 213, 214
as genre (*roman fantastique*) 208, 219

Female sexuality 92, 99, 129, 203

Feminism 10, 12, 101, 103
Western 101
global 13, 101

Francophone Studies 7, 39

Francophonie 6

Frankenstein 10, 24, 201-204, 213

Gender 11-13, 18, 22, 23, 93, 99, 102, 105, 110, 127, 129, 132, 144, 181, 189, 209, 217, 219, 220, 227, 228, 236
roles 189, 217
and stereotyping 228

Genealogies 23, 87, 105, 163, 165-67, 169-175, 192
family tree 23, 148, 159-175
lineage 137, 152, 160, 161, 164, 166, 171, 174
roots 7, 8, 23, 52, 81, 107, 119, 123, 128, 130, 134, 159-164, 166, 171, 172, 174, 175, 186, 190, 242, 244, 248, 250

Ghana 4, 5, 187

Guadeloupe 3, 4, 6-8, 14, 16, 34, 35, 51, 124, 127, 128, 130, 136, 149, 154, 160, 164, 166, 168, 170-173, 181, 185-187, 189-193, 195, 201, 202, 206, 207, 212, 218, 228, 242, 246, 248, 249, 253, 258-261, 263, 265, 266, 269, 272, 275, 277, 278, 280-283, 286
history of 277
independence movements in 187

Guilt 218, 219, 226, 234, 236

Haiti 40, 189, 228

see also Literature (Haitien)

History
Caribbean 49, 50, 59, 88, 90, 103, 253, 278
meta-history 88, 90, 92, 100
nonhistory 87-89, 92, 94
nostalgia for 242
Official 20, 277
of the Jewish people 90, 91
personal 20, 112, 188, 226, 271

Homosexuality 78

"Hybridity" (Homi Bhabha) 10, 14, 19, 22, 24, 65, 75, 202, 213, 214, 279

Identity
Caribbean 50, 54, 87, 124, 163, 166, 174, 183, 272
Creole 41, 57, 271, 272
cultural 9, 11, 20, 23, 24
gender 11
politics 183, 285
racial 23, 107, 108, 112, 147, 149, 264, 285

Ideology 187, 261, 277

Imagination 8, 37, 73, 76, 89, 100, 114, 130, 171, 212, 213, 249, 250

Incest 150

Intertextuality 37

Irony 10, 11, 52, 78, 119, 148, 160, 163, 226, 227, 285

Lactification 23, 143

Language 6, 13, 14, 16, 20, 21, 33, 36, 37, 39, 40, 42, 43, 49, 53, 54, 56, 59, 64-66, 70-72, 78, 114, 174, 195, 217, 221, 262
colonial language 13
Dutch 40-42, 92
English 7, 15, 19-22, 26, 33, 36-44, 47-55, 57-59, 68, 79, 80, 92,

319

93, 110, 144, 147, 160, 181, 188, 232, 243, 253, 276

mother tongue 265

Spanish 16, 40-42, 92, 253, 254, 257, 272, 278, 279, 284

Ashanti 48, 49, 67, 187, 263

Bajan English 49

American English 49

see also Creole

Lineage, see Genealogies

Literature 3, 5, 6, 10, 11, 15, 17, 20, 24-26, 40, 59, 64, 65, 68, 70, 71, 79, 81, 82, 88, 89, 91, 98, 127, 181-183, 217, 231, 236, 250, 272, 287

African-American 65, 71

American 40, 65, 71, 98

West Indian 5, 11, 91

Haitian 40

Oral 127

Love 7, 10, 16, 38, 67, 77, 78, 81, 117, 118, 130, 131, 136, 137, 149, 152, 154, 181, 182, 194, 206, 220, 222-225, 227, 228, 231, 233, 235, 236, 269, 271, 275

Marilisse 129, 130, 133, 136, 137

see also Lactification

Maroon 15, 53, 54, 67, 90, 91, 103, 243

Marronnage (Marooning) 50, 91

Marxism 4, 9

Maternal 75, 94, 118, 162, 163, 171, 173, 174, 217, 220, 223, 236

line 162

as metaphor 25

Matriarch, matriarchy 218

Memory 25, 71, 87, 98, 100, 103, 146, 147, 149, 150, 153, 155, 221, 241, 242, 244-251, 276-278, 280

cultural 71

Métissage 18, 19, 23, 24, 143-153, 155, 157, 183

Middle Passage 94, 121, 127, 162, 169, 174, 186, 245

Miscegenation 152, 213

Mixed race 147, 148, 203, 213, 259

Monsters, monstrosity 146, 174, 201, 203, 204, 208-210, 213

Mother 8, 9, 14, 24, 25, 37, 58, 67, 68, 78-80, 92-94, 112, 117-119, 122, 124, 131, 133, 145, 146, 149, 150, 153-155, 163, 164, 166, 170-173, 182, 185, 189-191, 193, 194, 212, 213, 217-223, 225-228, 231-236, 243, 248, 265, 268-271, 275

Mother tongue, see Language

Motherhood 213, 220, 232

maternity 163

Multiculturalism 14

Myth 127, 151, 193, 194, 220, 245, 246

Naming 70, 95, 169

Narrative 11, 16, 18, 20, 22, 24, 25, 41, 46, 47, 52, 64-66, 68, 70, 71, 76, 79, 80, 88-90, 94, 95, 97, 102, 103, 111, 114, 119, 139, 144, 145, 147, 148, 151, 153, 160, 162, 164, 166, 168-172, 208-213, 219-221, 223, 235, 244, 245, 248, 251, 256, 258, 277, 278, 285, 286

voice 22, 144, 145

structure 258

counter-narrative 286

see also Slave narrative

Narrator 9, 66, 70, 80, 107, 109, 110, 115, 131, 143, 145, 147, 149, 153, 155, 157, 163, 168, 170, 182, 195, 226, 227, 233, 234, 260, 261, 264, 265, 277-279

Négritude 16-19, 23, 107, 108, 117, 120, 121, 134, 139, 148, 157, 181-183, 194

Index

Nomadism 236

Nostalgia 193, 219, 225, 242
   for history 242
   for mother 225

Oedipal 24, 219, 220, 224, 227, 228, 232

Opacity 21, 49, 53, 57

Oppression 5, 10, 23, 90-92, 96, 129, 143, 144, 150-152, 155, 243, 261, 285
   racial 144, 150
   sexual 23, 143

Oral literature, see Literature

Origins 22, 74, 87, 107, 111, 115, 134, 135, 144, 149, 157, 159, 163, 164, 169-171, 174, 175, 183, 184, 189, 190, 207, 213, 214, 262, 263

Otherness 21, 70, 214

Paratextual elements 1, 4, 11, 16, 17, 22, 26, 34, 39, 42-48, 50, 51, 55, 56, 59, 64, 68, 181, 182, 189, 202, 211

Parody 10, 11, 48, 184

Patriarch, patriarchy 93, 94, 99, 101, 119, 145, 147, 149, 150, 152, 153, 159, 160, 269

Politics 13, 91, 93, 110, 134, 149, 183, 207, 277, 284, 285

Postcolonial Studies 285
   revision, revisionism 25, 78, 171, 276

Procreation 213

Puritanism, see Religion

Race 4, 10, 13, 14, 18, 19, 23, 63, 69, 75, 78, 93, 96, 99, 102, 110, 127, 130, 132, 133, 135, 136, 143, 144, 147, 148, 150, 189, 203, 213, 214, 229, 232, 258, 259, 262, 272, 285

Racism 6, 10, 12, 19, 22, 65, 81, 129, 139, 147, 154, 155, 282

"Relation" (Édouard Glissant) 161

Religion 72, 78, 94-96, 182, 220, 262
   African 95
   Puritanism 94, 95
   White Christian dogma 96

Resistance 47, 48, 90, 91, 144, 146, 218, 255, 256, 276, 280, 283, 285, 286
   cultural 255

Revolution 12, 101, 139, 188, 282

Rhizome 7, 8, 175, 242

Roman fantastique, see Fantastic

Roman fleuve 189

Roots, see Genealogies

Scapegoat 73, 77, 255, 256

Scarlet Letter, The 67, 73, 97, 98, 184
   and Hester Prynne 10, 67, 77, 97

Self, search for 65, 119, 153, 192

Sexuality 13, 22, 73, 76-78, 92, 93, 99, 100, 129, 136, 203, 206, 209

Slave narrative 70, 71
   see also Autobiography

Slavery 10, 15, 21, 64, 70, 78, 79, 88, 91, 92, 99, 103, 111-113, 124, 129, 133, 182, 184, 185, 242, 243, 245, 248, 253, 255-257, 261, 263, 275, 284
   abolition of 253, 261

Sorcery 46, 51, 203

Sorcière (Witch) 22, 45-49, 68-70, 73, 78, 184, 195, 249
   see also Voodoo

Spirituality 95, 96

Stereotypes 11, 76, 77, 99, 102, 108, 110, 112, 143, 144, 283

Subject/subjectivity 22, 26, 33, 47, 57, 63, 65-67, 69, 71, 73, 75-77, 79, 81, 89, 96, 97, 97, 99, 103,

109, 114, 133, 149, 163, 172, 221,
232, 250, 283, 285, 286
Supernatural 74, 208, 209, 211, 212
Syntax 14, 57, 58, 66, 79, 80, 149,
163, 230

Titles 3, 43, 160
Transgression 24, 201, 203-209,
211, 213
Translation 19-22, 31, 33-37, 39-43,
47-50, 52-54, 56-59, 81, 110, 120,
130, 132, 144, 181, 259
cannibalism 19, 22, 229, 231,
232, 235
pitfalls 23, 42, 138

"Untranslatability" 43

Violence 21, 73, 80, 81, 92-95, 98, 130,
139, 224-226, 231, 255, 256, 271
Voodoo/obeah/quimbois 67, 69,
276

West Indian 3-5, 11, 12, 16-18, 75,
91, 92, 123, 127, 128, 130, 133-
135, 139, 146, 162, 175
West Indian literature: and francophone women writers; see
Literature
West Indies 7, 18, 50, 66, 69, 71, 81,
129, 144, 162, 163, 167, 170
White Christian dogma, see Religion
Whiteness 73, 99, 131
see also *Békés*
Witch 10, 16, 35, 37, 43, 45-48, 51,
55, 64, 67-69, 73-75, 87, 88, 90,
93, 95, 96, 101
see also *Sorcière*
Womanism 101
Womb 14, 67, 115, 162, 218-220,
222, 224, 225, 269